CLASHES

CLASHES

Air Combat over North Vietnam 1965–1972

Marshall L. Michel III

NAVAL INSTITUTE PRESS

Annapolis, Maryland

Naval Institute Press
291 Wood Road
Annapolis, MD 21402

ISBN-10: 1-59114-519-8
ISBN-13: 978-1-59114-519-6

The Library of Congress has cataloged the hardcover edition
as follows:
Michel, Marshall L., III, 1942–
      Clashes : air combat over North Vietnam, 1965–1972 /
    Marshall L. Michel III.
              p. cm.
      Includes bibliographical references and index.
      ISBN 1-55750-585-3 (alk. paper)
      1. Vietnamese Conflict, 1961–1975—Aerial operations.
    2. Fighter planes—Vietnam.   I. Title.
    DS558.8.M53   1997
    959.704′3—dc21
                                                      97-9279

Printed in the United States of America on acid-free paper ∞

18 17 16   8 7 6 5

Contents

Acknowledgments

MANY PEOPLE generously gave their time to assist in the creation and completion of this book. They are too numerous to mention by name, but I would like to express my special thanks to some of those who took the time to read the manuscript at one stage of its development or another and critically comment on it. They include, from the Washington, D.C., area, Bob Haley, a friend of many lives and a former OV-10 pilot during the Vietnam War; Don Mace, who offered many observations about the EC-121 College Eye program, as well as many useful comments on style and substance; John McGregor, a friend from Georgetown and my F-4 days and someone very knowledgeable about air-to-air combat; and Skip Miner, whose observations about the Navy systems were especially useful, as well as Randy Knott and Doug Johnson, who offered support on a variety of issues. I would also like to thank Gen. Charles Gabriel, USAF (Ret.), the wing commander of the 432nd TRW at Udorn in 1972, when he was a colonel. Special thanks go to Von Hardesty and his colleagues at the Smithsonian's Air and Space Museum, without whose encouragement at an early stage the book might never have been written.

In New Orleans, Louisiana, there was Chip Carpenter, a high school classmate and former Marine aviator who flew the A-6 over North Vietnam and later the F-4, and Kathy Kohnke, the first person to read any of the manuscript.

In Cambridge, Massachusetts, I am particularly grateful to Les Brown, a past director of the Center for International Affairs at Harvard University and a former member of the State Department, who offered his considerable expertise in a variety of areas as he reviewed the manuscript.

Although I have not met them in person (yet), I would like to thank Jim Shaw of Platte City, Missouri, and Gerald Miller of Eau Claire, Wisconsin, who shared their Linebacker experiences and provided information about chaffing and smart bombs. If mistakes appear in those sections, it is because I was not smart enough to ask the right questions.

Many people helped with declassifying the large number of documents that made the book possible; these include the staff at the Office of Air Force History at Bolling Air Force Base in Washington, D.C., and at Maxwell Air Force Base in Montgomery, Alabama. Especially helpful in this area was Roy Patterson, the Freedom of Information manager for the 554th Mission Support Squadron at Nellis Air Force Base, Nevada. Amy Morgan of Designer Ink SPRL, Brussels, Belgium, assisted with the drawings, and Jay Miller of Arlington, Texas, provided several unique photographs of MiG aircraft.

Large numbers—certainly hundreds, perhaps thousands—of U.S. Air Force and Navy staff officers and civilians labored over the reports that I used during my research. The bibliography lists only a small part of these reports. I am sure that almost none of these people ever thought that their efforts would be used for anything other than another general's briefing, to be forgotten in a week, yet their work was almost universally of extremely high quality. To all of you, long since forgotten, thanks and my deepest respect for your professionalism. I hope that your efforts got you a good Officer Effectiveness Report (or its equivalent).

I also owe a great deal of thanks to my acquisitions editor at the Naval Institute Press, Mark Gatlin, whose patience with a new author was Olympian and who watched with amazement—as did many others—as outside events in my personal life unfolded, with the concomitant delays as the book drew to a close.

To all of these that I have mentioned, and to the many others I have not, I hope the book is good enough that you are not unhappy to be associated with it.

Finally, I must acknowledge that while this is an academic history, the flak-, SAM-, and MiG-filled skies over the Hanoi area were real. Many died there, on both sides. I have deliberately chosen not to make this a personality book, and so very few names are mentioned in it. This does not mean that the men who fought there are irrelevant, or that I have forgotten them. My greatest hope for *Clashes* is that the veterans of Rolling Thunder and Linebacker will give it to their friends and say, "This is a good book." If they do, the book will have been successful.

CLASHES

Introduction

IN MOST HISTORIES of the Vietnam War, the air war over North Vietnam is overshadowed by the political controversy that surrounded it. Other than the importance of the brief Christmas bombing in 1972 (which many believe finally brought Hanoi to sign a peace agreement and effectively end America's part in the conflict), the bombing of North Vietnam, especially the Rolling Thunder campaign from 1965–1968, is viewed as a political issue rather than a military one. Politically, it highlighted the doctrine of "gradual escalation" where North Vietnamese targets were struck, not in one mass blow, but a few at time to try to "send a message" to the Hanoi government. Rolling Thunder also highlighted the slowly widening differences between President Johnson's advisors as the war dragged on and ultimately came to be seen as a symbol of the futility of the war itself, and this view extended to the Nixon administration's relatively unrestricted 1972 bombing campaign, Linebacker I.

In fact, without attempting to judge the bombing's influence in the overall war, the air campaigns over North Vietnam had great military significance in the larger context of the Cold War and a possible military U.S.-Soviet military confrontation in other parts of the world. In this context, the other military aspects of the Vietnam War were unimportant. Naval surface and submarine war were virtually nonexistent. The ground war in South Vietnam was an unconventional war with few lessons in either equipment or tactics for a possible war with the Soviets in Europe, and the air war in South Vietnam was conducted in a permissive environment that would never exist in central Europe.

The air war over North Vietnam was different; it was the one area of the Vietnam War that had military significance in the global balance of power. Both the United States and the Soviet Union put some of their best weapons into play in the skies over North Vietnam. U.S. pilots were using many of the latest U.S. systems and tactics against a Soviet-style air defense system that integrated SA-2 Guideline surface-to-air missiles (quickly and universally known as SAMs), radar-controlled anti-aircraft guns, and late-model MiGs under close radar guidance, all closely imitating the Soviet system in Europe. If an American ground unit inflicted a defeat on a North Vietnamese unit in the jungles of Vietnam, it had little bearing on whether or not that U.S. unit was capable of defeating a similar Soviet unit in Germany. If American air forces could operate with impunity in a Soviet SAM environment, this had serious implications for Soviet forces in Europe. If North Vietnamese MiG-21s could shoot down American F-4s on a regular basis, this indicated how American F-4s might fare against Soviet-flown MiG-21s.

The air war over North Vietnam was the first "modern" air war—one where missiles were the main weapons in air combat. The SA-2 missiles were the major component of the North Vietnamese air defense system and were a dominating force throughout the war. Initially the SA-2s caused relatively heavy losses, but most of the problems they presented proved to be one-dimensional, technical ones. Almost alone, technology could negate the SA-2s, and by late 1966, the advent of the external electronics countermeasures (ECM) pod allowed the U.S. Air Force to dramatically reduce losses to SAMs for the rest of Rolling Thunder. During the Linebacker I campaign, different techniques—chaff corridors—had the same result. However, when U.S. forces failed to use their technology properly—as they failed to do in the early part of the Linebacker II campaign—the SA-2s exacted a heavy toll.

But even though ECM was effective against the SA-2s, the proper use of the countermeasures forced the American fighter bombers to use less than optimum tactics and formations when they went into SAM areas, so even after the direct losses to the SA-2s dropped, the anti-SAM tactics forced on U.S. aircraft led to serious losses to other defensive systems. The tactics used to counter the SAMs made the U.S. Air Force aircraft especially vulnerable to North Vietnamese MiG fighters, and from late 1966 the MiGs began major, continuous attacks on U.S. air strikes. From that time, for the first time in warfare, U.S. air strikes were facing an integrated air defense system, where ground radar and command and control systems coordinated missile-firing interceptors with SAMs and radar-controlled anti-aircraft guns to provide a complete and complex variety of threats to American strikes.

The air-to-air battle against the MiGs, like the battle against the SAMs, was one that could be expected to be fought over Europe in the event of a major war. But, while the challenge posed by the SAMs was mainly a technical one, the MiG threat was entirely different. It was the test of a much broader area of American air combat performance—the skill of the pilots, the performance of the aircraft and missiles, the effectiveness of its command and control—and provided a much more difficult test for American air power.

The American view of air-to-air combat had changed considerably since World War II and the Korean War, when U.S. fighter pilots had run up impressive scores and kill ratios in close-in turning battles—"dog-fights"—using aircraft machine guns and cannon to score their kills. From the late 1950s, air-to-air missiles—both heat seeking and radar guided—appeared to become practical weapons and gradually took over the role of the gun in U.S. aircraft fighter design. By the time the Vietnam War began, the newest and primary U.S. air-to-air fighter, the F-4 Phantom II, did not even carry internal guns.

Despite the high expectations of the Defense Department civilians and the U.S. military leadership, from the beginning of the war the air-to-air missiles caused U.S. fighters a number of problems; combat experience showed the missiles were extremely unreliable and unable to follow a maneuvering fighter at low altitude, and the F-4s had to resort to a hurried modification to provide them with a cannon to use against the maneuverable MiGs. But, despite the missile problems, through the summer of 1967 U.S. fighters were able to keep a healthy kill ratio and keep the North Vietnamese fighters from being a serious threat to U.S. air strikes. When the MiGs proved especially difficult, U.S. forces turned their full attention to them and administered sharp defeats. In two operations in early January 1967, U.S. Air Force F-4s shot down nine MiG-21s for no losses. In April, May, and June of 1967 the MiGs became aggressive again, and the American air forces again turned their attention to them and gave the North Vietnamese Air Force another sharp slap, as U.S. Air Force and Navy fighters shot down thirty-two MiGs for only two losses. In both cases, North Vietnamese losses were so heavy that the MiGs disappeared from the skies for several months.

In the thrust and parry of these air battles, the Americans learned some disturbing things about their training, aircraft, and weapons, but it seemed that when the U.S. forces were willing to focus on the MiGs, they could be countered relatively easily. This seemed especially true in the summer of 1967, when several new American systems entered the battle that were expected to increase the U.S. advantage. Surprisingly, in spite of the new American technology, in late August and September 1967 the North Vietnamese Air Force returned from its beatings of May and June and again began seriously to challenge the American air forces. In October 1967 the U.S. fighters once again administered several sharp defeats to the MiGs, and it appeared the same cycle would repeat itself.

But despite their losses, the North Vietnamese were nothing if not tenacious, and this time the MiGs reacted differently. They did not stand down, but continued aggressively to attack U.S. strike flights and their escorts using their exceptionally good close radar control—GCI—with new tactics. The results of the new tactics were electrifying—from late 1967 until the end of Rolling Thunder, North Vietnamese MiG-21s shot down over five U.S. Air Force fighters for every MiG-21 lost.

After the end of Rolling Thunder, the Air Force and Navy came to very different conclusions about their performance. The Navy instituted a rigorous air combat training program, called Topgun, for its F-4 crews, determined to prepare them for future air-to-air combat. The Air Force, on the other hand, limited its improvements to technical ones. It did nothing to improve the skill of its F-4 crews in air-to-air combat; in fact, despite the losses at the end of Rolling Thunder, the Air Force deemphasized air combat training.

The second air war over North Vietnam began again in earnest in April 1972 after the March invasion of South Vietnam, first as Operation Freedom Train, then, beginning May 9, as Linebacker I. Once again American aircraft bombed North Vietnam every day and engaged MiGs, and the battles followed much the same cycle as they had in Rolling Thunder. First the U.S. fighters, led by new technology in Air Force F-4s and by well-trained Navy F-4 crews, had the advantage, but by June the North Vietnamese simply stopped engaging Navy flights and reverted to tactics against the Air Force that had proven so successful at the end of Rolling Thunder. For most of the summer the MiGs dominated the engagements with Air Force aircraft, but by September a series of U.S. improvements made the contest even again, and it remained so until the end of Linebacker I in October 1972.

The most intense and important phase of the air war began on December 18, 1972, when B-52s began an eleven-day night bombing campaign, known as Linebacker II, into the heart of North Vietnam. Surprisingly, the North Vietnamese MiG force had little effect on the nighttime B-52 raids, but in the few day missions flown, the North Vietnamese MiG pilots again demonstrated they were equal to the Air Force F-4 crews, and when the air war over North Vietnam ended at the end of December, only the must ardent chauvinists could say the U.S. fighter force had achieved air superiority.

The postwar assessments by the Air Force made it clear where their problem was—lack of training. Beginning almost as soon as the war was over, the Air Force—led by its young and not-so-young combat veterans of the air war over North Vietnam—followed the Navy's lead and began a dramatic shift in its tactics and training programs, and soon the Air Force's programs were the equal of any in the world. This is the often-painful story of the trip from the first battles over Hanoi to these last battles in the United States.

Part 1
ROLLING THUNDER

1

Opening Fire

O N AUGUST 5, 1964, sixty-four U.S. Navy aircraft from the carriers *Ticonderoga* and *Constellation,* stationed in the Gulf of Tonkin, bombed North Vietnamese torpedo boat bases after the North Vietnamese allegedly attacked the U.S. destroyers *Maddox* and *Turner Joy.* After these raids, for almost forty months U.S. strike aircraft from the Air Force and the Navy bombed North Vietnam on a regular basis, and by early 1965 the bombing campaign of North Vietnam had a name—Rolling Thunder.

When the first U.S. bombs hit in 1964, North Vietnam had a very simple air defense network consisting of about twenty early-warning radars, 1,500 automatic anti-aircraft guns, and no SAMs. There were only two jet-capable airfields, the international airport of Gia Lam near Hanoi and the field at Cat Bi near Haiphong, though another airfield near Hanoi—Phuc Yen—was under construction. The North Vietnamese quickly took steps to improve their defenses, and soon U.S. intelligence identified about thirty-six Soviet-made MiG-17 fighters in North Vietnam. By February 1965, the North Vietnamese Air Force had increased to about sixty MiG-17s. U.S. intelligence also reported that the Soviets were supplying the North Vietnamese with the radars and other equipment for a system of fighter radar control for Ground-Controlled Interceptions (GCI). The North Vietnamese were to use a Soviet-style GCI system calling for strict radar control that guided interceptors to a point behind the target where they could attack from the most advantageous position.

Still, the MiG-17 was not really a modern fighter. It was an improved version of the MiG-15 that the Communist forces used during the Korean War, and American F-86s had rolled over the MiG-15s—often Russian flown—for a 10:1 kill ratio. The current U.S. fighters—the Air Force's Republic F-105 Thunderchief, the Navy's Chance Vought F-8 Crusader, and a fighter used by both services, the McDonnell F-4 Phantom II—were all a generation advanced from the F-86 and appeared to be markedly superior to the MiG-15's successor flown by third-world pilots.

First Shots

Rolling Thunder began on March 2, 1965, with strikes on North Vietnamese targets south of 20°N latitude. On April 3, a large American force of Navy and Air Force aircraft attacked the Than Hoa bridge in the center of North Vietnam. It was a hazy day with very limited visibility, and out of the haze the North Vietnamese Air Force made its move; in a well-executed attack MiG-17s struck Navy A-4s and F-8s bombing the bridge, damaging one F-8 and escaping unscathed.

The next day a force of forty-eight U.S. Air Force F-105Ds made another strike on the same bridge. Besides the F-105s, there were F-100s in the area flying combat air patrol (MiGCAP) to protect against MiG attack, as well as thirty or more Navy F-4Bs and rescue aircraft patrolling to pick up downed pilots. The weather still was very hazy between 12,000 and 15,000 feet, and all of the eighty-plus U.S. aircraft involved were trying to talk on a single radio frequency, clogging it with calls.

Four F-105s, Zinc flight,* were one of the middle flights in the strike force loaded with eight Mark 117 750-pound bombs and external wing fuel tanks. When they arrived in the target area, they found the entire strike force crowding together over the target waiting to bomb. Although MiGs had attacked the strike the day before, the mission commander instructed Zinc and two other F-105 flights to circle about ten miles south of the target and wait their turn.

Zinc flight arrived at the designated point and began to circle in the haze at 15,000 feet, but because of their heavy bomb and fuel load, the F-105s had to fly at a very slow speed—325 knots. As the F-105 flight began to turn at the orbit point, Zinc 3 saw two aircraft in a shallow dive approaching about a mile behind the F-105s. Zinc 3 could not immediately identify the aircraft, but as they closed inside 4,000 feet, he saw they were MiG-17s attacking Zinc 1 and Zinc 2. Zinc 3 called, "Zinc lead, break—you have MiGs behind you. Zinc lead, break! Zinc lead, we're being attacked." Zinc 4 followed with a similar warning. Neither Zinc 1 nor Zinc 2 reacted to the warning calls. (Although the radio frequency was cluttered with calls, Zinc 3 and Zinc 4 felt they were close enough to override the more distant transmissions, and the other aircraft in the area heard the break calls.)

---

* For the simple reason that the information was not available, not all of the call signs used by U.S. flights in the engagement descriptions are the ones actually used on the missions. Many of the call signs are correct; a significant number, however, are generic ones.

A Soviet MiG-17F. Note the bubble canopy, which gave it good visibility to the rear, and the bombs on the wing stations. North Vietnamese MiG-17s often carried external fuel tanks on these stations. *Jay Miller*

Two MiG-17s passed in front of and above Zinc 3 and Zinc 4 at high speed, and the MiG leader began firing about 1,500 feet behind Zinc 1 while the second MiG, flying about 1,000 feet off to the side of the first, fired on Zinc 2 at almost the same time. The heavily loaded, slow-flying F-105s never had a chance. Both Zinc 1 and Zinc 2 were hit; as the MiGs struck, Zinc 2 called to Zinc 1, "Lead, you have a MiG behind you—[pause] —I've been hit." Zinc 3 saw several hits in back of Zinc 1's aircraft and flames coming from the aft section of Zinc 2. The two MiGs pressed their attack inside 800 feet, then ceased firing, rolled wings level, and continued straight ahead to disappear in the haze.

As the lead pair of MiGs was attacking Zinc 1 and Zinc 2, a second pair of MiG-17s was trailing and began to attack Zinc 3 and Zinc 4. Zinc 3 saw the trailing MiG element, and the two F-105s turned into the attack. The two MiGs passed over and behind Zinc 3 and Zinc 4 and continued ahead and also disappeared into the haze, too fast for the F-105s to follow.

Zinc 3 and Zinc 4 then tried to find Zinc 1 and Zinc 2, both damaged but still flying. Zinc 4 found Zinc 2, but because of the haze, he did not see the damaged, slow-flying F-105 until he was very close—less than 1,500 feet. Zinc 4 overshot, flew past Zinc 2, and lost sight of him in the haze. As Zinc 4 turned back, Zinc 2 called that he was going to eject. Zinc 4 circled the area and thought he saw Zinc 2 crash in the water; later an Air Force rescue aircraft conducted an unsuccessful search for the body of Zinc 2's pilot.

Meanwhile, Zinc 3 was attacked by more MiGs; after defeating the attack, he resumed searching and found Zinc 1, still flying. The two F-105s began to climb as high as possible so Zinc 1 could glide to an American airfield if his engine failed. Leveling at about 21,000 feet, Zinc 3 flew around Zinc 1 to check the damage from the MiG's cannon fire. There was a large hole in the bottom rear of the F-105's speed brake, some damage to the top of the speed brake, and a large hole about a foot across in the left trailing edge flap. The drag chute door was open, but the chute was still inside. The damage to the speed brakes indicated that Zinc 1 probably had hydraulic problems; he confirmed he had partial hydraulic failure.

Zinc 4 joined Zinc 1 and Zinc 3, and the three F-105s headed for an emergency landing at Da Nang Air Force Base in South Vietnam. When they were about ten miles from Da Nang, Zinc 1 reduced power to begin his descent, but the engine lost oil pressure and "froze." He then leveled out and called that he was ejecting.

The ejection appeared normal, but Zinc 1 came out of the cockpit without his helmet, and the parachute did not seem to open. Zinc 3 followed the pilot and stayed in the area until a rescue helicopter arrived. A Navy ship then moved into the area and recovered Zinc 1's body. His chute had deployed, but apparently not in time to check his fall. Low on fuel, Zinc 3 and Zinc 4 landed at Da Nang. The air-to-air war over North Vietnam had claimed its first U.S. victims.

The Antagonists

The mainstay of the Air Force's bombing raids over North Vietnam during Rolling Thunder would be the Republic F-105 Thunderchief, known universally as the "Thud." The first F-105, the F-105B, originally had been designed as a low-altitude, long-range tactical nuclear bomber for use in Europe; it had small wings for high speed at low level and a bomb bay to carry a nuclear bomb. The F-105D, almost identical in appearance, was developed later as an all-weather ground-attack aircraft with a fuel tank in the bomb bay. Originally, the large, sophisticated fighter was a maintenance nightmare, but by the time of Rolling Thunder, most of the major problems had been solved. Most F-105s used during Rolling Thunder were the single-seat F-105D model, but the Air Force also made extensive use of the two-seat F-105F for special missions. The F-105 was the fastest aircraft in the theater at low altitude, and despite being used almost exclusively as a strike aircraft, during Rolling Thunder it was to have more MiG engagements than all the other U.S. aircraft combined.

A formation of four F-105 Thunderchiefs carrying wing and centerline fuel tanks. Note the lack of camouflage, indicating the photograph was taken either prior to or early in the war. *USAF (courtesy of the National Archives)*

The F-105 carried an internal 20-mm M-61 Vulcan cannon, with a rate of fire of 6,000 rounds per minute, and when used as a fighter (which was very rarely), could carry four AIM-9 Sidewinder[1] heat-seeking missiles on two double pylons. The double pylons generated a great deal of drag and meant carrying less ordnance, so F-105s rarely carried AIM-9s on strike missions. The F-105's small wings gave little lift in a turn, making the Thud notoriously unmaneuverable, but despite its poor turning capability, the Vulcan cannon and the F-105's high speed after it had dropped its bombs made a well-handled Thud a useful air-to-air fighter against the MiG-17.

About half of Navy air-to-air squadrons were equipped with the single-seat F-8 Crusader, an uncompromising air superiority fighter. It was fast and agile, carried four 20-mm Colt Mark 12 cannon and two or four Sidewinder missiles on "cheek" launchers, and had a limited air-to-air radar set. F-8 pilots were extremely well trained in maneuvering air combat—"dogfighting"—and were proud (some might say they were arrogant) of their skill; they believed they and their aircraft were the best in the world in air-to-air combat.[2] The F-8s flew from the Navy's smaller carriers, the Project 27-*Charlie* class: These were World War II *Essex*-class carriers—the *Oriskany, Bon Homme Richard, Hancock, Intrepid, Lexington, Ticonderoga,* and *Shangri-La*—that had been modified in the 1950s to operate jet aircraft.

A classic photo of an F-8 Crusader. This is an F-8U-2N, later designated the F-8D. Note the double "cheek" AIM-9 rails on the right side of the fuselage. *USNI Photographic Collection*

Both the Air Force and the Navy used the two-seat F-4 Phantom II. The F-4 originally was designed to give the Navy a radar-equipped, missile-armed fleet interceptor, but the Phantom II's overall performance was so impressive that the Air Force accepted it as a multirole fighter. The Navy designation for its F-4s was the F-4B; the Air Force designation was the F-4C, but they were essentially the same aircraft. At the beginning of the war, both services used the F-4 primarily as an air-to-air fighter, but while the F-4C had become the air-to-air backbone of the Air Force, the Navy F-4Bs—which operated from the larger *Forrestal*- and *Midway*-class carriers—divided the air-to-air mission with the F-8s.

The F-4 was in most ways an excellent aircraft. It had superb acceleration, was capable of flying twice the speed of sound at high altitude and supersonic at low altitudes, and had a powerful air-to-air radar operated by a second crew member who sat in the F-4's back seat. In Navy F-4s, the back seater was a navigator, called a RIO (radar intercept officer). In Air Force F-4s the back seater was a pilot recently graduated from pilot training, commonly known as the GIB (guy in back). Air Force F-4s also carried a limited set of flight controls for the GIB; Navy F-4s did not. For air combat the F-4 could carry up to eight air-to-air missiles, four AIM-9 Sidewinder heat seekers, and four large long-range, radar-guided

A U.S. Air Force F-4C takes off early in the war with a standard air-to-air ordnance load: two 370-gallon wing fuel tanks, a 600-gallon centerline fuel tank, four AIM-9Bs between the fuel tanks, and four AIM-7s under the fuselage. *USAF (courtesy of the National Archives)*

AIM-7 Sparrows. Designed as an interceptor, the F-4 followed the current trend in armament and did not carry an internal cannon. The lack of a cannon did not appear to unduly disturb the F-4 aircrews; in fact, many supported it.[3]

The air-to-air missiles carried by the U.S. fighters were expected to dominate air combat. All three U.S. fighters could carry the Sidewinder, a relatively old heat-seeking missile used effectively in combat in 1958 by the Nationalist Chinese. The AIM-9B model carried by Navy and Air Force fighters at the beginning of Rolling Thunder was light—only 164 pounds—had a 25-pound warhead (10.5 pounds of which was explosive), and was simple to operate. When the infrared seeker in the head of the AIM-9 sensed the heat from the target's engine exhaust, the missile gave the pilot a tone signal in his headset. The pilot flew his aircraft into the missile "envelope"—basically a 30-degree cone a mile or less behind the enemy aircraft—then fired the missile, which homed in on the hot exhaust. There were significant tactical advantages to the heat-seeking missile. Now, instead of having to close to inside 2,000 feet for a cannon attack, the missile-armed fighter could attack from almost a mile away from a large area in the rear of the target.

AIM-9B Sidewinders are loaded onto an F-8 Crusader. *USN (courtesy of USNI Photographic Collection)*

The Sidewinder did have some disadvantages. Fighters could only carry a few AIM-9s (four on the F-4 and F-105, and two or four on the F-8s) on external pylons, and the AIM-9 pylon/missile combination caused extra drag that reduced performance. Fighter pilots also were aware that the AIM-9 had been tested against relatively nonmaneuvering bomber targets at high altitude; the AIM-9's performance against low-altitude or maneuvering targets was still unproved. (Almost as soon as the first AIM-9s were operational, American fighter squadron tactics manuals recognized the problem with missiles in air-to-air combat and were telling pilots to get low and turn to negate a heat-seeking missile attack[4]—almost certainly the same thing that North Vietnamese MiG pilots were to be told later in Rolling Thunder.) Still, the AIM-9 dramatically increased the potential lethality of a U.S. fighter, and an enemy aircraft had to "honor" the heat seeker, thus limiting his maneuvers.

The radar-guided AIM-7 carried on the F-4 appeared to offer even greater advantages than the AIM-9. It was an "all-aspect" missile that theoretically could be fired from all around the target instead of just from behind. This was a real tactical breakthrough—Soviet fighters did not have this capability, so an F-4 could fire long before its Soviet opponents. The AIM-7 also had much greater range than the AIM-9—about twelve miles in a head-on attack and about three miles from the rear. The Sparrow had a

An AIM-7 Sparrow is fired from a U.S. Navy F-4. Note how the missile has dropped down vertically from the fuselage before the rocket engine fires.
USN (courtesy of USNI Photographic Collection)

65-pound warhead;[5] while the missile weighed over 400 pounds, to minimize drag and not take up a weapons station, it was carried partially submerged in the Phantom's belly.

The AIM-7 was a "semi-active" beam rider missile that worked in combination with the F-4 radar, which detected a target and then "locked on." If the radar in its normal mode was like a light bulb in a room, when it locked on, the light narrowed to a flashlight beam that stayed on the target. The AIM-7 followed the beam of the radar toward the reflection of the light off the target.

On the minus side, to guide the AIM-7 the radar had to stay locked on the target the entire time the missile was in the air, and the AIM-7 launch sequence was time consuming and complex. Additionally, the F-4's radar and the AIM-7 did not operate very well against a target flying below the F-4, especially at low altitude, because of a phenomenon known as "ground clutter" that affected all radars at this time. When the radar beam hit the ground, the ground produced a reflection—the ground return, or ground clutter—that hid aircraft radar returns and made it almost impossible to find an aircraft on radar at low altitude or looking down from above. Because of this ground clutter, as a rule the target had to be at the same altitude or above the F-4 for radar and the AIM-7 to be effective; the higher above the ground, the better. Ground clutter affected all types of radars and was one of the main problems with using radars during the Vietnam War.

The warheads on both the AIM-7 and AIM-9 had proximity fuses that were supposed to detonate when the missile passed close to the target, making a direct hit unnecessary. On the down side, both missiles also had significant minimum ranges. The minimum ranges were the result of safety features to prevent detonation of the missile immediately after launch, which might damage the launch aircraft. Inside these minimum ranges—about 3,000 feet—the missiles' proximity fuse warhead would not arm; a missile fired inside that range was simply a large, dumb, and expensive bullet. It was not noticed that the minimum range of the missile was the beginning of the effective envelope of aircraft cannon (nonexistent on the F-4), which were more effective the closer the range. Cannon were considered passé; Secretary of Defense Robert McNamara reportedly said, "In the context of modern air warfare, the idea of a fighter being equipped with a gun is as archaic as warfare with bow and arrow."[6]

The MiG-17

On paper, all of the American fighters appeared to be vastly superior to the MiG-17 in performance and armament. All three U.S. fighters were capable of speeds well above the speed of sound, while the MiG was subsonic, though the MiG-17 could turn much better than the American fighters. North Vietnamese MiG-17s were not expected to carry air-to-air missiles and would have to rely on the same armament the Korean War MiG-15 had carried: two 23-mm and one 37-mm cannon. These cannon were much heavier than those carried on Western aircraft because of the MiG's primary role as a bomber interceptor but were slow firing. A two-second burst from the MiG-17's three cannon delivered only 69 rounds, while in the same two-second burst the U.S. M-61 Vulcan (carried in the F-105) fired about 175 rounds and the F-8's four Mark 12 cannon fired about 160 rounds. But the MiG-17's cannon had very long range—out to 5,000 feet—and the weight of fire from the MiG's cannon was very heavy—70.3 pounds in a two-second burst, while the Vulcan had a weight of fire of only 38.6 pounds and the F-8s only 35.2 pounds.[7] American fighter pilots in the Korean War believed that these heavy cannon were too slow-firing for fighter versus fighter combat, but the heavy cannon made it possible for a MiG-17 to score a single lucky hit—a "golden BB"—at very long range and down or disable a U.S. fighter. However, the MiG-17 only had enough ammunition for about five seconds of firing, while the F-105 and F-8 each had about ten seconds of firing time.

A U.S. Air Force F-86H of the type used in the Feather Duster tests. Note the superb visibility from the bubble canopy and its general resemblance to the MiG-17. *USAF (courtesy of the National Archives)*

Feather Duster

Despite the apparent performance superiority of its aircraft, the Air Force believed that, since the 1960s, its air-to-air combat skills had deteriorated, and at the beginning of the Vietnam War the performance of current Air Force fighters against the smaller and more maneuverable MiG-17 was a source of serious concern.[8] Shortly after the war started, the Air Force began a program called Feather Duster to find the best tactics for the Air Force's first-line fighters, including the F-105 and F-4C, to use against a MiG-17 type of aircraft.

Unfortunately, at the beginning of the war no MiG-17s were available for testing, but old F-86Hs, provided and flown by pilots from the New York, Maryland, and Puerto Rican Air National Guard, proved to be ideal aircraft for simulating the MiG-17.

The first part of the program, Feather Duster I, consisted of about 180 engagements between the small, maneuverable F-86H and the major U.S. fighters. The various engagements had the F-86H and the current U.S. fighters alternate as attacker and defender, and simulated visual detection at two ranges—one to one and a half miles and 3,000 feet. The engagements were at high altitude (20,000 and 35,000 feet) and mainly were one on one. By May 1965 Feather Duster I was complete, and Feather Duster

II quickly followed. Feather Duster II flew the same engagements at the more realistic combat altitudes of 5,000, 1,000, and 500 feet and used formations of two and four aircraft to assess the effect of current American flight formations and tactics against attacks by a MiG-17.[9]

After the engagements, the Feather Duster report said "big [U.S.] fighters have a definite fighting region and have problems if they move out of it."[10] U.S. fighters, relatively larger and heavier than the Soviet fighters, had advantages over the smaller MiGs at higher speeds and lower altitudes, whereas the light, well-turning MiGs had advantages at lower speeds and/or higher altitudes. As long as the U.S. fighters did not turn with the MiGs, they had an advantage, but in a turning engagement, especially at slow speed, the advantage turned to the MiGs.

Feather Duster supported the Air Force's "energy maneuverability" theory, a formal, analytical method of quantifying fighter performance to define what speeds, altitudes, and types of turns and maneuvers gave a particular aircraft its maximum performance. Using the energy maneuverability theory, Vietnam-era U.S. pilots looked for altitudes and airspeeds where U.S. fighters had excess power (called P_S) advantages against a certain type of MiG so that the U.S. fighter could use his excess power either to out-climb, out-accelerate, or, in certain circumstances, out-turn the enemy. Energy maneuverability performance was displayed in a series of complex charts; by overlaying the charts of two particular aircraft, it was possible to locate areas where each aircraft's performance was significantly different (see appendix 2). Despite the complexity of the charts, American fighter pilots were able to draw from them a few "rules of thumb" about where their aircraft performed best against a certain type of MiG. Equally important, the American pilot knew where the MiGs had relative superiority and could avoid those areas.

The Feather Duster tests were similar to those conducted in World War II, when the U.S. tested its fighters against captured German and Japanese aircraft and issued guidelines for fighting various types of enemy aircraft. For example, the World War II tests compared a German FW-190A with the P-51D Mustang and advised U.S. pilots that "the FW-190 is nearly 50 mph slower at all heights. . . . [T]he Mustang and FW-190 turn circles are almost equal. . . . A FW-190 could not be evaded by diving alone. In defense a steep turn followed by a full throttle dive should increase the range before regaining height and course. Dog-fighting is not altogether recommended. Do not attempt to climb without at least 250 mph showing initially."[11] The instructions to Navy F6F Hellcat pilots fighting the very maneuverable Japanese Zero stated that "the maneuverability of the Zero is remarkable at speeds below about 205 mph, being far superior to that of the F6F. Its superiority, however, diminishes with increased speed, due to its high control forces, and the F6F has the advantage over 235 mph."[12]

Overall, the Feather Duster tests suggested some rather pessimistic projections about U.S. fighter performance against the MiG-17 and another, more advanced Soviet fighter, the MiG-21, which the North Vietnamese were expected to receive soon. The final report said that both MiGs would out-turn and generally outperform all U.S. fighters at .9 Mach[13] and below, and, the slower the speed, the greater their turn advantage against the F-4 and F-105. As the speeds increased, the MiGs' turn advantage decreased, but it never completely disappeared.

The basic characteristics of a turning dogfight made this slow-speed turning advantage very important. As an aircraft makes a hard turn, the gravity forces—called G forces—increase, and the aircraft becomes heavier. A mild two-G turn means the aircraft weighs twice as much as in straight and level flight; in a dogfight, six-G turns were the norm, which meant that an aircraft weighed six times as much as it did in a steady state. Since the engines were designed to push the aircraft in a steady state, as the weight increased with G forces, the aircraft inevitably slowed down. The lift produced by the wings was another factor in a turning fight. Since the fighter was much heavier in a hard turn, the wings had to lift more weight, resulting in much less lift from the wings and less relative thrust for a hard-turning fighter (since it was now six times as heavy). Consequently, in a turning dogfight, a fighter in a hard turn did not have the thrust to push its increased weight, so it slowed down. To keep its speed up, the fighter had to descend, so dogfights inevitably got lower and slower.[14] The light weight of the MiGs gave them a significant turn advantage over modern U.S. fighters in a slow, close fight—commonly called a "knife fight"—and the MiG's cannon armament was much more effective in a close engagement. The Feather Duster report emphasized that U.S. pilots should not turn with MiG-17s for long periods of time, but instead should keep their speed up and conduct hit and run "slashing" attacks.

The Feather Duster II tests made another significant point when they examined Air Force tactical formations to see if these formations could offset the MiGs' superior maneuverability. Feather Duster II pointed out that proper U.S. flight tactics cut into the MiGs' advantages, but also noted that the standard Air Force tactics were not the proper ones. Air Force flight tactics at the beginning of the Vietnam War were the same tactics used in World War II and Korea, a formation called "fluid four," where two pairs of two fighters supported each other. Each pair was divided into a leader and a wingman, and the wingman flew close but off to one side of the leader and behind the leader in a position known as "fighting wing." The pairs worked together, but the wingmen generally did not participate in offensive action; the wingman's sole role was to protect the leader. Based on the engagements with the F-86s, Feather Duster II said that the fighting wing formation was close to useless,[15] but since fluid four and fighting wing had been used for years and had strong support from high-ranking officers, the Air Force continued to use them throughout the war.

Other Air Force theoretical studies, like Feather Duster, were pessimistic about the results of air-to-air combat against MiGs, especially against the MiG-21. In the spring of 1966, the Air Force published the Southeast Asia Counterair Alternatives (SEACAAL) study; this study predicted that the MiG-21 would have a 3:1 kill ratio over the F-4 and a 4:1 kill ratio against the F-105, which was "hopelessly out-performed by the MiG-21C."[16] Against the MiG-17, SEACAAL predicted Air Force fighters would fare better; the study said that the MiG-17's only chance of shooting down an F-4 was to catch the F-4 unaware, and it projected an 18:1 kill ratio for the F-4 over the MiG-17 under the conditions over North Vietnam. The study concluded that the F-105:MiG-17 exchange ratio would be about even.

One drawback to the general predictions of how well the U.S. would do against the MiGs was that the Feather Duster tests had been flown by experienced U.S. fighter pilots; if the MiGs were flown by poor pilots, the results were expected to be different. Additionally, to be truly accurate, the tests should have been based on the performance of actual enemy aircraft, not U.S. substitutes. The energy maneuverability techniques told American pilots where their aircraft performed best and gave a rough idea of how they would do against the MiGs, but accurate relative comparisons would have to wait until the U.S. had real MiG-17s—and especially real MiG-21s—to test.

The Battles Begin

The first Rolling Thunder engagements between the opposing fighter forces had been surprisingly sharp and, with the loss of the two F-105s and an F-8 damaged, came as an unpleasant surprise to the U.S. air forces. The fights showed that the MiG-17's heavy cannon armament could be very effective and that the MiGs could be a dangerous adversary. As the U.S. increased the tempo of the bombing of North Vietnam, MiG activity increased, and on April 9, 1965, four Navy F-4Bs engaged four MiG-17s at very high altitude, over 40,000 feet. The F-4Bs fired eight AIM-7s and two AIM-9s; the last AIM-7 scored a hit and downed a MiG-17, but the victorious F-4B did not return—either a victim of one of the MiGs or an American missile.[17] On June 17, two Navy F-4Bs engaged four North Vietnamese MiG-17s and shot down two with AIM-7s in a head-on pass. These two engagements must have been a sobering introduction to the capabilities of the AIM-7 for the MiG-17 pilots.

By late May 1965, more and more strikes took place north of the 20° line. As Air Force F-105s began to strike regularly deep into North Vietnam, North Vietnamese MiGs became active, and soon this MiG activity began to fall into a pattern. MiGs would take off when the U.S. strikes were seen refueling, but when the first strike flights entered the target area, the MiG flights would move away. Then, as the last flights began to depart the area after the strike and the F-4 escorts were low on fuel, the MiGs moved back to follow the strike flights out.

The MiGs had not yet attacked the departing flights, and U.S. intelligence speculated that these were training flights for the MiGs and their GCI controllers, but it was clear that unless U.S. fighters interrupted this pattern, it would just be a matter of time before the MiGs caught some of the departing F-105s or their F-4 escorts, making U.S. losses a distinct possibility. To prevent this, the Air Force F-4 pilots developed a plan to surprise the MiGs, using for the first time what would be their most successful air-to-air tactic of Rolling Thunder—fooling the North Vietnamese radar controllers into thinking that their air-to-air armed F-4s were either heavily loaded strike or unarmed reconnaissance aircraft.

For this first deception mission, the F-4s were to simulate a delayed F-105 strike flight. The F-4s would launch later than normal and fly the same course and altitude as a delayed F-105 strike flight would, arriving in the target area as the strike flights were departing and hoping to surprise the MiGs with fully fueled air-to-air F-4s instead of low-fuel F-105s. On July 10, 1965, the morning strike flights had MiGs follow them out of North Vietnam, and that afternoon Mink, a flight of four F-4Cs, executed the plan.

All of Mink flight's air-to-air missiles received extra checks on the ground and in the air in an attempt to increase their reliability, and the flight flew at F-105 speeds, altitudes, and headings to give the appearance of being the last F-105 flight on target.

Mink arrived in the target area approximately fifteen minutes after the normal F-4C escort arrival time and began to orbit, but saw no MiGs on radar. Finally, low on fuel, the F-4s decided to make one more pass toward the North Vietnamese air bases before heading for home. After completing the turn, Mink 1 picked up a radar contact at thirty-three miles and the F-4s turned to make a head-on pass. Because of the large

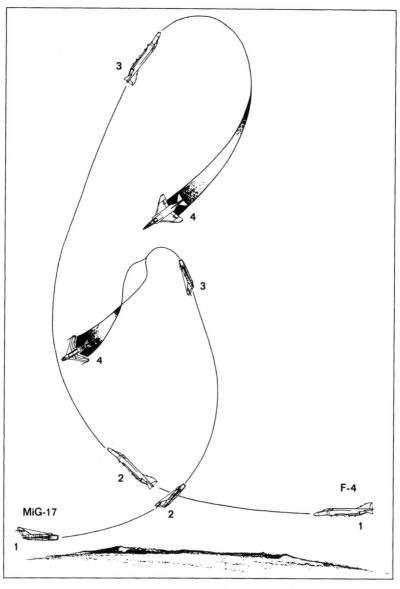

An example of "vertical flight," where an F-4 pilot uses his superior energy to out-zoom a MiG-17, then dive on the MiG when the MiG drops off. This tactic was highly effective until the MiG pilots learned not to climb with the F-4 but instead to stay low in horizontal turns. From *Fighter Combat: Tactics and Maneuvering*

numbers of American aircraft in the area, the F-4s had to visually identify the radar targets as MiGs before they fired; the F-4s' plan was to split
into two flights of two, one pair well in front of the other. The first pair of
F-4s, Mink 1 and Mink 2, was to lead in and make a head-on pass to identify the radar contacts; if they were MiGs, the F-4s would break away to a
safe distance while the second, trailing pair of F-4s, Mink 3 and Mink 4,
fired their AIM-7s head on at the North Vietnamese MiGs.

Mink 3 and Mink 4 dropped back to get the proper spacing; as the F-4s
closed on the radar contacts, Mink 2 identified them as MiG-17s in close
formation passing off his left wing. Unfortunately, Mink 3 and Mink 4
were not far enough behind the first two F-4s to fire safely; the plan to
shoot AIM-7s head on was dead. The MiGs started to turn as they passed
Mink 1 and Mink 2, but rolled out and turned back toward the second
element of Mink 3 and Mink 4. As the two flights passed head on, Mink 3
and Mink 4 dropped their external fuel tanks and turned into the MiGs;
the MiGs did likewise. The MiG-17s quickly turned inside the F-4s and
pulled behind Mink 3 and Mink 4; both F-4s saw the noses of the MiGs
light up with flashes as the MiGs began to fire their big cannon. The F-4s
were exactly where they did not want to be: namely, in a turning engagement with the agile MiG-17s. Mink 1 and Mink 2 had lost sight of the
engagement and left the area.

The harried F-4s put the energy maneuverability concepts and the
Feather Duster lessons to work and tried to exploit the MiG-17s' limitations. The faster Phantoms accelerated in the turn and began to outrun
the MiGs behind them; as the MiGs fell back, the F-4s split up to try to
trap the MiGs between them, but the MiGs also split, with one following
each F-4. At that point Mink 3 rolled into a dive to outrun his MiG; the
MiG tried to follow and wound up almost a mile behind the F-4, well out
of gun range and falling back. Mink 3 then began a pull up over the MiG;
the MiG tried to follow the F-4 up, but did not have enough power and
soon ran out of airspeed well behind and below the F-4.

The MiG rolled off and started a slow descent toward the clouds. Mink
3 was now high above the slow moving MiG-17; he pulled down to put
the North Vietnamese in front of him and fired an AIM-9B from a range
of 7,000 feet. It missed, and Mink 3 fired his three remaining AIM-9s in
a period of ten seconds, all with a good tone. The second missile detonated with a large fireball just to the right of the MiG's tail; the third
exploded slightly to the right of the MiG, and the fourth missed. The MiG
became a fireball as it entered the clouds; Mink 3, low on fuel, broke off
and headed for home.

Meanwhile, the second MiG was pursuing Mink 4, who went into a dive from 20,000 feet in afterburner, accelerated, and pulled away from the MiG. At 12,000 feet the F-4 started a climb; the MiG had lost ground but continued to try to follow the Phantom in the climb. At 33,000 feet Mink 4 saw that the MiG-17 had been unable to follow and was now several thousand feet below, dropping off in a slow, descending left turn. The F-4 made a slight turn and started down after the MiG, firing a Sidewinder from the heart of the missile envelope when the MiG was about a mile in front of him. The missile went past the MiG's tailpipe and detonated about five feet from the left wing tip; the MiG rocked his wings six or seven times rapidly and rolled slowly into a left bank with a fire in the tailpipe. Mink 4 fired a second AIM-9 without a tone that missed, then got a good tone and fired a third. The missile tracked well and exploded short of the tailpipe but in line with it. The fireball expanded until only the MiG's wing tips were visible; when the fireball subsided, the MiG started spewing dense white smoke from its tailpipe. The MiG-17 was now about 6,000 feet above the ground and rolled upside down and pulled into a steep, nose low dive as Mink 4 fired his last Sidewinder and departed the area without seeing the result. He later was credited with a kill. Mink 3 and Mink 4's departure was timely; after the F-4s landed, they learned that a large group of MiGs had been pursuing them as they left North Vietnam.

The post-mission analysis of the battle showed that the energy maneuverability ideas worked in real combat. Now the F-4s knew exactly how to fight the MiG-17—keep fast and climb away. If the MiG-17 was foolish enough to try to follow, he would not be able to climb as high, and when he fell behind, the F-4 could then drop down on him and kill him with a missile.

Later experience would show that the vertical maneuvering was not as easy as it first seemed, because the distance from the MiG when the F-4 could turn back was almost the same distance where the small MiG became very difficult to see. It took highly experienced pilots—which the Air Force had in the theater at this time—to execute the maneuver properly.

U.S. Air Force Basing

As the air war over North Vietnam intensified, more and more U.S. aircraft arrived, and the air bases in South Vietnam began to fill up. In February 1965 the Thai government had given permission for aircraft based there to be used in strikes against North Vietnam, and soon there were three F-105 squadrons based at the Royal Thai Air Force Base at Korat. They soon were joined by an F-4 squadron at the Royal Thai Air Force Base at Ubon, more F-105s at the Takhli air base, and reconnaissance aircraft at the base at Udorn. From late 1965, the Air Force based most of the fighter aircraft that were to strike North Vietnam in Thailand. For political reasons, all the U.S. air bases in Thailand were officially Thai bases, all carried the suffix of RTAFB (Royal Thai Air Force Base), and all were under the nominal command of a Thai officer who provided base services and who commanded a small Thai military detachment. In exchange, U.S. Air Force aircraft were allowed to fly freely into North Vietnam from these bases.

As the war developed, each of the Air Force bases in Thailand took responsibility for certain types of operations. The vast majority of the air strikes came from two F-105 wings, the 388th Tactical Fighter Wing (TFW) based at Korat RTAFB and the 355th TFW based at Takhli RTAFB. Takhli also was the home of the EB-66 electronic warfare aircraft and, at times, eight KC-135 airborne tankers. Most of the F-4s that flew escort and strike missions over North Vietnam came from the 8th TFW at Ubon RTAFB,[18] but often F-4s from bases in South Vietnam took an active part in Rolling Thunder and scored several MiG kills. The reconnaissance RF-4s and RF-101s were part of the 432nd Tactical Reconnaissance Wing (TRW) at Udorn RTAFB, just south of Vientiane, Laos. Udorn was the closest jet base to North Vietnam and was often used for recovery of battle-damaged aircraft, and later in Rolling Thunder it was home to a squadron of F-4s. All operations were under the command of Seventh Air Force Headquarters in Saigon, which was, in turn, under Pacific Air Command (PACAF) Headquarters in Hawaii.

Because of the relatively long distance to the targets in North Vietnam, Air Force fighter aircraft operating out of Thailand always had to have pre-strike air refueling over northern Thailand and southern Laos or the Gulf of Tonkin with KC-135 tankers before entering North Vietnam, and they often needed post-strike air refueling after the mission. The KC-135s came from various bases, but the main tanker base in Thailand was U-Tapao, on the Gulf of Siam. The pre-strike refueling of large numbers of fighters before a Rolling Thunder mission put the U.S. forces at a severe tactical disadvantage because the force of fighters and tankers showed up clearly on the North Vietnamese radar scopes and provided plenty of warning of a large Air Force raid from the Thai bases.

The long distances flown by Air Force aircraft also meant the fighter and strike aircraft always carried heavy external fuel tanks under their wings and fuselage to give them enough fuel to complete the mission and return to their base or a tanker. Full, these external tanks were very heavy

Six U.S. Air Force F-4s refuel from a KC-135 tanker over Laos. *Author's collection*

and limited the fighter's maneuverability, and even when empty they produced a great deal of drag. Once engaged by a MiG or SA-2 SAM, U.S. pilots needed to jettison these external tanks quickly for maximum maneuverability, but herein was a problem: The external tanks were designed for peacetime operations, and jettisoning them at combat speed or in a hard turn could result in damage to the aircraft, or even in its loss, if the tank hit the aircraft's control surfaces.[19] The restrictions on jettisoning an F-4 centerline tank were especially severe,[20] with the result that when attacked, U.S. fighters often had to delay their first defensive maneuver a few critical seconds until their tanks were completely clear of the aircraft.

U.S. Navy Carrier Operations

To strike targets in North Vietnam, the Navy located aircraft carriers off the coast of North Vietnam in an area known as "Yankee Station."[21] From early in Rolling Thunder, the Navy usually kept three carriers on Yankee Station, with one more on the way to the area and one on the way home. Besides the F-8s and F-4s, Navy carriers carried A-4, A-1, and A-6 strike aircraft, and the carriers offered tremendous flexibility. The position of the carriers close offshore reduced the need for air refueling, which was important because the Navy had few tankers on the carrier and ordinarily used them only for emergencies.[22] Additionally, Navy aircraft could carry out strikes with a much greater element of surprise than the Air Force because the carriers could be moved close to the targets, cutting down on the North Vietnamese warning time. Another advantage the Navy had was the radar on its ships, which provided GCI to give its strike forces MiG warnings and guide Navy fighters to attack MiGs near the coast.

While the carriers allowed great tactical flexibility, they also had their share of problems. The number of carriers committed to the war put a great strain on the Navy's carrier resources. Initially the war was fought by the carriers from the Pacific Fleet, but by mid-1965 Atlantic Fleet carriers were making the long trip to participate in the conflict, and in 1966 the carrier *Enterprise,* the Navy's only nuclear carrier, was transferred from the Atlantic Fleet to the Pacific Fleet to assist in the war effort. To further offset the shortage of carriers, the Navy extended the time the carriers remained on Yankee Station and cut the time they were allowed to "turn around" between deployments. The long deployments and limited time for refit caused severe problems, because most U.S. carriers dated from World War II and were reaching the end of their careers or required major refit. The high operational tempo of the war made their withdrawal from combat for an extended period impossible, and the carriers gradually wore down.[23] As an added problem, the long cruises in the combat area and short time in home port before returning to combat began to cause morale problems with the sailors and airmen.

Natural forces and accidents also cut into the carriers' effectiveness. Periodic typhoons forced the carriers to cease operations, and several tragic fires on carriers put some of the big ships out of action for long periods of time. The carriers disabled by fires increased the pressure on the available carriers, further contributing to maintenance problems.

Tactical Problems

Initially, Air Force tactics caused many problems. While Navy strike aircraft were trained for conventional strike missions with relatively high altitude entry into the target area for dive-bombing passes, the Air Force—especially the F-105 crews—had been trained for treetop-level attacks with nuclear weapons against Warsaw Pact targets in Europe. The feeling was that these very low-level, high-speed attacks were the best way to achieve surprise and that the jets' high speed would make them immune from ground fire. Additionally, bombing accuracy was good at low levels, and many Air Force conventional weapons were designed for such delivery.[24]

However, as the air war continued, the North Vietnamese early warning system improved, and low-altitude attacks no longer gave the fighters any element of surprise. At low level, U.S. aircraft were in range of every type of North Vietnamese weapon—including small arms—that could not reach them at higher altitudes. Additionally, because of political restrictions, there were a limited number of targets U.S. aircraft could bomb, and the routes to these targets became very predictable. As the number of flights over the same areas of North Vietnam steadily increased, the North Vietnamese concentrated their AAA in the known target areas, and Air Force losses began to increase dramatically. By mid-1965 Air Force tactics had begun to change; Air Force formations penetrated at relatively high altitudes and losses declined.[25]

The Arrival of Surface-to-Air Missiles

By mid-1965 U.S. intelligence noted that the North Vietnamese had more than doubled the number of warning radars, and the number of radar-guided guns was increasing rapidly. More importantly, during April intelligence detected electronic signals that indicated the North Vietnamese were significantly improving their air defense system with the Soviet-

An SA-2 *(insert, upper left)* and an SA-2 site, showing two missiles on launchers and the Fansong radar. Note the prepared roads beyond the missile launchers; these allowed trucks and carriers to load the equipment rapidly for redeployment. Later in the war the SA-2 sites were well camouflaged. *USAF (courtesy of USNI Photographic Collection)*

made SA-2 Guideline SAM, and on April 5 a Navy RF-8 brought back pictures of an SA-2 site under construction fifteen miles southeast of Hanoi. The SA-2 was a large, radar beam-riding missile designed to shoot down single, high-flying nuclear bombers such as the B-47 and B-52. At this role it was effective—it already had brought down the CIA U-2 flown by Francis Gary Powers over the Soviet Union in 1960, a U-2 over Communist China, and an Air Force U-2 over Cuba during the Cuban missile crisis. A typical active SA-2 site consisted of one Fan Song guidance radar, several long-range early-warning radars to detect incoming aircraft beyond the Fan Song's range, and six missile launchers. Each site normally had twelve missiles: six missiles on launchers and six held in reserve on transporters in a nearby holding area.

The SA-2 had a range of seventeen nautical miles and was effective from 3,000 feet to well above 50,000 feet; generally, the higher the target, the better the SA-2 performed. The missile itself was large and heavy and had small wings, so it was relatively unmaneuverable; it performed best against nonmaneuvering bomber-type targets and had serious tactical limitations against maneuvering, fighter-type aircraft. Additionally, below 3,000 feet, the Fan Song guidance radar had difficulties seeing and tracking fast-moving aircraft, and inside about five miles the SA-2 had a "dead zone" where it could not engage a target.[26] To cover this dead zone, the SAM sites were heavily protected by anti-aircraft guns.

U.S. Countermeasures

With the improvement in the North Vietnamese defenses and the increasing tempo of the air war, the Air Force decided to send EB-66 electronic warfare aircraft to Southeast Asia to support strikes into North Vietnam. The EB-66 was a large, swept-wing twin-jet bomber adopted from a mid-1950s Air Force reconnaissance aircraft and light bomber.[27] Two types of EB-66 were available, the EB-66C, which did both radar jamming and electronic reconnaissance, and the EB-66B, which was exclusively a jamming aircraft.

Six EB-66Cs were ordered to Thailand, but before they deployed, the aircraft received an extensive upgrade program to give their electronic equipment a reconnaissance and ECM capability against most North Vietnamese radars, as well as a radar homing and warning (RHAW) system, the APR-25/26, which provided the big aircraft with electronic warning that they were being tracked by SAM radars or were being fired on. The EB-66Cs began to support Rolling Thunder operations in May 1965. Their first mission was electronic intelligence gathering, but their role soon changed to providing real-time electronic intelligence and jamming for the strike force. The EB-66Cs were followed by five EB-66Bs in October 1965. The B model had twenty-three jammers to the C model's nine, and the B model's jammers were more powerful, but the B's jamming frequencies had to be set on the ground, while the C could alter its jamming pattern in the air.[28] The EB-66 jammers were especially effective against the radars, known as Fire Can, that controlled the larger North Vietnamese anti-aircraft guns.

Tactically, over North Vietnam the EB-66B and EB-66C were best used in combination. The EB-66C used its intelligence-gathering systems to locate the SAM sites and direct the jamming of the EB-66B so it could provide the most effective jamming angles to cover the strike force's attack; the EB-66C also provided SAM launch warning and augmented jamming.[29]

Even with the improvements to their defensive electronic systems, the EB-66s were vulnerable to North Vietnamese defenses, and protecting them was an ongoing concern. There were a limited number of EB-66s in the Air Force inventory, so each one was very valuable, but the big air-

An EB-66 in flight. *USAF (courtesy of the National Archives)*

plane was helpless against MiGs and did not have the capability to jam the SA-2 Fan Song guidance radars or outmaneuver the missile,[30] so all of its orbits had to be set up outside of SAM operating areas. Additionally, when the jammers were on, they blanked out the aircraft's radios, so the EB-66 crews could not hear warnings that MiGs were in the area or that SAMs were being launched. These vulnerabilities severely cut into the EB-66's usefulness as the war went on.

Navy carrier-based aircraft also had electronic warfare aircraft to protect their strikes, and during Rolling Thunder the Navy's mainstays were the EA-3B (similar to the EB-66) and the single-engine, propeller-driven EA-1F. The EA-3Bs collected electronic intelligence, and the EA-1Fs provided jamming support for strikes. The slow, propeller-driven EA-1Fs did excellent service through 1967, loitering in pairs a few miles off the coast of North Vietnam in easy range of MiGs. When the EA-1Fs detected a threatening radar, they flew toward it at top speed—about 130 knots—while jamming the signal. Briefly, another electronic warfare aircraft, the U.S. Marine Corps' EF-10B, was embarked on the carriers, but it soon was moved to the base at Da Nang in South Vietnam to make maintenance easier.

The SAMs Engage

By June 1965, the SA-2 sites were completely laid out with the launchers in the open and the cables laid; it simply was a matter of hooking up the cables to the consoles and bringing in the missiles to make the sites operational. They were perfect targets, but the Johnson administration did not believe the North Vietnamese would actually use the missiles and feared that the Chinese or Soviets might be helping with the construction or even manning the sites, so U.S. aircraft were not permitted to attack,[31] even though some in the U.S. military pressed to do so.[32]

On July 24, 1965, Leopard, a flight of four Air Force F-4s, was in the area of one of the SA-2 sites when the site's Fan Song radar locked on. The F-4s had no electronic systems to warn them that the site was preparing to fire; an EB-66C in an electronic reconnaissance orbit saw the signals from the site and called a SAM launch, but, despite the warning, SA-2s hit the F-4 formation, downing Leopard 2 and damaging the other three F-4s. After the loss, permission was given to attack several sites; three days later a strike force of F-105s, with heavy jamming support from EB-66Cs, made an ill-advised low-level attack on two missile sites. It was too late: Only one site was occupied; the other site was a flak trap whose AAA tore into the American strike. Six F-105s were lost, and the sites essentially were undamaged.

The SAMs became more active, and on the night of August 11–12 the Navy lost an A-4 to a SAM. Permission was given to attack this particular installation, and two days later the Navy repeated the Air Force's mistake by sending a large strike force to find and attack the site. Not only did the attackers not find the SAM site, but North Vietnamese guns in the area shot down six of the Navy aircraft.[33] In a little over three weeks, the SAMs had been responsible for the loss of fourteen U.S. aircraft, and a U.S. report noted "the difficulty of identifying an active SAM site, and eradicating the SA-2 threat was quickly emphasized."[34]

After these initial successes, the North Vietnamese rapidly built a network of SAM sites all over North Vietnam. Originally the SAM sites were set up in a unique "star of David" pattern that allowed the support vehicles maximum accessibility to the missiles and launchers so the site could be moved quickly. Most of the sites were unoccupied, but the SA-2 and its associated systems were easy to move, and an entire battery easily could be taken down at one site, transported, and set up at another site overnight. A deadly shell game began as each day American electronic warfare aircraft tried to find the Fan Song radar emissions so they could tell which sites were occupied before the strike flights arrived in the area.

SAM Countermeasures

The SAMs now had become the major component of the North Vietnamese air defense system, and the medium altitudes where U.S. fighters had been flying were in the heart of the SA-2 envelope. During the next few weeks another U.S. aircraft was downed. Since only twelve SA-2s had been fired and since U.S. aircrews had very little experience with missiles, reports noted the crews had an "uncomfortable feeling . . . that the kill probability [P_k] was of the SA-2 missile was quite high."[35]

One thing that contributed to the feeling that the SAMs were very effective was U.S. military perceptions formed in the joint American Air Force/Army exercise Desert Strike, conducted in California in 1964. Army Hawk missiles—a missile much superior to the SA-2—were used then, and after the exercises there was some feeling that "tactical aircraft could no longer survive in a SAM environment."[36] Aircrew "concern over its [the SA-2] employment caused immediate changes in flight tactics,"[37] and throughout the war the tactical countermeasures forced on U.S. strikes by the SA-2—not the number of aircraft that it shot down—were the true measure of its effectiveness.

After the first SA-2 kills, U.S. fighters began flying at very low altitude—below 3,000 feet—as they moved into areas protected by SAMs. The Nui Tam Dao mountain range, a thin strip of relatively high (about 5,000 feet) hills running from the highlands close to the Chinese border southeast almost to Hanoi, became the favorite American approach route, since the small range blocked some of the North Vietnamese radars; the F-105 pilots soon named the green spine "Thud Ridge." As the strike flights approached the target at low level, they would pull up (POP) to a higher altitude (above 10,000 feet), make their dive-bombing pass on the target, then descend again to low level until out of the SAM area.[38] While limiting losses to SAMs, low-level attacks still had the same disadvantages they had earlier in the war, and it later was noted that "the cure was worse than the disease"[39] as American losses to AAA increased dramatically.

Not only were the North Vietnamese defenses more effective against low-flying U.S. aircraft, but for the strike flight leaders low altitude navigation and target location presented severe problems, especially in marginal weather. It was difficult for pilots to come into the target area at low level, POP sharply to high altitude, locate the target in a few seconds while hanging nearly upside down, and set up for a dive-bombing pass. If the bomb load was heavy, the aircraft could not POP to a high altitude and was forced to make a shallow-angle dive-bombing pass, decreasing accuracy and increasing its vulnerability to the defenses. Worse, at the top of the POP, the U.S. aircraft was at high altitude right over the SAM-defended target, vulnerable to an SA-2. One of the F-105 wing commanders commented during this period that "numerous targets have not been hit because the strike force could not go in at the desired altitude and [aircrews] were forced to use pop-up tactics that allow a few seconds to acquire the target and [thus] decreasing bombing accuracy."[40]

Meanwhile, U.S. fighters found they could outmaneuver the SA-2 by making a hard turn down and into it, followed by a sharp pull up and change of direction if the missile followed their first move down. Unfortunately, these maneuvers were impossible to execute in a fully loaded fighter, and if a strike aircraft was attacked by SAMs before it got to the target, to survive it had to jettison its bombs so it could outmaneuver the missile; in such a case the SAM would have accomplished its mission.

A major aid for U.S. strike aircraft against the SAMs was RHAW equipment. Like the EB-66s, the F-105s (but not the F-4s) were equipped with an RHAW system that told them the direction of SAM radars and when the SA-2 site was preparing to fire, and it gave an extra warning when the SA-2 was launched. The RHAW equipment took advantage of the fact that the SA-2's Fan Song radar took about seventy-five seconds to acquire a target, lock on, and fire. The radar had to change its power output significantly for thirty to forty seconds before launching the missile to "lock on" to the target, and then the Fan Song had to turn on its missile guidance signal—which also had a unique electronic signature—within four seconds after missile launch. The F-105 RHAW equipment detected each of these changes in the radar signals from the SAM sites and gave the pilot an aural tone that changed as the Fan Song proceeded with its launch sequence, and it gave him the direction of the missile site on an indicator in the cockpit and a bright red "launch" light when the Fan Song signals showed a launch. This meant, in principle, that the F-105 pilot knew where to look for the missile as the SA-2 lifted off, when it was easy to see the very large flame from the booster rocket. Once the pilot saw the missile, it was relatively easy to tell if it was guiding on his aircraft, and if necessary, the F-105 could either dive below the SAM's minimum altitude or jettison his ordnance to outmaneuver it. Later in the war, as the number of North Vietnamese radars proliferated, the RHAW systems gave so many warnings that they became less and less useful.

Jamming from the EB-66s also helped the F-105s' low-level approaches to their targets. The EB-66s normally operated singly or in pairs, escorted by F-4s, during U.S. bombing raids (the F-4 escort was required because the EB-66s could not hear radio warnings if MiGs were approaching). To provide their jamming, the EB-66s had set up two orbits, one over the Gulf of Tonkin and one northwest of Thud Ridge, flying in a racetrack pattern at around 30,000 feet for maximum jamming range and effectiveness for their systems. The EB-66s used "noise" jamming, which simply matched the power of their jammers against the power of the North Viet-

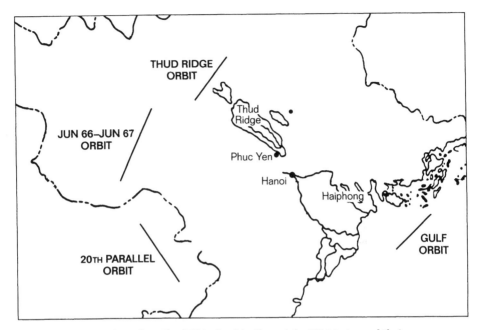

EB-66 Orbits. Note how the "Thud Ridge" orbit allowed the EB-66s to send their jamming signals parallel to the ridge into the Hanoi area. In June 1966 North Vietnamese defenses forced the EB-66s to move the orbit to the west, where they were much less effective.

namese radars on the same frequencies.[41] The farther away from the radars the jamming source was, the less effective the jamming, but the two orbits were close enough for effective jamming and well out of range of SAMs. They provided excellent coverage over the Hanoi/Haiphong area, where the North Vietnamese had most of their radars and radar-controlled defenses.[42] The Thud Ridge orbit was especially valuable because it provided the EB-66 jammers a straight line of jamming down the ridge to the North Vietnamese defenses around Hanoi. This jamming augmented the protection the strike flights got from the masking of the ridge.

To supplement the protection of standoff jamming and flying at low level, both the Navy and the Air Force began using specially modified fighters to attack SAM sites on a mission called Iron Hand. The Navy used mainly the single-seat A-4, while the Air Force opted for two-seat fighters with special electronic gear and an electronic warfare officer in the back seat to locate and attack the SAM sites and their Fan Song radars. Besides electronics to find the SAM sites, beginning in March

A two-seat F-105F Wild Weasel. Note the rear canopy of the second seat for the
electronic warfare officer and the Shrike missile under the right wing.
USAF (courtesy of the National Archives)

1966 these special fighters carried a missile that homed in on the Fan
Song radar emissions, the AGM-45 Shrike.[43]

The Air Force aircraft were called Wild Weasels, and the first aircraft
used were two-seat F-100Fs, but their performance was inadequate, and a
two-seat F-105, the F-105F, quickly replaced them in early 1966.[44] Air
Force tactics called for one or two flights of Iron Hand aircraft—all
F-105Fs or a mixture of F-105Fs and single-seat F-105Ds—to move into
the target area before the strike flights arrived to search for and attack the
SA-2 radars. The North Vietnamese had four times as many prepared
sites as active sites, so the Weasels could not go directly to a site; while
the strike flights were in the target area, the Weasels had to remain to
watch all the SAM sites that might try to attack, and they stayed until the
last strike flights left. Since the target area had the heaviest defenses, the
long periods the Weasels had to spend there gave them the most exposure
to the defenses and resulted in the highest losses. Also, operating in single flights and focusing on their hunt for the SAM sites, the Iron Hand
flights were attractive targets for MiGs throughout the war.

With the aid of jamming, RHAW, and Wild Weasels, the Air Force felt
the strikers, flying around 5,000 feet and in wide long trail formations,

could operate with a fairly low risk of SAM intercept.[45] If engaged by SAMs, the strike flight would drop down to low level to try to escape, then as a last resort jettison their ordnance and outmaneuver the missile. This long train of aircraft over a wide area meant the strikers arrived over the target one flight at a time, giving the AAA gunners around the target the opportunity to concentrate on just a few aircraft. Later, as the MiGs became more active, the long train of strikers gave them plenty of chances to sneak in without being detected by the small fighter escort, and the slower MiG-17s could begin their attacks from above the low-flying U.S. strike flights, using the altitude advantage to accelerate to a speed where they could close for a gun attack.[46] Even with these tactics, however, losses to SA-2s and especially AAA were still very high, and the missiles were still forcing the U.S. strikes away from optimal tactics; clearly the solution was some sort of electronic countermeasure for the SA-2.

One answer was an aircraft that could fly with the strike flights and jam the SAM sites as they went, rather than orbiting some distance away. The Navy had the Marine EA-6A, a jamming aircraft with performance similar to the Navy's A-6 attack aircraft, which could accompany the Navy strikers at least part of the way to their targets; this was especially helpful because the closer they came to the radar, the more effective the EA-6A's jammers. The Air Force, on the other hand, did not have a jamming aircraft of comparable performance (and had not been interested in buying the EA-6A). Another possibility was chaff—thin strips of tin foil cut to specific lengths. During World War II, it had been found to be the simplest, cheapest, and most effective weapon against radar. Chaff was light, compact, and could have been carried easily in fighter aircraft, but it had not been developed for internal carriage on Air Force fighters (Navy aircraft carried chaff, and later Air Force F-4s carried small amounts of chaff in their speed brakes for a "one time" use if needed).[47] Chaff could be carried externally—either in chaff dispensers or in chaff bombs—but these caused a great deal of drag, took up stations that could be used for bombs, and generally were not considered cost effective.

The Air Force and the Navy decided in the late 1950s that the most desirable solution was to have the strikers carry their own jamming system, so they tried to develop small jammers that could fit in a fighter aircraft, but in the era before microelectronics, such jammers were very difficult to design. By the end of 1963, the Air Force was testing a family of externally carried countermeasure pods, the QRC-160, based on countermeasures packages developed earlier for strategic bombers. In July 1965, the first QRC-160 jamming pods for fighter-type aircraft arrived in Southeast Asia for use by Air Force RF-101 and RF-4 reconnaissance aircraft, but they were unsatisfactory and were returned to the United States after a few months.[48]

The Navy was quicker to field an operational electronic jamming system, and by the end of 1965 its ALQ-51 jammer was internally mounted on the underside of A-4 and A-6 strike aircraft, where it did not take up a weapons station.[49] The ALQ-51 was not particularly powerful and was a "deception jammer" that depended on sending a false return to the SAM or anti-aircraft gun radar rather than jamming the signal; the theory was that the confused operator would not be able to figure out which radar return to fire on. The Air Force tried the ALQ-51 on some of its reconnaissance aircraft, but found that when the radar operators saw the false targets they simply fired more guns and missiles; the chance of damage from this barrage of fire offset the ALQ-51's usefulness, and the Air Force dropped it. Throughout 1965 and most of 1966 U.S. aircraft lacked a truly effective jamming system against the SAM radars.

Route Packages

The air strikes continued to intensify. On September 20, 1965, the first strikes were made against the northeast railway that ran from China to Hanoi and over which a larger percentage of the North Vietnamese supplies moved, but from December 25, 1965, until January 30, 1966, the bombing was halted to give the North Vietnamese a chance to respond to U.S. peace overtures. During this lull, the Navy and the Air Force tried to simplify the command arrangements by dividing the target areas in North Vietnam geographically and formalized what had been a U.S. Navy/Air Force working agreement prior to this time. The Air Force took responsibility for strikes over Route Packages I, V, and VIA (the Hanoi area), and the Navy took Route Packages II, III, IV, and VIB (the Haiphong area). Despite its apparent complexity to civilian decision makers[50] the Route Package system worked reasonably well; the main problem was that when the weather was bad in Route Packages V and VI, the Air Force had to go all the way to Route Package I rather than the more lucrative areas of Route Packages II through IV, which belonged to the Navy. Practically, the Route Package divisions meant Air Force aircraft from bases in Thailand had to fly long distances over North Vietnam and thus had a greater chance of being engaged by—and engaging—MiGs. Engagement patterns by the end of 1965 reflected this: The Air Force had twenty-five encounters with MiGs, the Navy nine. On a personal level, to American aircrews in the Vietnam War, the Hanoi-Haiphong area—"Route Pack Six"—became synonymous with the toughest missions one could fly.

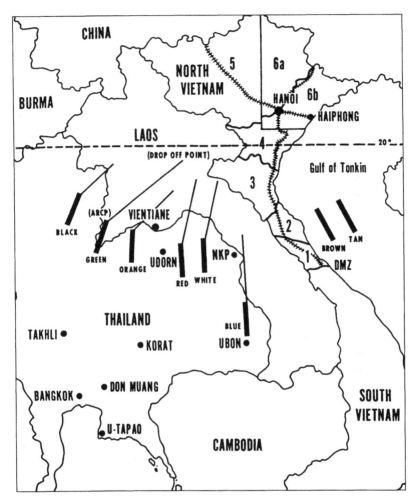

USAF Bases in Thailand, Air-Refueling Tracks, and the Route Package Division of North Vietnam. Note the large number of refueling tracks over Thailand/Laos that would pick up strikes from the U.S. Air Force bases in Thailand and drop them off at the 20th parallel. Note also how Route Package VI was divided into VIA (for the Air Force) and VIB (for the Navy).

2

The Battles Begin

AFTER THE BATTLES of July 1965 air-to-air encounters slowed, and U.S. aircraft would not heavily engage MiGs until April 1966. U.S. radar and intelligence indicated that the MiGs would follow U.S. strikes when they were leaving their targets but break off before they were close enough to engage. It seemed—and North Vietnamese radio transmissions tended to confirm—that the MiGs and the GCI radar controllers were in a training cycle.

The perception that training was necessary certainly was understandable. Notwithstanding their well-executed first attacks in April 1965, the North Vietnamese Air Force had little success against U.S. forces, losing six MiG-17s without shooting down any more U.S. aircraft. There were several reasons for this. As expected, the MiG-17 was slow compared to all of the U.S. aircraft—even when carrying a full bomb load—and the combination of slow speed and lack of missile armament meant the MiG-17 was no threat to U.S. aircraft at ranges greater than 3,000 feet. Even when a MiG-17 was behind a U.S. aircraft, often it could not get close enough to attack. Additionally, U.S. aircrews considered the North Vietnamese to be inferior pilots and thought their poor flying and lack of aggressiveness had prevented them from taking advantage of the occasions when their GCI put them in an excellent position to attack. When the North Vietnamese *did* get into a close-in, turning engagement with less-maneuverable U.S. fighters, they did not take advantage of the excellent turning ability of the MiG-17.

The MiG-21 Arrives

In the beginning of 1966, the air-to-air war over North Vietnam began to change dramatically as North Vietnamese MiG-21s started to appear. The MiG-21s had arrived in North Vietnam in November 1965 and had not participated in combat, but on January 15, 1966, a Navy RF-8 reconnaissance aircraft and its escort reported sighting a MiG-21. In February, a

Three MiG-21F-13s, known as the MiG-21C by American pilots. Note the two Atoll missiles under the wings. *Jay Miller*

MiG-21 pursued a U-2 over North Vietnam, and in March a MiG-21 attempted to attack an F-105 flight.

The MiG-21 was the Soviet Union's most modern fighter and represented a quantum leap in the capabilities of the North Vietnamese fighter force. It was evaluated as equal to—and in some aspects superior to—the F-4 and F-8 in maneuverability and acceleration and was vastly superior to the F-105 in every performance area except maximum speed at low altitude. Additionally, while the MiG-21Cs[1] carried a single 30-mm cannon with sixty rounds, the MiG-21's main armament was two Soviet K-13 (U.S. designation AA-2 Atoll) infrared missiles, a missile roughly equal in performance to the AIM-9B carried by the U.S. fighters at this time.[2] The MiG-21/Atoll combination would force a drastic revision in U.S. tactics; before the MiG-21's arrival, U.S. fighter maneuvers against MiGs assumed a gun-only fighter.

Escalation

Frustrated by the lack of response from North Vietnam and under pressure from the military to increase air strikes into North Vietnam, the Johnson administration launched a significant escalation in the bombing campaign on March 2, 1966: Now all of North Vietnam (except the prohibited and restricted areas) was open for attack.

As the bombing increased, the North Vietnamese defenses responded by significantly increasing MiG activity. Toward the end of April 1966, the MiGs made their first regular, concentrated attacks, beginning with an effort to intercept and destroy the Air Force EB-66s in their Thud Ridge orbit, and from April 23 to April 30, MiG-21s made their first active interventions in the war as they joined MiG-17s in attacking both the high-flying EB-66s and Air Force strike flights.

The attacks on the EB-66s probably reflected the effectiveness of EB-66 standoff jamming and showed the priority the North Vietnamese put on having their radar network unobstructed during American air raids. On April 23, 1966, Denver, a flight of Air Force F-4Cs, was escorting two EB-66s in their Thud Ridge orbit when they saw a single MiG-21 closing from behind the flight. When the MiG was about a mile and a half behind the flight, Denver 1 jettisoned his external fuel tanks and turned back into the MiG while Denver 2 stayed with the EB-66 to guard against other MiGs that might be in the area. When it was clear that the MiG-21 was alone, Denver 2 told the EB-66 to leave the area, then jettisoned his external fuel tanks and turned back toward the fight.

The MiG-21 had turned on his attacker and now was chasing Denver 1 in a right turn, but he could not stay with the U.S. fighter and drifted to the outside of the turn. As Denver 2 approached the fight, he had a radar lock on and saw two aircraft about six miles ahead, but because of the distance, he did not know which was the MiG and which the F-4. Unable to contact Denver 1 on the radio, Denver 2 chose one of the aircraft and began an attack. As he closed saw he was on the MiG-21, but now he was too close to fire a missile and began to maneuver to drop back. About 5,000 feet behind the MiG, he tried to launch two AIM-7s, but the missiles did not fire (the maintenance ground crew had not connected the missile ejector mechanism). Still behind the MiG, Denver 2 changed his switches and fired two AIM-9Bs; he felt the missiles leave the aircraft but did not see the missiles in the air. He maneuvered again to keep from overrunning the MiG, then fired his last two AIM-9s from behind the MiG, again feeling the missiles leave the aircraft but not seeing them in the air. Still behind the MiG-21 but low on fuel, out of AIM-9s, and with AIM-7s that would not fire, Denver 2 turned away, and the MiG escaped.

On April 26, two F-4Cs were escorting an EB-66 when they were met head on by two MiG-21s. After the two flights passed, one of the MiGs apparently lost sight of the F-4s and began a gentle climb away. The F-4s pulled behind him, and one of them fired three AIM-9s; the first passed close and the MiG pilot ejected; the second missed, and the third went up the MiG's tailpipe and exploded. This was the first MiG-21 kill of the war. As the F-4s followed the MiG down, the second MiG attacked but missed, and flew in front of the lead F-4, who fired his last AIM-9 from close behind the MiG in the heart of the envelope. The missile passed over the MiG's left wing but did not explode. On April 29, F-4Cs downed two MiG-17s, one with an AIM-9; the other crashed trying to avoid an F-4 attack. To end the week, on April 30 an F-4C shot down another MiG-17. It had been a big week for the Air Force F-4s with one MiG-21 and three MiG-17s downed for no losses, but this was only part of the story.

Missile Problems

Despite their success in air combat thus far, U.S. aircrews could see potential problems ahead because the Air Force air-to-air missiles, especially the radar-guided AIM-7, were performing poorly. In April and May, Air Force F-4s fired thirteen AIM-7s and twenty-one AIM-9s. Of the thirteen AIM-7s fired, only one was a hit, for an 8 percent hit rate; the F-4s had tried to fire three more AIM-7s, but the missiles did not even leave the rail, so the actual performance was one out of sixteen (about 6 percent). Out of the twenty-one AIM-9s fired, six hit (two on the same MiG) for five kills, for a 28 percent hit rate—respectable, but less than expected.[3] Poor AIM-7 performance was beginning to be seen as the norm by American pilots, and by the end of May, Air Force F-4 aircrews reported losing much of their confidence in the Sparrows. The Navy had fared better with the AIM-7—four hits in twelve firings—but this was little consolation to the Air Force.

It was very frustrating for U.S. crews to work their way into position for a kill and have the missiles malfunction, and the lack of a cannon made Air Force F-4s especially sensitive to missile problems. (The problem was not as serious for the Navy, because the missile-armed F-4Bs split the air-to-air mission with the cannon-armed F-8s). One solution often mentioned in Air Force aircrew combat mission debriefings was to mount a gun on the F-4, and there had been several opportunities for F-4s to use a gun during the early engagements. Still, equipping the F-4 with a gun was a much-debated topic at this point in the war and was not a universally accepted idea. Not all Air Force F-4 crews believed a gun was necessary, or even desirable. Some crews believed that a cannon would tempt F-4 pilots to slow down and get into the MiG-17's best arena—a slow-speed, gun-only dogfight. Air Force combat debriefings report F-4 crews making such comments as, "It would be undesirable and possibly fatal for an F-4 to use a gun in fighting with a MiG because the MiG is built to fight with guns and an F-4 is not,"[4] or "A gun is not particularly desirable [because] one might make the mistake of getting into a turning engagement if a gun was available."[5]

Consequently, for the time being the F-4 crews were stuck with the poorly performing missiles; the situation was well summed up by an Air Force F-4 squadron commander who said, "Guys, they don't call them 'hittles.'"

North Vietnamese GCI

The North Vietnamese radar system continued to improve and now consisted of a diversified surveillance radar net and weapons-control radars. These radars gave the North Vietnamese the capability to detect Air Force strikes early and to track U.S. aircraft continuously while maintaining control of their MiGs. The system was not flawless; among other shortcomings, the North Vietnamese appeared unable to control SAMs and MiGs at the same time. The presence of MiGs in the vicinity of U.S. aircraft usually indicated an absence of SAMs and vice versa, and U.S. aircrews began to refer to "MiG days" and "SAM days."

It is difficult to overstate the advantages that GCI radar control gave the North Vietnamese fighters; it was able to tell the MiGs the location of the U.S. aircraft and was usually able to position them behind U.S. aircraft, so the MiGs had time to maneuver to set up an attack, often giving them the advantage of surprise. North Vietnamese GCI also warned the MiGs when they were about to be attacked by U.S. fighters, making it difficult for U.S. aircraft to surprise the MiGs.

Jamming the GCI

The United States understood that the North Vietnamese radar system and GCI were key to the North Vietnamese defenses and therefore tried hard to counter them, especially with jamming from EB-66s. But while the EB-66 was effective against fire control radars, it was not as effective against the North Vietnamese early warning system. For early warning, the North Vietnamese used two high-powered, multibeam Bar Lock radars, which were relatively immune to EB-66 jamming. One Bar Lock in the western part of North Vietnam gave early-warning and GCI coverage at least 90 miles into Laos, covering the refueling tracks of U.S. strikes coming out of Thailand, and a Bar Lock near Haiphong covered Yankee Station and gave early-warning coverage well out over the Gulf of Tonkin. The Bar Lock required only eight hours to become operational after moving; this mobility made destroying them very difficult. As an additional countermeasure, the North Vietnamese used a truck-mounted radar, the Flat Face, as a backup to the Bar Lock and a gap filler; the Flat Face could be operational in about ten minutes.

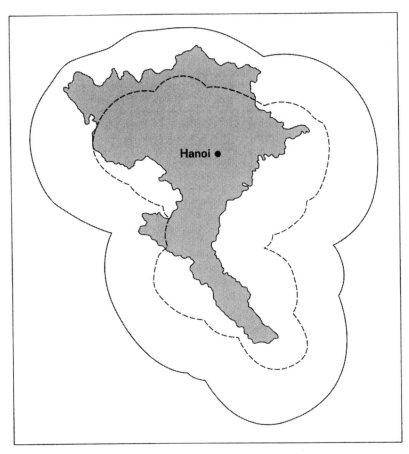

North Vietnamese GCI Coverage. The outer, solid line shows the detection range of the North Vietnamese radar for an F-105-size target flying at 15,000 feet—the normal altitude for a strike force to enter the country. This radar coverage gave the North Vietnamese considerable warning that a U.S. Air Force raid was inbound. The inner circle shows a detection range of an F-105–size target flying at 5,000 feet.

The GCI net was hard to jam for a variety of other reasons. Typically, the North Vietnamese reacted to the U.S. standoff jamming effort by concentrating radar activities in bands not jammed at a particular time, and by constantly changing frequencies to evade the jamming. The system had overlapping radar coverage, some anti-jamming devices, and effective communications; this was combined with rapidly improving radar operator proficiency in an ECM environment. Throughout the war, U.S. intelligence analysts believed the North Vietnamese air defense could maintain the overall picture of the air situation, even if degraded by jamming.

U.S. Radar Coverage

While the North Vietnamese benefited from excellent radar coverage, over most of North Vietnam the U.S. forces did not. The coastal area could be covered by the Navy with radar from its ships, and from July 1966 the Navy set up a system called the PIRAZ (Positive Identification and Radar Advisory Zone) off the coast. The PIRAZ had a radar ship, Red Crown, located about 25 miles from the mouth of the Red River, and two more radar ships, one south of Red Crown and one north, for additional coverage. At first the PIRAZ ships used the SPS-30 radar, but it proved unreliable, and from early 1967 the ships were upgraded to the SPS-48 radar, which was a vast improvement and had a greater capability to pick up aircraft at low level.[6] With the introduction of the SPS-48, the PIRAZ generally gave U.S. forces excellent GCI coverage in the areas it could cover throughout the war. The Navy carriers also carried an early-warning aircraft, the E-1B, whose radar was best over water but that did have a limited capability over land.

The Air Force did not have any ground stations close to North Vietnam to set up radar sites, so it set up a radar station on the northeastern Thailand/Laos border at Nakhon Phanom RTAFB, which offered some coverage into North Vietnam to the area south of Hanoi. Unfortunately, both the U.S. ground- and sea-based radars were "line of sight" and, because of the curvature of the earth and the terrain, could not see low-flying aircraft over the Hanoi area.

The Air Force recognized this problem early in the war and brought in the Big Eye Task Force, a small group of EC-121D airborne radar surveillance aircraft, to provide airborne radar coverage over North Vietnam. The EC-121D was a military version of the Lockheed Super Constellation, adapted to carry long-range radar, and was originally designed to fly orbits off the coast of the United States to provide an extension of the ground-based, early-warning radar network for the defense of North America against Soviet nuclear bombers. The EC-121D was, to be polite, ungainly. In a large hump under the long, sleek fuselage, it carried a long-range, early-warning search radar that had a range over water of about 150 miles. In a fin on top of the fuselage, the EC-121D carried an altitude-measuring radar with a practical range of only 70 miles. The two radars protruding above and below the slim fuselage led some to call the EC-121 the "pregnant guppy."

The Big Eye Task Force was sent to Tan Son Nuit Air Base in South Vietnam in early April 1965, and beginning April 16, two EC-121Ds began to fly orbits in the Gulf of Tonkin to provide radar coverage of

An EC-121. Note the graceful lines marred by the large upper and lower radomes, resulting in its nickname, the "pregnant guppy." *USAF (courtesy of the National Archives)*

North Vietnam. North Vietnam was a special challenge to the EC-121Ds because its radar system was designed to look for hostile aircraft over the water, and ground clutter from the mountains and terrain seriously interfered with the radar picture. Fortunately, many of the EC-121s' previous missions had involved watching Soviet aircraft over Cuba, and there EC-121 crews found that their radar had some limited capability to track aircraft over land. From their Cuban experience, the EC-121 radar operators knew that if they flew over water at very low altitude—under 200 feet—they actually could "bounce" the radar beam of the search radar off the water. This allowed them to avoid some ground clutter and detect medium-altitude targets over land at ranges out to 150 miles. To bounce their signals off the water and get this range over North Vietnam, the EC-121Ds set up one of their orbits about fifty miles from the coast. One EC-121D flew this orbit, a search pattern known as the Alpha Track, at low altitude—50 to 300 feet—over the water, while a second EC-121D flew an orbit called the Bravo Track at medium altitude farther from the coast. However, even in the Alpha orbit, most of the EC-121's radar contacts were beyond the seventy-mile range of the EC-121's altitude-measuring radar, so while the EC-121Ds could detect aircraft flying over North Vietnam at altitudes above 8,000 feet and pass general MiG locations and

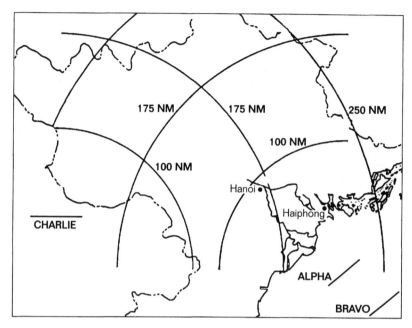

EC-121 Orbits. The effective range of the EC-121 radar was generally less than 100 miles, but with the advent of the QRC-248 enemy IFF detector, the range was extended to about 175 miles, and the low-altitude Alpha orbit became unnecessary.

heading information, they could not pass the critical information about the MiGs' altitude.

While flying the radar orbits off the coast of North Vietnam sounded simple, it was not. Maneuvering the large, underpowered EC-121s at the low altitude required by the Alpha orbit, often in marginal weather, was not a trivial matter, and from time to time weather forced the EC-121s so low that they literally were dodging the masts of the many fishing sampans in the area as they tried to fly their orbit. There also were constant problems with the large, complex systems on the EC-121s.[7] Maintenance was difficult; the seawater and the hot, humid Thai bases wreaked havoc on the EC-121's sensitive electronics. The equipment and the crews on the low-level Alpha orbit especially suffered; flying low over the water on the hot Asian days, the air conditioning was practically useless, and the heat generated by the electronic equipment sent temperatures soaring. The situation became so bad that often a flight surgeon was carried on Alpha orbit flights.[8] Additionally, there was the constant threat of interception by MiGs, which would have found the EC-121 a tempting and helpless target. Each EC-121 in orbit had to have a fighter escort; if the escort had to leave or did not show up, the EC-121 had to abort the mission.

Early in the war the EC-121s tried to give a type of coverage called "close control" on a separate frequency for MiGCAP aircraft, but for technical reasons the aircraft's radar was not capable of the precise tracking needed to guide U.S. fighters the way the North Vietnamese GCI controlled their MiGs. By February 1966 it was clear they could not control the fighters to an interception, or even identify the U.S. flights that MiGs were attacking. Because of these problems, the EC-121s changed their procedures and began to give the MiGs' location, first in grid areas and then, later, in range and bearing from Hanoi, which had the code name Bullseye. A typical call might be, "Bandits, Bullseye 270 for twenty"; this meant there were MiGs on a bearing of 270° (due west) 20 miles from Hanoi. The EC-121s called the radar contacts' position every five minutes or when there was a change in position, but they did not try to guide U.S. fighters to the MiGs or even warn specific flights they were under attack. U.S. flights over North Vietnam were forced to perform the mental gymnastics of determining where they were in terms of Bullseye and then figuring where the MiGs were relative to themselves based on the EC-121's Bullseye calls.

Communications between the EC-121s and the MiGCAP and strike forces they were supporting were a constant problem. The warnings issued by Big Eye and the quality of the control varied from day to day, depending on how well the radios and/or radio equipment functioned, the weather, and the amount of traffic. The EC-121 radios usually did not have the range to communicate with the Air Force aircraft coming into North Vietnam from Laos, so radio messages had to be broadcast by ground radio relay stations. The need for a radio relay delayed passing of vital information to aircraft under attack and probably contributed to U.S. losses, but it was not until September 1966 that a specially configured C-135 was deployed to Southeast Asia for this purpose—yet even this aircraft proved unreliable.

To help the EC-121s and other radar operators identify aircraft, all of the radars read a signal electronically generated by a piece of aircraft equipment known as the transponder, or IFF (Identification Friend or Foe). Transponders dated from the beginning of World War II; as that war progressed, and radar became vital for controlling fighters, there was a critical need to be able to distinguish between the radar returns of friendly and enemy aircraft. The transponder was a simple electronic device developed to meet this need. To determine if an aircraft was friendly, the radar sent out a special pulse that triggered the transponder, a procedure called "interrogating." The electronically enhanced radar return from the transponder-equipped aircraft gave a unique signal, clearly distinguishable from a "raw" radar return, on the "interrogating" radar screen showing if the aircraft was friendly. As an added benefit, transponder-equipped aircraft could be seen at greater ranges and lower altitudes than nontransponder-equipped aircraft. By the time of the Vietnam War, all military aircraft carried transponders, and both the United States and North Vietnam used them to control their aircraft. Each system was unique: U.S. radar could not read the Soviet transponders on North Viet-namese aircraft, and the Soviet-supplied North Vietnamese radar could not read U.S. transponders. Since the transponders were unique, their security was important—if one side could read the other's transponders, they would have a tremendous advantage in locating the enemy.

Despite its utility, the transponder was not universally popular with American pilots. One fear was that the North Vietnamese were able to interrogate and read the U.S. transponders on their radars. In May 1966, one U.S. headquarters speculated that the North Vietnamese (perhaps with Soviet or Chinese assistance) might be able to interrogate U.S. transpon-ders on their radar by dissecting and examining the Mark X transponder sets taken from downed U.S. aircraft.[9] If the North Vietnamese could read U.S. transponders, they could track U.S. strikes at very low altitudes, and more seriously, the SA-2's Fan Song radar could read the transponders. If that were the case, it was estimated that the minimum effective altitude of the SA-2 would drop from 3,000 feet to 1,000 feet.[10]

U.S. pilots also might choose not to use their transponder because one of the EC-121's duties was to report U.S. planes that entered the "prohib-ited" and "restricted" areas in North Vietnam and the Chinese "no-fly" zone, which extended 30 miles south of the Chinese border. Any no-fly zone violations had to be reported to higher headquarters—often up to the White House—with serious consequences for the offending pilots. Many fighter pilots were not willing to put their careers at risk by using their transponders as they violated the no-fly airspace fighting their way in and out of North Vietnam.[11] The relatively undefended no-fly areas, especially the mountains in the Chinese buffer zone, beckoned as a way to get in or out of the heavily defended Red River delta around Hanoi and Haiphong; all a U.S. fighter had to do to fly there was turn off his trans-ponder to prevent detection by the EC-121s. Later in the war, when the EC-121s were able to give individual flights their own transponder codes and could warn and control them more precisely, U.S. pilots began to see the benefits of the transponder, and they became more willing to use it.

On May 10, 1966, an American F-105D pursued a MiG-17 twenty-five miles into China and shot it down.[12] The kill—the first by an F-105—was hushed up and is not listed in the official records of U.S. kills in

Southeast Asia, but it had major consequences. After this border violation, the Seventh Air Force decided the EC-121s in their Gulf of Tonkin
orbits could not see into enough of the Chinese no-fly zone, and they
ordered another EC-121 orbit set up just north of Vientiane, Laos. The
purpose of this orbit was not so much to assist U.S. aircraft with MiG
warnings, but more to report U.S. violations of the Chinese no-fly zone.[13]
Called Charlie Station, the orbit began on October 1966 but proved to be
a great strain on the limited EC-121 force; consequently, it took a low priority and was flown only irregularly. In order regularly to fly the orbit, the
Big Eye Task Force leadership said the force would need to increase from
seven to eleven aircraft and crews, but this was not to take place until
later in the war.[14] In addition to the Charlie orbit, the Air Force set up
additional radars at a Tactical Air Control Center North Sector, with the
call sign of Motel, at Da Nang Air Force Base in South Vietnam. Motel
monitored all Air Force flights over Route Packages V and VI, mainly
retransmitting Big Eye information such as MiG and border warnings.[15]

The Big Eye Task Force led a nomadic life. Their main operating base
was in Tainan Air Station in Taiwan, Nationalist China,[16] but this was too
far away for operations over North Vietnam, and it quickly became clear
that the EC-121s required a forward-operating base in the theater. They
began their operations at Tan Son Nuit Air Base close to Saigon, but Viet
Cong attacks on the base made Seventh Air Force decide in early 1966 to
send the EC-121s to a U.S. base in Thailand. It was not a popular move;
the EC-121s were large, complex, difficult to maintain, and required a
large support group, which put a severe strain on the facilities of the
small Thai fighter bases. The task force was very much a "hot potato" and
spent time at a number of fighter bases in Thailand before settling at
Korat RTAFB in mid-October 1967.[17]

The F-8 Crusaders Engage

In June and July 1966 there were twelve engagements between U.S. aircraft and MiGs, and Navy F-8 Crusaders scored well, shooting down four
MiG-17s for two losses. The F-8 was designed as an air superiority fighter
and manned by the Navy's best-trained and most experienced air-to-air
pilots. In contrast to many Air Force pilots and Navy F-4 pilots, the F-8
pilots expressed great confidence in their training. In all of their combat
debriefings after air-to-air engagements, F-8 pilots never mentioned that
they needed more or better air combat training, even when they suffered
losses;[18] this training and confidence stood them in good stead as they
began regularly to engage MiGs.

On June 12, 1966, Nickel, a flight of four F-8s, was covering a strike leaving a target north of Haiphong when Nickel 2 saw two MiG-17s about three miles ahead and slightly to the left of the F-8s. The F-8s turned left into the MiGs, and as the F-8s and MiGs passed head on, Nickel 1 and Nickel 2 turned on the lead MiG, and Nickel 3 and Nickel 4 split off to engage the second MiG. Nickel 1 got behind the first MiG and fired approximately 150 rounds of 20-mm with no apparent results, then worked into the AIM-9 envelope about 4,000 feet behind the MiG. The F-8's first AIM-9 appeared to guide temporarily, but then fell off to the right without detonating (the missile probably guided on one of the scattered clouds in the background). Nickel 1 fired his second (and last) AIM-9 from dead astern at a range of 3,000 feet. The missile knocked off parts of the MiG-17's wing, then the tail came off as the North Vietnamese went down, out of control, and crashed. Nickel 1 came off his kill and saw two more MiG-17s off to his right and slightly high. Apparently unseen, the F-8 pulled behind the MiGs and easily closed behind the second MiG, firing about thirty rounds of 20-mm into the right wing of the MiG-17 before he unexpectedly ran out of ammunition. Out of missiles and cannon ammunition, Nickel 1 left the area and returned to his ship. Maintenance checks revealed that an electrical malfunction had prevented Nickel 1's lower pair of cannon from firing, but he later was given credit for a kill on the second MiG—the first American double-MiG kill of the war.

As Nickel 1 was maneuvering for position on the first MiG, Nickel 2 saw a third MiG-17 flying straight and level 3,000 feet away and turned behind the MiG, got a good tone, and fired both of his Sidewinders from a range of 4,000 feet. The first AIM-9 hung, and the second missile did not guide. Nickel 2 turned away to leave the area, but as he departed, he saw another MiG-17 pass in front of him, slightly low. Nickel 2 easily took position behind this MiG and fired about thirty rounds of 20-mm. He continued to close to a range of about 1,000 feet and opened fire again, but the cannon jammed after fifteen rounds, so Nickel 2 departed the area.

Nickel 3 had fired a few ineffective rounds of 20-mm at the second MiG-17 on the initial head-on pass, and as they passed, he saw the MiG dive for the ground with an F-8 (Nickel 4) in pursuit. The MiG recovered from the dive with a sharp, low-altitude pullout, with the other F-8 still following, but Nickel 3 was able to pull in behind the MiG and then attempted to launch two AIM-9s from a distance of about 1,500 feet; both Sidewinders missed.

Meanwhile, Nickel 4 was still behind the MiG and fired an AIM-9; the missile guided well but fell short of the target, and the MiG escaped into the clouds. Nickel 4 began to depart the area but on his way out saw a fourth MiG-17 and launched his second Sidewinder from a range of about 9,000 feet; the missile did not guide. In this engagement, three of the four F-8s had gun malfunctions, and only one of the eight AIM-9s fired hit the target.

On June 21, 1966, four F-8s, also designated Nickel flight, were searching for a downed reconnaissance pilot. Forced to search at low altitude (1,500 to 2,000 feet) below an overcast, the F-8s soon began to receive intense AAA fire from a railroad line just west of the downed pilot's location. Nickel 3 took a hit in his right elevator, but he elected to remain and continue the search. Shortly thereafter Nickel 3 and Nickel 4 sighted the downed RF-8 pilot just east of a ridge line; the downed pilot acknowledged the sighting by firing an orange flare. A fuel check from both sections showed that Nickel 3 and Nickel 4 were approaching minimum fuel, so Nickel 1 sent them to the tanker.

As Nickel 3 and Nickel 4 departed the area, Nickel 1 and Nickel 2 began a left orbit near the downed pilot at 2,000 feet. In the turn, Nickel 1 called "MiGs" as a pair of silver MiG-17s dropped out of the clouds and made a head-on pass very close to the F-8s. Nickel 2 quickly pulled up into the MiGs and fired seventy-five rounds of 20-mm almost head on from very close range at the second MiG. The cannon hits started fuel streaming from the MiG's wing, and the two MiGs split, with the damaged MiG diving for the ground; Nickel 2 followed this MiG and fired a Sidewinder at a range of one mile, but the MiG pulled up sharply as Nickel 2's missile closed. It missed, but the MiG crashed, either as a result of the maneuver or the cannon hits. After his kill, Nickel 2 saw two MiG-17s closing behind him, but he outran the MiGs and left the area.

Nickel 3 and Nickel 4 had been on their way to the tanker when they heard Nickel 1's MiG call, and immediately turned back to join the fight. Nickel 3's damaged F-8 could not turn as hard as Nickel 4, so he dropped back in the turn. He had dropped almost two miles behind Nickel 4 when he saw an F-8—later determined to be Nickel 1—with a MiG close behind, heading in the opposite direction at very low altitude. Nickel 3 called, "Low F-8 you have a MiG on your tail," but immediately after he made the call, Nickel 3 saw the MiG fire his cannon; the F-8's tail burst into flames, and the F-8 pilot ejected.

Meanwhile, as Nickel 4 rolled out of his turn, he saw two more MiGs diving out of the clouds slightly to his right, and as the first MiG passed in front of him, he opened fire with his 20-mm cannon, but the guns jammed after firing twenty-five rounds. As Nickel 4 finished his firing pass on his MiG, he heard Nickel 3's call for an F-8 low to break; thinking the call was for him, he broke, separated from the MiG, and left the area. On his way out he saw a fireball on the ground, later confirmed to be Nickel 1.

After seeing the F-8 pilot eject, Nickel 3 checked his own tail and saw a MiG-17 behind him at close range and firing. He broke into the MiG but could not outmaneuver him because of his damaged elevator, so he accelerated to 600 knots and separated. As the F-8 opened the range, the pilot saw the MiG apparently give up and break off the attack, turning away in an easy left turn. Despite his low-fuel state and battle damage, as soon as Nickel 3 saw the MiG had turned away, he turned back to reengage. He closed to about 4,000 feet behind the MiG and attempted to fire his Sidewinders. The first missile would not leave the launcher, but the second missile guided and detonated to the left of the MiG's tail. Critically low on fuel, Nickel 3 immediately left the area, but he did see the MiG roll into a steep dive, right wing down, smoking badly. The MiG later was confirmed as destroyed.

On July 14, 1966, three F-8s covering a strike mission got into a tight turning fight with three MiG-17s; one F-8 was shot down while one MiG was hit several times, but it escaped when the pursuing F-8's cannon jammed. One of the F-8 pilots later commented that "the F-8 had little capability to shoot down the MiGs in this encounter because the [F-8] cannons were completely unreliable and the MiGs stayed inside missile minimum range."[19]

Sadly, the F-8 cannon failures were not a surprise. Well before the war, the F-8's Colt Mark 12 cannon had a history of jamming, and when the F-8 went into combat, the problem still existed. The most common problems were jammed ammunition belts and failure of the pneumatic air system that charged the guns; these became especially severe during high-G maneuvering, when the guns were needed most. Additionally, while the F-8 air-to-air gunsight was designed for air combat, it computed insufficient lead when the aircraft pulled over three Gs.[20] Since many dogfights involved turns twice that hard, often F-8 pilots fired by "Kentucky windage." The F-8's cannon originally carried between 125 and 144 rounds per gun, but modifications—mostly improved electronic warfare equipment—reduced the combat ammunition load to about 100 rounds per gun, or about six seconds of firing.[21] Finally, early versions of the F-8 only carried two AIM-9s: While most were modified to carry four, in combat, for various reasons, the F-8 often carried only two AIM-9s; the F-4, in contrast, usually carried four AIM-9s and four AIM-7s.

The AIM-9D

One thing that helped the F-8s was the Navy's introduction in June 1966 of an improved Sidewinder, the AIM-9D. Because of the limitations of the earlier AIM-9s, the Navy had sponsored development of this missile, which was a significant improvement over the AIM-9B; it had a streamlined nose to cut down drag, a new rocket motor that provided higher speed and longer range,[22] a much shorter minimum range, and a much more destructive warhead. The AIM-9D's seeker head was cooled by liquid nitrogen to increase its sensitivity and make it easier for the seeker to pick out the heat from the MiG's engine; additionally, the head sensed radiation in a band that made it less likely that heat radiation from the ground or clouds would divert the missile, and it had a much narrower field of view, which meant it was less likely to be drawn off by a false heat source.[23] The overall result of the improvements was that the AIM-9D's launch envelope was roughly twice the size of the AIM-9B's.

After some early difficulties, the AIM-9D was a resounding success, and the AIM-9D/F-8 union would give the well-flown F-8s the highest kill per engagement ratio of any American fighter; this kill per engagement ratio is especially remarkable considering the problems with the F-8's cannon armament. The AIM-9D went on to have the highest hit ratio of any U.S. air-to-air missile during Rolling Thunder, but for reasons to be discussed later, the Air Force did not adopt the AIM-9D for use on its fighters and continued to use the vastly inferior AIM-9B.

The Thuds Meet the MiGs

In April 1966, in response to an assessment that the bombing of North Vietnam was still ineffective, the United States began to consider bombing the North Vietnamese petroleum, oil, and lubricant (POL) storage sites, which seemed particularly vulnerable to air attack.[24] After some delay, President Johnson approved the plan, and on May 29, 1966, the United States began a major bombing campaign against POL sites in North Vietnam. Sadly, the POL campaign was typical of the ambivalent nature of Rolling Thunder. The first POL sites bombed were the smaller ones; the North Vietnamese realized from past U.S. political decision patterns that the larger sites would be attacked next, so they began dispersing the bigger sites to protect them from later, larger U.S. strikes. Even though the United States began by bombing only the small sites, the MiGs moved in and began to meet U.S. strike flights on a regular basis. These attacks on the strike flights eased the pressure on the EB-66s; despite numerous attacks, the North Vietnamese had failed to shoot down any of the jamming platforms.

The United States expanded its attacks to the main North Vietnamese POL storage sites on June 29, 1966, and for the rest of the summer the main aim of Rolling Thunder was the destruction of North Vietnam's oil storage capacity. At the same time the United States intensified the bombing, U.S. reconnaissance began to note new MiG-21s as the Soviets replaced North Vietnamese losses.

As the POL campaign continued, the North Vietnamese saw that the U.S. strikes were flying predictable routes and times, and the pace of air-to-air combat picked up steadily. U.S. pilots noticed a steady improvement in the North Vietnamese GCI as the MiGs turned their attention to the F-105 strike flights, marking a change in air war. From the beginning of the war until late June 1966, F-105s had encountered MiGs only fourteen times; from June 29 until the end of July, there were seventeen engagements between F-105s and MiGs.

The F-105s now were flying almost exclusively strike missions as they carried the burden of the attacks into North Vietnam, while the F-4Cs took the MiGCAP escort missions (though they still carried bombs in case they did not engage MiGs). Despite their strike role and their lack of an air-to-air missile, the F-105 pilots still considered themselves "fighter jocks," and it had been a source of considerable frustration to them that, despite several losses, they had not shot down any MiGs (except for the unacknowledged kill over China). Now the MiGs challenged them more often, and in late June the F-105s got their first "official" kill.

The Iron Hand F-105s on their SAM suppression missions always were the first in the target area, and as such they drew much of the MiGs' attention. On June 29, four Wild Weasels, Bison flight, were on an Iron Hand mission around Hanoi. As they began their hunt for SAM sites, Bison 1 divided the flight into two elements, with Bison 3 and Bison 4 about a half mile behind and a half mile to the right. Bison flight was looking for the SAM sites when Bison 4 saw a flight of three MiG-17s closing from about half a mile behind and several thousand feet below the F-105s. Bison 4 called "MiGs," and Bison 3 called for a left break. Bison 1 and Bison 2 did not see the MiGs or hear the break calls, and continued flying straight and level. The first MiG-17 fired at the turning Bison 3 but missed, and the three MiGs continued straight through after Bison 1 and Bison 2. The battle was beginning to unfold like the disastrous first engagement between the MiG-17s and the F-105s.

This time, however, the F-105 leader saw the MiGs as they closed and called, "Break left, go afterburner and jettison ordnance." The leading MiG opened fire on Bison 2 as he turned and hit the F-105 several times on the left side; one 23-mm cannon shell passed through Bison 2's cockpit, knocking the pilot's hand off the throttle and wrecking most of the instruments, including the gunsight. After firing, the MiG overshot and flew directly in front of Bison 2. Taking advantage of the MiG's mistake, Bison 2 (without a gunsight) fired about 200 rounds of 20-mm and saw about ten hits on the MiG's left wing root. The MiG-17 rolled over and dove straight down into the low clouds just above the ground, for the first official F-105 MiG kill of the war. After his kill, Bison 2 saw the second MiG-17 about 200 feet to his left firing on Bison 1. Bison 2 saw the MiG hit Bison 1 several times in the tail, but as he turned to help his leader, another MiG-17 dropped behind him and began to attack; Bison 2 was forced to break off and escape into the clouds. Meanwhile, Bison 3 and Bison 4 briefly sparred with a fourth MiG-17 and then turned to depart the area. As they were exiting, Bison 3 saw Bison 1 with the MiG-17 still on his tail. Bison 3 turned toward the MiG and fired 100 rounds of 20-mm. The cannon fire apparently missed, but the MiG-17 broke away from Bison 1, and the F-105s departed the area.

On July 14, two MiG-21s attacked an Iron Hand flight, but the F-4 escort intervened and, in a close, turning dogfight, shot down both of the MiGs. By the end of July, the air-to-air score still was significantly in favor of the American forces. F-4s had shot down fourteen MiG-17s (five by Navy F-4Bs) for only one loss, and two MiG-21s for no losses, giving the F-4 a 16:1 kill ratio. In just a few engagements, two F-8s had been shot down by MiG-17s, and F-8s shot down four MiG-17s in return, while the F-105s shot down one MiG-17 and damaged four, for three losses (two in April 1965) and seven damaged. In August 1966 the United States ended the POL bombing campaign and returned to its interdiction campaign; U.S. intelligence estimated the strikes had destroyed 70 percent of the North's POL, but they conceded that North Vietnam still had enough stored in tiny, hard-to-find storage areas to remain functional.[25]

At this time, the North Vietnamese moved SAMs northwest from Hanoi closer to the EB-66 jamming orbits; this increased threat forced the vulnerable EB-66s to leave their Thud Ridge orbit and set up a new orbit farther to the south and west, a move that placed them farther from the North Vietnamese radars and thus made their jamming less effective. When the EB-66s moved away from the most heavily defended areas, the Air Force reduced their F-4 escorts; the North Vietnamese detected this, and soon MiGs began to press the EB-66s again. Still unable to hear the MiG warnings from Big Eye and other agencies because of the impact of their jamming on their radios, the EB-66s were forced to move their orbits even farther south and west, further reducing their effectiveness.

The Battle Increases

In August 1966 the total number of MiG engagements dropped off to ten, but in September the MiGs made a serious, concerted effort to attack U.S.

strike forces, and that month the number of engagements increased to thirty-seven, with twenty-five of the attacks on F-105 flights. From the beginning of September until early January 1967 MiGs were airborne virtually every day.[26]

On September 21, a force of forty F-105s and eight F-4s attacked the Dap Cau bridge, and the first large, significant air battle of the war took place. The weather was very hazy, and the North Vietnamese GCI sent a large number of MiG-17s into the battle for the first time. The tactic did not work; the North Vietnamese GCI apparently was overwhelmed trying to control such a large fight and could not warn the MiGs that they were being attacked by American aircraft. In the melee, F-105s were able to make at least six apparently unobserved attacks on MiG-17s, shooting down two and damaging three more, notwithstanding some cannon problems—in seven firing attempts, three of the F-105s' cannon jammed.

But even while the MiG-17s were being roughly treated, a few MiG-21s appeared and showed the F-105s they were a force to be reckoned with. One MiG-21 gave a clear demonstration of his performance superiority when an F-105 surprised him from behind. As the F-105 opened fire, the MiG dove, accelerated away, then pulled up high above the F-105; as the American pilot watched helplessly, the MiG completed a loop and dropped in behind him. The MiG opened fire with his cannon as the Thud dove for the ground; after a harrowing few minutes, the F-105 escaped.

In another disturbing development on September 21, North Vietnamese GCI controllers began to vector Atoll-armed MiG-21s behind U.S. aircraft, where the MiG's small size made it very difficult to see. Edsel, a flight of two F-4Cs, was part of the September 21 strike mission when, inbound to the target, Edsel 2 saw a silver MiG-21 close behind Edsel 1. As the MiG began firing his cannon, Edsel 2 called, "MiGs at 6 o'clock" and jettisoned his bombs and external fuel tanks. As he jettisoned his ordnance, he saw a second MiG-21 directly behind him and overtaking quickly. The MiG fired an Atoll, which passed close but missed high and to the right, then followed up with cannon fire. The gunfire missed, and the second MiG accelerated past Edsel 2 and disappeared.

Meanwhile, Edsel 1 had not heard Edsel 2's call and continued flying straight ahead with the first MiG about 500 feet behind him. The MiG now fired an Atoll, but the missile missed (it probably was fired inside minimum range). He then resumed firing his cannon, apparently emptying it without a hit, while Edsel 1 continued on, blissfully unaware that he was under attack. The MiG finally dove away, and as the MiG disappeared, Edsel 1 finally heard Edsel 2's calls and jettisoned his ordnance. The two F-4Cs turned to pursue the MiGs, but they were unable to regain visual or radar contact. When they returned to base, the F-4Cs were found to be undamaged; during the entire time Edsel 1 was under attack from close range with guns and missiles, neither the front seater nor the back seater saw the MiG, nor had they realized they were being fired upon.

The missile-firing MiG-21s marked the beginning of a new stage in the development of overall North Vietnamese fighter tactics. Gradually, the MiG-21s would become responsible for high-altitude, high-speed interceptions, while the other types of MiGs would be responsible for low-altitude dogfights.

F-105 Problems

As F-105s began regularly to engage MiGs, the Thud pilots' debriefing comments after their engagements sounded several themes. Like the F-8 and F-4, the F-105 had its share of air-to-air weapons systems problems. The F-105 could carry two AIM-9Bs on each of its outboard wing pylons, but because the F-105's salvation was its speed, the high-drag pylon was unpopular,[27] and at this point in the war F-105s almost never carried air-to-air missiles on strike missions, relying exclusively on their cannon in air-to-air combat. Eventually, the F-105 TFWs in Thailand developed a low-drag pylon to carry a single AIM-9B,[28] but it was not until mid-December 1966 that at least some F-105s in each flight regularly carried an AIM-9B.[29]

Fortunately, the F-105 had an excellent internal cannon, the 20-mm Gatling-gun type M-61 Vulcan. Carrying 1,029 rounds, with a high rate of fire (6,000 rounds per minute), a heavy shell, and a maximum effective range of about 3,000 feet, the M-61 was a very effective weapon with eleven seconds of firing time—about twice the firing time of the MiG gun systems. Unfortunately, a flawed gunsight system on the F-105 seriously limited the M-61's capability and made it awkward to use in air combat.

Like every fighter, the F-105 used its optical gunsight for both dive bombing (the standard method of bomb delivery) and air-to-air combat. In the air-to air mode, the F-105 gunsight computed lead on the target with a gyroscope that sensed how hard the aircraft was turning and compensated for the turn to give the proper lead on the target. The F-105 also had a radar ranging set, and when the range to the target from the radar and the turn rate from its gyroscope were combined, the sight was quite accurate.

Unfortunately, in combat the system did not function well. The F-105's normal setting for the gunsight inbound to the target in North Vietnam was the bombing (air-to-ground) mode, not the air-to-air mode, and this setting made the gunsight virtually useless in air-to-air combat. To be effective against MiGs, the F-105 pilot had to have the sight in the air-to-air mode, but changing the sight from bombing to air-to-air was a complicated, time-consuming task—even under normal circumstances—that involved changing five switches,[30] several of which were in hard-to-reach spots in the cockpit. When under attack or engaged in a turning dogfight with a MiG, such an operation was almost impossible. Consequently, most F-105 cannon attacks were made without a gunsight—just pointing the airplane at the MiG, getting in as close as possible, and letting fly.

This gunsight problem was especially serious because of the F-105's M-61 cannon, ironically because it was so accurate. The "Gatling gun" arrangement of six rotary barrels gave the cannon a high rate of fire, but the bullets all came out in a single stream, with virtually no dispersion. If the bullet stream stayed on the target, the destruction was terrific, but if the stream was even slightly off, there was no spread of the bullets to increase the chances of a hit.[31] The M-61 cannon also had some reliability problems; overall, it malfunctioned about once out of every eight times it was fired (12 percent). Considering how close the F-105s were to the MiGs when they tried to use the gun, these malfunctions probably cost several kills.

The F-105 had clear speed and acceleration superiority over the MiG-17, but the pilots were very conscious of how maneuverable the MiG-17 was, and, if possible, they avoided turning engagements, using their speed and acceleration to engage or escape from MiG-17s. With its high speed, the F-105 was able to close quickly on the MiG-17s, and with the cannon—even with no missiles and no gunsight—the F-105s could get close enough to have some hope of a kill. When a Thud faced a MiG-21, however, it was a different story. The MiG-21 could out-accelerate, as well as outmaneuver, the Thud, so the F-105 had virtually no chance for a kill with the cannon.

Over and over again during this period, the F-105 pilots expressed frustration at engaging in air-to-air combat without an air-to-air missile and with a very poorly designed gunsight system. Perhaps they should have been grateful they had a gun at all. Early in the F-105's career, an Air Force design board made a serious attempt to remove the gun—as well as the RHAW equipment and an explosion suppression system in the fuel tanks—as a weight and cost-saving measure.[32] In the end cooler heads prevailed; what would have happened to cannon-less F-105s over North Vietnam is not pleasant to contemplate.

Introduction of ECM Pods

By the late summer of 1966, the Air Force's low-level approaches sent losses to SAMs and the AAA soaring, and the North Vietnamese defenses

An F-105D takes off with a QRC-160 pod on the right wing station. Note the standard load of two wing tanks and six 750-pound Mark 117 bombs on the centerline station. *USAF (courtesy of the National Archives)*

were on the verge of denying the Air Force the ability to operate in the areas where SAMs were highly concentrated.[33] As the fall northeast monsoon moved over North Vietnam the weather worsened, and in October— "in the nick of time," one source said[34]—one of the most tactically significant events in the Rolling Thunder campaign took place. In September 1966, the first twenty-five QRC-160s[35] arrived in the theater, and the F-105s of the 355th TFW[36] began a test program known as Vampyrus.

The QRC-160 ECM pods were designed to jam the North Vietnamese SAM and AAA fire control radars. The QRC-160 was a fairly small, low-drag pod that was carried on the extreme outboard right wing pylon of the F-105. Each pod contained four jammers, two programmed to jam the Fan Song radar for the SA-2 and two to jam AAA radars.[37]

From the beginning, the ECM pods proved very effective and simple to operate, and the test program went quickly. A dramatic demonstration of the pods' effectiveness occurred on one of the early test missions on October 8, 1966, when twelve pod-equipped F-105s in three flights of four attacked the Nguyen Khe POL storage area. Taksan, the first flight of pod-equipped F-105Ds, was the flak suppression flight and split into two elements, Taksan 1 and 2 and Taksan 3 and 4. Taksan 1 and Taksan 2 did not have operable pods, while Taksan 3 and Taksan 4 did. During the

mission, Taksan 1 was hit by radar-controlled AAA, attacked by a missile-firing MiG-21 (who missed), and fired at by a SAM, while Taksan 2
received heavy fire from radar-controlled AAA but was not hit. Taksan 3
and 4, with working pods, reported light to moderate uncontrolled AAA.
Neither of the other two F-105 flights—both of which had working
pods—reported being attacked by SAMs or radar-guided AAA.

The F-105 pilots found that a single pod would make the SA-2 miss,
but not by enough to prevent damage from the warhead's explosion, so
several pods had to be used together to provide enough jamming to make
the SA-2 miss completely. The two Thailand-based F-105 wings, the
388th and 355th, quickly developed formations where the pod-jamming
patterns overlapped and supplemented each other, and the revolution
was on. The F-105s began to penetrate at higher altitudes, above the light
and medium AAA, and the pod jamming dramatically cut their losses to
SAMs. As the number of pods in the theater slowly increased, the F-105
strike flights began to enter North Vietnam in larger and larger flights
packed close together to maximize pod coverage and protection. The two
F-105 wings made different decisions on penetration altitudes and formations. The F-105s from the 388th TFW at Korat moved quickly to an
altitude of 15,000 to 18,000 feet and flew large, very tight pod formations
with two-minute spacing between formations. The higher altitudes
flown by the 388th gave them better protection against guns, but bomb-
loaded F-105s were unwieldy at this altitude, and the formation was
more difficult to maneuver.[38] The F-105s from the 355th TFW at Takhli
moved up more slowly, moving first to 6,500 feet and then gradually
higher, until June 1967, when they were operating between 8,000 and
12,000 feet. The 355th also flew a loose trail formation in the pod formation (about one mile separation between flights), with about one
minute between formations.[39] The 355th's tactics exposed them more to
AAA fire and offered less pod protection, but they were more flexible
and maneuverable.

Whatever the formation, the effect of the pods was dramatic. In 1965,
the SAMs shot down one aircraft for every sixteen SAMs fired; in 1966 it
dropped to about one kill for every thirty-three missiles fired, then
decreased to one kill per fifty in 1967 as pods came into general use, and
in 1968 it took more than 100 missiles to bring down an Air Force aircraft.[40] Not only did losses drop, but flying into North Vietnam at medium
altitude improved navigation to the target and bombing accuracy, and
most importantly, it kept the Thuds out of the AAA. The tradeoff: The
tight ECM pod formations were not as good for the type of visual lookout
needed to detect MiGs before they attacked.

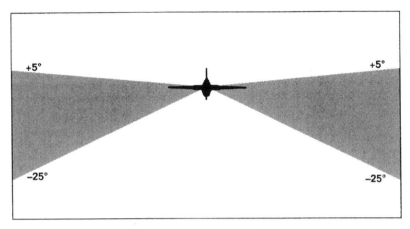

QRC-160 Pod-Jamming Pattern. The QRC-160 provided jamming out to the sides of the aircraft in the pattern shown, so to give fully effective coverage, it had to be used in a formation.

The Atoll Draws Blood

There were few MiG engagements in October because of bad weather, but two F-4s were shot down, and it appeared there might be an increase in the MiGs' capabilities, thereby somewhat offsetting the effect of the ECM pods on the SAMs. Prior to October 1966, the MiG-21/Atoll combination had not scored a kill despite several excellent opportunities, but the two F-4 losses in October were probably the first successes of GCI-controlled MiG-21s firing Atolls. On October 5, 1966, two F-4Cs, Tempest 1 and Tempest 2, were escorting two EB-66s jamming for strikes around Hanoi. There were numerous warnings that MiGs were in the area as the F-4Cs took up an escort position on the side of the flight of EB-66s at 30,000 feet. While in orbit, one of the EB-66s looked to his left and saw an aircraft— later determined to be Tempest 1—going down in flames. There were no radio calls, and no one in the flights saw any MiGs. The back seater from Tempest 1 was rescued, and he said he thought they had been hit by Sidewinder-type missiles. This was probably the first U.S. aircraft to be shot down by an air-to-air missile over North Vietnam.[41] Four days later, on October 9, a MiG shot down a Navy F-4B. The back seater became a POW and later said he had been attacked and shot down by a MiG firing a missile.[42] Both of these losses probably were attributable to Atoll-armed MiG-21s, and in both instances—as was to be the case so often later in the war—the first indication of an attack was the impact of the missile.

While the new MiG-21 tactics gave them more opportunities to surprise U.S. aircraft, the North Vietnamese MiG-21s still dissipated their advantage by poor flying and poor missile performance. On November 3, 1966, a pair of MiG-21s surprised three Air Force F-4Cs escorting an EB-66. The F-4s did not see the MiGs until one of the MiG-21s fired an Atoll at the lead F-4. The Atoll missed, and in the chase that followed the lead F-4 fired seven missiles (three AIM-7Es and four AIM-9Bs) from well within the envelope; all missed. One of the MiG-21s pulled close behind one of the other F-4s but did not fire his cannon, leading the F-4 crews to speculate that it was a later-model MiG-21D without an internal cannon.[43]

Despite the North Vietnamese GCI, from time to time U.S. aircraft could surprise the North Vietnamese. On October 9, 1966, the same day the Navy F-4B was shot down, four F-8s were in a low altitude MiGCAP orbit over North Vietnam. A Navy E-1B early-warning aircraft advised the F-8s of MiGs in the area, and the F-8s turned to engage. As they moved toward the contact, the F-8s saw a single MiG-21 high and slightly to their right crossing from right to left. The low altitude of the orbit must have hidden the F-8s from the North Vietnamese GCI, and the MiG did not appear to know the F-8s were there. The first two F-8s pulled in behind the MiG, but the North Vietnamese either was warned by GCI or saw the F-8s and rolled over and dove for the ground. As the MiG started down, the lead F-8 rolled upside down to follow and fired two Sidewinders from close to the heart of the envelope. One blew off a wing; the second flew up the tailpipe and exploded, for the Navy's first MiG-21 kill.

In engagements where neither side had the advantage of surprise, the MiG-21s that tried to engage did poorly. On November 5, 1966, four F-4Cs, Opal flight, were escorting a single EB-66 electronic warfare aircraft providing support for strikes in Route Package VI. During the jamming orbit, the F-4s had seen radar targets approximately 22 miles away, then saw the radar targets change course and begin to close on the U.S. flight. Shortly thereafter Opal 1 saw a silver MiG-21 off his right wing; the MiG-21 ignored the F-4s, turned very rapidly behind the EB-66, and fired an Atoll. Opal 1 called "break right" to the EB-66, and the EB-66 turned into a hard right diving turn. The MiG's missile missed, but the MiG followed the EB-66 into his turn. Opal 1 followed the MiG; a second MiG-21 appeared and turned behind Opal 1, and Opal 2 pulled behind the second MiG. The engagement was now a "daisy chain"—EB-66, MiG-21, Opal 1, MiG-21, Opal 2—going down in a tight right spiral, all at close quarters. The MiGs reduced power in an attempt to keep behind the slower EB-66, and Opal 1 and Opal 2 maneuvered to keep behind the MiGs and get enough distance to fire their missiles outside minimum range.

Opal 1 attempted to fire a Sparrow at the first MiG-21, but the missile motor failed. Opal 1 tried to set up his armament switches to fire a Sidewinder, but he disarmed the system instead, so he switched back to his AIM-7s and launched a second AIM-7. The missile passed over the MiG but did not detonate, and the MiG continued to press the EB-66. Opal 1 now was so close to the MiG that he flew alongside the North Vietnamese fighter and overlapped wings in an attempt to force him to break away. The MiG moved out but immediately moved back behind the EB-66. Opal 1 again dropped back to gain separation from the MiG, got a full system radar lock on, and launched a third AIM-7. The missile passed close behind the MiG but again did not detonate. As the EB-66 entered a thin cloud layer at 9,000 feet, Opal 1 called for him to reverse his turn to the left. The EB-66 did so and pulled up into a climb.

The first MiG-21 ignored the EB-66, and the North Vietnamese continued down in a right-hand spiral. Opal 1 followed and launched his last Sparrow, which appeared to miss and detonated in front of the MiG. Suddenly the MiG decelerated very rapidly, apparently from an engine flameout after ingesting the debris and smoke from the AIM-7 explosion, and as Opal 1 passed, the pilot ejected.

Meanwhile, the second MiG-21 had broken off his attack on Opal 1 and pulled up in a climb, still in front of Opal 2. The F-4 maneuvered behind the climbing MiG, pulled his throttles to idle to keep outside the AIM-9B's minimum range, and launched a Sidewinder. The missile detonated near the tailpipe of the MiG. Now in idle power, Opal 2 found himself in a steep climb, decelerating rapidly. As he maneuvered to regain airspeed, he saw the MiG-21 with an empty cockpit and the MiG pilot in a parachute.

While the F-4s shot down the two North Vietnamese fighters, both American fighters had been so close to the MiGs that they had to execute a series of convoluted maneuvers to get far enough behind the MiG to launch a missile. Clearly, now the MiGs understood that the F-4s did not have a cannon and could not fire at them from close range, and there was a noticeable change in the post-engagement comments of Air Force F-4 aircrews. Earlier in the war, F-4 crews were split on the desirability of a cannon, but from May 1966 on, all the Phantom crews that commented about a cannon said the F-4 needed one.[44] This reflected the increasing number of engagements with the MiG-21, whose turn the F-4 could match, and the fact that the F-4s were finding it very difficult to successfully attack low-flying, hard-turning MiG-17s with the unreliable American missiles.

By October 1966 the MiGs had completed developing patterns that would hold for the rest of Rolling Thunder. From this point on, MiG-17s engaged at low altitude and MiG-21s at high altitude, and when U.S. fighters fired missiles at the MiGs, their tactics (if they saw the missile) were to turn hard and dive for the ground. The MiGs also seemed to understand their primary mission was to disrupt the bombing, and when their attacks forced a U.S. strike flight to jettison their bombs, the MiGs would break off their attack and move on to harry another bomb-loaded flight. To try to counter this tactic, U.S. strikers began jettisoning their external fuel tanks first when under heavy MiG attack, hoping the MiGs would mistake the jettisoned tanks for the strikers' bombs.

After the 1966 U.S. presidential elections, the bombing of North Vietnam escalated again. On November 12, 1966, U.S. aircraft began to strike the North Vietnamese power plants; at the same time, a new problem for Air Force strike forces arose as Air Force F-4C losses to SAMs began to increase dramatically. Beginning in October 1966, many F-4Cs had been flying full time as bombers in Route Packages V and VI instead of their previous primary MiGCAP role, and as bombers they were exposed to more and more SAM attacks. The F-4Cs had not received ECM pods and were just beginning to receive RHAW equipment; since the pod-equipped F-105 strike flights were jamming the SAMs, the podless F-4 flights now were the most attractive SA-2 targets. Without an electronic warning that they were being fired on by SAMs and with no capability of jamming the Fan Song radar, the F-4s were relatively helpless; from late November to early December 1966, SA-2s downed three F-4Cs, two in one day. Losses continued to rise, and on December 2, U.S. forces lost eight aircraft—five Air Force and three Navy—their worst day of the war. Five of the losses were to SAMs, but no ECM pod-equipped F-105s were shot down. Faced with these losses, Seventh Air Force immediately prohibited F-4Cs that had no RHAW capability—which was most of the fleet—from operating in SAM areas. Now the F-4C MiGCAPs escorting F-105s into Route Package VI could only escort the strikers to the edge of a SAM area; there they had to break off their escort and pick up the F-105s as they came out of the area.

The limitations on the F-4 MiGCAP had an immediate impact on air-to-air operations when, in early December, there was another escalation in bombing as American aircraft struck targets in the Hanoi prohibited area for the first time. North Vietnamese GCI controllers took advantage of the unescorted F-105s in the target area and concentrated their MiG attacks on them, since they now were almost immune to SAM attacks. Forty-two of the forty-seven engagements in December involved F-105s, but the F-105s were aggressive against the older MiG-17s and shot down two; in one engagement two F-105s attacked sixteen MiG-17s, shooting down one and escaping unscathed. The Thud pilots still found the MiG pilots inferior, timid, and unaggressive, but without air-to-air missiles, the F-105 pilots were unable to take full advantage of the situation.

But while the F-105s were doing well against the MiG-17s, the MiG-21 threat continued to increase. On December 12, Fosdick, a flight of four F-105Ds, was part of a strike mission attacking the Yien Vien railroad yard near Hanoi. After bombing the target, Fosdick left the area at high speed and climbed on top of the clouds in a line abreast formation. Shortly after Fosdick flight leveled off, two silver MiG-21s attacked from behind. The F-105s went to afterburner to try to outrun the MiGs, and the flight descended into the clouds. Under the clouds the F-105s began to receive intense flak. After jinking for several seconds and reaching the mountains southwest of Hanoi, Fosdick again climbed on top of the clouds. A few seconds later Fosdick 2 saw a MiG-21 flying along side the F-105s and beginning to turn to attack Fosdick 4. Fosdick 2 warned Fosdick 4, who dropped down into the clouds with the MiG after him. A short time later, Fosdick 4 popped back through the clouds without the MiG.

As the SAM and flak activity subsided, the F-105s began to climb and spread out for a better lookout against a MiG attack. Fosdick 2 looked back to clear the flight and saw two MiG-21s behind the F-105s, one attacking Fosdick 1, the other Fosdick 3. Before Fosdick 2 could make a radio call, he saw the second MiG fire an Atoll that blew off Fosdick 3's tail; the MiG-21 broke off and disappeared.

As Fosdick 3 ejected, Fosdick 2 turned to attack the other MiG on the tail of Fosdick 1. The MiG broke off his attack and dived for the ground with the F-105 in hot pursuit. Fosdick 2, with his sight in the air-to-ground mode, fired a single burst of 350 rounds of 20-mm from very close behind the MiG-21—a few hundred feet—but missed. Fosdick 2 broke off from the MiG as they neared the ground and turned back toward Fosdick 3's chute. He immediately was engaged by another MiG-21, so the F-105 dived to the deck in afterburner, accelerated away from the MiG, and escaped.

Fosdick 3 was the first F-105 shot down by a MiG-21, and it came after several MiG-21s had caught the F-105s from behind. The Thud's speed was not offering as much protection as hoped; the F-105 had a higher top speed than the MiG-21, but to get to this speed the F-105 had to be in full afterburner, which burned so much fuel that the F-105 could use it only for a few minutes. The Thuds had to wait until they were attacked before they used the afterburner, and if a MiG-21 could get in fairly close before the F-105 saw him, the MiG's acceleration advantage would let him get into Atoll range before the F-105 could get to maximum speed. Once the MiG fired a missile, the F-105 was in a "Catch-22" situation: If he turned to avoid the missile, he allowed the MiG to close in to cannon range; if he kept going, he might be hit by the heat seeker.

On December 14, 1966, two MiG-21s attacked four F-105s from behind and above. The Thuds saw the MiGs' contrails just as the MiGs reached firing range; the MiGs fired two Atolls as they closed, but both missiles exploded short. The MiGs followed up with a cannon attack on the last F-105, but missed again. As the F-105s tried to give chase, the MiGs simply rolled over and accelerated away into the clouds. The F-105 pilot who had been the target of both a missile and cannon attack commented that he "was lucky to be alive."

An AIM-9 missile would have given the F-105s some chance against the MiG-21, but although a new low-drag, single AIM-9 pylon was finally ready, the arming of the Thuds with this equipment was proceeding slowly. For most of the raids in December 1966, few F-105s carried air-to-air missiles, and on several occasions in early December F-105 pilots felt they lost kills because they did not have a missile. The most egregious example happened on December 14, when an Iron Hand flight— one F-105F and three F-105Ds—was on a SAM suppression mission in the Hanoi area. The F-105s were at 14,000 feet when they saw two MiG-21s approaching from behind them about 10,000 feet above. The MiGs apparently did not see the F-105 flight as they slowly overtook the U.S. fighters and flew directly over them heading in the same direction. The MiG-21s were flying slightly faster than the F-105s, who, with their heavy ordnance loads, could not climb to catch them. The F-105s watched in frustration as the MiGs moved slowly in front of them, in perfect AIM-9 range, for almost three minutes.

By December 19, 1966, most flights of F-105s had the number 1 and number 3 aircraft in the flight carrying AIM-9Bs but, as might be expected on the F-105, firing the AIM-9B was not easy. As with selecting the air-to-air mode on the gunsight, in order to launch a Sidewinder, the F-105 pilot had to throw five switches (different from those that set up the gunsight) in the correct sequence.

U.S. Detection Problems

While the North Vietnamese pilots had GCI radar to detect and guide them to U.S. aircraft, U.S. fighters usually had to rely on visually sighting the MiGs. This was a serious problem; the MiGs were small, and seeing them below 15,000 feet was especially difficult because low-altitude weather—haze and clouds—often limited visibility. Additionally, seeing MiGs was only one of the many things that U.S. aircrews had to do—they also had to look for SAMs and AAA, as well as fly formation and navigate. The visual lookout load was especially heavy for single-seat aircraft, the F-8s and F-105s.[45]

F-4s and F-8s carried radar to help pick up MiGs, but the radar only looked in front of the aircraft, and its capabilities were limited. The mix of defenses at low altitude forced the aircrews continuously to be "heads out"—looking outside the cockpit—visually searching the area for SAMs, anti-aircraft fire, and MiGs rather than looking at the radar inside the cockpit. The F-4 had the luxury of a back seater who could spend part of the time looking at the radar scope, with the result that almost all MiG acquisitions on radar were made by F-4s.[46] Flying at low level also severely limited the fighters' radar because of the ground clutter.

Even when a U.S. fighter *did* pick up a target on radar, he could not fire immediately, except under rare circumstances. Usually there were a large number of U.S. aircraft—and only a few enemy aircraft—flying over North Vietnam, and during Rolling Thunder there was no way electronically for a U.S. fighter to tell the difference between a MiG and a U.S. aircraft. American radar operators could not assume that any aircraft not showing the proper transponder return was hostile; the transponder may have failed, or the pilot may have turned it off. Consequently, to prevent attacks on friendly aircraft, the U.S. Rules of Engagement required that, under most circumstances, a radar target had to be visually identified as an enemy aircraft before it could be attacked. The rules were modified at various times later in the war, when more reliable systems appeared that could electronically identify the MiGs, but positive identification in one form or another before firing a missile remained a requirement for the entire war.

Unfortunately, these identification requirements caused tactical problems. In order to identify visually a radar target as a MiG, a U.S. fighter usually had to make a pass close enough—generally within a mile—to identify the type of aircraft or see the markings. This significantly reduced the F-4's long-range radar acquisition advantage by limiting the chances of using the AIM-7 in the head-on and most effective attack angle,[47] and eliminating any chance of surprise. Additionally, when the U.S. fighter got close enough to identify a target as a MiG, he usually was too close to employ missiles anyway; this was an especially serious problem for the F-4, which lacked a cannon for short-range attacks.

Defensively, the main difficulty was that a MiG-21 with Atolls could attack very quickly. Even if the U.S. fighter did see the MiG-21 before he

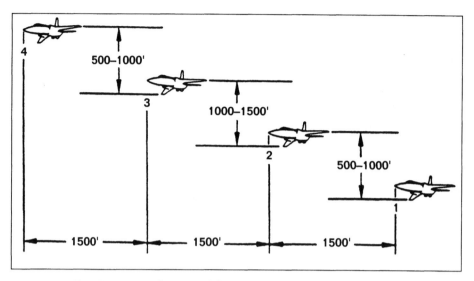

Four F-105s in a classic "pod formation" that allowed mutual QRC-160 jamming protection for the flight.

opened fire, the U.S. pilot had far fewer options because he could not simply accelerate away—the MiG-21 already had a speed advantage, and often the U.S. fighter had external loads that had to be jettisoned before he could accelerate—and by then the MiG-21 would be very close. Conversely, when the slow MiG-17 attacked a U.S. aircraft, it took a good bit of time at combat speeds—about two minutes—to close from 12,000 feet (where it first could be seen) to 2,000 feet (where it could fire cannon accurately). This made the chances that the MiG would be seen by the U.S. aircraft quite good. Once the U.S. fighters saw the MiG-17, often it was a simple matter for the U.S. fighter to accelerate away if he chose not to fight.

Another U.S. handicap was the poor rear visibility of Vietnam-era U.S. fighters, which had their canopies streamlined into the fuselage. These were good for high speed, but provided very poor rearward visibility compared to their Korean War–era predecessors. The F-105 had especially poor rear visibility; the close ECM pod formations flown by the F-105s only added to the problem because these formations required more concentration to fly and thus cut down on the time the pilots could take to look back for MiGs. Also, F-105s in pod formation were so close together, it created a blind spot behind them that could be exploited by

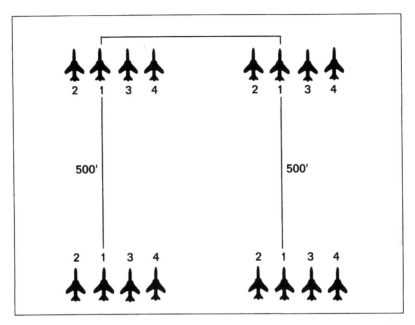

Top view of one variation of a mass pod formation. Note how close together the aircraft were, creating a large blind spot to the rear of the formation that MiGs continually exploited.

the MiGs. The visibility problem was less severe in F-4s because it had a back seater who spent most of his time looking out the back while in MiG areas. Navy F-8s also had relatively poor visibility aft, but its pilots did not complain for a variety of reasons: They were well trained in looking out for attacking aircraft, flew in formations designed for maximum lookout against MiGs (unlike the pod formations), and rarely encountered MiG-21s.

Overall Assessment

Despite the MiG's improvement and the problems combat had highlighted for Americans, as 1967 began, the overall battle against the North Vietnamese defenses was going fairly well. At the end of 1966 there were fifty-one QRC-160 pods in Southeast Asia, with more on the way,[48] and the ECM pods carried by the F-105s were showing extremely good results. Earlier, from April 1 through September 26, 1966, fifty-two Air Force aircraft had been lost in Route Package VI, for a loss rate of 28.3 per

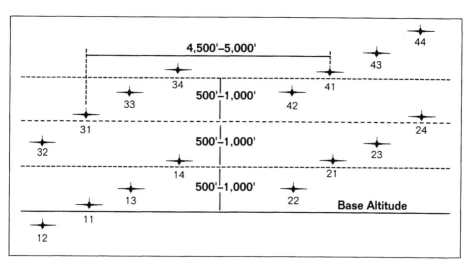

4,500'–5,000'

34

500'–1,000'
33   42

31   24

32   23

500'–1,000'

14   21

500'–1,000'

13   22   **Base Altitude**

11

12

44

43

41

42

Front view of the formation shown in the diagram on page 71.

1,000 sorties. Forty-five of the aircraft—or 86 percent—were F-105s. After the introduction of the ECM pods on the F-105s, the F-105 loss rate dropped to 16.4 per 1,000 sorties (6 in 365 sorties), and only one pod-equipped F-105 was lost to SAMs between mid-October (when the pods were first carried) and early December 1966.[49] One wing commander said, "Seldom has a technological advance of this nature so degraded the enemy's defensive posture. It has literally transformed the hostile defense environment we once faced, to one where we can now operate with a latitude of permissibility."[50] The commanders weren't the only ones to recognize the effects: An F-105 pilot commented, "When I got my orders in 1966 the sortie rate until you could expect to get shot down was 66 missions for a '105' pilot." (A tour was 100 missions.) But this individual was lucky enough to arrive after the ECM pods, and continued, "We had very few [pilots] shot down the whole time I was there. . . . [E]lectronic warfare just turned the attrition rate upside down."[51]

In the air-to-air arena, by the end of December the MiGs were aggressively contesting all U.S. strikes in the areas of Hanoi, Haiphong, and Kep, and the assumption was that the North Vietnamese would continue to be aggressive and increase the number of MiG-21/Atoll attacks in the coming year. The pure U.S.-MiG kill ratios were encouraging, but clearly the U.S. could not count on the poor performance of the North Vietnamese pilots and missiles to continue, and there were other costs from the increased MiG activity besides losses—in December, for example, 20 percent of the strike flights attacking targets in Route Package VI had to jettison their bombs because of MiG attacks.[52]

Operation Bolo

Since airfield attacks were still forbidden by the White House in January 1967, the Air Force began an aggressive air-to-air campaign to preempt more MiG attacks. Since early in the war—as early as April 1965—the U.S. high command had been interested in conducting a large decoy air raid into North Vietnam to lure the MiGs up, then shoot them down in the air.[53] The regular, aggressive attacks by MiG-21s indicated that the time now appeared right for such an operation, and in January Air Force F-4Cs flew two carefully planned missions where they simulated other types of aircraft to fool the North Vietnamese GCI; the plans worked, and the F-4s shot down nine MiG-21s without a loss.

On the first of these missions, Operation Bolo, the F-4s simulated a large F-105 strike, hoping the MiGs would come up to attack what they thought were bomb-loaded F-105s, only to be surprised by air-to-air loaded F-4s. The 8th TFW at Ubon RTAFB meticulously planned the mission: The F-4s would fly the same profile as an F-105 strike—similar times, altitudes, airspeeds, and routes. Additionally, for the first time the F-4s would carry QRC-160 jamming pods so that they would show up on radar as F-105s.[54] The 8th TFW crews led the mission, which called for fifty-six F-4Cs, eight F-104s, and twenty-eight F-105s to participate. When the engagements started, the plan called for other U.S. fighters to cover the MiG airfields and pick off the MiGs as they returned to base low on fuel. For several days before the mission, the crews studied all parts of the operation—weapons envelopes, RHAW and pod operation, and all phases of air-to-air tactics.

The careful planning and the intense training and preparation of the 8th TFW aircrews paid off. Despite bad weather and some coordination problems—only thirty-two F-4Cs, four F-104s, and twenty F-105s completed the mission—eleven MiG-21s came up, and the 8th TFW F-4Cs shot down seven; no U.S. aircraft were lost. The F-4s had all the advantages: The crews were well prepared and experienced; the engagements were all at relatively high altitude (above 10,000 feet), where missiles and radars performed well; the MiGs were easy to see (skies were clear with a solid cloud layer below) and easy to identify (they were silver, while the F-4s were camouflaged). The fight was fast (which was to the F-4s' advantage) and involved little close-in maneuvering, and the F-4s fired many of their AIM-7Es under ideal conditions—with a full system lock-on and at such high altitude that ground clutter was not a problem. Finally, from the beginning of the fight, the F-4s were above the MiGs and had an energy advantage, which they exploited.[55]

In this operation, U.S. missile effectiveness was high—about as high as reasonably could be expected in fighter-versus-fighter combat. Four of twenty AIM-7s and three of twelve AIM-9s hit, and the hit rate showed that the crews used the missiles properly. The AIM-9B rates were especially impressive, since three of the Sidewinders were deliberately fired out of the envelope to distract a MiG attacking another F-4, so the success rate of AIM-9Bs could be considered 33 percent.

Despite their losses, however, for the next two days after Operation Bolo, North Vietnamese MiG-21s chased a single RF-4C weather reconnaissance aircraft on its regular mission over North Vietnam and forced the RF-4C to abort the route. On January 5, the 8th TFW decided to try another trap and sent a flight of two air-to-air armed F-4Cs to fly a route identical to that of the RF-4C. The two F-4Cs would fly in a very close formation so that the radar return would look like a single aircraft; in this way they hoped to fool the North Vietnamese radar operators into thinking the two F-4Cs were the single RF-4C weather reconnaissance aircraft. The mission would operate in a "missile free" environment where visual identification was unnecessary to allow the F-4Cs to fire their AIM-7s at long range. No MiGs came up.

The next day Crab, a flight of two F-4Cs, was to escort an F-105 strike flight, but when the F-105 strike was canceled because of weather, Crab was reassigned to fly the previous day's decoy mission and see if they might have better luck. Once again, a "missile free" zone was established so that anything seen on radar could be assumed to be hostile. Again the two F-4s flew in very close formation in order to appear on the North Vietnamese radar as one target, and again they flew the standard RF-4C weather reconnaissance route. Crab was intercepted by four MiG-21s, and in a well-flown engagement, the F-4s shot down two of the MiGs.

By the end of January 1967, despite the advantages of GCI, the kill ratio showed that the North Vietnamese fighter force still was not measuring up. The MiG-21s especially had been disappointing; U.S. fighters had shot down sixteen MiG-21s for only three losses to the late-model MiG, and Air Force F-4Cs had a 15:1 record against the MiG-21.

3

The American Victory

MiG Tests

By early 1967 the Air Force and the Navy were testing real MiG-17s and MiG-21s—the MiG-17 under a project known as Have Drill and the MiG-21C under project Have Donut. The MiGs had been provided to the United States by the Israeli government: The MiG-21 had been flown to Israel in August 1966 by an Iraqi defector, and the MiG-17 had been provided by a Syrian defector. With actual MiGs to fly, the U.S. pilots had a much more precise idea of what they were up against, making it possible to construct an accurate set of energy maneuverability charts to compare U.S. fighters to the MiGs.

The MiG-17 test program showed that the old Soviet fighter was still a formidable opponent. The report said that the MiG-17's "afterburner gave it a [superior] performance [to] US aircraft with a similar turn rate";[1] nevertheless, the test pilots found the MiG-17 had numerous shortcomings. The engine was limited to five minutes at full power and three minutes at afterburner, and high speeds caused many problems: Above 400 knots at low and medium altitudes, the MiG-17 began to roll uncontrollably, making it almost impossible to keep the gunsight on a target; during turns above 3.5 Gs the aircraft vibrated and buffeted around the longitudinal axis; and the MiG-17's maximum speed was limited to 575 knots because of its controllability problems. The MiG-17's armament of one heavy 37-mm cannon and two smaller 23-mm cannon also received mixed reviews. The report said that "the effectiveness of the MiG-17's cannon is good, and they are accurate and reliable," and U.S. fighters had to avoid crossing the MiG's "gun line inside of 5,000 feet when passing head on since one 'golden' 37-mm projectile can end the engagement."[2] Still, overall the test pilots felt the MiG-17 had a poor gunsight and slow-firing cannon; when combined with the control problems, U.S. test pilots assessed the MiG-17 as a poor gun platform in a high-speed turning engagement. In fact, U.S. pilots often commented on the MiG-17's poor shooting—as one wing commander said, "The one thing I think they lack,

Top view of a Syrian MiG-17F painted with Israeli markings. This aircraft was later given to the United States for the Have Drill program. *Jay Miller*

thank God, is the ability to shoot,"[3] and an F-105 pilot commented, "They have serious technological problems with their sight system. They have been relatively ineffective with their gunfire."[4]

The test pilots noted that, unlike the MiG-21 and all the U.S. fighters, the MiG-17's "overall visibility [from the cockpit] is quite good with no blind area above the horizontal plane" (although it did have poor visibility over the nose and out of the side), and as expected, the MiG-17 turned remarkably well at slower speeds. These two characteristics meant the MiG-17 was able to perform well in a low-speed turning engagement; more than one U.S. pilot had been a mile behind a MiG-17 setting up to fire a missile when the MiG pulled a sharp turn and pulled behind the U.S. fighter as he passed. Even experienced U.S. pilots were constantly impressed with this turning ability. One Air Force pilot said, "I was firing a Sparrow at a MiG[-17] that I thought I had dead to rights. I launched my missile. . . . As the missile accelerated the MiG started turning—[and] made a firing pass on me."[5] A Navy F-4 pilot said, "I saw two MiG[-17]s [meet us head on and] pass 200 feet over my canopy. . . . My concentration was on the MiG [in front]. . . . [My RIO called] 'MiGs behind us and shooting!' 'Impossible,' I thought, 'no plane can come around that fast.' . . . Yep, impossible, but there they were, firing at us."[6] U.S. test pilots also assessed the MiG-17 as very difficult to shoot down because of its simple

The Have Donut MiG-21F-13 over the Nevada desert. The government of Israel provided the United States with this MiG-21 after it was flown to Israel by an Iraqi defector. *Jay Miller*

systems and lack of hydraulics; usually a kill required destruction of a main structural member.

The MiG-21 had some of the same characteristics as the MiG-17. For example, like the MiG-17, it had engine limitations; its engine acceleration was very poor, and the afterburner took from five to seven seconds to light. The MiG-21 did not have any control augmentation devices, and the test pilots thought it was very difficult to maneuver below 215 knots and above 510 knots, even by a skilled pilot. Above 510 knots, high control forces made the controls very heavy, and the pilot could not pull the nose up to a high pitch angle. The MiG-21 was limited to 595 knots below 16,000 feet—a speed well below most U.S. fighters at that altitude—because of severe airframe buffeting and structural problems.

The visibility from the MiG-21 cockpit received the most criticism. The rearward visibility of the MiG-21 was even worse than that of the U.S. fighters, with a blind 50-degree cone behind the aircraft. The pilot could see only the leading edge of the 57-degree swept delta wing, and a flight leader could not see his wingman much farther back than line abreast, so he could direct the flight only in simple maneuvers.[7] The pilot sat very low in the seat, with a thick bulletproof glass windshield, large gunsight, and glare shield—all of which severely restricted his forward visibility. The MiG-21 also had a narrow canopy, and its rails restricted

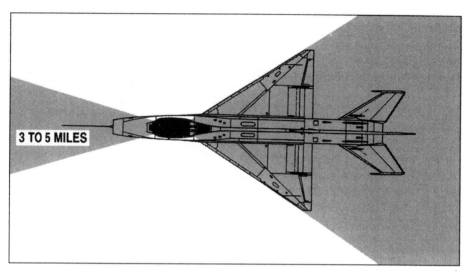

MiG-21 cockpit visibility to the front and rear.

the pilot's downward visibility to 20 degrees out of the side of the aircraft. Additionally, the pilot had a very restricted view above him out of the top of the canopy because of a protective head cover on the ejection seat.

The Atoll heat-seeking missile was the MiG-21's primary weapon, and the missile's envelope (and limitations) were much the same as the AIM-9B, from which it was copied. The MiG-21C carried a "High Fix" radar that provided Atoll range information. The radar had a detection range of about seven kilometers (four miles), but there was no radar scope—only a meter to show the MiG-21 pilot the range to the target after the radar locked on. There were two range lights to give cues when to launch the missiles. The first light came on at about 3.5 kilometers (2.7 miles), showing the missile's maximum range (although the MiG pilot was told to launch the Atoll from no more that 1.9 miles), while the second light came on at about 800 meters (3,000 feet) to tell the pilot to break off the missile attack because he was inside minimum range. From the time the radar locked on, the MiG-21 needed between three and five seconds before getting the indication to launch the Atoll (about the same delay the F-4 had in launching the AIM-7), and Soviet tactical doctrine called for the MiG-21 to conduct a follow-up attack with the 30-mm cannon, opening fire at about 3,000 feet from the target.[8] The MiG-21C carried a single 30-mm cannon[9] with sixty rounds of ammunition, or about five seconds' worth of firing time. The MiG-21's gunsight—like the gunsights in all

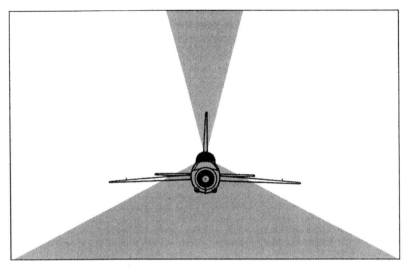

MiG-21 cockpit visibility downward and upward.

Vietnam-era MiGs—was designed to be used against a straight and level bomber target, not for maneuvering combat, and U.S. pilots rated the gunsight as "inadequate" because, in a turn greater than three Gs, it did not compute adequate lead and because the gunsight jumped violently when firing the cannon. The later-model MiG-21D had a distinctive, much larger radome than the MiG-21C that contained a larger radar, the "Spin Scan." The Spin Scan had a search range of 15 miles and a lock-on range of 10 miles (but only two to three miles below 10,000 feet). The MiG-21D carried only two Atolls, with no cannon.

U.S. test pilots felt the MiG-21's greatest asset was that it was extremely hard to see at combat ranges. Besides being very small, the MiG-21's engine did not leave a smoke trail at any power setting, and many times during the tests, the only way the U.S. aircraft was able to see the MiG-21 was by looking for the smoke from the engine of the American fighter flying with it. These characteristics made the MiG-21 especially effective in the most critical aspects of combat: head on, when the MiG-21 was attacking, and tail on, when he was running from a U.S. aircraft. From these positions, the MiG-21 was practically invisible at combat ranges, and this was commented on again and again in U.S. combat and test reports.

U.S. test pilots also found that at all airspeed and altitudes—except as noted—the MiG-21 had exceptional turn capability despite its control

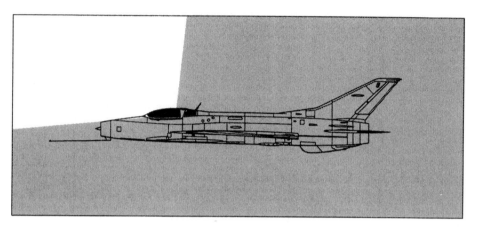

The MiG-21's Blind Spots. The poor visibility from the MiG-21 made it very vulnerable to attack from the rear; this shortcoming probably was responsible for many—if not most—MiG-21 losses.

problems. The MiG's armament controls were considered easy to use (although they were scattered randomly throughout the cockpit), and changing from missiles to cannon took only two switch changes. The MiG-21, like the MiG-17, was considered more survivable than U.S. fighters. The MiG-21 had simple flight controls and hydraulics, and while all the surfaces were hydraulically boosted, only the horizontal stabilizer required hydraulic boost for flight. The MiG-21's bladder fuel tank offered good protection from incendiary hits and, unlike U.S. aircraft, the pilot was protected by armor plate.

While the test projects were very helpful in making energy maneuverability charts and highlighting the Soviet fighters' specific weaknesses and strengths, tactically they yielded few changes in the recommended ways U.S. fighters should fight the North Vietnamese MiGs. The U.S. test pilots recommended that U.S. pilots in combat continue to exploit the low energy and slow speed of the MiG-17 by climbing and diving—"fighting in the vertical"—and by keeping their speed high. Above 500 knots, the MiG-17 was considered "relatively easy prey," but below 475 knots it was "a formidable opponent."[10] The 8th TFW tactics manual said after the tests: "Do not attempt to turn with the MiG-17. . . . The F-4 can . . . accelerate away from the MiG-17 at almost any time. . . . Use the three advantages available to the F-4D over a MiG-17: acceleration, zoom and speed."

Against the MiG-21, the Have Donut U.S. test pilots thought that, despite its speed and maneuverability, the poor visibility from the cockpit made the MiG-21 vulnerable in a turning engagement as long as the U.S. fighter could be keep it in sight—a very significant caveat. The final report recommended keeping the fight low and fast, and a great deal of emphasis was put on taking advantage of the MiG-21's very poor rearward visibility. U.S. aircrews considered these visibility problems very tactically exploitable in a turning fight,[11] and a careful reading of the accounts of American kills on the MiG-21 during Rolling Thunder and later indicates that the MiG-21's poor visibility from the cockpit probably was responsible for the majority of its losses. The 8th TFW tactics manual recommended that, when fighting a MiG-21, "Force the fight as low as possible and work toward the blind area," but it also acknowledged the MiG-21's excellent performance by saying bluntly, "If the MiG-21 has the advantage, disengage."[12]

Many U.S. fighter pilots, especially Navy pilots, had the opportunity to fly against the MiGs in these practice engagements and found the experience invaluable. One later commented (after shooting down a MiG-17), "You can sit around and talk at the bar . . . about the square corner the MiG-17 can turn, but until you've seen it with your own eyes you can't visualize the way this thing [the MiG-17] can turn. . . . It wasn't that big a surprise to me. . . . [I]t looked the same as it did in Have Drill."[13]

Aircraft Comparisons

The drawing on page 82 compares the characteristics of the six fighters in use over North Vietnam in 1966. It shows U.S. fighters were significantly larger (thus could be seen from a much greater distance) and also were from three to five times heavier than the MiG-17 and from two to over three times as heavy as the MiG-21. This was not, however, just dead weight—U.S. fighters had much greater range and more sophisticated electronics than the MiGs, which were designed for very short-range interception missions under GCI control (unfortunately, this is just what they were doing over North Vietnam). The U.S. aircraft also carried more missiles and more cannon ammunition—for example, U.S. fighter cannon carried enough ammunition for about ten or eleven seconds of firing time, while MiGs carried enough for between five and six seconds, or about two firing passes.

The drawing also shows the relative performances of the six aircraft. Maximum speed at high altitude had little meaning over North Vietnam, since most combats were at medium to low altitudes. On the other hand, maximum speed at sea level was significant since it allowed the faster fighter to disengage from the low altitude battles over North Vietnam. All

U.S. F-105D
Gross Weight 52,000; Max Speed Sea Level 730 knots; Thrust/Weight .745; Wing Loading 92.5

U.S. F-4
Gross Weight 53,000; Max Speed Sea Level 710 knots; Thrust/Weight .79; Wing Loading 81

 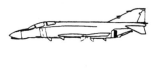

U.S. F-8
Gross Weight 30,000; Max Speed Sea Level 650 knots; Thrust/Weight .69; Wing Loading 69

NVN MiG-21
Gross Weight 16,300; Max Speed Sea Level 595 knots; Thrust/Weight .88; Wing Loading 58

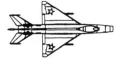 

NVN MiG-17
Gross Weight 12,000; Max Speed Sea Level 575 knots; Thrust/Weight. 64; Wing Loading 44

NVN MiG-19
Gross Weight 16,500; Max Speed Sea Level 620 knots; Thrust/Weight .84; Wing Loading 51

The six main fighters involved in air-to-air combat in the Vietnam War.

of the U.S. fighters were faster than the MiGs at low altitude, but real combat experience indicated the difference might not be as great as the charts indicated. The airspeeds shown for U.S. fighters were chart data for new aircraft, whereas many U.S. fighters in Southeast Asia had been battle damaged or had suffered other forms of structural stress and consequently were not as fast as they were when brand-new.

Thrust-to-weight ratio (the ratio of the thrust of the engine to the combat weight of the aircraft) was a good general test of climbing ability and acceleration for each aircraft; a higher relative thrust-to-weight ratio meant better climb and acceleration. The advantage U.S. fighters had over the MiG-17 in this area was the main reason they had been able to dominate the older Soviet fighter. Defensively, U.S. fighters used their superior thrust-to-weight ratio to out-accelerate the MiG-17 and get a speed advantage quickly, allowing them to disengage or separate and reenter the fight if they found themselves at a disadvantage. Offensively, a significant thrust-to-weight advantage meant the U.S. fighters could climb faster and longer than the MiG-17 and then attack from above. The MiG-21, on the other hand, had a thrust-to-weight advantage over the U.S. fighters and could stay with them if they tried to accelerate or climb away. Additionally, with the Atoll missile, the MiG-21 could shoot down U.S. fighters who were trying to outrun or outzoom it.

The final number on the drawing, wing loading (the ratio of the combat weight of the aircraft to the area of the wing), is a good general measure of an aircraft's turning ability; in principle, the lower the wing loading, the better a fighter's turn performance. The MiG-17 had a very low wing loading—almost half that of the F-4 and much less than half that of the small-winged F-105—and at low speeds (below 400 knots), the MiG-17 was by far the most maneuverable fighter in the skies over North Vietnam. The MiG-21 also had a low wing loading, and at high altitude it was more maneuverable than the U.S. fighters. However, turn performance is complex[14] and depends on other factors (including altitude and the aerodynamics and flight control systems of the aircraft), and at 15,000 feet and below, aerodynamic limitations made the MiG-21's combat maneuverability about equal to that of the F-8 and F-4. But at any altitude and airspeed the MiG-21 still was far more maneuverable than the F-105.

During Rolling Thunder, there were two clear aircraft performance differences. The MiG-17 was inferior to all of the U.S. fighters and suffered losses that reflected this fact. Despite having excellent GCI and often attacking bomb-loaded U.S. aircraft, about eighty-seven MiG-17s were shot down, while they in turn shot down only twenty-three U.S. aircraft. On the other hand, the MiG-21 clearly was superior to the F-105: They shot down fifteen F-105s, while F-105s did not shoot down a single

MiG-21. But with the F-8, F-4, and MiG-21, the differences in aircraft performance appeared to cancel each other out, with the outcome of a given battle depending on other factors.

U.S. Crews Evaluate Their Fighters

Now, after a large number of engagements with MiGs, U.S. pilots were able to assess the relative merits and disadvantages of their own aircraft. Air Force and Navy F-4 crews considered the performance of the F-4 its important asset,[15] especially its speed and acceleration. Although it could not out-turn the MiG-17, its superior thrust permitted vertical maneuvers that the MiG-17 could not follow. Against the MiG-21, the F-4 also had a small turn advantage below 15,000 feet. Some reports[16] indicated that this advantage was insufficient to be exploited tactically; combat pilots disagreed,[17] however, and Air Force F-4s were consistently successful against the MiG-21 in turning engagements. Nevertheless, it was difficult to determine if this was due to the F-4's performance, the relative superiority the American pilots, or—probably most important—the MiG-21's poor cockpit visibility. Whatever the reason, the F-4's performance made its pilots willing to stay and turn with a MiG-21, often with good results.

F-4 crews also liked the air-to-air radar and complementary capabilities of the heat-seeking and radar-guided missiles.[18] They appreciated the large firing envelope and long-range capability of the AIM-7, which they found useful in a variety of situations despite reliability problems and the restrictions of the rules of engagement. The F-4's radar capability, despite limitations at low level, sometimes was useful over North Vietnam in detecting MiGs to begin an engagement, and F-4 crews found a radar lock on helped them keep the small MiGs in sight during a hard-maneuvering fight.

The F-4's back seater provided the fighter with another advantage, and his assistance to the pilot often decided an engagement. The back seater's usefulness went far beyond operating the radar; his primary contribution was his ability to provide additional visual surveillance—"another pair of eyes." Many times the back seater saw the MiGs first and helped the aircraft commander in combat by warning of attacks from the rear, making fuel checks, and checking other items often overlooked in the heat of a dogfight.

The two other fighters used by the United States had fewer advantages. The Navy's F-8 pilots liked their aircraft's performance (mainly its turning capability and high speed): F-8s were successful against MiG-17s and

MiG-21s in all types of engagements and seldom seemed outperformed. The F-8 pilots liked their cannon armament (when it worked), but they rarely used the radar because of its susceptibility to ground clutter and because of the need for the pilot to look continually outside the aircraft for MiGs and SAMs. Interestingly, F-8 pilots often said they felt that a two-seat fighter was unnecessary—probably more of a chauvinistic dig at their F-4 rivals than an objective observation. F-105 pilots thought the Thud's performance advantages were limited to its high speed at low altitude and its ability to take structural damage. Still, many F-105 pilots felt that a clean, AIM-9-armed F-105 was capable of giving a good account of itself in air-to-air combat.

Despite the strong points of U.S. aircraft, there were several serious complaints about them, besides their missile and weapons systems problems. For example, converting the fighter's performance into some exploitable tactical advantage depended in part on aircraft handling qualities; if these characteristics were poor, the pilot had to pay extra attention to flying the aircraft and limit his aircraft's performance to those conditions that he could control. Both the MiG-21 and MiG-17 had control problems—lack of controllability at speeds above 400 knots and 3.5 Gs for the MiG-17, difficulty maneuvering above 510 knots and below 210 knots in the MiG-21—that gave the U.S. fighters some areas of advantage, but many F-4 pilots found the Phantom difficult to maneuver because it had an undesirable flying characteristic called "adverse yaw." In very hard turns, especially at slower speeds, the F-4 could not be rolled in the normal fashion by moving the stick (which controlled the ailerons) in the direction of the turn. To turn under these conditions, the F-4's control stick had to be held in the center and the aircraft rolled with the rudder foot pedals; if the F-4's stick was not held in the center position in a hard turn, at best the aircraft would turn poorly, and it easily could go out of control and perhaps into a spin, often fatal in combat. As the F-4 flight manual said: "The natural tendency to turn with aileron must be avoided . . . [or there will be] departure from controlled flight followed by a rapid spin entry."[19] Centering the stick in a hard turn was counterintuitive for most pilots, and it required good training for a pilot to be comfortable maneuvering an F-4 to get maximum performance in a dogfight. Most new Air Force F-4 pilots did not get this type of training, however. The adverse yaw problem had a maintenance component as well—if an F-4's ailerons were out of alignment, the aircraft turned poorly even if the pilot used his controls properly.

Fear of the F-4s' adverse yaw kept many U.S. pilots from getting the maximum performance out of the Phantom. Compounding the real problem was a distinctive beeper that sounded as the aircraft approached the critical adverse yaw zone, which required turning with the rudder. For experienced pilots, the beeper was just a reminder to use the rudder and was helpful in ensuring that they got the maximum turn. But inexperienced pilots often considered the beeper a warning that they were turning too hard and, on hearing the tone, relaxed their turn—a potentially fatal mistake when being pursued by a MiG or dodging a SAM.

Another significant problem was that, while U.S. fighters could take heavy structural damage, they were highly vulnerable to hits in their hydraulic systems—much more vulnerable than the simpler MiGs. In the F-4, for example, a hit in the hydraulic system often caused loss of hydraulic pressure; when this happened, the stabilator locked, and the F-4 would pitch straight up and go out of control.[20] The F-105 had a similar problem; one pilot said, "This was the curse of the Thud. . . . She was prone to loss of control when the hydraulic system took even the smallest of hits. There is just no way to steer her once the fluid goes out. . . . You can lose two of the three hydraulics systems that run your flight controls by the time you realize you are hit . . . [and] once they have a vent they are gone."[21] Later in Rolling Thunder there were combat modifications to make the hydraulics systems more survivable, but the problem never went away.

One of the U.S. aircrews' major complaints about their fighters was that they were easy to see. Not only were they were much larger than the MiGs, but their engines also smoked heavily, making them easily visible from the ground or air. This especially was a problem with the twin-engine F-4, and it was not uncommon for F-4s to be seen from as far as 30 miles away.[22]

Radios were another special problem on the F-4. One American MiG killer said, "[T]hat's our greatest problem: the UHF radio. . . . It is our single most important piece of equipment in [Route Package] 6 . . . and radio failure . . . is unacceptably high."[23] Because of the antenna placement on the F-4, in certain phases of flight the antenna was blocked by the aircraft structure, completely cutting out radio calls,[24] and it seemed to be especially bad under maneuvering conditions, such as a dogfight, when the radio was most needed. Making matters worse, during a heavy rain—very common in Southeast Asia—the water drained from the cockpit directly on the F-4's radio control box, causing problems of epidemic proportions.[25] Additionally, since the F-4 radio was located under the Phantom's back seat, repairing it meant the entire back ejection seat had to be removed.[26] It was believed that many F-4 losses were caused when the crew missed a critical "break" call when under attack,[27] but despite this, the F-4's radio problems largely were ignored throughout the war.

Radio communications in general were a major difficulty for Rolling Thunder (and later Linebacker) strikes. U.S. fighters had only one two-way radio, and on a normal strike mission much of the strike force had to be on the same frequency so they could exchange warnings and other information. During a mission it was necessary for the crew to switch radio frequencies several times, and if a flight member missed a frequency change—all too easy when under attack—he could not communicate with the rest of his flight. The simplest solution—adding another radio—was never tried, despite the fact that many single-seat nonfighter U.S. aircraft carried two (or more) radios.[28] Additionally, all U.S. aircraft radios had a separate receiver set on a special frequency called Guard. In theory, this channel was monitored by every aircraft in the theater and was used for emergencies, such as notifying rescue forces that a pilot was down. Unfortunately, many agencies and support aircraft, such as the EC-121s and EB-66s, used Guard channel for MiG and SAM warnings, so as the strike force entered the area and MiGs and SAMs came up, the force not only had their own transmissions, but also often extraneous MiG and SAM warnings, crowding the radios. Finally, when a U.S. pilot ejected, a loud, shrill "beeper" in his ejection seat went off on Guard channel; not only was this chilling, but it also blocked other transmissions. The confusion caused by these "beepers" going off on Guard during a critical moment, such as when a large strike flight was attacked by MiGs and SAMs while trying to bomb a target, can be imagined. Post-strike analyses of U.S. losses indicate that many U.S. aircraft were lost because radio transmissions cut out a SAM or MiG attack warning. The large number of aircraft and other agencies on the radios blocking vital calls was one of the major problems throughout the war, and it was never satisfactorily resolved.

However, the F-4 did have a little noted but important advantage because, unlike other U.S. fighters, it carried an extra radio receiver, called the auxiliary (or aux) radio. The F-4 MiGCAPs could listen to the strike flights with their aux radio receiver to see where the action was, and at the same time keep their two-way radio free for their own conversations.

New MiG-17 Tactics

Beginning on February 14, 1967, there was a massive increase in strike activity, and for the next ten months the U.S. attempted the sequential destruction of North Vietnam's industrial base. Major power plants were destroyed, most military airfields were attacked, and systematic attacks were made on rail transportation yards and repair facilities. Over the course of the campaign the White House would approve strikes into the "restricted" and "prohibited" areas, and rail and highway bridges in the Haiphong area were destroyed, along with the longest railroad/highway bridge in the country. Unfortunately, the attacks were not made in a single massive stroke but—still in accordance with "gradual escalation"— gradually increased in intensity.

By this time in the war Air Force F-4Cs were receiving their own QRC-160 pods and no longer had to depend on pods borrowed from the F-105 wings. Once again the MiGCAP F-4s could escort the F-105s all the way to the target instead of orbiting outside the SAM areas, and the pods helped the F-4s as much as they had helped the F-105s, with the loss rate of F-4s to SA-2s dropping measurably. From September to December 1966, SAMs shot down six F-4s in 226 sorties in Route Package VI; from January to March 1967, SAMs shot down only one F-4 in 306 sorties in the same area—a drop in losses similar to that of the F-105s when they began to carry the QRC-160s.

For most of February 1967 the weather was bad; there were no air-to-air losses on either side. The MiG-21s appeared to be standing down, probably because most of the MiG-21s in the North Vietnamese inventory had been shot down in the last few months, and single flights of four F-4s began to cap the MiG bases during strikes in hopes of catching the MiGs taking off. The EC-121Ds of Big Eye now moved to Ubon RTAFB, the home base of the 8th TFW, whose F-4s flew most of the MiGCAPs over North Vietnam. (Shortly after their arrival at Ubon, the EC-121 operation changed its name from the Big Eye Task Force to the College Eye Task Force.) While the base staff did the ritual grumping about the large early-warning aircraft and their substantial support requirements, the 8th TFW's F-4 pilots, always looking for an edge, began to examine the EC-121D's capabilities and showed an interest in using it for MiGCAP control rather than just MiG warning.

In the few February engagements with the North Vietnamese, Air Force F-4s began to note an improvement in MiG-17 tactics. On February 5, four F-4Cs were flying MiGCAP, protecting an F-105 strike in the Hanoi area. The weather was moderately hazy and the F-4s were capping at low altitude, about 3,000 feet. In one of their orbits they sighted two MiG-17s in front of them; as they turned to attack, the F-4s were attacked by two trailing MiG-17s. The engagement turned into a low-level, hard-turning fight where neither side could gain an advantage. Every time an F-4 pulled behind one of the MiGs, a trailing MiG would force him off. When the MiG pulled behind him, the F-4 would use the standard tactic of pulling into a steep climb, which the MiGs could not follow. In the past, the MiGs would try to follow the F-4s in the climb, then fall off, allowing the F-4s to drop down behind them and fire a missile. But in this engagement, when the F-4s climbed, the MiGs stayed low in their level turn and refused to climb with the F-4s. The MiG-17 pilots had developed an understanding of energy maneuverability; by no longer trying to climb with the F-4s, the MiG-17s took away the F-4s' most effective tactic. The result was a stalemate. The frustrated F-4s fired eight missiles (three Sparrows and five Sidewinders), but none came close.

The North Vietnamese realized that low-altitude fights reduced the effectiveness of both types of American air-to-air missiles, and an analysis of the trends in MiG engagements showed that the average altitude of the engagements had been going down steadily, especially for the MiG-17.[29] From this point on, the MiG-17s tried to lure the F-4s into slow-speed turning fights, and as 1967 moved on, U.S. fighters began to find the MiG-17s waiting in a circling formation, quickly christened a "wagon wheel," at very low altitude over the most likely routes of the F-105 strike force; from this formation the MiGs would attack as the F-105s ingressed or egressed the target area. The wagon wheel was very effective defensively against the escorting F-4s; the MiG-17s spaced themselves around the circumference of the circle, and if the F-4s tried to slow down to enter the circle to get behind the MiGs for a missile shot, the trailing MiGs in the wheel would attack.[30] The ground clutter prevented the F-4 from getting a radar lock on to launch AIM-7s, and the low altitude drastically shrunk the AIM-9B envelope. (At 10,000 feet, the AIM-9B had a range of about 6,000 feet and could be fired in a 40-degree cone behind the target, but at sea level its maximum range was reduced to 4,000 feet, and the cone shrunk to 30 degrees.) The envelope limitations, combined with the MiGs' tight turns and the infrared radiation from the ground, made the AIM-9B almost useless. While the F-4s continually were able to avoid MiG-17 attacks and reattack by diving and climbing in and out of the wheel, rarely was there enough time to maneuver for a missile attack, and the F-4s had no cannon for close-in attacks. Once again, the F-4 crews groused about the lack of a gun. The MiG-17s, on the other hand, stood little chance of shooting down an F-4 unless they got a lucky cannon hit or could make an unobserved attack, or unless the F-4s slowed down and tried level turns.

But while the MiG-17s could not threaten the F-4s, they were relatively safe from F-4 missiles in their low-altitude wheels and could wait for the strike flight's approach. As the strike flight came in range, the MiGs would break out of the wheel and climb to the strike flight's altitude to harry the bomb-loaded strikers, trying to force them to jettison

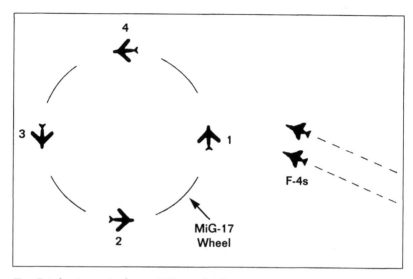

Two F-4s begin an attack on a MiG-17 wheel.

their bombs and engage in turning dogfights. Often U.S. aircraft saw a single MiG-17 in the area of the wheel, and it was hypothesized that this was a "lead" or "director" aircraft.[31] This director was believed to be telling the MiGs when they were under attack and when to break out and engage the American strike flights, and U.S. pilots commented that this formation let the North Vietnamese effectively use and protect a large number of inexperienced MiG-17 pilots and a small cadre of experienced ones.[32]

In March the northeast monsoon kept the weather bad and limited the number of strikes, but the strikes escalated when, on March 10, the Thai Nyugen steel works were bombed for the first time. In Washington another battle continued: Rolling Thunder was becoming ever more controversial and had resulted in a sharp division between the military and the secretary of defense, with the president in the middle. The military continued to press for an increase in the bombings and the relaxation of other restrictions, including the mining of Haiphong harbor; Secretary of Defense McNamara believed the bombing was achieving its objectives and still feared a confrontation with China or the Soviet Union.

The MiGs of April

The spring 1967 northeast monsoon lasted longer than normal, and through early April the weather remained bad. On April 18 the weather

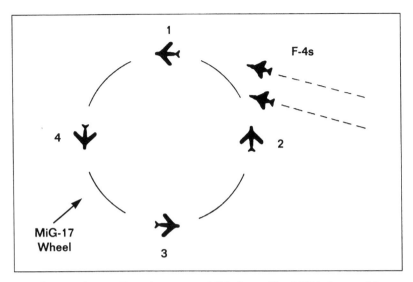

Note how, as the two F-4s close on one MiG, the trailing MiG is in a position to attack the U.S. aircraft.

began to clear, and the battles for the rest of the month made it one of the most intense periods in the Rolling Thunder campaign. The MiGs and SAMs were out in force, and there were a record number of MiG engagements and SAM firings. U.S. reports noted that the MiG pilots were "more aggressive and proficient," that "MiG flight tactics have shown remarkable improvement over the last few months," and that through April and May MiGs constantly attacked U.S. forces on ingress and egress.[33] The "SAM days" and "MiG days" were over; the North Vietnamese air defense system began firing SAMs and committing MiGs nearly simultaneously against U.S. aircraft. The North Vietnamese also appeared to be protecting their low-altitude MiG-17 wheels by fusing their AAA to explode at 12,000 feet and above, and by having the MiG-17s stay below that altitude. The combination of SAMs and AAA above 12,000 feet cut down the F-4s' most effective way of attacking the MiG-17 wheel; now, when they attacked a wheel from above or climbed away from an attack, they were vulnerable to flak and SA-2s.[34]

U.S. tactics also changed. In early April, to increase the number of bombs that could be put on the North Vietnamese targets, more F-4s were used as strikers. The combination of F-4 sweeps and the use of other F-4s for bombing meant that often there were not enough F-4s for MiGCAP, so for added protection against the MiGs the first F-105 strike flight off the target became a MiGCAP flight[35] to help cover the rest of the strike flights as they bombed. With their bombs gone and carrying AIM-9s, the F-105s were helpful against MiG-17s; this tactic stayed in effect through May.[36]

On April 19 a series of a wild dogfights began that continued until the end of the month. Six American F-105s and an A-1 were downed, while U.S. fighters shot down nine MiG-17s and a MiG-21.

For the first four days after the weather cleared, the MiG-17s tried to assert themselves, whereas the MiG-21s were rarely seen. On April 19 a large U.S. force attacked the Xuan Mai army barracks and insurgency school located at the foot of the mountains about 12 miles west-southwest of Hanoi. As usual, the Iron Hand F-105Fs were first in the target area to try to shut down any SAM sites in the area. Kingfish was the first Iron Hand in and was attacked by MiG-17s shortly after entering the target area. The MiGs shot down one F-105F, Kingfish 2, and lost a MiG-17 to Kingfish 1. As the strikers moved in to attack the target, there was a large, inconclusive melee between the F-105 MiGCAP and a large number of MiG-17s over the target area. While the battle raged, Kingfish 1 located Kingfish 2's two-man crew on the ground and began to orbit over them; it appeared it would be possible to pick up the crew, so a rescue operation began.

Tomahawk, a flight of F-105s, struck the target and was heading for post-strike refueling when it heard that Kingfish 2 was down. Once he arrived at the tanker Tomahawk 1 volunteered to take his flight back to the area to cover the rescue, but the rescue controller was reluctant to grant permission because Tomahawk did not have external fuel tanks (they had been jettisoned earlier when Tomahawk had engaged MiGs) and therefore would be able to stay over the downed crew for only a short time. However, since no other aircraft were available to return to the area, the rescue controller told Tomahawk flight to fill up with gas and return to the area to cover the rescue. When the flight completed refueling, Tomahawk 1 headed back into the area at high altitude to conserve fuel because "it was obviously a MiG day."

As U.S. search and rescue forces moved to pick up the downed crew of Kingfish 2, MiG-17s came up in force to stop the rescue, and a large air battle developed between the U.S. rescue forces and the MiG-17s. The rescue forces were led by "Sandys," slow, propeller-driven A-1s that escorted the ponderous rescue helicopters. The Sandys normally held an orbit close to North Vietnam timed with the air strikes so that they would be in the optimum position to assist in any rescue attempts. As soon as an aircrew was reported down, the A-1s' mission was to proceed to the downed crew's location, determine whether a rescue was possible based on the position of the crew and enemy defenses, then take charge of the rescue attempt. During the rescue attempt the Sandys would direct the rescue helicopters, known as the "Jolly Green Giants" or "Jollies" (from their large size and green camouflage color scheme), to the downed crew and direct any available fighter flights in the area to attack enemy troops or guns; the Sandys also attacked targets with their own weapons. Needless to say, taking a slow, low-flying aircraft like the A-1 or the rescue helicopter into Route Packages V or VI was a difficult and risky business. The risk increased because the North Vietnamese listened to U.S. radio transmissions; they knew when an aircraft was down and when a rescue was going to be attempted. U.S. forces only attempted rescues outside areas of heavy ground defenses, so the only way the North Vietnamese could intervene was with MiGs, but they did so regularly—and effectively—throughout the war.

On April 19, two A-1s, Sandy 1 and Sandy 2, part of the search and rescue force, were in orbit when informed that Kingfish 2 was down. The A-1s headed to a point about 32 miles southwest of Hanoi, met Kingfish 1, and began to look for Kingfish 2's crew. Sandy 2 saw the F-105 burning and located one of the downed aircrew. The A-1s began to orbit at about 1,000 feet and were just rolling out of a turn when Sandy 2 saw four MiG-17s behind and slightly above them; the MiGs were in two pairs, with one pair attacking each A-l. The MiGs started firing almost immediately after Sandy 2 saw them. Sandy 2 called, "Break right," as he broke right over Sandy 1 into the MiGs. The MiGs missed Sandy 2, but as he broke he saw Sandy 1 take cannon hits and roll rapidly to the left with pieces coming off his left wing, then crash into a mountaintop without a chute or a beeper.

Kingfish 1 also was attacked by MiGs and warned the inbound Tomahawk flight that there were "MiGs all over" and that he was under MiG attack. As Tomahawk flight let down about 20 miles west of the area, Kingfish 1 called and said he was out of fuel and departing for a tanker. Sandy 2 contacted Tomahawk and said that MiGs had shot down Sandy 1 and that at least four MiGs were attacking him, and he requested— "rather excitedly"—that the F-105s come and help him. The F-105s advised Sandy 2 to stay low as they homed in on the A-1's radio transmission, dropping down to 5,000 feet and accelerating to 700 knots.

The MiG-17s by now had surrounded Sandy 2 and were making individual passes from around the circle. They had made at least five firing passes before Sandy 2 saw the four F-105s and called, "F-105s, I'm at your [right side] 3 o'clock; come right, come right, come right." Sandy 2 made another turn to avoid a MiG pass and next saw the four F-105s in loose trail with a MiG-17 behind them. Sandy 2 called, "F-105s break; one's on your tail."

Tomahawk flight broke right and picked up a group of MiGs close in front of them. Tomahawk 1, in an attempt to divert the MiGs from the A-1, aimed the four F-105s for the center of the MiGs, who scattered as the Thuds roared through their formation. One MiG recovered and rolled back in behind Sandy 2, but Tomahawk 3 and Tomahawk 4 turned to press the MiG and immediately got into a low-altitude "daisy chain" with several more MiG-17s: MiG-17, Tomahawk 3, MiG-17, Tomahawk 4, and two more MiG-17s. The fight slowed to an airspeed below 300 knots, ideal for the MiGs and very dangerous for the F-105s.

In the daisy chain Tomahawk 3 hit the MiG in front of him with cannon fire in the left wing and on the fuselage just aft of the canopy, but as he started firing, Tomahawk 4 called, "Tomahawk 3 break right; Tomahawk 3 break right—F-105 break right now; MiG-17 firing on you." Tomahawk 3 saw "big orange balls going over the canopy and decided that it was time to break right," and dived into a nearby cloud, "hoping that there wasn't a mountain on the other side." The MiG behind him continued to fire as Tomahawk 3 entered the cloud; when he came out the MiG was gone.

Meanwhile, Tomahawk 1 had turned back to the main battle and immediately saw the daisy chain of Tomahawk 3 and Tomahawk 4 and the four MiG-17s. As he approached he saw Tomahawk 4 firing from about 200 feet behind the MiG-17 attacking Tomahawk 3, but Tomahawk 4 apparently missed. Another MiG pulled in behind him, and Tomahawk 4 called, "Somebody come help me; I have a MiG on my tail and I can't shake him." Tomahawk 1 had now closed on the fight and was easily able to slide in behind the MiG that was firing on Tomahawk 4. He moved to about a thousand feet behind the MiG and opened fire, immediately hitting the North Vietnamese fighter on the fuselage behind the canopy. As he closed to within 100 feet, the MiG started a slow roll; Tomahawk 1 pulled up hard to avoid a collision and was passing over the stricken MiG when it exploded. The explosion snapped Tomahawk 1's head down on his chest; thinking he had rammed the MiG, Tomahawk 1 called, "I hit him—Tomahawk lead is hit." He then moved off, checked his aircraft over, and, finding no indications of damage, called, "Tomahawk lead is okay," and went back into the fight.

The fight now was between 3,000 feet and the treetops, with the F-105s desperately trying to keep the MiGs away from Sandy 2 while the A-1 continued to maneuver around small rock formations in the valley.

Sandy 2 knew that his only hope for safety lay in reaching the large mountain range that led all the way to Laos, but to reach the mountains he would have to make a four-minute trip across a flat, ten-mile-wide valley that was between his position and the mountains, and in the flat valley the MiGs would have a clear shot at him.

Tomahawk 1 made Sandy 2's decision for him when he called, "Sandy, you better go home; we're running out of gas and can't stay much longer." By this time the MiGs were firmly engaged with the F-105s, and Sandy 2 started out across the flat valley floor as fast as he could—160 knots. One MiG set up for a pass on the A-1 but, distracted by the F-105s, never completed the run. As Sandy 2 neared the far side of the valley, he saw a deep, narrow gorge with the tops of the mountains in a cloud layer about 300 feet above the valley floor. The A-1 ducked under the cloud layer, followed the gorge, and escaped undamaged; the F-105s then disengaged and returned to their base.

For the next few days MiG activity continued to increase, and their growing aggressiveness finally persuaded Washington to allow the bombing of some—but not all—of the MiG bases. On April 24 a small U.S. force was given permission to bomb the MiG airfields at Kep and Hoa Lac. Shortly after these bombing raids, most of the North Vietnamese MiG-17s moved out of the country, but the MiG-17s continued to engage U.S. aircraft from bases in China. Also later in April, Air Force F-4s began to enter the target area about five minutes prior to the strikers to "sweep" the area for MiGs, then orbit between the target and the MiG bases to try to cut off the MiGs before they reached the strike flights. This was not successful; neither the F-4 radar nor the EC-121 radar could pick up the low-flying MiGs, and the North Vietnamese GCI simply vectored the MiGs around the F-4s to the strike flights. Additionally, the early entry left the F-4s low on fuel when the last strike flights were hitting the target, and the orbits exposed the F-4s to AAA and SAMs for long periods of time.[37]

Unfortunately, during the last two days of April MiG-21s returned to the fray, and they conclusively demonstrated their superiority over the F-105. On April 29, Lightning, a flight of four F-105Ds, was the flak suppression flight leading the strike force in an attack on a target near Hanoi. The weather was good—scattered to broken clouds with bottoms at 16,000 feet and tops at 20,000 feet with good visibility (about 15 miles). After hitting the target, Lightning 1 and Lightning 2 broke off in a futile pursuit of two MiG-17s while Lightning 3 and Lightning 4 departed the area. Lightning 3 and Lightning 4 were exiting at 18,000 feet and 500 knots when they saw an unidentified silver aircraft come out of the clouds about two miles away behind them and slightly to their left. The aircraft was at the same altitude and closing rapidly. The F-105s started a left level turn into the unidentified aircraft and jettisoned their fuel tanks. As the aircraft closed, they saw it was a clean MiG-21 and continued their left turn, diving to accelerate as the MiG-21 turned in behind them.

The MiG closed, and Lightning 4 felt a thump as the MiG's cannon shells hit. The MiG overshot slightly, and the two F-105s watched helplessly as the MiG-21 moved high and repositioned about a mile behind them as they continued their descending turn. Passing through 10,000 feet, Lightning 4 saw the MiG closing again and then saw the MiG's underside as he pulled lead and began firing his cannon. At the same instant, Lightning 3 called that he was hit and immediately started to slow down. Lightning 4 saw fire and smoke in Lightning 3's aft section and began to call for him to abandon the aircraft. Lightning 3 continued to descend and shortly erupted into flame from the right wing back. Lightning 4 followed him down and tried to keep him and the MiG in sight; he saw the MiG a few times during this period, but the MiG (probably out of cannon ammunition) did not press another attack. At 1,000 feet Lightning 3 ejected; Lightning 4 saw two black objects separate from the aircraft and then saw the F-105 hit the ground. Lightning 4 stayed in the immediate area for about two minutes, then, having lost sight of the MiG and unsure of the damage to his own aircraft, egressed.

The debriefing was depressing. It was bad enough that the North Vietnamese GCI had put the MiG-21 in an excellent position and the MiG had been able to run down two clean F-105s after they had dropped their bombs. What was truly disturbing was that, contrary to most MiG-21 pilots seen before, this MiG pilot demonstrated considerable skill in using his speed and maneuverability advantage over the two F-105s in pressing his attack. This was a bad omen, and it was fortunate that the MiG had shot down only one of the Thuds.

The next day the MiG-21s struck again. Tomahawk, a flight of four F-105s, was flying the Iron Hand support for a strike on the Hanoi transformer station. Tomahawk was the first flight in the target area when they received a MiG-21 warning for their area. A few minutes later Tomahawk 1 observed Tomahawk 3 (an F-105F with a two-man crew) on fire. Tomahawk 3 flamed out shortly afterward, and the aircraft went out of control. Tomahawk 1 and Tomahawk 2 saw two good chutes and heard two beepers, then began circling the chutes as they descended. The F-105s made voice contact with Tomahawk 3's pilot and went into an orbit over the area to try to set up a rescue. At this point Tomahawk 1 and Tomahawk

2 realized that Tomahawk 4 was not with them. Neither had seen Tomahawk 4 hit or had heard any radio transmissions; they attempted to contact him but got no response. Tomahawk 1 reported the downed crew to the search and rescue command center, adding that Tomahawk 4 also was probably down. Intelligence analysis later determined that both F-105s were victims of the same MiG-21.

The inbound strike force commander heard that there was contact with the downed crew and believed the possibility of a rescue was high, so he aborted the entire strike mission to set up a rescue for the crews of Tomahawk 3 and Tomahawk 4.[38] Carbine was one of the F-105D flights inbound with the strike force, and after the mission aborted, the four F-105Ds set up a high cover at 16,000 feet over the downed aircraft while a second flight of four F-105s set up as low cover. When the low-cover aircraft called that they were leaving for the tankers to refuel, Carbine 1 and Carbine 2 dropped down to low cover while Carbine 3 and Carbine 4 stayed in the high orbit.

While in the orbit Carbine 4 "felt a jolt and heard a thud" and immediately told Carbine 3 to break left "because of MiGs." As Carbine 3 broke left and down, he saw a MiG-21 sliding out high off his left wing. He turned into the MiG, and as he did so he saw a second MiG-21 engaging Carbine 4. The two F-105s lit their afterburners and dived for the comparative safety of some clouds a few thousand feet below, then turned and headed out of the area. On the way out Carbine 3 asked Carbine 4 several times if he "had him in sight;" each time Carbine 4 confirmed he did. Approximately ten seconds after one such request, Carbine 3 looked back and saw a ball of flame; it was Carbine 4. Carbine 1 and Carbine 2 called Carbine 3 and reported they saw Carbine 4 going down and a chute with a man waving. The F-105s returned to base without further incident.

MiG-21 versus the F-105

The loss of four F-105s in two days to MiG-21s—without firing a shot in return—showed what had been clear for some time: that the F-105 was no match for the late-model MiG. The performance differences between the F-105 and MiG-21 sharply contrasted with those between the F-105 and MiG-17. While the F-105 could not come close to outmaneuvering either the MiG-17 or the MiG-21, it had a significant acceleration and maximum speed advantage over the MiG-17, which permitted the F-105s to engage and disengage at will. The MiG-17 could exploit only limited tactics—usually hard turns—because of the F-105's superior speed.

On the other hand, while the F-105 had a higher maximum speed than the MiG-21—730 knots versus 595 knots—unfortunately, North Vietnamese GCI was becoming increasingly skillful at putting the MiG-21s high behind the F-105s, giving the diving MiGs a significant speed advantage at the beginning of the fight. Additionally, the MiG had better acceleration, and its performance gave it the ability both to maneuver offensively and easily counter F-105 attacks.

The MiG-21's missile armament also gave it more capability against the F-105, especially if the U.S. fighter tried to escape by simply running away. The F-105s' straight-ahead accelerations to separation, which were effective against the MiG-17s, were no longer recommended, because a straight-ahead separation in afterburner merely solved the Atoll's problems with maneuvering aircraft. Now, the recommended defensive maneuver was for the F-105 to turn hard into the attacker to defeat an Atoll and dive to accelerate away. If the MiG-21 returned to the attack, the F-105 repeated the maneuver. Another successful tactic was the diving spiral. This kept the F-105 out of the Atoll's small envelope; unfortunately, eventually the F-105 got so low he had to roll out and run for it. If he had not gathered enough speed, the MiG would be on him.

If the MiG-21 was close, the F-105 did have one last-ditch maneuver that had been successful in the past. The F-105 would make a hard break into the attacker and continue his turn to roll upside down, as if he were starting a dive; at this point the pilot would pull the throttle to idle and open his speed brakes while completing the roll. Properly done, the maneuver lost 5,000–8,000 feet, dropped the F-105's speed to 200 knots, and left the MiG high and in front. From that position it was hoped the F-105 could dive away and escape.

If a MiG-21 attacking an F-105 missed its first attack, its speed and overall performance allowed it to accelerate, gain separation, make a climbing high-G turn that the F-105 could not follow, and reattack. If the F-105 was in good position behind the MiG-21, the MiG made a diving high-G turn—considered its best defense against the F-105's missiles or gun—then pulled back up behind the fighter. As a result, in a similar situation, an F-105 pilot might choose to run from a MiG-21 where he might attempt to shoot down a MiG-17. A hard statistic showed the difference. While more and more of the F-105 engagements involved MiG-21s, very rarely did the F-105 get a shot at a MiG-21; 90 percent of their firing attempts were at MiG-17s.[39] The Thailand-based F-105 Wing Tactics Manuals did not offer much encouragement to F-105 pilots attacked by MiG-21s. One manual said that when a MiG-21 was behind an F-105, "the F-105 will not out-accelerate the MiG-21 until past the 21's Q [maximum speed] limit. The F-105 will not turn with the MiG[-21] so do not expect an overshoot. Maneuver to survive and leave the enemy's lethal range."[40]

May 1967

In May 1967 the air war continued to escalate, with a significant increase in the number of politically approved targets and in U.S. strikes in Route Package VI. Bad weather over the other target areas in North Vietnam and the increasing strikes led the North Vietnamese to shift the bulk of their AAA and SA-2s to the Hanoi area. The increase in their defenses and the high MiG activity during April had prompted more changes in Air Force tactics; at the end of April the decision was made to change the mission of the F-4Cs from the strike/CAP role, where they carried bombs and jettisoned them if MiGs attacked, to a strictly MiGCAP role, where they carried only air-to-air armament—no bombs. Seventh Air Force also decided to increase the number of F-4 escorts to eight for each strike force,[41] and to supplement the Ubon-based F-4s of the 8th TFW, which had been flying most of the escort missions over North Vietnam, with the Da Nang-based F-4s of the 366th TFW. The 8th TFW took over the task of escorting the F-105s of the 355th TFW, and the 366th TFW escorted the 388th

A MiG-17 shoots down an F-105. Note the stream of flame from the F-105's tailpipe, just visible in front of the cloud backdrop. *USAF (courtesy of the National Archives)*

TFW F-105s. Additionally, a few F-105 flights were configured as fighters armed only with AIM-9Bs—no bombs—in the hopes of surprising the MiGs.[42]

The QRC-248

By May 1967, several new systems were entering service on the U.S. side that would tip the battle scales in its favor. The first was a system that would have a tremendous impact on air-to-air combat for the rest of the war: the QRC-248 enemy IFF transponder interrogator. The QRC-248, developed during the continuing American surveillance of Soviet-supplied Cuban MiGs, was able to read the SRO-2 transponder used on exported Soviet fighter aircraft.[43] The system was tested by an experimental EC-121, Quick Look, in a brief visit to Southeast Asia from mid-December 1966 to mid-January 1967.[44] The North Vietnamese were using the same SRO-2 transponder as the Cubans, and the test showed the QRC-248 could read the North Vietnamese MiG transponders. This was a tremendous breakthrough; with the QRC-248 reading the North Vietnamese transponders, the EC-121s could see the MiGs at low level out to a range of more than 175 miles and could tell which of the many radar returns over North Vietnam were MiGs. Since the North Vietnamese GCI net depended on SRO-2 transponders to control the MiGs, the QRC-248 was expected to be very effective, and sets were quickly sent to the College Eye EC-121Ds; by the end of May 1967 all EC-121Ds had QRC-248s.[45]

Unfortunately, the promise of the QRC-248 was limited by U.S. government rules that restricted its effectiveness over North Vietnam. The most effective mode for the QRC-248 was the active mode, where it could actually interrogate the MiG's IFF,[46] but in an attempt to avoid alerting the North Vietnamese of the QRC-248's existence, U.S. radar operators had to operate the system in the passive mode. Operating in this mode meant that the EC-121Ds had to wait for the North Vietnamese radars to interrogate the MiGs to see the transponder return, so they could not keep the MiGs under constant surveillance. This meant the EC-121 could not use the QRC-248 offensively to guide U.S. fighters to attack MiGs, but only as part of their general "Bullseye" warnings.[47] The National Security Agency (NSA), which was generally responsible for all signals intelligence (SIGINT), and the Joint Chiefs of Staff did not give the EC-121Ds authority to use the QRC-248 actively to interrogate the MiGs' IFF until July 21, 1967.[48]

But now the MiGCAP F-4s knew the EC-121's Bullseye calls were meaningful. The EC-121Ds still were based with the 8th TFW and its air-to-air F-4s at Ubon RTAFB, and the pilots from the 8th TFW began lobbying to get permission from Seventh Air Force Headquarters to have EC-121s pass the information directly to the F-4s over North Vietnam.

The QRC-248 proved to be very accurate and extremely reliable, and it gave U.S. intelligence a whole new look at North Vietnamese MiG activities. It showed that the MiGs orbited over three general areas as the U.S. forces approached: one northwest of Hanoi at the foot of the mountains along the Red River at the airfield at Yen Bai, one west-southwest of Hanoi around the village of Hoa Binh in a valley called (because of its shape) "Banana Valley," and one north of Haiphong over the small ridge of mountains called, variously, "Little Thud Ridge" or "Phantom Ridge." This new, accurate picture of MiG activity was somewhat disconcerting; the College Eye commander commented, "With the advent of the QRC-248 we were able to detect aircraft we had not previously seen. It was somewhat frightening to realize that in the past there had been so many aircraft we hadn't seen."[49]

F-4 Cannon

Another major change to the Air Force's F-4 air-to-air capabilities occurred when the 366th TFW at Da Nang decided to carry a 20-mm M-61 Vulcan

An M-61 Vulcan cannon pod mounted on the centerline station of an F-4.

gun pod on its F-4s for its escort missions. The Air Force had begun experimenting with an external cannon pod for the F-4, called the SUU-16, in mid-1964.[50] The SUU-16 could be carried in any one of three positions on the F-4 (the centerline and the two outboard wing stations) where the external fuel tanks were carried, and F-4s used the gun pods in combat for air-to-ground strafing operations from at least November 1966, but the pods had not been used for air-to-air operations. In April 1967, after being notified of their MiGCAP role, the 366th TFW asked Seventh Air Force for permission to carry the cannon pods on their MiGCAP missions, saying, "This Wing has lost a minimum of seven kills in the past ten days because of the lack of a kill capability below 2000 feet altitude and inside 2500 feet range," and that they considered the pod-mounted M-61 Gatling gun "the only air to air weapon that can be employed against a very low altitude aircraft."[51] On April 27 permission was granted to test the idea on training flights.[52] The 8th TFW—which had by far the greatest number of MiG kills—was, by some reports,[53] quite skeptical of the gun pod, clinging to the idea a cannon would get the F-4s into trouble against the more maneuverable MiGs. It also had been noted that in the past "the SUU-16 pod was considered to be disadvantageous in that it would tend to reduce maneuverability, increase drag, and increase fuel consumption."[54]

It was true the F-4C/SUU-16 combination had many limitations in the air-to-air role. The 366th TFW F-4s carried the cannon pod on the centerline station, and a potential problem was fuel: The centerline station normally carried a 600-gallon fuel tank, which meant F-4s with the cannon pod carried 600 gallons less fuel than an F-4 with a normal air-to-air weapons load. In addition, it was difficult to align the gun to the gunsight accurately enough to be used for air-to-air combat, and high speed and firing of the cannon also caused the pod to vibrate, so it was not as accurate as the fixed Vulcan in the F-105.

On May 2, 1967, 366th TFW F-4s flew test flights to check the fuel problem, with the element leads (number 1 and number 3) carrying the cannon pods and the wingmen (number 2 and number 4) carrying a centerline fuel tank. The test found the wingmen used more fuel than the element leads, because the wingman had to use his throttles more to stay in formation, and, like a car, the rapid acceleration and deceleration used more gas than a steady speed; over the course of the mission that evened out the difference in fuel. The test found that the lack of the centerline fuel tank generally meant the cannon-armed leader and wingman with a centerline fuel tank had the same effective time in combat.[55]

The main problem with the cannon pod was not the pod itself, but the F-4 gunsight. The F-4 did not have a lead-computing air-to-air gunsight;

instead, it had a fixed sight that did not compensate for turns and had roughly the same capability as the gunsight on an early World War II fighter. To offset the sight shortcomings, the 366th TFW pilots were told to "overlead" their target by putting the sight well in front of the MiG when they opened fire, then lessen the lead as they closed, hoping the MiG would fly through a stream of bullets. The 366th TFW calculated that there was only 30 feet between bullets in the stream and that the chances of a MiG flying through the stream without being hit were "nonexistent."[56] Like the F-105, the F-4s had to get in very close to be sure of a hit, but many F-4 pilots thought the fact that the pod vibrated at high speed helped their shooting because it increased bullet dispersion.

Beginning May 3, 1967, the 366th TFW F-4s began to carry the cannon pod on their escort missions into Route Packages V and VI. The F-4s were configured with two 370-gallon external wing tanks, four Sidewinders on the inboard wing stations, an ECM pod under the right inboard wing station, and four Sparrows; the number 1 and number 3 aircraft in each flight carried an SUU-16 cannon pod on the centerline station, and number 2 and number 4 carried a 600-gallon centerline fuel tank.

In addition to increasing their numbers, the F-4 escorts changed their tactics. Now, instead of flying ahead of the strikes and setting up cap points, they flew with the strike force into the target area, then split off and converged with the strikers on their way out. The decision to increase the MiGCAP forces was a wise one, because May turned out to be biggest air-to-air month so far; it also was a stunning victory for U.S. fighter forces. There were 110 encounters between U.S. fighters and MiGs, and American fighters shot down twenty-three MiGs for a loss of three Air Force F-4s, all to MiG-17s. F-4s shot down ten MiG-17s and five MiG-21s for their three losses, while F-105s shot down a further eight MiG-17s without loss. Almost as important, in May only fifteen strikers jettisoned their ordnance because of MiG attacks, whereas in April, in far fewer engagements, sixteen strikers were forced to jettison their ordnance.

May opened with a good day for the Navy when a sixteen-plane A-4 Alpha strike on Kep airfield brought up MiG-17s *en masse*. Despite heavy flak and pursuit by at least four MiG-17s during their bomb runs, the A-4s destroyed three MiG-17s on the ground. In the air battle that followed, two more MiGs were shot down, one by an F-8 and one by an A-4. That same day, the Air Force attacked Hoa Loc airfield, and two F-4s attacked eight MiG-17s in a low-altitude defensive wheel. The wheel was effective; the F-4s fired nine missiles without a hit, although one MiG-17 crashed into the ground while maneuvering to avoid a missile. On May 4, Air Force F-4s engaged MiG-21s and MiG-17s. An F-4 fired three AIM-

7s and three AIM-9s from behind a MiG-21 before the last Sidewinder hit and destroyed the MiG, and later the same flight ran into a wheel of MiG-17s and fired three more AIM-9s without a hit. In two days of engagements, only one of eighteen missiles fired by Air Force F-4s hit a MiG.

Over the next few days action slowed somewhat, but May 12, 13, and 14 produced the largest air battles of the war thus far. The podded cannon finally was brought into combat on May 12, when a U.S. strike force penetrated very heavy defenses to attack the Ha Dong army barracks. An F-105 shot down a MiG-17 with his cannon, and the 366th TFW, with their cannon pods, got into their first engagement. The 366th F-4s engaged five MiG-17s while covering a downed F-105 pilot. The lead F-4 got in close to one MiG-17, but the cannon malfunctioned and the MiG escaped unscathed, while one F-4 was lost. This F-4 had reported an engine problem—one afterburner would not light—before the engagement, and he later was seen being caught from behind by two MiG-17s.

An even larger air battle took place the next day during an Air Force attack on the Vinh Yen railroad yards around Hanoi. For the first time, F-105s scored with their AIM-9Bs, bringing down two MiG-17s. F-105s also shot down three MiG-17s with cannon fire and damaged two more. MiGCAP F-4s downed two MiG-17s, one with an AIM-7 and one with an AIM-9. Returning pilots reported the MiG-17s had now modified their wheel tactics. Now the MiGs were setting up two wheels, one at very low altitude and one at about 5,000 feet, apparently to try to catch U.S. fighters between them. The new tactics were of little help—the seven MiG kills and two damaged for no losses made May 13 the biggest day for U.S. forces against the MiGs—even bigger than Operation Bolo.

On May 14, the 366th TFW F-4s escorting an F-105 strike on the Ha Dong army barracks four miles southwest of Hanoi got what they had been waiting for—gun kills. Speedo, one of the cannon-armed F-4 flights, was flying behind and above the last strike flight of F-105s when they saw two F-105s leaving the target area being pursued by four MiG-17s in two flights of two. Speedo 1 and Speedo 2 turned to attack the lead pair of MiGs, and Speedo 3 and Speedo 4 turned on the trailing pair. As the F-4s approached, the MiGs broke down into the clouds. Speedo 1 and Speedo 2 broke off, and as they leveled off saw many more MiG-17s—about sixteen—in the area.

Speedo 1 began to pick out MiGs and attack. He fired an AIM-7 at one MiG-17; the missile dived into the ground, and Speedo 1 followed up with a gun attack but missed as the MiG dived into the clouds. Speedo 1 found another MiG and fired another Sparrow—which again dived into the ground—and again followed up with an unsuccessful gun attack. The

F-4 attacks had prevented the MiGs from setting up a wheel, and Speedo 1 saw two more MiGs off to his right and slightly low. Singling out one of the MiGs for a cannon attack, he closed and started firing 2,500 feet away with the gunsight well in front of the MiG, letting it drift back along the MiG's fuselage as he moved closer. As the F-4 closed, the MiG-17 tightened his turn, and the F-4's windscreen "filled with MiG." Speedo 1 saw the shells hit close to the canopy; fire broke out, and the MiG exploded in his face. As Speedo 1 and Speedo 2 turned to leave the area, they saw another MiG-17 just off their nose in a shallow left turn. Speedo 1 pulled behind him and, at a range of about 3,500 feet, launched an AIM-9B, but the missile passed about 200 feet behind and below the MiG. Speedo 1 attempted to follow up with a gun attack but found he was out of ammunition. With MiGs reported along the egress route, Speedo 1 and Speedo 2 decided to exit the fight with enough gas to fight their way out.

Meanwhile, Speedo 3 and Speedo 4 had pursued the second pair of MiGs. Speedo 3 fired an AIM-7, but the missile did not guide; he tried to follow up with a gun attack but could not set up the switches in time, and the MiGs escaped into the clouds. The two F-4s saw two more MiG-17s and pulled behind them; Speedo 3 fired another Sparrow, but again the missile did not guide. The F-4s broke off and attacked three more MiG-17s attempting to set up a wagon wheel. One of the MiGs was trailing well behind the other two, and Speedo 3 set up for a gun attack on the trailing MiG. The F-4 opened fire about 2,500 feet from the MiG and saw hits immediately in the middle of the fuselage; the MiG began to burn on the right side from the wing aft. As the Phantom pulled off and high, the MiG exploded into flames and plunged into the undercast in a steep dive.

About the same time, another F-4 flight also attacked the MiGs and shot one down with an AIM-7, but two other AIM-7s and seven AIM-9s missed. That day the AIM-7s scored one hit in seven launches; the AIM-9Bs were zero for eleven, or one missile hit for eighteen fired. The cannon pod had two kills in four tries. One of the victorious F-4 pilots commented, "I'll bet those MiG pilots have a tactics meeting at Phuc Yen tonight."

Evaluation of the Cannon

Many Air Force F-4 pilots long had believed that the North Vietnamese were exploiting the "safe zone"—the approximately one-half mile in front of a Phantom created by the lack of a cannon—and the SEACAAL study had stated that "the lack of an F-4 gun is considered one of the factors in the low kill rate in MiG encounters."[57] An Air Force report examined in detail many of the air combats over North Vietnam and highlighted the need for a short-range weapon in the F-4. Defining "short range" as less than missile minimum range—something closer than 2,500 feet—and using the characteristics of the 20-mm M-61 Gatling gun, the report looked at twenty-nine Air Force F-4 versus MiG engagements. It found that in twenty-three of the engagements the F-4s had cannon-firing opportunities, and often the lack of a cannon appeared to have cost a kill.

The study concluded that in approximately half of the twenty-nine engagements, North Vietnamese fighters benefited from the F-4's inability to shoot them at close range, and that even if the only effect of the cannon was to keep the MiGs from getting close, it would help because then the MiG would be in the missile envelope.[58] When the 366th TFW F-4s began to carry the cannon pod in the air-to-air role, combat confirmed the conclusions of the study. The first eight times the SUU-16 cannon pod was fired in the air-to-air mode it scored four kills; this was especially encouraging since these firings included two cannon malfunctions.

The cannon provided an additional benefit. If an F-105 was shot down, other F-105s used their cannon to strafe approaching North Vietnamese to protect the crew until a rescue helicopter arrived. A downed F-4 crew, on the other hand, had to hope that there were F-105s in the area because the air-to-air missiles carried by the other F-4s were useless in covering the rescue. Despite the cannon pod's obvious utility and the Air Force's success using it, for a variety of technical reasons the Navy did not attempt to carry the centerline cannon on its F-4s.[59] The lack of such a cannon would cost the Navy several kills for the remainder of the war.

On May 20, 1967, the MiGs were up in force again, and two flights of MiGCAP F-4s, Ballot and Tampa, were escorting another F-105 strike when they saw two large groups of MiG-17s, one off to the left, the other to the right. The F-4s split, with each flight engaging one of the MiG-17 groups. The MiGs used their new tactics and set up two wheels, one at about 1,000 feet and the other at about 5,000 feet. The two wheels came together, and the fights merged into a huge "furball"-style melee as the F-4s dived and climbed, trying to break into the wheels for a missile shot (these were the 8th TFW F-4s that were not carrying a cannon pod).

The MiGs were very aggressive; one of the MiG-17s closed quickly on Tampa 2 and hit him with cannon fire. The F-4 burst into flames, the right wing and tail came off, and the crew ejected. After this first loss the twisting melee went the F-4s' way. There were no SAMs in the area, so the F-4s were free to climb above the MiGs and dive to attack. The F-4s also tried a new tactic, where one pair of F-4s left the fight and returned at low level below the wheel.

Using these tactics, Ballot 1 and Tampa 3 each shot down a MiG with Sidewinders, and Tampa 1 shot one down with a Sparrow. As the fight broke off and the combatants were leaving, Tampa 1 saw a lone MiG-17 flying very low in the area, apparently the "director" for the wheels. Tampa 1 turned as if he were egressing, then turned back and, after a brief pursuit at very low level, shot the MiG-17 down with an AIM-9B for his second kill of the day. One of the F-4 pilots in this engagement had flown in Operation Bolo and, commenting on the MiG-17 pilots' aggressiveness, said, "[T]he MiG-21s on January 2 were not the problem these MiGs were today."

There were no engagements on May 21, but on May 22 MiG-21s were up again. Wandes, a flight of four F-4s (Wandes 1 and Wandes 3 armed with cannon pods), was behind the strike force as an escort when they saw a MiG-21 behind the flight. The MiG went straight thorough the F-4s, fired an Atoll at one of the F-105 flights (it missed), then pulled up in a steep climb. Wandes 1 pulled up behind the MiG and fired an AIM-9 from long range as the MiG was entering a thin cloud layer. Wandes 1 followed the MiG up through the clouds, but when he popped through the top he found no sign of the MiG, only smoke and debris.

As they rejoined the strike force, Wandes flight saw another MiG-21 slightly to the right about a mile away. Thinking this was the MiG he had just attacked, Wandes 1 turned and fired a Sidewinder. The missile did not guide and the MiG-21 dived for the ground, twisting and turning, with the four F-4s in hot pursuit. The MiG led the F-4s over Hoa Loc airfield, where North Vietnamese anti-aircraft guns opened fire, and five SAMs passed through the F-4 formation. Wandes 1 closed and pressed a cannon attack, firing a 235-round burst from his cannon pod, apparently without result. The MiG-21 then rolled out in what appeared to be a shallow glide; Wandes 1 pulled high to reposition and slid down close behind the MiG for another cannon attack. The gun jammed.

Wandes 1 was out of AIM-9Bs and called for Wandes 2 to take the MiG, but Wandes 2 was too close for an AIM-9 shot and did not have a cannon pod. As the MiG drifted away, Wandes flight had to break off the chase because they were very low on fuel. The MiG continued straight ahead and crashed just north of the Red River. When they landed, Wandes 1 learned that a trailing F-105 flight saw MiG parts falling through the clouds, so his first attack was confirmed as a kill. This was the first double MiG-21 kill of the war.

Toward the end of the May and into June, there was a noticeable decrease in MiG, AAA, and SAM activity. U.S. intelligence speculated that the intense activities of the last two months had depleted the North

Vietnamese stocks of ammunition and SAMs, and their losses in the air and from the bombing of the airfields had forced much of the North Vietnamese Air Force to withdraw to China and regroup. All the remaining MiGs in North Vietnam moved to the fields at Phuc Yen and Gia Lam, which were still off limits to U.S. attacks.

F-4D and AIM-4D

Late in May 1967 a new-model Air Force Phantom, the F-4D, arrived at the 8th TFW at Ubon RTAFB. This was the first pure Air Force F-4 (the F-4C had been a slightly modified Navy model), and it incorporated numerous modifications, mainly improved bombing systems. The F-4D had been in the Air Force inventory for over a year, and equipped a wing in Germany and one in the United States, so the 8th TFW was expecting a new but well tested weapons system. The change that had the most impact on air-to-air operations was the new heat-seeking missile carried by the F-4D, the Hughes AIM-4D Falcon.

The AIM-4D appeared to have several improvements over the AIM-9B, including an expanded envelope and an internally cooled seeker head

Two AIM-4D Falcon missiles mounted on an F-4. The Falcon was the most unsuccessful U.S. Air Force missile of the war. *USAF (courtesy of the National Archives)*

that picked up the heat of a jet engine more efficiently. The Air Force had used early models of the AIM-4 for U.S. Air Force Air Defense Command interceptors for some time, and Hughes had convinced the Air Force the AIM-4D was the answer for maneuvering air combat. As a sign of the Air Force's commitment to the missile, the AIM-4D and the F-4D were mated;[60] the F-4D was not wired to carry the AIM-9B Sidewinder. Once the Air Force committed to the AIM-4D to replace the AIM-9B, it elected not to participate in the development of the AIM-9D, leaving that to the Navy. By the time the AIM-4D arrived in theater, the Navy had been using the AIM-9D for over a year, and it was hitting at a much higher rate than the AIM-9B.[61]

The 8th TFW engaged MiGs for the first time with their new F-4D/ AIM-4D combination on June 2, 1967, when four F-4s (two F-4Ds and two AIM-9B-armed F-4Cs) attacked a wheel of eight MiG-17s. The F-4s fired two of the new AIM-4s (as well as four AIM-7s and three AIM-9s) but scored no hits.

On June 5 the AIM-4s had another opportunity. Olds was a flight of F-4s (Olds 1 and Olds 3 were F-4Ds; Olds 2 and Olds 4 were F-4Cs) covering an egressing F-105 strike when they heard one of the strike flights call that they were engaged with MiGs. As they came in sight of the fight, Olds saw a single MiG-17 off to the right and another off to the left. Olds 1 and Olds 2 went after the MiG on the left while Olds 3 and Olds 4 went after the other.

Olds 1 and Olds 2 pulled behind their MiG, and Olds 1 fired two AIM-4s from well within the envelope; the first did not guide, and the F-4s never saw the second missile. Olds 1 repositioned and, still behind the MiG, launched four AIM-7Es in boresight mode; none guided. Considerably frustrated by this time, Olds 1 repositioned and let Olds 2 take an AIM-9B shot. The MiG started a slight climb as Olds 2 fired two of the old Sidewinders; one hit on the MiG's tail and the other about three feet ahead of the tail. The MiG rolled left and crashed.

Meanwhile, Olds 3 and Olds 4 had turned behind the second MiG. At a range of 3,500 feet in a level left turn well within the envelope, Olds 3 fired an AIM-4. The missile appeared to guide but missed by twenty feet. Now, several other MiG-17s joined this one and set up a wagon wheel, so Olds 3 and Olds 4 separated and reattacked. Olds 3 maneuvered directly behind another MiG-17 and, from 3,000 feet and again in the envelope, fired another Falcon. The missile passed ten feet behind the MiG without detonating. Olds 3 fired a third AIM-4, but the missile did not leave the launcher, and the two F-4s broke off and climbed away. As they did so they saw another MiG-17 flying very low (about 500 feet), apparently returning to base. Olds 3 and Olds 4 dropped behind the MiG unobserved and began to follow. As the MiG approached a hill he began to climb and silhouetted himself against the sky. In the heart of the envelope, with a clear shot from dead astern and a good tone, Olds 3 fired his last AIM-4 at the nonmaneuvering MiG-17. The missile guided but passed ten feet behind the MiG without detonating.

On that day, the 8th TFW's F-4Ds had fired six AIM-4s under ideal conditions; five missed and one aborted on the launch rail. To make matters worse, the pilot of Olds 1, who had missed an easy kill when his AIM-4s malfunctioned, was the 8th TFW wing commander and had four MiG kills to his credit. Had the AIM-4s functioned properly—or if he had been carrying AIM-9Bs—he almost certainly would have gotten his fifth kill, making him the first American ace in Vietnam. Anecdotes indicate the wing commander was understandably furious; one account says he told his crew chief after this mission that the AIM-4D was "a piece of shit,"[62] and another says that he called Seventh Air Force and demanded to be allowed to replace the AIM-4Ds with AIM-9s immediately.[63]

The AIM-4D's advanced features were of little use in the fast-moving, hard-turning dogfights over North Vietnam, and many of the AIM-4D's other advertised improvements did not seem to be improvements at all. The system for cooling the AIM-4D's seeker head—which was supposed to prevent the missile from being diverted by clouds or the ground—was touted as one of the Falcon's main advances, but in practice it was seriously flawed. The liquid coolant was in a small bottle in the missile, and once the pilot armed the AIM-4D, coolant began to flow to cool the seeker head. The sequence of switches to start the coolant flow was complicated, but more importantly the coolant flow to the seeker head was continuous and could not be stopped; when the coolant was used up, the missile was effectively dead. However, the missile had only two minutes of coolant available, and since the coolant flow began when the missile was armed, *the AIM-4D had to be fired within two minutes after arming, or it was useless.* The F-4D pilot had a choice: Either arm the AIM-4D early in the engagement and hope he would get a chance to use it within the next two minutes, or wait and try to remember to arm it after the fight began and when there was a target available. In a turning dogfight where shot opportunities were fleeting, such restraints on a missile clearly were unacceptable.[64]

There were still other problems with the AIM-4D. It claimed a very short minimum range, 2,500 feet, but the shortest successful minimum range test launch had been from over of 5,000 feet[65]—a much greater minimum range than the AIM-9B. Additionally, there were several switches involved in firing the AIM-4D, and its firing sequence was the most complex of all the missiles in the inventory (for example, in its most effective mode it needed to have two buttons depressed before the trigger was pulled, whereas the AIM-9 required only a trigger squeeze—no buttons), and the minimum time from the start of the launch sequence to actual launch was 4.2 seconds,[66] as compared to less than a second for the AIM-9B. The AIM-4D did not have a proximity fuse, so the missile had to score a direct hit on the target to detonate the warhead. The warhead itself was very small—less than three pounds of explosive compared to the almost 11-pound warhead of the AIM-9. Frustrated 8th TFW crews sarcastically remarked that "to kill a MiG with the AIM-4D it had to hit the pilot in the heart."

Then there was the question of reliability. In the first fifteen combat launch attempts only ten AIM-4Ds even left the aircraft; this 67 percent launch reliability was well below the AIM-9B (over 90 percent). Seventh Air Force Headquarters agreed that the AIM-4D was a failure and reported that the "tactical limitations of the AIM-4D render it unsuitable for operations over North Vietnam. We have experienced the majority of our kills with Sidewinders and are reluctant to give it up unless the deficiencies of the AIM-4D are overcome." In September 1967 Pacific Air Force (PACAF) Headquarters told Air Force Headquarters that it intended to rewire the F-4Ds to carry the AIM-9B in place of the AIM-4D.[67]

The failure of the AIM-4D made the Air Force finally recognize that its heat-seeking missiles were not satisfactory. But instead of simply adopting the Navy's proven AIM-9D or creating an AIM-9 with a new motor, warhead, and fuse, the Air Force elected to begin an upgrade program on the AIM-9B, designated the AIM-9E. The AIM-9E was only a small improvement—it added a cooled seeker head while keeping the old AIM-9B motor, warhead, and fuse.[68] Despite these modest improvements, the first AIM-9E did not arrive in Southeast Asia until after Rolling Thunder (over two years from the deployment of the AIM-9D),[69] while the unreliable AIM-4D stayed in Southeast Asia and was used in combat as late as 1972.

Fortunately, to offset the AIM-4D, the F-4Ds had an air-to-air lead-computing sight for its SUU-23 cannon pod (the SUU-23 essentially was the same as the F-4C's SUU-16). Although the F-4D's sight was much better than the fixed sights on the F-4C, initially the 8th TFW did not carry the cannon pod, but by June 1967 the success of the cannon pods and the failures of the AIM-4D overcame the 8th TFW's skepticism, and they began to try to mount cannon pods on their F-4Ds.

Initially the wiring in the 8th TFW's F-4s caused a problem. These F-4s were wired to carry their ECM pod on an outboard wing station (one that

normally carried a 370-gallon fuel tank), so they carried only two external fuel tanks—one on the outboard wing and one on the centerline. Carrying the gun on the centerline in this configuration would mean that the
F-4s could not carry enough fuel for combat over North Vietnam.[70]

The 366th TFW had solved the problem by changing the wiring on
their F-4s' inboard pylons to carry the QRC-160, and they carried the
ECM pod on the right inboard pylon, the fuel tanks on the outboard stations, and the cannon pod on the centerline.[71] The modification was
cheap (about ten dollars in parts) and simple (about eight hours of labor),
so with the help of the 366th TFW the 8th TFW modified the inboard
pylons of its F-4Ds for the ECM pods. Now the centerline station was free
for the gun pod, and the 8th TFW F-4s began to carry a cannon as standard on the number 1 and number 3 aircraft on their MiGCAP flights.

Tactics against the MiG-17 Wheels

The 8th TFW F-4s continued to try new tactics for breaking into the latest
MiG-17 formation, the two-level wagon wheels. This formation, with one
wheel one at about 5,000 feet and the other at about 1,000 feet, was giving
MiGCAP flights a great deal of difficulty. SAMs still were being used from
time to time in combination with the low flying MiGs, and often F-4s
using the climbing and diving attacks were engaged by SAMs as they
went high. The 8th TFW's initial solution was to have one pair of F-4s
engage the wheel and try to make the MiGs climb while the other pair
separated out and dropped down low. The second flight then would
come back at low altitude, hoping to find the MiGs above them for an easier missile shot.

The North Vietnamese then moved the wheels over areas heavily
defended by AAA, which would engage the F-4s if they tried to come
back at low altitude below the wheel. To counter this, one group of F-4s
would engage the MiG-17s while the other would separate from the
wheel at medium altitude and then turn back into the engagement from
another direction. As the separated F-4 flight turned inbound, it called
the engaged F-4s to break off. As the MiG-17s pursued the disengaging
F-4s, the inbound flight attempted to get behind them for an unobserved
missile shot.[72] These new F-4 tactics required good coordination and
some luck, but they did offer at least some hope of breaking into the
wheels. Gradually, as more and more of the F-4 MiGCAPs began to carry
gun pods, they began to use the cannon as the primary weapon against
the low wheels.

June and July 1967 Slowdown

There were no MiG engagements from June 6 to June 30, 1967, and in July bombing attacks on the North Vietnamese bases forced more of the North Vietnamese aircraft into China. At the end of the month there were only seven MiG-21s and twenty-eight MiG-17s based in North Vietnam. Most of the MiG engagements so far in 1967—94 percent—had involved attacks on Air Force aircraft, but on July 21, after no kills for close to two months, Navy F-8s were back in action. The F-8 pilots did not agree with the F-4s' philosophy of not turning with a MiG-17, and with their cannon armament and reasonably reliable AIM-9Ds, F-8 pilots were willing to mix it up with the agile Soviet fighter when the opportunity arose. There was just such an opportunity this day, and it showed the pluses and minuses of getting into a tight turning engagement with the small Soviet fighter, even for the skilled F-8 pilots.

Page Boy, a flight of four F-8s, was the MiGCAP for an Alpha strike on the Ta Xa fuel storage depot 30 miles northwest of Hanoi. In their MiGCAP orbit, Page Boy saw about eight MiG-17s drop out of the clouds, so they attacked. Page Boy 1 pulled behind a MiG-17 and fired an AIM-9D; it failed to guide. He fired a second AIM-9D, which aborted on the launcher, but a third AIM-9D guided well and destroyed the MiG. As Page Boy 1 made the kill, another MiG-17 attacked him and hit the F-8 in the right wing, severing hydraulic lines and starting a small fire.

Page Boy 2 went after the other MiG-17s and fired two AIM-9Ds at different MiGs; both missed. He then turned after another MiG-17, fired a third Sidewinder, and missed again, then closed for a gun attack. Pressing his attack to 600 feet, Page Boy 2 scored 20-mm hits all over the MiG; the pilot ejected as the F-8 went by. Shortly thereafter, Page Boy 2 was hit and severely damaged, losing three-quarters of his right stabilator.

Page Boy 3 attacked another MiG-17 and took an AIM-9D shot but did not see the missile hit; later, however, a MiG pilot was seen in a parachute and Page Boy 3 was credited with a kill. Despite their damage, Page Boy 1 and Page Boy 2 recovered safely.

While the Page Boy F-8s were battling their MiG-17s, Nickel, a single F-8, was on an escort/flak suppression mission with an A-4C Iron Hand SAM suppression flight. In this flak suppression role, Nickel carried air-to-ground unguided Zuni rockets and a single AIM-9D. MiGs attacked the A-4s and Nickel engaged a MiG-17; he missed with his AIM-9D, and his follow-up gun attack resulted in hits but no kill. Two more MiG-17s crossed in front of the F-8, and he turned after them. Out of cannon range, Nickel fired four Zunis at one of the MiGs, hoping for a lucky hit. He got it: A Zuni appeared to hit one of the MiGs, and it rolled out of turn. Nickel closed and emptied his cannon into the MiG; the pilot ejected.

Rivet Top

During the summer of 1967 the Air Force took another step toward countering the MiGs when a new model of the EC-121, the EC-121K, arrived in Southeast Asia. This new EC-121, called Rivet Top, originally was conceived as an electronic intelligence collector but now carried new equipment that could provide SAM warnings and help locate SAM sites.[73] More importantly, Rivet Top carried four special consoles where Vietnamese-speaking air force "Security Services"[74] specialists monitored communications between MiGs and their GCI; Rivet Top could tell when MiGs were taking off, climbing, sighting U.S. aircraft, and attacking, and when they were low on fuel. Like the other EC-121s, Rivet Top carried the QRC-248, but it also carried other equipment that could interrogate two other Soviet transponders, the SRO-1 and the SOD-57, which the College Eye EC-121Ds could not.[75] Rivet Top had many advantages—it carried a crew of ten in the operations compartment instead of the four in the regular EC-121, and its equipment was specialized, unlike the off-the-shelf, commercial equipment of the regular EC-121s.[76] Another major advantage of Rivet Top was that it combined the SIGINT and IFF interrogators into one aircraft and made it easier to collate and pass the MiGs' position to the strike forces. Rivet Top was so successful that its initial, 120-day temporary duty assignment extended through 1969, and it was flown virtually every day; as a measure of its success, from the time it was deployed until the end of Rolling Thunder, Rivet Top contributed to thirteen MiG kills out of a total of twenty.[77] The superiority of Rivet Top over the standard EC-121s was clear, and PACAF Headquarters began to press to upgrade its standard EC-121s to Rivet Top standards.[78] To give the College Eye EC-121Ds the same capability as Rivet Top, the four security service stations, known as Rivet Gym, were installed in the EC-121Ds, but these aircraft were not available until May 1968, when the Air Force portion of Rolling Thunder was over.[79]

Rivet Top and Rivet Gym highlight one of the most useful sources the United States had to monitor MiG activity—radio transmissions between the MiGs and their GCI control. Because the North Vietnamese used the Soviet system, where the pilot was directed to do virtually everything, it was very easy for U.S. SIGINT operators to tell exactly what was going on—to listen to the MiGs start and take off, and to hear GCI guide him to the U.S. forces, then tell him to climb, turn, and select afterburner. U.S.

listeners also could hear the MiG pilots call when they had sight of the U.S. forces, when they were attacking, and what the results of the attack were.

While SIGINT gave U.S. intelligence a precise, real-time picture of what the North Vietnamese MiGs were doing, it was not necessarily useful. There were several problems. For example, it was difficult to determine which flight the MiG was attacking. When the MiG called that he was going to attack, the U.S. translator heard only one side of the conversation; he did not have a radar scope, so he could not tell which U.S. flight the MiG was attacking. Security was another problem. The fact that the United States was listening to North Vietnamese transmissions was a closely guarded secret. How long could this be kept secret if, every time a MiG was about to attack, the U.S. aircraft was warned over the radio? The North Vietnamese—and the Soviets and Chinese—were listening to U.S. radio transmissions, so the question was how to use the SIGINT information without compromising it. This troubling situation was compounded by the fact that SIGINT was generally the responsibility of the NSA, not the military, and it had its own rules. In fact, compiling and handling any kind of electronic intelligence information—radio transmissions, radars, etc.—was the NSA's responsibility. Even though much of the information was actually gathered by military people from military platforms, the military could not use it freely.

The problem was a ticklish one; what the North Vietnamese said was not as sensitive as the fact that the U.S. was monitoring the communications. The question of how to use and still protect this very valuable information operationally remained throughout the war. That American government personnel were listening to North Vietnamese radio transmissions and not passing the information on to the aircrews—thereby possibly saving their lives—was a source of great irritation to the high-ranking military officers aware of the situation. Throughout the war these officers continued to press to get this information to the combat aircrews, and gradually the rules on using intercepted North Vietnamese communications were loosened, though the problem never was completely solved.[80] Ironically, once the Rivet Top information began to be passed to the aircrews, it was not as useful as had been hoped. The aircrews did not have the proper security clearances and therefore could not be told the source of the new MiG warnings, so they lumped it into the category of all the other information they received, much of which was at best marginally reliable. Finally, even when real-time information on MiG attacks was available, the EC-121s' radios were still so bad that the warnings had to be passed through a radio relay aircraft, often delaying the information until it was too late.

By the latter part of July most of the restrictions on the targets in North Vietnam had been lifted, and the bombing increased in intensity, but despite this, MiGs rarely engaged U.S. strikes. The MiGs had stood down before after periods of heavy losses, and U.S. intelligence assumed that during these periods the North Vietnamese were analyzing their tactics and training new pilots to replace the ones they had lost. The MiGs' standdown was so marked that the number of F-4s on MiGCAP was reduced, and the Phantoms began to return to the strike role.[81]

Mid-Summer Analysis

The Rolling Thunder forces could look back over their air-to-air operations during the first half of 1967 with satisfaction. The North Vietnamese had lost about fifty-five MiGs in the air and another thirty on the ground—the equivalent of their entire inventory.[82] In April and May alone the North Vietnamese had lost thirty-eight fighters in air-to-air combat, while U.S. losses had been low and the MiGs had forced relatively few strikers to jettison their ordnance.

The Air Force credited the success of their air-to-air campaign to three developments. First was the introduction of ECM pods for the F-4s. By May all F-4 Wings had pods, enabling the F-4 escorts to go anywhere the strikers went. The pods allowed the F-4s to penetrate the SAM environment in tight formation with the strikers; since the North Vietnamese GCI kept their MiGs away from obvious F-4 sweeps and MiGCAPs, the Phantoms had a better chance of engaging when they were part of the strike formation. Second, with the introduction of the gun pod, F-4s could engage the MiGs in close-quarter battles, and this offset to an extent the continued poor performance of the missiles, especially against the MiG-17s. Finally, the introduction of the QRC-248 interrogator in the EC-121s gave a significant improvement in the ability of the EC-121s to detect MiGs and to guide U.S. aircraft to attack them.[83]

The Navy had played its part as well, scoring twelve kills since April and vastly increasing its missile effectiveness with the AIM-9D, which had scored nine of the kills.

An analysis of the Air Force weapons results during the April–June engagements showed that the missile problems remained. In sixty-one engagements, Air Force F-4s had fired seventy-two AIM-7s for eight hits, for an 11 percent success rate, and fifty-nine AIM-9Bs for ten hits, for a 17 percent hit rate. Surprisingly, the F-105s scored on three of their eleven AIM-9 firings, for 27 percent—much higher that of the F-4s (seven of forty-eight for 14 percent). Ten AIM-4Ds were fired for no hits. Meanwhile, the cannon results were encouraging. F-105s made twenty-one cannon attacks and scored six kills for 28 percent effectiveness; F-4s made nine cannon attacks and scored five kills, for an effectiveness rate of 55 percent. In addition to the eleven kills, four MiGs were damaged by cannon fire, giving the cannon a hit rate of 50 percent. The excellent cannon results appear to be the result of several factors. F-105s were being used more in a MiGCAP role and many of their engagements were expecting to meet MiGs, so their gunsights were set up in the air-to-air mode. For the F-4s it appeared the MiGs were maneuvering to counter an expected missile shot and were not expecting a cannon attack; these anti-missile maneuvers brought them close to the F-4 and in range for a cannon attack. The F-4's maneuverability and the skill of its pilots also appeared to be major factors in the cannon's success.

4

The MiGs Strike Back

IN AUGUST the Senate Subcommittee on Defense Preparedness held hearings and listened to a number of present and past military officers talk about the war. At this hearing, Gen. William W. Momyer, former commander of Seventh Air Force (responsible for U.S. Air Force operations over North Vietnam) commented on the Air Force's air-to-air successes that summer, saying, "We have driven the MiGs out of the sky for all practical purposes. If he comes up, he will probably suffer the same fate [being shot down]."[1] Unfortunately, like most public U.S. general officer projections about the future course of the Vietnam War, it was wrong.

General Momyer's statement was incorrect because he ignored some basic cautions about the air war. The QRC-248 still could not be used in the most effective way. Overall air-to-air missile performance continued to be poor, and there were no indications that it would improve in the future. The F-4D/AIM-4D combination especially had been unsuccessful, yet the AIM-4D still was the only heat-seeking missile the F-4D could use; consequently, the new Phantom offered only a very limited increase in air-to-air capability. The MiG-21 had demonstrated conclusively that it was far superior to the F-105, and, even more disturbing, a report by a group that had analyzed all the air combat engagements so far stated that the North Vietnamese GCI system had the potential for considerable improvement.[2] Finally, and perhaps most importantly, there was a real change in the quality of the U.S. Air Force aircrews: During the first half of 1967 the United States had possessed a very experienced F-4 force with exceptional leadership, while the MiGs were flown by inexperienced pilots using very poor tactics. By the beginning of August, however, this began to change as internal Air Force policy decisions had a severe impact on Air Force combat effectiveness. New Air Force pilots coming into the combat theater were not nearly as well trained in air-to-air combat as their predecessors. The first U.S. Air Force fighter squadrons sent to Vietnam had been some of the best in the Air

Force and had flown together as a unit and knew each others' capabilities. But the Air Force soon adopted a policy allowing crews to rotate home after one hundred missions over North Vietnam or after one year of combat in South Vietnam; as a result, unit cohesion disappeared. At first the fighter pilots who rotated after their Southeast Asia tours were replaced by experienced fighter pilots from squadrons in Europe and the United States, but that source soon was exhausted, forcing the Air Force to look elsewhere.

By 1966 the Air Force began to send pilots without a tactical fighter background to the combat fighter wings. While many of these pilots were from Air Defense Command fighters or from fighter-type aircraft in the Air Training Command, others were from multi-engine aircraft such as bombers or transports who had a difficult time getting used to flying the more agile fighters. Statistics reflected this. Before June 1966, the average Air Force fighter pilot in Southeast Asia had flown more than 500 hours in his combat fighter; by June 1968 this average had dropped to 240 hours. More significantly, from April 1965 to June 1967, 77 percent of the aircrews in the war had come from either the Tactical Air Command (which had most of the Air Force's fighters) or directly from pilot training, where they had flown fighter-type aircraft. From June 1967 to March 1968, only slightly more that half of the new fighter pilots in Southeast Asia came from these two sources. However, these percentages are deceptive and do not reflect the depth of the problem. Virtually all who came from pilot training went to the back seat of F-4s, where their pilot skills were meaningless. Thus, when only the true fighter pilots—F-105 pilots and F-4 front seaters—are considered, the percentage of pilots in combat who had previous tactical fighter experience was only 30 percent in mid-1967, compared to 65 percent earlier.[3]

The Thailand-based combat units were not impressed with the "instant fighter pilots" with bomber or transport backgrounds, but since it was Air Force policy, they had little choice but to accept them. Officially, the tactical fighter wings said such pilots performed well, but anecdotal evidence suggests otherwise. While they were well trained and professional, they simply did not have the fundamentals that were second nature to an experienced fighter pilot.[4]

Carrier Operations

By early 1967 the U.S. carrier operations had settled into a pattern. The Navy normally had three carriers operating off Yankee Station, though sometimes the number rose to as high as five during periods of overlap—

when a new carrier arrived and one prepared to leave. Each carrier carried out air operations for twelve hours (noon to midnight or midnight to noon), then stood down for twelve hours for maintenance. The carriers conducted two types of operations: cyclic operations and Alpha strikes. During cyclic operations, a carrier would launch about half its aircraft (between twenty-five and forty) every hour and a half (or eight cycles for every twelve-hour period); the maximum number of aircraft committed to a particular target was about twenty. The Navy conducted mainly cyclic operations in Route Packages II, III, and IV, which provided a number of relatively small but lucrative targets along the transportation networks.

When a target required a major strike for maximum results and protection, the carrier went to the Alpha strike. In an Alpha strike all aircraft from a single carrier were organized into one strike group for a mission against a given target, usually in Route Package VI. Alpha strikes generally were coordinated with the other carriers and the Air Force units in Thailand through Seventh Air Force, and there might be several Alpha strikes combined with Air Force strikes against important targets. For an Alpha strike, the carrier suspended air operations for a time before the launch—usually about two hours—to prepare for the operation. After Alpha strike recovery, it took about the same amount of time for the carrier to begin cyclic operations again.

Air Force officers acting as liaison officers on the carriers sometimes were critical of the Navy's tactics. To the Air Force, it seemed the Navy put a tremendous number of support aircraft up for a few strike aircraft. Regarding Navy cyclic operations, one liaison officer noted, "On a routine strike, within twenty miles or less of the North Vietnam coastline, a force of eight attack aircraft [A-4s or A-6s] launched, followed by a barrier CAP of four to six F-4Bs, a flight of two or four F-8s armed with two AIM-9Bs as target CAP, four to six A-1s or A-4s as flak suppressers in addition to two tankers and at least two ECM aircraft of various sizes and capabilities are launched also. Frequently the only aircraft actually to deliver ordnance are the A-4s and A-6As. . . . support efforts, other than an occasional emergency refueling, were seldom necessary for successful accomplishment of the mission."[5]

By mid-1966 the Navy was having severe personnel problems, especially with pilots and aircrews. The Navy's policy on aircrew tours to Southeast Asia was, in general, to not limit the number of combat missions an aircrew could fly over North Vietnam and, since a Navy aircrew's tour of duty on a Pacific Fleet carrier was about three years, it was normal to make two or three cruises to Vietnam during that time. During

Rolling Thunder and later during Linebacker, Navy carriers flew most of their missions from Yankee Station over the dangerous skies of North Vietnam.

This extensive exposure to North Vietnamese defenses was a two-edged sword. While Navy aircrews became very experienced (their bombing and air combat results reflected this), Navy combat losses over North Vietnam nevertheless were high; soon the pilot supply began to dwindle, forcing the survivors to participate in more combat cruises—which affected their morale.[6] Although the Navy tried to train more carrier-qualified attack/fighter pilots, structural limitations (described later) made it very difficult to significantly increase the numbers quickly. This was noted by Air Force liaison officers; one commented in the fall of 1966: "There appears to be a definite shortage of fighter and attack pilots, many flying two missions during a twelve hour period."[7]

Air Force Operations

The standard U.S. Air Force daily mission into North Vietnam was an Alpha strike-type raid into Route Package VI, when weather permitted. The Air Force continued to receive more ECM pods[8] and by mid-1967 had enough to equip all strikers and most escorts. Since the four-ship pod formations worked so well, the F-105 wings began to form strike groups of four or five flights of four, closely grouped for maximum pod coverage. With the pods and the appropriate formations, the strike force could enter North Vietnam above 10,000 feet, safe from light and medium anti-aircraft fire (85 percent of losses from AAA were below 6,000 feet).[9] The large strike formations all rolled in to make the dive-bombing attack on the target together, forcing the ground gunners to choose among a large number of targets that were all bombing at the same time. To add to the gunners' problems, the first flight of F-105s in the strike usually acted as flak suppression and dropped cluster bombs on the AAA positions to keep them occupied, while the other flights struck the target.

The Iron Hand and MiGCAP support aircraft also benefited from the large, tight formations of such a compressed strike force. Iron Hand F-105Fs led the strike flights and would approach the targets a few minutes early to check the weather and attack SAM sites, then stay until the last strikers were out. Compared to the long, strung-out pre-pod formations, the large, compact flights were in and out in very quickly, significantly reducing the time the Iron Hand flights had to stay in the defended area. Additionally, the F-4 MiGCAP escorts benefited from flying very close to the strike force—they shared the benefits of mutual ECM cover-

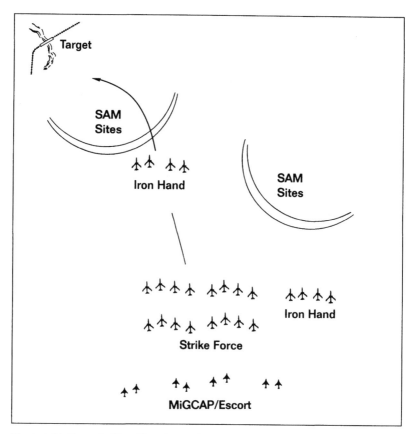

Typical Air Force Rolling Thunder Strike

age and had performance advantages over the MiG-21 below 15,000 feet, where the strike flights flew. Also, as few as two F-4 flights, one just behind the lead strike flight and the other behind the last strike flight, could protect the whole force. This was much easier and more effective than trying to protect the long stream of strike flights of the pre-pod days. One wing commander called the ECM pods and the new formations "the most significant development in the air war over North Vietnam during my tour," and said, "It is now commonplace for us [the F-4 escorts] to be part of a 28 to 32 aircraft strike force which roars in at 520 to 560 knots at 13,000 to 17,000 feet, strikes one to three closely spaced targets with all the aircraft on and off the target in less than a minute, and then withdraws in [a] deceptively well ordered gaggle at up to 600 knots until out of the high threat area."[10]

Just as some Air Force officers were critical of Navy tactics, some Navy officers thought these Air Force tactics were inflexible.[11] Naval aviators were used to relatively small, flexible attack formations with heavy escort that flew without effective ECM pods, launching from carriers close to the target. Navy strike flights were on and off the target quickly, and the idea of massing jet fighter-bombers in large, tight formations resembling World War II bomber formations was strange indeed.

Air Force strikes going into Route Package VI now had standardized most of their tactics. Normally the Air Force scheduled four major strikes each day, two in the morning from five to thirty minutes apart and two in the afternoon. A typical strike consisted of four flights of F-105 or F-4 strike aircraft, two flights of F-4 MiGCAP, and two flights of F-105F Iron Hand. Each strike required eight KC-135 tankers for pre-strike air refueling. With EB-66s, EC-121s, search and rescue aircraft, and other aircraft that supported the strike, the total number of aircraft involved came to about 110.[12] Often the number of strike flights was doubled to eight, and the second four-flight strike came in with very little separation along the same route to take advantage of the jamming, Wild Weasels, and MiGCAP; it then would bomb targets in the same general area as the first, then exit along the same route.[13] These strikes allowed the Air Force to double the number of bombs on targets for almost the same support package, but they increased coordination problems.

The strikers usually were F-105s carrying six 750-pound Mark 117 bombs on a centerline rack, two wing fuel tanks, and either two ECM pods or one ECM pod and one AIM-9B on the extreme outboard pylons. An alternate bomb load would be a centerline fuel tank in place of the Mark 117s and two 2,000-pound Mark 84 or 3,000-pound Mark 118 bombs in place of the wing tanks. If the first flight of the strike was flak suppression, cluster bomb units (CBUs), which dispersed a large number of small bomblets over a wide area, were substituted for the other bombs. F-4s flew MiGCAP and often were strikers in the force.

The F-4s carried heat-seeking missiles—either AIM-4Ds or AIM-9Bs—and an ECM pod on each inboard pylon, four AIM-7Es, and two wing fuel tanks. For MiGCAP missions the centerline station carried either a fuel tank or a cannon pod; for strike missions or strike escort, the F-4s carried a bomb rack with either six 500-pound Mark 82 bombs or five 750-pound Mark 117 bombs on the centerline station. On strike missions, as soon as the F-4s dropped their bombs, they were ready for MiGCAP.

Whether the Air Force strikes entered North Vietnam from the east from the Gulf of Tonkin or west from Laos depended on the tanker orbits, called "tracks," assigned to the strike force. The tracks were chosen based on a variety of factors, and Air Force planners took special care to make sure specific tanker tracks were not linked with specific targets or target areas, in order to prevent the North Vietnamese from connecting tanker tracks to targets. Pre-strike refueling took place between 14,000 and 22,000 feet, and the strike dropped off the tankers at about the 20°N latitude line. If the flights refueled over Laos, they came in over a clandestine radio navigation station in Laos known as TACAN Channel 97,[14] then through western North Vietnam. If the strikes refueled in the Tan or Brown anchors over the Gulf of Tonkin, they entered North Vietnam from the coast at Isle Cac Ba, east of Haiphong, and proceeded up a small mountain range known as "Little Thud Ridge" or "Phantom Ridge" to the target. Because of the large number of aircraft involved in the air refueling, the radio conversations, and the appearance of aircraft jamming the early-warning radars, it was virtually impossible to deny the North Vietnamese early warning that a strike was coming.

While it was impossible to deny the North Vietnamese the information that a large strike was on the way, jamming of the North Vietnamese radars was not designed to give the strike force real protection but rather to degrade North Vietnam's GCI and make it more difficult for the GCI controllers to judge the size of the force and its probable target. While the jamming might have seemed only marginally effective, the speed of the strike force meant the time that elapsed from when the force entered North Vietnam until it hit the target was only seven to ten minutes. If the North Vietnamese defenses could be denied information for even one or two minutes, it could be significant.[15]

The other form of electronic jamming, the ECM pods, offered significant protection against SAMs, but they also imposed a significant tactical disadvantage on the strike flights. Because of the jamming pattern and limited coverage of the pods, the force was restricted to turns of 15 degrees of bank in AAA/SAM areas and 20 degrees of bank outside these areas, so after ingress only small heading corrections were possible. This limitation on the strike force was a significant liability because it prevented a major feint toward another target area; the virtually straight course of the strike force helped the North Vietnamese GCI controllers predict the target area early and start moving the MiGs in that direction.

The strike force entered between 11,000 and 16,000 feet (18,000 feet was a practical maximum altitude for a fully fueled, fully loaded F-105), and once in the defended area, flew at high speed (about 540 knots). The strike force was led into the target by two Wild Weasel F-105F flights that arrived a few minutes before the strike flights. Each flight of Wild Weasels took one side of the inbound course and performed one of two roles. The initial role was Iron Hand, where the Weasels suppressed and/or attacked SAMs and

AAA radar systems during the force's ingress, strike, and egress. If Iron Hand suppression was not required, the Weasels took on a hunter-killer mission, where they actively sought out the radars and tried to attack them.

Two flights of four F-4s usually escorted each strike. The ability of the North Vietnamese GCI to identify MiG sweeps and other forms of wide ranging "preemptive" escort tactics had negated these tactics, so usually one F-4 escort flight was stationed in or near the lead formation, with the other in close trail or line abreast of the last formation; alternately, both flights could be placed on the rear flanks of the strike. From June 1967 QRC-248-equipped EC-121s could give reliable information on MiG activity, and they were able to warn strike and CAP flights of MiG attacks by the flight's individual call signs. If MiGs threatened the strike inbound, one of the MiGCAP flights would engage the MiGs while the other stayed with the strike. After parrying the MiGs, the engaged MiGCAP flight rejoined the strike force. If MiGs engaged all of the F-4 MiGCAP flights, the strike flights assumed responsibility for their own protection. At that point, the strike force took up a "box" (or very rarely a "diamond") formation; if MiGs attacked, the rearmost flight closest to the attack would jettison their ordnance and engage while the rest continued to the target. If attacked by MiGs, the flight leader decided whether to jettison ordnance based on how serious the threat was to the flight. After a MiG engagement, the flights reformed to pod formation as quickly as possible. Strike and CAP flights were on different radio frequencies, but the F-4s used their aux radio to monitor the strike flight frequency.

The F-4 wings gradually began to realize that their position behind the strike flights was unsatisfactory—the trailing F-4s flights generally were unable to ward off MiGs attacks and were in effect just another set of targets—but the limited MiG activity in the third quarter of 1967 made them slow to change the formation.[16]

As the strike force approached the targets, the MiGCAP F-4s usually split up, one flight moving ahead to cover the Wild Weasel flight until they departed, the other waiting for the strikers on their exit route as they came off the target and following them out of the target area. The strike force proceeded to the target and executed their dive-bombing attack together in pod formation, minimizing the time over the target. A formation dive-bombing attack of twenty-four to thirty-six aircraft was impressive and effective, but it took great skill by the strike force leader to get everyone in position. After bombing, the strikers exited at high speed and continued to post-strike refueling.

While the larger, medium-altitude strike flights had many advantages, they had some tactical disadvantages as well, mainly because they were very easy to detect. Besides the radar signature of the larger flights as they refueled and the relatively straight course to the target dictated by ECM pod coverage, these strike flights also magnified a significant problem with all U.S. aircraft—the dense smoke trail from their engines. As one fighter wing history pointed out, because of the "relatively poor combustion and burning characteristics of the U.S. axial-flow turbojet engines . . . U.S. pilots regularly saw each other at 20–30 miles, and MiGs use them for their attacks; a large force leaves a veritable corridor of smoke in the sky."[17] The smoke trail was especially helpful to the MiG-21s, with their poor cockpit visibility.

During bad weather a highly unpopular variation of these strike tactics was the notoriously inaccurate Commando Nail or Commando Club strikes, where one or two strike flights, supported by two MiGCAP flights and one or two Iron Hand flights, flew in pod formation over the clouds and dropped their bombs by radar. Commando Club attacks were controlled by a ground radar site in Laos;[18] Commando Nail strikes used the fighters' internal bombing system, designed for delivering nuclear weapons. The system was not accurate enough to be effective with conventional weapons, but the official position was that the bombing kept "pressure" on the North Vietnamese. On the other hand, most pilots felt the missions were flown to give the Air Force as high a number of sorties as the Navy (who was suspected of doing much the same thing). The Commando strikes were hazardous because they required long, straight and level runs at medium altitude in tight formations at a constant speed over the most heavily defended areas in North Vietnam; they were tempting targets for MiGs and SAMs, and periodically heavy losses halted these types of missions.

Defenses and ECM, Mid-1967

The North Vietnamese continued to improve their defenses, and by mid-1967 they had over 200 early warning and GCI radars, 175 AAA fire control radars, and approximately 25 Fansong B missile control radars, heavily concentrated in the Hanoi-Haiphong area. By now the North Vietnamese air defense command and control system had achieved a high degree of sophistication. The radar surveillance and weapons controllers now were coordinated and could simultaneously employ AAA, SAMs, and MiGs. North Vietnamese GCI controllers were able and willing to employ their MiGs at greater distances from Hanoi than ever before, and this put great pressure on the U.S. fighter escort to protect the entire force throughout the strike. U.S. aircraft were faced with the possibility of MiG attack as soon as they penetrated the coastline from the east or crossed the Laotian border from the west.

For some time more aggressive MiGs and the westward moves of the SAMs (the EB-66Bs could jam only one SAM site at a time and were restricted from operations where multiple SAM sites provided overlapping coverage) gradually forced the EB-66s away from the Hanoi-Haiphong area to south of 20°N latitude—so far south that they could not effectively jam the defenses in the Red River Valley area. Finally, in mid-1967, the EB-66s received new radios that allowed them to hear MiG warnings even when their jammers were operating and with the improved MiG detection available from the QRC-248, the EB-66s were able to move back into North Vietnam to 21°N latitude.[19] To increase the jamming of the North Vietnamese radars, an improved EB-66, the EB-66E, deployed to Southeast Asia in August 1967, and by October the number of EB-66s in the theater rose from about twenty to twenty-six. While the EB-66E carried two fewer jammers than the EB-66B, like the jammers on the EB-66C, they allowed the electronic warfare officers in the aircraft to change the jamming frequencies in flight. By mid-November, the EB-66s had moved back to their Thud Ridge orbit. This was too much for the North Vietnamese; MiGs began to attack the EB-66s, forcing the jamming aircraft to move south and west again.[20]

The Air Force continued to be satisfied with its anti-SAM tactics and equipment. At this point the Air Force was not expecting its SAM loss rates in 1967 to exceed the 1966 rates, which had been about 2.4 aircraft shot down for every 1,000 sorties. On the other hand, the Navy had not matched the Air Force's success against the SA-2. Navy aircraft had not adopted the external ECM pods or the pod formations and were still taking a pounding from the missiles. In Route Package VI from January 1 to September 31, 1967, the Air Force's pod-equipped forces lost only five aircraft to SAMs, while the Navy lost about twenty. In 1966, in the same area, SAMs usually accounted for half of the losses; since January they were claiming only about 16 percent of Air Force losses but still 50 percent of the Navy's.[21]

New MiG Tactics

The weather in August 1967 was good, and the Air Force and Navy continued their intense strikes, with the majority of the effort concentrated in Route Package VI against lines of communication, especially the two rail lines running northeast and northwest from Hanoi to China and the transportation network from Hanoi to the port city of Haiphong. The

MiGs had not been very active since June, and as far as the combat wings knew, there were no indications of changes in MiG tactics.[22] Unfortunately, the wings were wrong.

On August 23, 1967, a large U.S. force—nine flights of F-105s and four flights of F-4s (one MiGCAP and three strike)—attacked the Vinh Yen railroad yards. The F-105 force took the lead, with the F-4 MiGCAP on their left rear and the three F-4 strike flights in a "V" formation well behind them. The weather was good with an overcast at 25,000 feet. Unbeknownst to the U.S. force, two MiG-21s were launched from Phuc Yen at low level to intercept. The MiGs stayed in the ground clutter to avoid detection by U.S. airborne radars, but their transponders were picked up by one of the orbiting EC-121's QRC-248. The EC-121 called out the MiGs' location, but the escort did not react. Once the North Vietnamese GCI saw the MiGs were abeam the strike flight and outside the radar range of the MiGCAP F-4s, they instructed the MiGs to climb quickly to 28,000 feet. This put the MiGs above the overcast and on one of the flanks of the strike force, still unseen by the F-4 radars. The MiG-21s closed on the force and, on GCI's command, dived out of the overcast and swept down at high speed on Ford, one of the rear F-4 strike flights. The MiGs attacked with Atolls; the first warning the F-4s had was when Ford 3 saw a missile hit Ford 4, which blew up in a ball of flame. At the same time, Ford 2 watched an Atoll pass by his wing and destroy Ford 1. The MiGs escaped unscathed.

But the battle was not over; in the target area, more MiG-21s and MiG-17s attacked using conventional tactics. One F-4 launched an AIM-7 at another F-4 he had misidentified but was able to break lock before the missile hit. To round out a bad day for the F-4s, another F-4 was lost to AAA, and Ford 3 ran out of gas trying to reach a tanker, bringing the day's total F-4 losses to four, three of them from Ford flight. Ford 3's crew was picked up; at least three chutes were seen from Ford 1 and Ford 4, but none of the crewmen were recovered.

The MiG-21s' deadly attack on Ford flight was especially disturbing because the fighter wings learned afterward that U.S. intelligence had watched the MiG-21s practicing their new tactic for ten days before the attack but had not reported this to the wings. The wing commanders—to put it mildly—were outraged. They would have been more distressed had they known the attack on Ford flight was just the beginning of what would be a radical change in North Vietnamese MiG-21 tactics.

It soon became apparent that the reason the North Vietnamese stood down in late June, July, and early August 1967 was to work on their training and tactics—and their efforts were very successful. From early 1967

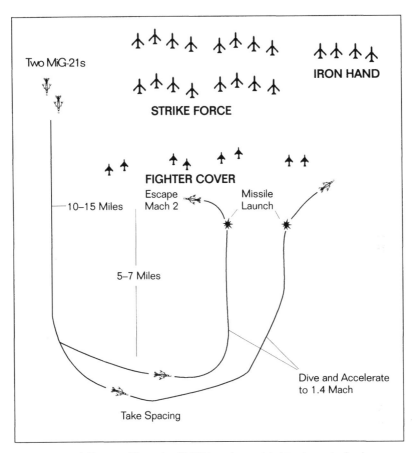

MiG-21 Attack Pattern. The pair of MiG-21s always tried to stay out of radar range and sight of the American flights until they had begun their attack from the rear. Note how the split let them attack in trail or attack two flights at the same time.

it was clear the MiGs had to pick up the main burden of air defense when the ECM pods came into general use and the SAMs became less effective, and the North Vietnamese first had tried the obvious solution of using more and larger formations of MiGs. They kept these large MiG forces within a thirty-mile radius of Hanoi—where most of the targets were— and attempted to intercept every U.S. strike, attacking aggressively and provoking a large number of dogfights.

But after several months of heavy losses, it was obvious these tactics were not working. The large volume of engagements overloaded the

North Vietnamese GCI controllers, and the MiGs lost much of the benefit of their GCI system. The MiG-17 was not equal to the American fighters, and it was clear the MiG-21, despite its excellent performance, was not a match for the F-4 in a dogfight. The F-4s usually outnumbered the MiG-21s, and U.S. tactics exploiting the MiG-21's poor rearward and downward visibility gave American F-4 pilots superiority in turning engagements. Additionally, the F-4 carried much longer-ranging and heavier armament, especially with the cannon pod.

The North Vietnamese learned from their losses, and from August 1967 until the end of Rolling Thunder they changed their procedures for using the MiG-21s. They realized the MiG-21 was fast, hard to see, and ideally suited for hit-and-run attacks as long as it had good GCI to vector it to its target and protect its tail. The GCI controllers became much more disciplined and concentrated on selectively intercepting U.S. flights with a smaller number of MiG-21s guided by much more skillful controllers.

By September, as one F-4 squadron history put it, "The MiG pilots grew more skillful and aggressive overnight."[23] Now MiG-21s attempted closely controlled intercepts only at high speed from high and behind the strike flights when they had a clear advantage. As they approached, the MiG-21s would make a supersonic diving pass against trailing or isolated U.S. flights; when they reached missile range they had both speed and positional advantages and also were set up for a high-speed escape. Another major change was that now the MiG-21s took the most isolated target (which often was the F-4 in the trailing escort element), whereas in the past they would fly past the escorting F-4s to attack the strike aircraft. As an added benefit, the increased effectiveness meant the North Vietnamese could base fewer MiG-21s in country, where they were vulnerable to U.S. bombing.

To react to this high-speed, rear-quarter attack, U.S. aircraft had to jettison their fuel tanks and bombs to evade the attackers; once the bombs were jettisoned, the attack was successful even if the MiG-21s' missiles missed. The MiGs' high-speed dives away from this type of attack made it almost impossible for the U.S. fighters to catch the MiGs before they ran out of fuel. The MiG-21s studiously avoided turning dogfights. Their motto now, as one American pilot put it, was "one pass and haul ass."

Meanwhile, to keep the pressure on the American strikes from all angles, small flights of MiG-17s without GCI control would continue to set up low-altitude wheels close to expected targets and try to split up the formations, make the strikers jettison their ordnance, and try to draw U.S. aircraft into dogfights. The MiG-17s simply were given information on where the American strike was and then ordered to attack it.

Using their new tactics, the MiGs forced forty-seven strikers to jettison their ordnance in only sixteen engagements in September—almost double the number of jettisonings of any other previous month, including the "MiG months" of April and May. In addition to harrying the strike flights, the MiG-21s began to take a special interest in U.S. reconnaissance flights. Several times MiG-21s pursued them well to the west toward Laos, and on September 16 a MiG-21 shot down an RF-101 on a reconnaissance mission over North Vietnam for the only air-to-air loss of the month. To counter these new attacks, most F-4s now were moved back to MiGCAP, but despite the added MiGCAP and the heavy MiG reaction, no MiGs or strikers were shot down during September.

October 1967/Active QRC-248

Meanwhile, the ground war in South Vietnam escalated as North Vietnamese forces became more aggressive in attacking U.S. troops. With no solution to the escalating ground war, the United States increased the bombing of North Vietnam until the military had virtually every option they asked for except the mining of Haiphong harbor.

In October 1967 the weather was good despite the northeast monsoon, and the MiGs continued to be aggressive. In one day, on October 2, MiG attacks forced sixteen F-105s to jettison their bombs. The next day two F-4Ds were escorting an RF-4 reconnaissance mission when one of the escorts was hit by flak; he made a radio call that he had been hit and had lost an engine. The North Vietnamese were listening to the radio transmissions, and thirty seconds later MiG-21s launched out of Phuc Yen. A few minutes later the MiGs caught the F-4 flight limping along at slow speed and, in a high-speed rear pass, shot down one of the F-4s. MiG-21s shot down F-105s on October 7 and 9, and their successes led the White House to authorize the first U.S. strikes on the MiG base at Phuc Yen. On October 24 and 25 combined Air Force and Navy strikes hit the bases, destroying about twelve MiGs (seven MiG-17s and five MiG-21s) and damaging eight more on the ground. Strikes also hit the other MiG-capable airfields regularly, and now the only major airfield that had not been bombed was Hanoi's international airport at Gia Lam.[24]

The Air Force tried several ways to counter the MiG-21s' stern attacks. The MiGCAP F-4s no longer flew in formation with the strike flight; rather, they dropped back to a mile behind the strikers and offset to one side, and some strikes were provided with two escort flights. Additionally, the United States continued to improve its use of technology to try to counter the MiG attacks. Reinforcements of the College Eye force allowed them to fill all three EC-121 orbits on a regular basis, but there was still a need to remove the restrictions on the EC-121's QRC-248 IFF interrogator. The QRC-248 could pick up the IFF signals of the MiGs as they approached the U.S. strikes, but the EC-121Ds still were unable to give close control because of security restrictions on the QRC-248 actually interrogating the MiGs' IFF. Finally, on October 6, Seventh Air Force received permission for the EC-121s to use the QRC-248 to interrogate the MiGs' IFF more efficiently. Now Rivet Top and College Eye EC-121s could directly vector U.S. MiGCAP F-4s—using a separate frequency—to intercept the MiGs before they attacked.[25] On October 23, 1967, two F-4D pilots from the 8th TFW went to the EC-121D unit for orientation on the QRC-248 and to set up procedures. The next day, one of the pilots flew that afternoon's MiGCAP mission for the first strike on Phuc Yen, while the other F-4D pilot rode in the QRC-248-equipped EC-121. The EC-121 located a MiG-21 with the QRC-248 and warned the F-4D escorts—led by their previous day's guest—of a high, rear MiG-21 attack while the MiG was still well out of range, then guided the F-4s to the attack. As the visiting 8th TFW pilot in the EC-121 watched, the F-4s turned into the MiG, and after a brief dogfight the F-4D leader shot the MiG-21 down with his podded cannon.[26] Three days later, F-4Ds were escorting a post-strike reconnaissance escort mission at 20,000 feet near Phuc Yen airfield when they received a QRC-248 warning that they were about to be intercepted. The attackers were six MiG-17s, and at that relatively high altitude the F-4s had an even greater performance advantage over the MiG-17 than at low altitude, and their missiles were more effective. The F-4s had a relatively easy time, shooting down three of the MiGs for no losses. The much maligned AIM-4D scored two kills, its first of the war.

The offensive use of the QRC-248 was off to an auspicious start, and overall it was so successful that the QRC-248-equipped EC-121Ds in the Bravo and Charlie orbits found they could cover all of Route Packages V and VI. By the end of December the low altitude EC-121D Alpha orbit in the Gulf of Tonkin was canceled, and the Bravo orbit moved closer to North Vietnam at an altitude of 11,000 feet.[27]

As the QRC-248-equipped EC-121s began to use their systems to guide the F-4 escorts to attack the MiGs, they found it was more difficult than expected. To counter the high-flying MiG-21s as they moved behind the strike force, the EC-121s had to turn the F-4s at exactly the right time to get into position for the attack. If the F-4s began to turn toward the MiG-21s too early, North Vietnamese GCI would warn the MiGs to break off the attack; from there the MiGs would escape or simply reposition for another attack. If the F-4s started their intercept too late, by the time they were in a position to attack, the MiG-21s would have started their diving acceleration, and their speed would allow them to blow past the F-4s and break through to the strike force. Experience showed that the ideal range for the F-4 MiGCAP to leave the strikers and turn to attack was when the MiGs were about 20 miles from the strike force.

Surprisingly, even with Rivet Top and permission to use the QRC-248 more actively, there was no immediate, dramatic increase in kills against the newly aggressive MiGs; with regard to Rivet Top, this was attributed in post-Rolling Thunder reports to the unfamiliarity of the Rivet Top crews with the strike force tactics and the general combat situation. The information was all there; it was a matter of using it properly, and there were numerous conferences and meetings to try to solve the problems.[28]

Navy F-4Bs scored at the end of the month, but the engagements did not go smoothly. On October 26, a section of F-4Bs was vectored by *Harbormaster*, a Navy GCI ship, toward MiGs and cleared to fire without a visual identification. The lead F-4's radar failed just as he was about to fire an AIM-7; the second F-4 attempted to fire, but the AIM-7 failed, and a hurried AIM-9D shot went ballistic. As the F-4s closed, they saw the MiGs were in fact other F-4s from the same squadron. After some "anxious discussion" with *Harbormaster*, the F-4s were turned to another radar contact, and after a visual identification, the number two F-4 shot down a MiG-21 with an AIM-7.[29] On October 30, the AIM-7's malfunctions reached tragicomic portions. With good vectors from *Harbormaster*, two Navy F-4Bs engaged four MiG-17s; the leader shot down a MiG-17 with an AIM-7, then closed on a second MiG and fired another AIM-7 from well within the envelope. The missile came off the F-4 and began to turn toward the MiG; the F-4 pilot thought, "Great, I've got another one," when the Sparrow detonated prematurely about fifty feet in front of the Phantom. The debris from the missile caused such extensive damage to the hydraulic system that the crew had to bail out, but fortunately they were quickly picked up.[30]

North Vietnamese losses in October were so high—eight MiGs shot down in the air and about twelve more destroyed on the ground—that American intelligence expected the North Vietnamese to stand down again,[31] but the losses were deceptive. A closer look indicated the new MiG-21 tactics were quite successful. Only two of the eight MiGs destroyed in October were MiG-21s, and all three U.S. losses were to MiG-21s, giving the MiG-21 a success ratio of 3:2 with their new tactics.

November 1967

The November 1967 northeast monsoon was worse than normal, and for much of the month the Rivet Top EC-121, the most effective of the American control agencies, had to stand down for modifications,[32] leaving the U.S. strike forces without their most effective MiG warning tool. The MiG-21s took advantage of Rivet Top's absence and were increasingly effective with their hit-and-run attacks. In an attempt to counter the MiGs, U.S. aircraft restruck Phuc Yen on November 5 and hit the other major MiG airfields whenever possible, forcing the North Vietnamese to keep fewer and fewer MiGs in the country. By the end of the month, only four MiG-21s and twelve MiG-17s were based in North Vietnam.

U.S. escorts sometimes were able to force the MiGs to break off some of their high-speed attacks, but it was noted that "the skill level of the enemy pilots is high," and often the MiGs "were positioned perfectly"[33] to avoid the U.S. MiGCAP, even when the U.S. aircraft were assisted by the QRC-248. On November 7 an F-105 was hit by an Atoll in a stern attack, but he was able to recover with half the missile imbedded in his tail section. On November 8 a flight of MiGCAP F-4s, Olds, was covering a strike when it began receiving garbled MiG warnings. A MiG-21 attacked from behind and "smoked" through the formation; Olds broke into the attack, then reformed to cover the strike. As they rolled out, a second MiG-21, using the classic "in trail" tactic, attacked, and Olds 3 took an Atoll in the aft section. The F-4 began to burn and the crew turned to leave the area, but the tail section broke off and the crew ejected.

The one bright spot for the month was that the 8th TFW's F-4Ds' lead-computing gunsight, combined with the SUU-23 cannon pod, was fulfilling its promise. On November 6, Sapphire 1, the leader of a MiGCAP flight, was covering an F-105 strike on Kep airfield and was able to surprise a MiG-17 firing on one of the F-105s. The F-4D attacked with his cannon, shooting the MiG down in a ball of flame. As he turned to egress, Sapphire 1 saw another MiG-17 and chased him at low level (200 feet) into a box canyon. As the MiG climbed to avoid hitting the end of the canyon, Sapphire 1 exploded him with 20-mm fire. These would be the only two U.S. kills of the month against the six U.S. losses to MiGs.

In the second half of November, overall U.S. losses soared: The North Vietnamese shot down seventeen Air Force aircraft—nine F-105s, four RF-4Cs, and four F-4s—as the North Vietnamese defenses coordinated their activities extremely effectively. On November 18 Waco, a flight of Wild Weasel F-105s, was inbound to the target to provide SAM suppression for a Command Club mission when they were warned that they had

MiG-21s two miles behind them. Unfortunately, the F-105s did not hear the call; they did not know they were under attack until Waco 4 was hit and his engine began to vibrate violently. About two seconds later the trailing MiG struck; Waco 1 took an Atoll and began shedding pieces and emitting black smoke. Waco 4 was able to get turned around and headed back out of North Vietnam before the crew had to eject, but Waco 1 was last seen engulfed in smoke and in a steep dive toward the clouds.

As the Commando Club mission approached the target, the North Vietnamese plan became clear. The SAM operators had realized that the close formations flown by the strike aircraft on these missions might be vulnerable to the SA-2, and once the MiGs had forced the Wild Weasels away, the SAMs began a mass attack against the strike flight using new techniques. Two of the strike F-105s were shot down, and the rest had to jettison their bombs to escape the missiles.[34]

The Navy was not immune to the newly aggressive MiGs. On November 19 a pair of F-4s, Switchbox 110 and 115, were being guided by Navy GCI to attack a formation of MiG-17s near Haiphong's Kien An airfield. As they turned to attack the MiGs, their garbled radio calls indicated they were surprised by other MiGs. A faint mayday call was heard, and other Navy aircraft reported seeing a bright flash followed by two fireballs falling to earth, leaving two columns of smoke rising two miles apart. Neither crew was recovered.

On November 20 poor communications cost the Air Force an F-105. A strike of F-105s with an F-4 escort was ingressing for attack on the Lang Lau bridge when Red Crown, a Navy GCI ship, warned them that two MiG-21s were attacking from behind. The F-4s were flying about a mile behind a strike of F-105s when two MiG-21s turned in front of them to attack the strikers, giving the F-4s a perfect set up. The F-4s did not warn the F-105s of the MiGs but closed for what they expected would be easy kills. As they closed, the back seater of the lead F-4 called, "Break left," and the F-4s, thinking other MiGs were behind them, scattered (as it turned out, the back seater had meant to say "turn left" to close on the MiGs), leaving the MiGs they were pursuing an unimpeded run on the unsuspecting F-105s. The MiGs attacked Dallas, one of the F-105 flights, and when the F-105s saw the MiGs Atolls were already in the air. Dallas 4 saw Dallas 3 take a hit from a missile fired by a camouflaged MiG-21; as Dallas 3 ejected, a second MiG closed and fired an Atoll at Dallas 4, but it missed. Several more MiG-21s fired missiles and forced all the F-105s to jettison their ordnance, but these Atolls missed.

In addition to the MiG-21s, there was a surge of success by the SAMs in November. The North Vietnamese began using other radars, unjammable by the ECM pods, to give the SA-2 the launch information, and they lowered some of their SAM radar frequencies below the jamming frequencies of the ECM pods. This, combined with the extremely tight formations flown by the U.S. aircraft on the Commando missions (to give maximum concentration of bombs), made their pod-jamming patterns too narrow and allowed the SAM radars to find a target even with the jamming.[35] On November 19 the North Vietnamese fired ninety-four SAMs in one day, shooting down four aircraft, and overall SAMs were much more successful than they had been for some time, scoring eight kills in four days, mostly against U.S. aircraft on Commando radar bombing missions.

The losses to SAMs and MiGs in November were so severe that PACAF Headquarters held a conference November 22–30 to try to develop tactics to reduce Air Force aircraft attrition. The conference resulted in several new tactics and procedures. Strikes in the Hanoi area were limited to one a day, with the target times varied as much as possible, and Commando Club bombing was halted while the Commando Nail formation size was reduced. With fewer raids in the Hanoi area, there were more Iron Hand and MiGCAP flights available to cover the strikers.

The Air Force also tried a variety of changes in MiGCAP procedures in an attempt to disrupt the MiG attacks. The EC-121s and Rivet Top streamlined their control procedures with the MiGCAPs and began to try to send the F-4s in active pursuit of MiG IFF contacts. Additionally, the F-4s set up a "MiG screen," with the last MiGCAP flight arriving late to cut off and engage any MiG-21s that followed the withdrawing strike flights. Because they were the last U.S. flight in the area, the MiG screen F-4s had a "missile free" zone where they could fire on targets without making a visual identification. An additional MiGCAP flight was sent in at very high altitude—40,000 feet—to try to draw the high-flying MiG-21s away from the strikers, and from time to time MiGCAP flights were sent in ahead of the strikers at various intervals—five, ten, or fifteen minutes early—or were allowed to freelance instead of staying close to the strikers. At other times F-4s tried to catch MiGs as they landed or went in very low, under North Vietnamese radar, to an area where the QRC-248 was reporting MiGs. Unfortunately, none of these measures met with any great success, mainly because of the real-time information available to the North Vietnamese pilots from their GCI and the availability of safe divert bases in China, but also because the MiGs were small and hard to see even when the F-4s were close. As one F-4 pilot said, "The QRC-248 could get us in the ballpark, but we still had to find our seat."

SAMs also came in for attention. To counter the new North Vietnamese SAM tactics, by late 1967 the United States was fielding a modified ECM pod, the QRC-160-8 (or ALQ-87). This pod was much more powerful than the earlier pods and jammed the SAM radars so well that the older pods were modified to jam another part of the SAM system, the electronic signals the North Vietnamese used to control the SA-2 missile itself, called the "guidance link." These modified pods, called "special pods," were quite successful, and when they functioned properly, the SA-2 lost guidance and went ballistic.[36] By the end of December, the "special pod" guidance link jammers were in general use over North Vietnam.[37]

December 1967

In December, the bad weather from the northeast monsoon continued and severely limited the number of air strikes into Route Packages V and VI. In mid-month the weather broke for a few days, and large Air Force strikes resumed. After their exposure to the new, highly aggressive MiG tactics in November, the U.S. planners tried to vary their attack patterns. The planners had found in the past that when the strike flights did not follow predictable routes or came from the land and sea together, reaction was less intense.[38] For the strikes in December, the U.S. strike forces attacked from different directions or with much different spacing, attempting to split and confuse the MiG forces and their GCI controllers. This had some success, but the more complicated tactics caused some confusion with the U.S. strike forces themselves, and using the new patterns in the bad weather caused "bunching of strike flights, broken formations and general confusion" and "tended to increase the effectiveness of the MiGs."[39]

Meanwhile, the North Vietnamese GCI controllers continued to refine and improve their tactics, and the MiG pilots' aggressiveness and proficiency continued to increase. The controllers now were able to control two pairs of MiG-21s instead of just one, and the MiG-21s began to coordinate their attacks with the MiG-17s. Additionally, the MiGs now were willing to make multiple attacks instead of single hit-and-run attacks. These multiple attacks put a major strain on the U.S. escorts; the Air Force reported that the "multiple MiG approaches and their decoying effects were particularly effective in degrading the protection of the entire strike force throughout the entire mission."[40] The strain increased as the MiGs began to fire Atolls in the general direction of the strike flights when they could not get into the proper range; the sight of an Atoll in the air often was enough to make the strikers to jettison their ordnance.[41]

On December 16, Olds, a flight of MiGCAP F-4s, intercepted a wheel of MiG-17s at low altitude over Kep airfield. The F-4s split into two flights of two to try to break up the wheel, but the fight turned into a tight turning battle with neither side scoring any hits. Olds 3 and Olds 4 broke off early, but Olds 1 and Olds 2 stayed too long and had to egress with very little fuel—not enough to use afterburner. The North Vietnamese heard Olds' radio calls that they were low on fuel; as the F-4s departed at slow speed, Olds 1 saw Olds 2 explode in flames. As he turned toward the stricken F-4 he saw a silver MiG-21 disappearing into the haze. The Olds 2 crew bailed out and was captured. It was Olds 2's second mission into Route Package VI, and he was not happy that his leader had nearly run him out of gas and gotten him shot down. The pilot later commented, "[I]n the silk, I thought to myself, 'I hope the hell they get those [mission] tapes and play them.' . . . [There was] gross negligence on the mission."[42]

On December 17, an Air Force strike force tried its first two-pronged "pincher" attack. It did not go well; when the first prong of the strike force found the primary target covered by weather, it turned toward the secondary target but merged with the other pincher of the strike flight, which also was trying to change course to the new target. As the U.S. flights passed through each other's formation and tried to avoid collisions, a large number of MiGs—eighteen to twenty—struck and overwhelmed the Rivet Top controllers, who could only call warnings to the F-4 escorts. For the first time, the North Vietnamese made coordinated attacks with MiG-17s and MiG-21s, as the MiG-21s synchronized their high attacks with the MiG-17's low attacks. One flight of MiGs would attack from one direction and draw the F-4 MiGCAP to them; when the MiGCAP reacted, another flight of MiGs would attack from another direction. If the F-4s reacted to the second group of MiGs, the first flight of MiGs would reattack. Hornet, one of the MiGCAPs, got into a turning engagement with a number of MiG-17s. The F-4s were split up, and Hornet 4 saw Hornet 3 take cannon hits on top of the fuselage and turn away, trailing smoke; he was not heard from again.

While the F-4 escorts were trying to counter the attacks, several of the F-105 strike flights were hit from behind by eight MiG-21s in a beautifully executed attack; four dived out of the sun from the left side of the formation and four more simultaneously executed a low-level pop-up attack from below on the right side. One of the high MiG-21s hit an F-105 with an Atoll and sent him spinning down in flames, and the other F-105s were forced to jettison their ordnance.

On December 19, the Air Force tried a different tactic. This time the two strike forces attacked from the same direction, but they were very widely spaced, with the second force much farther behind than usual. The first strike force was heavily engaged by MiG-17s in coordination with MiG-21s, and the MiG attacks forced all of the strikers from the first force to jettison their ordnance even though they failed to score any kills. The second strike force, coming in after most of the MiGs had departed, was able to make it through to the target and bomb. An F-105F shot down one of the MiG-17s; another MiG-17 kill was shared by an F-4D and an F-105.[43]

The Navy and the MiG-21s

While the Air Force was suffering heavily from the MiG-21 attacks, the Navy, for a number of reasons, was not. The large Air Force attacks from Thailand, with their requirement for air refueling over Laos or the Gulf of Tonkin, gave the North Vietnamese plenty of advance warning. Air Force strike flights also had to fly a relatively long distance over land at fairly high altitude to the target, giving the North Vietnamese GCI controllers time to set up the MiG-21s for an attack.

The Navy's area of responsibility, on the other hand, was the coast of Route Package VI around Haiphong. Because the carriers could move close to the coast, even large Alpha strikes from carriers in the Gulf of Tonkin needed little or no pre-strike refueling, which cut down advance warning to the North Vietnamese radar network. Because they were so close, Navy carrier-based strikes also could fly low over the water, below radar coverage, and get to the target in a matter of minutes, further limiting the warning available to North Vietnamese GCI controllers. Even when Navy aircraft struck in the Hanoi area, the time from the coast to target was much less than the time it took an Air Force strike force to get there from a refueling track. Against the Navy, it appeared that the North Vietnamese GCI did not have the time to set up their MiG-21s for the high, rear intercepts that were so successful against the Air Force, and generally the Navy strikers faced only MiG-17s in the target area. From the beginning of Rolling Thunder through the end of 1967, the Navy scored thirty-two kills, but only four were MiG-21s, or about 13 percent. The Air Force scored seventy-seven kills, twenty-one of them MiG-21s, or about 27 percent. Only about three Navy aircraft appear to have been shot down by MiG-21s during all of Rolling Thunder, while the Air Force lost about twenty-three.[44]

End-of-Year Balance

By the end of 1967 it was clear, at least for the Air Force, that the balance of power over the skies of North Vietnam had shifted. Since August, the United States had lost thirteen aircraft in exchange for twelve MiGs, but MiG-21s had claimed twelve of the kills for only one loss.[45] In the first half of 1967 the F-4:MiG-21 kill ratio was 13:0 in favor of the F-4; during the last half of the year the kill ratio was 5:1 in favor of the MiG-21. To exacerbate the problem, replacements had increased the North Vietnamese fighter force from 75 to 100 aircraft,[46] even with the October losses.

MiG Patterns

With the QRC-248, U.S. intelligence now had a very precise picture of how the MiGs were deploying to counter U.S. strikes.[47] When U.S. strikers were inbound, the alert flights of eight to twelve MiG-17s from several bases and two MiG-21s from Phuc Yen launched to get off the ground in case the U.S. aircraft were attacking their bases, then proceeded to specified orbit points. The North Vietnamese GCI controller chose the MiGs' orbit point based on the point the U.S. force crossed the North Vietnamese-Laos border, its heading, composition, the positioning of the electronic warfare aircraft, and other patterns.

The orbit points were different for each MiG type. The two MiG-21s went to a separate orbit at high altitude, between 22,000 and 32,000 feet. The orbits were pivot points; as the U.S. force moved farther into North Vietnam, the controller made the decision whether to attack with the two MiG-21s, keep them at the orbit point to possibly attack the force later, or withdraw them to China. If the GCI controller saw that the U.S. force was a fighter sweep rather than strike aircraft, or if the U.S. MiGCAP was in a position to protect the force, the MiGs then moved away.

When the U.S. forces were about 60 miles from Hanoi, a second pair of MiG-21s launched to a more advantageous orbit based on the GCI controller's "best guess" of the U.S. target. If these MiGs did not attack immediately and stayed at the orbit point, they often followed the U.S. forces out, occasionally as far as the Laotian border, waiting for an opening. For all the MiG-21 orbits, if the situation deteriorated and the controller decided not to attack, the MiGs went to a point in eastern North Vietnam, close to the Chinese border in the no-fly zone. From there the MiG-21s stayed out of the way of the F-4s and could land in North Vietnam or divert to Chinese bases.

MiG-21s from Kep generally were not as aggressive as the MiG-21s from Phuc Yen and orbited only north of the base. If they did attack, they usually attacked the F-4 MiGCAP as the force egressed, apparently hoping to catch the F-4s low on fuel.

MiG-17 Patterns

As the MiG-21s became more successful, the MiG-17s stayed closer to their home bases and at lower altitudes in a secondary or backup defensive role. When U.S. strike flights crossed into North Vietnam from Laos or reached forty miles offshore in the Gulf of Tonkin, alert flights of four MiG-17s launched from Gia Lam, Phuc Yen, and Kep. Each flight usually remained within 12 miles of its base orbiting in wheels between 3,000 and 9,000 feet. As the North Vietnamese GCI controller determined the inbound course of the U.S. strikes, he had the option of leaving the MiG-17s in their orbit, either to avoid contact or wait for the U.S. forces to run into them. He also could move the MiG-17s to block the strike flight's expected route of approach.

Phuc Yen MiG-17s usually launched ten to fifteen minutes later than the Phuc Yen MiG-21s. The MiG-17s engaged U.S. strike flights in coordination with Phuc Yen MiG-21s as the MiG-17s tried to break up U.S. force integrity and the MiG-21s tried to pick off stragglers or isolated flights. It is reasonable to assume that the Phuc Yen MiG-21 and MiG-17 pilots, sharing the same base, worked out these tactics together. The Phuc Yen MiG-17s also provided base cover for their MiG-21s on landing, and it was not unusual for all of the MiG-17s, if the situation demanded it, to be kept over or close to their base to act as cover for MiG-21s recovering with low fuel.

On almost every U.S. strike, four MiG-17s from Kep launched to an orbit point southeast of Hanoi. They engaged only about 10 percent of the time, usually inadvertently, and often these MiGs moved west or southeast to avoid an encounter.

Once the North Vietnamese GCI controller deployed the MiG-17s, he gave them little direction other than moving them between orbits and updating them on the location of the U.S. strike force. When the MiG-17 leader saw the U.S. force, he conducted his own attacks. In the attack, the MiG-17s protected each other, and often wingmen chased off U.S. attacks on their leaders. From time to time U.S. fighters were able to find and attack MiG-17s that were trying to avoid combat by holding out of the strike force's path, forcing the MiG-17s to escape or fight on their own.

MiG-21 Tactics

If the North Vietnamese GCI controller decided to try an intercept with the two MiG-21s, the pair made a high-speed run from their orbit point to a final turn point selected by the GCI controller; this put the MiG-21s between five and seven miles above and behind the strike force. In the turn, the MiGs took about three miles' separation and moved into a trail formation, one behind the other. This turn point was an important change from standard Soviet tactics, which turned the MiG-21 one to two miles behind the strike formation, offset to one side so the pilot could avoid the MiG-21's blind area in front and look for the strike force out of the side panel. The North Vietnamese apparently had decided that this position made it possible for the F-4 escorts to see the MiG-21 before it attacked, so they changed the pattern and turned the two MiGs much farther back and directly behind the strike force. This was too far out for the MiGs to see the strikers, but it also was so far behind the strike that the U.S. MiGCAP could not see the MiGs.[48]

GCI guided the MiG-21s to the tightly packed strike flight, with its highly visible smoke trail, and the MiGs made a sequential diving attack at very high speed, firing their Atolls at about one mile range. When the first MiG was seen (often only after he had fired his Atolls), it sometimes distracted the U.S. flights, and they did not see the second MiG-21, three miles behind the first, until too late.

After they fired, the MiGs accelerated straight through at high speed, then climbed and headed for the Chinese border as fast as they could go, about Mach 2. If the U.S. MiGCAP jettisoned its tanks and attempted to follow these MiGs, a second pair of MiG-21s could attack the strike force, especially it the North Vietnamese GCI controller detected an opening in the area the escorts had left.[49] The U.S. aircrews were totally frustrated by the MiG-21s' tactics. More than one Air Force pilot commented that "the best flying job in the world today is a MiG-21 pilot out of Phuc Yen."

January 1968

In January 1968 the weather remained generally bad, but MiG activity remained at a high level, with thirty-six engagements, all but one with Air Force aircraft. Now MiG-21s began to show an interest in the U.S. electronic support aircraft, an obvious move that many U.S. officers had expected much earlier.[50] On January 14, a North Vietnamese MiG-21 shot down an EB-66C over Laos. That same month, MiGs appeared to pursue the Rivet Top EC-121 as it returned from a patrol over the Gulf of Tonkin, and in February MiGs approached the EC-121s in the Laotian Charlie orbit several times, once closing to 25 miles. This activity forced the Air Force to move the EC-121 orbits south except for the specific time when strikes were to take place.[51] The MiG-21s began to range farther south and west to harry U.S. aircraft while continuing to fly and fight aggressively. They no longer fled to China after one pass; rather, they stayed, made another pass, and landed in North Vietnam. Additionally, the MiGs began to engage with larger and larger flights, with as many as four MiG-21s and four MiG-17s attacking U.S. forces. The MiGs often would position one group of four on one side of the strike flight and one on the other; generally they concentrated on the inbound strike forces in an attempt to force the strikers to jettison their bombs, but often the same group or another group would attack the U.S. force as it egressed. Additionally, the MiG-17s now received GCI control; they were no longer simply placed near suspected targets.[52] To counter these attacks, U.S. forces now used three dedicated MiGCAP flights for visual strikes and two MiGCAP flights for Commando operations.

On January 3 two large Air Force raids, one in the morning and one in the afternoon, hit North Vietnamese railroad yards. On the morning mission Tampa, a CAP flight of F-4Ds carrying cannon pods, was ingressing from the Gulf of Tonkin when a MiG-17 attacked an F-4 strike flight. Tampa 1 closed on the MiG at very low altitude and fired from close range, hitting the MiG-17 in the wing root. The MiG's wing broke off and the aircraft burst into the flames as the pilot ejected. Another F-4D from this force shot down a MiG-17 with an AIM-4D. On the afternoon mission the strike force of four flights of F-105s with two MiGCAP flights was inbound to the target when it was attacked from the rear by MiG-21s, who forced two of the flights to jettison their ordnance. More MiGs attacked as the last two F-105 flights turned to the target; one MiG-21 avoided the MiGCAP, closed on one of the F-105 flights, and fired an Atoll. It hit the number 3 F-105 in the tail and the Thud exploded in flames, rolled inverted, and hit the ground. The MiG easily ran away from the other F-105s.

The MiGs continued to show interest in the isolated Iron Hand flights. On January 5 a MiG-17 shot down an Iron Hand F-105F, and on January 14 another Iron Hand flight, Bobbin, was flying well ahead of a three-ship strike flight on a Commando Club mission against Yen Bai airfield. After the strike bombed, Bobbin began to egress the area when they heard MiG warnings from the escort flight behind them; suddenly two MiG-21s appeared and Bobbin 2 took an Atoll in the aft end. As the Thud began shedding parts, the pilot ejected. The F-105 flight jettisoned their ordnance and tried to pursue, but again the MiG-21s easily accelerated away.

Because of the continuing MiG successes, in mid-January the 8th TFW reconfigured one of the two MiGCAP flights that normally accompanied the strike flights. The new flight, called the "fast CAP," was armed to engage MiG-21s with the most reliable and lowest-profile configuration possible. The fast CAP replaced the AIM-4Ds with AIM-9Bs, dispensed with the non-jettisonable centerline cannon pod for a centerline fuel tank (which could be jettisoned when empty), and carried only a single ECM pod. The fast CAP usually took the first vectors to the MiG threat. The other CAP flight continued to carry two or three AIM-4Ds, the centerline cannon pod, and one or two ECM pods. But the new CAP configuration had little chance to prove its worth because the northeast monsoon had now arrived in full force, and from the end of January until the end of March, the weather was so bad that there were no large strikes in Route Packages V and VI.

February 1968

Over the northern part of North Vietnam the weather in February was some of the poorest in the past three years, and most strikes into Route Package VI were radar-directed Commando Nail missions. The United States continued to bomb the MiG bases of Kep, Kien An, Hoa Loc, Cat Bi, and Phuc Yen, as well as the southern airfield at Vinh, where MiGs had been sighted. The bad weather did not hamper the MiGs, however, and they began to display more new tactics. In the past MiG-21 attacks usually had involved more than one aircraft, but now single MiG-21s began operating with their transponders off. These "sleepers" would either fly alone or in the company of two other MiG-21s who were using their transponders. They were given only general GCI control and considerable discretion in which U.S. flights to attack, and consequently were very difficult to detect.[53]

Despite the MiG successes, U.S. aircrews thought that their MiG warnings, especially from Rivet Top, were very good.[54] One pilot said, "[P]rior to Rivet Top's arrival, our command and control was very poor. Rivet Top was a 500 percent improvement"; another commented that "the warning agencies had become very good. It was just like being under GCI control back home."[55] The F-4 escorts, guided by the EC-121 controllers using the QRC-248, were able to counter many of the MiG attacks, but even with the QRC-248 the skill of the North Vietnamese GCI controllers and the aggressiveness of the MiG-21 pilots allowed them to continue to get unobserved shots at the F-105s and their F-4 escorts.

In the few air battles in February the pendulum swung back and forth, with neither side able to gain the upper hand. On February 3 two F-102As, delta-winged Air Force fighters normally used for tanker escort, were orbiting over North Vietnam when the second F-102 said, "Something is wrong with my aircraft." The lead F-102 closed and saw an unexploded Atoll missile protruding from the tail. As they turned back toward Thailand, two MiG-21s attacked again; their missiles missed, but the damaged F-102 crashed in flames after avoiding the second missile attack. On February 5 a flight of four F-105s, Pistol, was scheduled for a Commando Club attack in the Thai Nguyen area. The small force was escorted by four Iron Hand aircraft and two MiGCAP flights—twelve escorts to protect four strikers. Inbound the F-4 MiGCAP received a call that two

MiG-21s had taken off from Phuc Yen, and the EC-121s kept QRC-248 watch as the MiGs approached the strike flight. Following the accurate calls the MiGCAP saw the MiGs off their right wing about five miles away, but when they turned to attack, they lost sight of the small North Vietnamese fighters. While the F-4s thrashed around trying to get sight of the MiGs again, the North Vietnamese had gone into a trail formation and closed on the F-105s. Pistol 3 looked to his left and saw the lead MiG's Atoll hit Pistol 4; the MiG pulled up to the left, rolled back to the right to confirm the hit, then accelerated away as Pistol 4 ejected. As the F-105 went down, the F-4s picked up the second MiG climbing away and attacked. The lead F-4 closed and fired a burst from his cannon pod but missed; he followed up with three AIM-7s—one that did not launch and two that did not guide—and two AIM-4Ds. The MiG was hit by one of the AIM-4Ds and went down, but as the F-4s watched, an Atoll flew past number 4, so close he could feel the jet wash from the missile; the first MiG had returned, but the poor performance of his second Atoll denied him an easy kill.

On February 6, a similar event occurred, but with better results. Four F-4Ds of Buick flight, a fast CAP with AIM-9s and no gun pod, were escorting an F-105 Commando Club strike when they were vectored to a QRC-248 contact on two MiG-21s approaching the strike flight. The F-4s climbed to 31,000 feet and passed the MiGs head on; as the F-4s turned to pursue, the MiGs split, one turning into a left descending turn and the other climbing away. The four F-4s continued after the descending MiG. Buick 1 tried to launch two AIM-7s; neither missile motor fired. The MiG then turned in front of Buick 3, who fired two more AIM-7Es, both of which missed, then Buick 1 fired two more Sparrows; again neither missile motor fired. Buick 3 then fired two Sidewinders, but neither guided.

Buick 2 now thought he had a clear shot at the MiG and fired an AIM-9, but the missile headed for Buick 4, who had to break violently to avoid being hit. Buick 2 then fired an AIM-7 without a radar lock on and the missile went ballistic; the MiG headed for his home base with the four F-4s still about a mile behind him. The comedy of errors ended as Buick 2, Buick 3, and Buick 4 fired a total of four missiles at the same time. Buick 2 fired two AIM-7s, Buick 3 fired two AIM-7s (one of which did not launch), and Buick 4 fired a single Sparrow. The MiG blew up from one of the missiles, and in the end the kill was awarded to Buick 4.

On February 14, Killer, a flight of F-4Ds, was MiGCAP for a Commando Nail bombing mission on the Phuc Yen airfield. Again the escort was heavy—two flights of Iron Hand F-105Fs and two flights of F-4 MiGCAP protecting a single flight of four F-4 strikers. The MiGCAP, under control from Rivet Top, engaged a wheel of MiG-17s, shooting down one with an AIM-7E and one with the cannon; these would be the last U.S. Air Force kills of Rolling Thunder.

On February 23, Honda, a MiGCAP flight of four F-4Ds, received several QRC-248 warnings for MiGs in their area. The MiGs apparently were hiding in a cloud layer at 7,000 feet; as the F-4s maneuvered to try to locate the MiGs, Honda 4—an inexperienced fighter pilot who previously had flown C-130 cargo aircraft—dropped behind the flight and was attempting to get back into position when he was hit by an Atoll from an unobserved MiG-21. A review of the mission tapes showed that the missile probably had been meant for Honda 3 and that an EC-121 had warned Honda flight that the MiG-21 was beginning to attack; the tapes also showed that Honda 4's back seater called a break just before the missile hit.

At the end of the month, U.S. fighters had shot down three MiG-21s and two MiG-17s for the loss of three U.S. aircraft, all to MiG-21s; clearly the problem was not solved. In March, the weather was still bad and limited the strikes over Route Package VI; the MiGs grew increasingly bold, and two MiG-21s attacked egressing flights at the Laotian border, but there were no air-to-air losses on either side.

As the good weather approached in early 1968, there were no counters for the MiG-21s on the horizon, and the prospects for Rolling Thunder looked bleak.

Bombing Halt

On March 31, 1968, President Johnson announced that he would not run for president again and also announced a bombing halt on targets north of 20°N latitude, which included all of Route Packages V and VI. Two more southerly moves of the "bomb line" quickly followed, finally leaving the line on 19°N latitude. This area was all in Route Packages II and III, which were still the Navy's responsibility, so the Air Force effectively dropped out of the air-to-air war and the Navy took over.

U.S. Navy versus MiGs

After the bombing halt, the MiGs slowly moved back to North Vietnam from China, and beginning in May 1968, flights of MiGs began to come south to harry Navy aircraft, showing the aggressiveness and confidence that had allowed them to successfully challenge Air Force strikes for the last six months. But the MiGs found the environment over the southern part of North Vietnam very different from the environment in Route

Packages V and VI; now it was the North Vietnamese fighters that were operating at the limits of their GCI environment, and Navy fighters had the advantages the North Vietnamese had enjoyed for so long—effective GCI and SAM support, provided by Navy ships just off the North Vietnamese coast. To make sure the North Vietnamese did not build up a GCI capability in the southern part of the country, U.S. strike aircraft regularly bombed a new GCI facility the North Vietnamese were trying to build at Vinh, in the center of the North Vietnamese panhandle.

Well aware of their advantages, the Navy planned to use two techniques if the MiGs came to attack Navy strike aircraft. First, all Navy strike aircraft would leave the area when the MiGs came down, enabling the F-4s to fire their AIM-7s at long range without a visual identification pass. Next, when the MiGs were in the area, the Navy would use communications jamming from aircraft and ships off shore to deny the MiGs the warning from their GCI that Navy fighters were attacking.

Despite the change of environment, initially things did not go well for the Navy fighters, especially the F-4s. On May 7, five F-4Bs engaged two MiG-21s in very hazy weather. Radar control and the F-4 response were confused, and the F-4s became separated. An EKA-3B electronic warfare aircraft was trying to jam North Vietnamese communications, but his jammers failed, so the MiGs had good GCI to vector them against the confused F-4s. One of the F-4s, Silver Kite 210, separated toward the coast alone, low on fuel. Shortly after he crossed the coast another F-4 saw him take a hit from an Atoll and crash in the water. On May 9, three MiG-21s came down to attack Navy strikes. The strike aircraft cleared the area to give the F-4s a chance to used their AIM-7s; two F-4s got good GCI control and fired four AIM-7s at the MiGs but apparently missed. On May 23, a mixed force of MiG-17s and MiG-21s penetrated south and was on the receiving end of what U.S. fighters had dealt with for the last three years, a SAM attack, as a Talos SAM from a U.S. Navy ship shot down a MiG-21.

But the F-4 woes continued. On June 14, two MiG-17s came down, and, as planned, the area was cleared; two F-4s engaged two MiG-17s and fired four AIM-7s without a hit. On June 16 another section of two F-4s, Milkvine, was vectored to attack two MiG-21s. The F-4s were forced to turn back as they approached the 19°N latitude line, and the two MiGs also turned back and attacked from behind as the F-4s headed south. Milkvine 102 saw them, broke away, and called for Milkvine 101 to break, but Milkvine 101 apparently had radio failure, and the MiG-21s closed easily. The lead MiG-21 fired an Atoll that went up the F-4's tailpipe and exploded, and the crew ejected. The F-4s had three more engagements during the rest of June and fired thirteen more AIM-7s, but despite good GCI and despite apparently firing the missiles in parameters, they did not score a hit.

The F-8s fared better—and were luckier. On June 26 a flight of four F-8s were vectored toward two MiG-21s when another two MiG-21s appeared behind them, firing missiles; the MiGs were in perfect position, but their missiles missed. Later that day three F-8s were coming off a tanker when they were vectored to a MiG contact near the North Vietnamese airfield at Vinh. As the MiGs passed 19°N heading south, Navy ships and aircraft began jamming the North Vietnamese GCI radar and radio transmissions. The F-8s saw a MiG-21 passing head on above them; the MiG turned into the F-8s, and they pulled up sharply as the MiG passed and turned behind him. The first F-8 fired two AIM-9Ds and blew the tail of the MiG completely off; afire from the wing roots back, the MiG-21 crashed. But the Crusaders had moved too soon; a second MiG was two miles behind the first and "sandwiched" the Navy fighters; fortunately the number 3 F-8 saw the MiG, and the Crusaders broke into the attack and escaped.

The MiGs continued aggressively to come south. On July 9, Feed Bag, a single F-8, was escorting an RF-8 on a reconnaissance mission in southern North Vietnam; despite indications that MiGs were in the area, there was no GCI warning until tracers began whizzing past the RF-8 from a MiG-17. The F-8 called for the RF-8 to break and attacked, damaging the MiG with an AIM-9D and shooting it down with a follow-up cannon attack. The planned jamming from an EKA-3B and an EA-6A did not begin until after the MiG was downed.[56]

The next day was better coordinated. Four MiG-21s came south, and the other Navy aircraft left the area as two F-4s moved to intercept, cleared to fire their AIM-7s without visual identification. As they closed on the MiGs, three ECM aircraft—an EKA-3B, an EA-6A, and an Air Force EB-66E—began jamming the radars and GCI radios. The MiGs were in two pairs, one high and a trailing pair low; the number 2 F-4 fired a Sparrow and an AIM-9, but both missed. He then followed up with another AIM-9 for the kill while the first F-4 turned and fended off the second pair of MiGs. It was later assessed that "ECM made a significant, if not vital, contribution to the success of this mission."[57]

On July 29, the North Vietnamese continued their sweeps when four MiG-17s tangled with four F-8s, and one of the F-8s shot down a MiG-17 with an AIM-9. On August 1, a single MiG-21 attacked two F-8s; after dodging the MiG's Atoll, the F-8s turned after the MiG, and each hit him with an AIM-9D, destroying the North Vietnamese fighter. On August 7 things again went poorly for the Navy F-4s when, in a dogfight with two

MiG-21s, an F-4 shot down his own wingman with an AIM-9. On September 19, Old Nick, a flight of two F-8s, launched from their carrier to attack a pair of MiG-21s. Vectored by Navy GCI, Old Nick came in from behind the MiGs, shot one down with a Sidewinder, then turned to pursue the second. The F-8s fired their AIM-9s at the fleeing MiG-21 and two detonated close by, but the MiG escaped. This MiG-21 kill would be the last air-to-air victory of Rolling Thunder.

On November 1, 1968, President Johnson—after a million sorties and the loss of almost 1,000 aircraft—ended Rolling Thunder by ordering a total halt to the bombing of North Vietnam.

5

The End of the Beginning

Looking Back

THE U.S. AIR FORCE assessment of air-to-air combat results for the last part of Rolling Thunder was bleak. From October 1, 1967, until March 31, 1968, the North Vietnamese had out-thought and out-fought the Air Force; and during this period the United States lost twenty-four aircraft while claiming twenty-seven kills. More importantly, sixteen U.S. aircraft were lost to MiG-21s while the United States shot down only five MiG-21s. This was a kill ratio of over 3:1 in favor of the MiG-21, despite the Air Force's use of QRC-248 and Rivet Top. Other numbers were equally stark. In 1965, losses to MiGs were only 1 percent of total U.S. losses over North Vietnam. That rose to 3 percent in 1966 and 8 percent in 1967, and in 1968, losses to MiGs were 22 percent of the total U.S. losses over North Vietnam. While these statistics are somewhat deceiving—new U.S. ECM equipment cut into the losses to SAMs and allowed the strikes to fly higher, reducing their losses to AAA—by March 1968 MiGs had become the biggest threat to Air Force strike flights over North Vietnam. In the most broad-ranging study of air-to-air combat over North Vietnam, the Air Force stated, "[In late 1967 and 1968] the USAF did not recognize and/or respond to changing NVNAF [North Vietnamese Air Force] tactics."[1]

The engagements from May to the end of Rolling Thunder had been equally traumatic for the Navy F-4 force. During that period, despite excellent GCI, communications jamming support, and a situation where they could often fire their AIM-7s head on without having to visually identify the target, Navy F-4s fired about twenty-six Sparrows (and sixteen AIM-9Ds) for only two MiG kills, while losing two F-4s to MiGs.

Weapons Results

AIM-7 Sparrow

The AIM-7 had two major variants, the AIM-7D and AIM-7E. Air Force and Navy F-4s used the AIM-7D from April 1965 until the AIM-7E, with

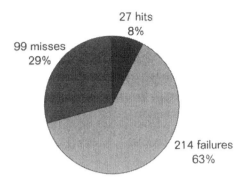

99 misses
29%

27 hits
8%

214 failures
63%

Rolling Thunder AIM-7 Results

minor performance improvements, replaced it in early 1966. During Rolling Thunder, about 330 AIM-7s were fired for about 27 kills.[2] Except for a spike in January 1967 (Operation Bolo) and one in late May–early June 1967,[3] there was a downward trend in the hits to firing attempts ratio.

The main problem with the AIM-7 was reliability: It simply failed to function properly at an alarming rate and, as the war went on, despite attempts to fix the problem, the AIM-7s steadily became less reliable. The AIM-7 failures hit 60 percent in April 1966 and dropped off to about 40 percent in mid-1967 (possibly influenced by the Bolo and May–June spikes), but from August 1967, the failure rate began to climb back up until it reached 80 percent.[4] Worse, the ability of the AIM-7 to fire when launched and to guide even when fired in the proper envelope was questionable. An Air Force team sent to examine missile performance in mid-1966 determined that, at low altitudes, the combat reliability of the AIM-7 was, at best, under 30 percent[5] and added, "[Even] assuming proper maintenance of aircraft and missiles, the probability of a kill with a Sparrow can be expected to be low." The AIM-7 missile malfunctions were due to its complexity: It contained a large amount of sensitive equipment, all of which had to function perfectly if the missile was to hit the target, and too often this was not the case.

Still other AIM-7 problems had shown up in combat. For the AIM-7 to guide, the F-4 radar had to "lock on" to the target to pass information to the missile so it would "know" where to go when launched. The F-4 had two lock-on options, a quick "dogfight" mode called a "boresight lock on" and a normal "full systems lock on." The boresight lock on allowed the missile to be fired quickly—in little over a second—and so was quite popular. Unfortunately, for a variety of complex reasons, this mode did not work as advertised and proved to be a complete failure: In the first sixty-five AIM-7 boresight firings of Rolling Thunder, there was only one hit.[6]

While the full systems lock on was more reliable, it took time. After the radar locked on to the target, it took four more seconds to feed all the information to the missile. This meant that, after the F-4 crew locked on to a MiG and received cockpit indications that they could launch an AIM-7, they still had to count "one thousand one, one thousand two, one thousand three, one thousand four" before they could squeeze the trigger. Then it took an additional 1.25 seconds from trigger squeeze until the Sparrow left the aircraft, so a proper launch took about five seconds from lock on to missile launch.[7] The F-4 crews all agreed that these delays were too long for maneuvering air-to-air combat in Southeast Asia.

Once the AIM-7 was launched, the problems were not over. The F-4 had to keep the radar locked on to the MiG the entire time the AIM-7 was in the air, so this meant following the MiG until the missile hit (or missed). Combat experience had shown that an F-4 following one MiG until its AIM-7 hit was an easy target for other MiGs, but if the F-4 was attacked while the AIM-7 was in the air and had to break away from the target, the missile lost guidance—"went ballistic"—and missed. F-4s lost several possible kills under these circumstances.

Additionally, ground clutter caused much greater problems than had been anticipated for the radar and the AIM-7. Combat experience showed that at altitudes below 8,000 feet, the F-4 radar beam began to bounce off the ground, often preventing the radar from sensing the target; or, if the radar was already locked on to a target, it would transfer lock to the ground or break lock because of ground return interference. Yet another problem was the AIM-7's distinctive "in the envelope" firing symbology that appeared on the F-4's radar scope. The F-4's weapons computer determined the proper AIM-7 firing envelope and "told" the crew when to fire by special symbols on the radar screen, but the symbols were correct only when the target was in straight and level flight (which MiGs rarely were). Against maneuvering targets, the computed AIM-7 launch envelopes displayed in the cockpit were not accurate, and a 1966 Air Force report noted that "the parameters for missile firing are not easily determined [by the crew] since missile parameters change for each change of target flight attitude."[8]

Finally, there were tactical frustrations with the AIM-7. The F-4 crews had expected a tremendous advantage in air-to-air combat with the AIM-7's long-range and head-on capability, but the requirement to visually identify the target as hostile before firing severely limited the opportunities to use the AIM-7 in the head-on mode. Also, the AIM-7 left a huge

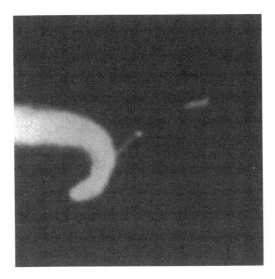

An AIM-7 Sparrow about to hit a MiG-21. Note the large smoke trail from the missile, which made it easy to see in flight—a tactical disadvantage. In this case, the MiG pilot probably did not see the missile because of the poor visibility from the MiG-21's cockpit. *Author's collection*

white smoke trail that was easy for the MiG to see, allowing him to maneuver to avoid the missile.

There were several other dimensions to the problem. Before entering combat, the AIM-7s ran a self-check called "tuning"; a missile that did not tune was dropped from the firing sequence. A considerable number of AIM-7s did not tune and could be considered failures, but since they were not fired, these types of failures were not counted in the statistics. Also, the F-4 radar itself had to work for the AIM-7 to work; the number of times the radar failed, rendering the AIM-7s useless, is not recorded, but the detailed accounts of the air-to-air engagements over North Vietnam[9] show that F-4 radar failure was not uncommon. The Southeast Asian humidity and the long supply line caused problems with all types of electronics, and the F-4's radar was no exception.

AIM-9 Sidewinder

The AIM-9 Sidewinder heat seeker was a popular missile because it was simple, easy to use, and much more reliable than the AIM-7. The Air Force used the AIM-9B throughout Rolling Thunder; the Navy used it for a time

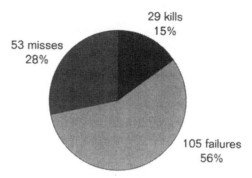

29 kills
15%

53 misses
28%

105 failures
56%

Rolling Thunder AIM-9B Results

but began to replace it in early 1966 with the much superior AIM-9D (although the AIM-9B was used on Navy aircraft well into 1967). During Rolling Thunder, about 187 AIM-9Bs were fired for about 29 kills (about 15 percent); about 105 were failures (56 percent) and 53 were fired outside the envelope (about 28 percent).[10] The AIM-9D—which was used by the Navy in 93 percent of its firing attempts—was fired 99 times for 18 kills, for a rate of about 18 percent.[11]

The AIM-9B could be fired quickly—in less than one second from trigger pull—but combat experience showed that, like the AIM-7E, it too had severe limitations, the main one being a very small firing envelope, particularly in a turning engagement. When a target was in straight and level flight, the Sidewinder launch envelope was roughly a cone extending from the tail, but when the target turned—the standard defensive maneuver—the AIM-9B envelope swung to the outside of the target's turn. It was tactically unsound to try to move outside an enemy's turn, so the attacking pilot was forced to wait until the MiG stopped his turn (which, surprisingly, often happened) or look for a MiG flying straight and level. A turn also affected the size of the envelope: A MiG turning at three Gs shrank the already small AIM-9B envelope by about 50 percent, and a MiG turning at more than five Gs—not an excessively hard turn in a dogfight—made the AIM-9B envelope disappear completely.

The infrared guidance system of the AIM-9B was another problem. The seeker looked for its heat source in an infrared radiation band that also contained the infrared radiation from clouds and ground. When fired with the ground, clouds, or sun as a background, the AIM-9B often homed on one of these instead of the MiG's exhaust. Additionally, if a MiG went into a cloud, the moisture hid its heat signature, so the AIM-9B stopped tracking and went ballistic.

Adding to the AIM-9's woes was its headset missile tone, which confused some pilots; they thought the tone meant the missile was in the firing envelope. In fact, however, the tone only meant the missile could sense a heat source, not that the missile could hit the target; the tone was necessary but not sufficient to launch the missile. The pilots needed the tone *and* to be in the missile envelope to have the missile guide.

Like the Sparrow, the Sidewinder had a minimum range of about 3,000 feet, but if the missile-firing aircraft was closing on the target or if their target turned into the attack—the normal defensive reaction—the minimum range increased. For an AIM-9B at low altitude this presented a further problem—there, the Sidewinder had a very short maximum range, and often the maximum and minimum ranges were within a few hundred feet of each other.

But unlike the AIM-7, the AIM-9 system gave the pilot no assistance in estimating the location of the missile's small, rapidly changing envelope. Additionally, a fighter had to be almost straight and level when firing an AIM-9B; if the launch aircraft was in more than a gentle two-G turn, the missile would not guide. Estimating the missile envelopes meant putting a premium on air-to-air training, which Air Force pilots were beginning to complain they had not received. PACAF Headquarters agreed the pilots were poorly trained,[12] and statistics bore them out—28 percent of the AIM-9B firings were out of the envelope, a much higher percentage than either the AIM-7 (11 percent) or the AIM-9D (13 percent). In fact, the AIM-9B/F-4 combination had a greater number of out-of-the-envelope firings than any other missile/aircraft combination in the Vietnam air war. There were several studies[13] about the high percentage of out-of-the-envelope firings, and they drew the following conclusions:

—pilots need more training to know when they are within the heat-seeking missile envelope
—pilots need an improved on-board indication of when they are within the firing envelope
—pilots need a missile with a larger launch envelope

While the AIM-9B was in many ways unsatisfactory, the Navy decided an improved AIM-9, the AIM-9D, would be better than developing a new missile. Because it had opted for the AIM-4D Falcon, the Air Force did not participate in the AIM-9D development; this resulted in a split in the services' missile development. While the Navy was aware of the advantages of cooling the seeker head, they were more farsighted than the Air Force, and even before the AIM-4D's problems, they realized the problem with cooling the seeker head lay in the amount of coolant, so the Navy decided to mount the liquid nitrogen coolant bottle for the AIM-9D's cooled seeker head in the missile launch rail itself rather than in the missile. A bottle mounted in the rail could carry much more coolant than one in a small missile; as a result, the AIM-9D and subsequent Navy missiles did not have the AIM-4D's problem with coolant. Since the Air Force had not worked on the project, they ignored this development; they did not notice until later that the new AIM-9D could not be carried on an Air Force aircraft because their missile launch rail did not carry a coolant source. From the development of the AIM-9D until the late 1970s, Navy AIM-9s were incompatible with Air Force AIM-9 rails and vice versa.

AIM-4D Falcon

The AIM-4D showed no improvement from its initial poor performance. From its introduction until the end of Rolling Thunder, fifty-four AIM-4Ds were fired for only five kills (9 percent), and the long, complex firing sequence caused many to be fired out of the envelope. Though the Falcon was used (unsuccessfully) through 1972, by 1970 virtually all of the F-4Ds were dual-missile (AIM-9/AIM-4) capable, but the heat seeker of choice was the AIM-9.

Prewar Missile Testing

The air-to-air missiles' combat results were startling to the people in the Department of Defense (DoD) and to the uniformed military who were responsible for making the F-4 entirely dependent on missiles. They had high expectations for the air-to-air missiles, because *prewar U.S. air-to-air missile test programs had predicted the AIM-7 would hit the target 71 percent of the time, and the AIM-9B would hit the target 65 percent of the time.*[14] Looking back at the air-to-air missiles' development, a combination of circumstances resulted in the discrepancy between performance predicted in the test program and actual performance in air-to-air combat.

The main problem with the test program appeared to be the "corporate" Air Force, Navy, and DoD assumption that the missiles would work; it followed logically, then, that when a missile did not work properly in a test, the only possible conclusions were either that the missile's maintenance was poor or that the test itself was improperly executed.[15] The managers of the missile programs were not stupid; they realized the missile tests were not tests of missile performance, but of missile maintenance and program management. Since by definition properly maintained and tested missiles "worked," the test program managers made sure the missiles were carefully handled and that the target maneuvers were as benign as possible to ensure the missiles produced the expected results. They were successful, because the tests showed a very high percentage of missile hits. Unfortunately, the top echelons of the Air Force, the Navy, and DoD were not aware of the flaws in the missile testing procedures, or else they ignored them in favor of a bias toward the high-tech weapons.

What the missile designers knew—but did not highlight—was that U.S. missiles were not intended for use against maneuvering enemy fighters. They had been designed and tested for high-altitude attacks against nonmaneuvering bomber targets, and the "book" envelopes for the missiles reflected that. Now a more careful analysis based on combat results showed a maneuvering aircraft changed the missiles' firing envelope. Instead of being fixed, as depicted on performance charts, the missile envelope was dynamic, continually moving, shrinking and expanding with each target maneuver.

Additionally, by testing at high altitude, the missile designers missed the fact that engagement altitude was a key factor in whether or not the missiles worked. As altitude decreased, the size of the missile envelope shrunk rapidly, mainly because of increased aerodynamic drag on the missile in the denser air at low altitude, so the ability of a maneuvering target to distort this smaller envelope also increased as altitude decreased. There was a significant statistical inverse correlation between the percentage of out-of-envelope firings over North Vietnam and altitude; that is, as the altitude decreased, the percentage of out-of-envelope firings increased. Low altitude also magnified the missiles' other flaws; for the AIM-7, the lower the altitude, the greater the problem of ground clutter, and for the AIM-9, the greater the possibility of the missile homing on a hot object on the ground. The North Vietnamese apparently realized this and, as the war continued, forced the fights lower and lower, with the expected results—a large decrease in the effectiveness of U.S. missiles. MiG-17s, especially, kept the fights at very low altitudes.

Combat conditions also were the opposite of the almost antiseptic conditions of the test programs. Once the missiles got to the combat area, they were no longer hand massaged, but treated as another round of ammunition. They were roughly handled, hung on aircraft for long periods of time with only the most cursory checks, and exposed daily to drastic changes in temperature and humidity—from the Southeast Asia ground climate heat to the extreme cold of high altitude—and often their seeker heads were damaged by rain and hail or by debris kicked up on takeoff by the aircraft in front of them. Conditions were worse on Navy carriers, where missiles were exposed to the salt air and more cramped conditions.[16] Finally, the MiGs were less cooperative than the test drones;

the North Vietnamese proved more interested in surviving than in demonstrating the effectiveness of U.S. missiles.

Consequences

The erroneous assumption that the missiles would work well had serious consequences and delayed the development of a wide variety of possible U.S. fighter improvements. One example was the decision to remove the guns from the initial version of the F-4 (the AH-1), made at a point when the F-4's main weapon, the AIM-7C (then known as the Sparrow III) was not even in production.[17] The Air Force had stopped the development of guns for fighter aircraft in 1957[18] (fortunately not until after the M-61 Vulcan was developed), and from that time until the 1970s most American fighters were not designed with internal cannon. This was not a phenomenon peculiar to the United States—the French Mirage III was designed without cannon (the manufacturer, Dassault, installed two 30-mm guns only at the insistence of the Israeli Air Force), and after the MiG-21C several generations of Soviet-built MiG-21s no longer carried an internal cannon.

Cannon Results

A post-Rolling Thunder official report observed that U.S. guns and missiles essentially had the same low effectiveness in kills-per-firing attempt—about 13 percent[19]—but the report was somewhat deceptive; in many ways scorned as an air-to-air weapon before the war, the cannon proved very effective. The F-105 scored 20 confirmed gun kills, including two head-on kills, in about 140 gun attacks. Because of the difficulty of setting up the gunsight, about 100 F-105 gun attacks were made without the aid of a computing air-to-air sight, producing about 10 kills, for a success ratio of about 10 percent. The F-105s made about 40 gun attacks with the sight in the air-to-air mode, also producing 10 kills, for a success rate of about 25 percent.[20]

The F-4C, which began carrying the cannon pod in the air-to-air modes from May 1967, had a non-lead-computing sight, but despite this problem, the F-4C had a high hit ratio with its SUU-16 cannon pod. The F-4D, which began to use the SUU-23 cannon pod in the latter half of 1967, had even better results with its computing air-to-air sight.

A closer look at the results of the U.S. gun attacks indicates the cannon was more effective than the statistics might indicate. The large number of cannon misses (100) when the F-105 fired without a sight skews the data. Dropping these cases, there were 148 cannon attacks with a gunsight; in those attempts, the cannon scored twenty-four kills, or more than 16 percent, which was considerably above the 11 percent kill rate for U.S. missiles. The argument could be made that with any sort of a gunsight, the cannon was the most effective U.S. air-to-air weapon in Rolling Thunder.

North Vietnamese Weapons Results

During Rolling Thunder American intelligence concluded that the North Vietnamese had about the same results as U.S. aircraft with weapons—a success ratio of about 13 percent. In fact, the North Vietnamese results probably were worse than reported because the numbers of reported firings were only those observed. It is quite likely that there were more firings on U.S. aircraft that were simply unseen.

During Rolling Thunder the MiG-17 scored all of its kills with cannon fire, while the MiG-21Cs scored very few kills—probably a maximum of three—with their cannon, although they frequently made cannon attacks, especially early in Rolling Thunder. The rest of the MiG-21 kills were made with the Atoll.

Pilot Performance

Besides systems performance, there also was the question of pilot performance. The accounts of the engagements over North Vietnam are full of occasions where U.S. fighters slowed down to turn with more maneuverable MiGs and not only survived, but won. While an F-105 in a turning engagement with a MiG-17 certainly was a mismatch that could have fatal consequences for the Thud, it did not happen automatically—the North Vietnamese pilot had to be good enough to take advantage of his aircraft's superior performance, and usually he was not skilled enough to do so.

Interestingly, on both sides pilot skill seemed to be less important defensively than offensively.[21] Defensively, the pilot only had to counter the opponent's attack and escape. Because of both sides' weapons limitations—unreliable air-to-air missiles and poor gunsights—countering an attack and escaping was commonplace, even when the enemy was not detected until he was in a firing position. There were few kills per engagement in Rolling Thunder, and for both sides a kill in an engagement, even from a position of significant advantage, was the exception rather than the rule.

Offensively, pilot skills were of varying importance, depending on how the engagement developed. Often pilots on both sides simply pulled behind an unsuspecting enemy aircraft and fired for a kill. Other times there was considerable maneuvering involved before a kill. Maneuvering to a position of advantage, staying there, and moving into the limited missile and gun envelopes for a kill took tremendous flying skills, and most—but not all—pilots who scored kills after maneuvering were American. Luck also was a factor; many times pilots on both sides were in position for an easy kill, only to have their weapons malfunction.

Skill in offensive air-to-air combat is marked by the ability to maneuver the aircraft in both the horizontal and vertical planes. Such three-dimensional maneuvers are quite difficult to judge and perform and have to be practiced again and again—accompanied by suitable instruction and critiques—to be executed consistently and successfully. In addition to maneuvering his own aircraft, a fighter pilot on the offensive had to be able to watch the enemy aircraft and anticipate his maneuvers, then maneuver his aircraft to a precise spot behind the enemy—or rather, where the enemy would be when he arrived—where he could fire his very limited weapons (and then hope they worked). As one American multiple-MiG killer described, "I had [a MiG] in sight at my ten o'clock, in a left turn. . . . I pulled sharp left, turned inside him, pulled my nose up about 30 [degrees] above the horizon . . . barrel rolled to the right, held my position upside down above and behind the MiG until the proper angular deflection and range parameters were satisfied, completed the rolling maneuver, and fell in behind the MiG. . . . Range was about 4500 feet, angle off [the tail of the MiG] 15 [degrees]. . . . I put the pipper on his tailpipe, received a perfect growl [missile tone], squeezed the trigger. . . . Suddenly the MiG erupted in a brilliant flash."[22]

Obviously, such maneuvering took considerable training, and part of the Air Force problem stemmed from its philosophy of making all of its tactical fighter pilots dual qualified—theoretically, equally skilled in both ground attack and air-to-air combat. The dual-role Air Force fighter pilot had to divide available training time between the two roles, so air-to-air combat training—which required both better weather and a much greater commitment of time and resources than air-to-ground training—tended to suffer. For example, in 1964 an Air Force dual-role pilot received six air-to-air combat training missions every six months,[23] as opposed to well over 100 ground attack missions in the same period. Additionally, the Air Force units in Thailand had a number of former bomber and transport pilots with no experience in fighter combat, especially air-to-air. From their debriefing comments, most of the Air Force F-4 and F-105 pilots felt they were poorly trained in air-to-air combat.

The Navy had a structural advantage over the Air Force when it came to air-to-air training. Navy squadrons were specifically divided into VF (pure fighter squadrons that did relatively little bombing) and VA (almost pure ground attack). Navy VF squadrons maintained their emphasis on air-to-air combat and made the necessary allocation of resources and training. Among the VF squadrons, those equipped with the F-4 tended to emphasize the intercept role of the F-4 using the AIM-7's all-aspect capabilities, while the cannon/AIM-9-armed F-8s' training emphasized close-in dogfighting.

Interestingly, a closer look shows that the difference between Rolling Thunder Air Force dual-role F-4 and F-105 pilots and Navy F-4 pilots was smaller than might be expected. The Navy F-4s' AIM-9B and AIM-7 out-of-envelope firings were statistically identical to the Air Force, although the Navy overall had a much smaller number of firings. Like the Air Force pilots, Navy F-4 crews also complained that they did not have enough air-to-air training (though Navy F-4s crews had more relatively nonmaneuvering AIM-7 interception training), but because Navy F-4s had far fewer engagements than Air Force F-4s—and thus fewer post-engagement interviews—it is unclear whether this feeling was as prevalent as with the Air Force F-4 crews, but anecdotes suggest it was.

The major difference in terms of air-to-air training was with the Navy F-8 pilots. Before the war, F-8 squadrons—equipped with cannon and the short-range AIM-9—emphasized the type of dogfighting that became the norm over North Vietnam,[24] and while the F-8s were developing their training program before the Vietnam War, they were carrying only the AIM-9B, with a limited envelope that put a premium on using precise air combat maneuvers to get into the proper position to fire the missile. F-8 pilots were the only American pilots that always seemed willing—even eager—to enter into a turning engagement with the MiG-17. Their performance was impressive even though they were fighting in the MiG-17's arena, and a subjective evaluation of F-8 maneuvering in their engagements leads to the conclusion that F-8 pilots knew what they were doing in a dogfight. Finally—and perhaps most conclusively—in all of the available post-mission interviews, F-8 pilots *never* said they needed more air-to air combat training.

Examining these and other measures—the F-8 pilots' kills per engagement (the highest of any fighter in the war) and their high percentage of in-the-envelope missile firings, it is not difficult to conclude that the F-8 pilots were the best air-to-air pilots in the theater during Rolling Thunder.

North Vietnamese Pilots

Through early 1967, the U.S. pilots respected the capabilities of the North Vietnamese GCI network but did not feel the North Vietnamese pilots were very skilled. U.S. pilots looked enviously at the North Vietnamese pilots' advantages—highly maneuverable aircraft and good GCI that allowed them to start almost every engagement with a tactical advantage—and many thought they would have been aces had the situation been reversed. U.S. pilots usually characterized the North Vietnamese pilots as "unaggressive" and very poor in maneuvering their aircraft and firing their weapons. Comments about the inferiority of the MiG-21 pilots at this time were especially common, and while MiG-17 pilots occasionally were described as "aggressive" and "capable," more often U.S. pilots commented that they did not know what they were doing. By April 1967, U.S. pilots noted that the MiG pilots were improving, and their comments changed dramatically beginning in September 1967 as the MiG pilots, especially the MiG-21 pilots, became more aggressive, skilled, and confident.

Despite their improvement, however, combat reports give little evidence that the MiG pilots ever developed real air combat maneuvering skills beyond attacking from behind and executing hard turns for both offensive and defensive maneuvers. The limited weapons capabilities of U.S. aircraft made these maneuvers perfectly acceptable; there are a few examples where MiGs used vertical maneuvers offensively, but these were isolated cases and seem to have been maneuvers executed on the spur of the moment, not as part of a plan. In only one engagement was a North Vietnamese pilot under attack able to maneuver to shoot down his American attacker. (In contrast, U.S. pilots scored twenty-eight kills when the fight began from a neutral position and shot down eighteen MiGs when the MiGs began with an advantage.)[25]

According to Russian advisor reports, another problem the North Vietnamese MiG pilots had was the physical difficulty of actually flying the aircraft. Russian cockpits and control forces were designed for fairly large European types, and the small, slender Vietnamese reportedly had difficulty maneuvering the MiGs because of the strength required. There are many combat reports of MiGs not maneuvering hard offensively or defensively where a hard maneuver would have given them an advantage, and certainly the physical ability of the North Vietnamese pilots in these situations was an issue.[26]

U.S. Training

U.S. Air Force

As it became clear that the war was going to be a long one, it also became clear that it was impractical and unfair to have it fought by only one group of pilots; the risks and rewards would have to be shared, but the length of Rolling Thunder and the inability to predict how long the war would last put a great strain on the Air Force and Navy personnel system to produce enough fighter pilots.[27] Prior to the war both services' personnel systems were designed to produce only enough pilots to man the fighters in the actual inventory, but from 1965 they had to produce enough pilots to fill these cockpits and to rotate aircrews in and out of Southeast Asia.

The Navy and the Air Force had different personnel policies for their aircrews. The Air Force made a decision early to spread combat experience wide rather than deep, and aircrew assignments to Southeast Asia were driven by a single policy—no aircrew should fly a non-voluntary second tour until every pilot had flown a first tour.[28] (A "tour" was defined as one year in South Vietnam [where the chance of being shot down was very low] or 100 missions over North Vietnam, which usually took about six months.) Because the war went on much longer than expected, this policy had a profound effect on Air Force manning in Southeast Asia, and, as one official postwar report put it, the Air Force wound up "fighting seven one-year wars instead of one seven-year war."[29]

The problems in replacing 100 percent of the Air Force fighter pilots flying out of Thailand every six months and 100 percent of the rest of the pilots in Southeast Asia every year were immense. Structurally, the Air Force had two advantages over the Navy when it came to producing additional fighter pilots for Southeast Asia. First, the Air Force pilot training philosophy was to produce a "universal" pilot who could go from pilot training to any type of aircraft—fighter, bomber, transport, or even helicopter—and later in his career be transferred to another type of aircraft. Second, Air Force pilots, unlike Navy pilots, did not have to meet any fixed skill levels. When the Air Force needed more pilots, it simply lowered standards, brought in more students, and graduated more pilots from pilot training. Many of these new Air Force pilots—who might have "washed out" from the pilot training course in earlier times—were sent to copilot positions in bombers or transports where they would not have to fly for long periods of time, freeing up the pilot they had replaced to be sent on a combat tour. This allowed the Air Force personnel system to replace combat fighter pilots with pilots from transports or bombers, and the burden of rapidly training most of these pilots fell on the Replacement Training Units—the RTUs.

RTU Training

The Air Force's RTUs were responsible for training most of the replacement pilots for the Southeast Asia fighter squadrons. The first classes in the RTUs were pilots who had some type of fighter background, who proved easy to train and did well in combat.[30] By mid-1966, the new RTU classes were beginning to get pilots with no fighter experience at all, many from large transports or bombers. Moving from a large aircraft to a fighter was extremely difficult. Many of the problems involved the type of flying itself: Fighters were expected to execute sudden, violent maneuvers (which large aircraft could not do) and usually flew in formation, often very close, and executed formation maneuvers. Missions in large aircraft were usually long, with extended periods of inactivity, whereas in a fighter everything happened quickly. Finally, responsibility in a large aircraft was diffused; the crew generally was in touch with a headquarters on the ground that could help them with aircraft problems or make decisions for them. In a fighter, even an F-4, the pilot had to make most of his own decisions. Training these large-aircraft pilots presented the RTUs with a difficult challenge; it was especially difficult for the F-4 RTUs, whose graduates had to be proficient in air-to-ground and air-to-air tactics and techniques. It quickly became clear that because each class of students had a wide range of experience and flying skills, the RTU could teach only certain basic skills—air refueling, tactical formation, dive bombing, and very basic air combat maneuvering. The RTUs certainly could have done more had they been given more time, but the Air Force artificially set the RTU course time at a maximum of six months; after that time, the graduates had to be on their way to Southeast Asia.[31]

While the RTUs were able to train their students adequately in air refueling, tactical formation, and dive bombing, many of the Air Force pilots complained about how little air-to-air combat maneuvering training they had received in the RTU. The evidence indicates that the RTUs had difficulty training in this area, for many reasons. The RTUs were on a tight schedule to finish classes so that the replacements could get to Southeast Asia and replace crews that were completing their tours, and the RTU commander's job and promotion prospects depended on getting the classes out on time. Air combat training slowed all phases of the RTU because, unlike all other training missions, it required that the aircraft be flown "clean"—no external fuel tanks—to allow the full range of high-G maneuvers. It took significant maintenance time to download these fuel tanks, meaning the aircraft could not be used for any other training missions until its tanks were put back on again. Another factor was that air combat maneuvering training was the last phase of RTU training because it was the most demanding and required the most skill in the aircraft, but this meant it came just before the classes were scheduled to graduate and go to Southeast Asia.[32] If there were periods of inclement weather (air combat training required good weather) during scheduled air combat maneuvering periods, or if the aircraft had maintenance problems, the

RTU crews could not complete their training and graduate on time. In such cases the RTU crews graduated and went off to their combat units with a "note from mother" stating that the pilot had not completed air combat training. Crews fresh from the RTUs commonly had to complete additional training after arriving at their combat units, taking them away from combat sorties and delaying the time new crews could get into combat.[33]

All of these difficulties could have been overcome, however. In the end, the biggest reason the RTUs produced poorly trained air-to-air pilots was the Air Force's corporate belief that air combat maneuvering among inexperienced pilots would lead to accidents.[34] The Air Force during this period was obsessed with flying safety; one of its official slogans was, "Flying safety is paramount to the completion of the mission"—even if that mission was training to go into real combat. Because of the F-4's adverse yaw problems, hard maneuvering could be a serious problem for inexperienced pilots; air combat training required hard maneuvering, so there was the fear that trying to teach air combat to inexperienced non-fighter pilots inevitably would cause accidents. The Air Force did not rate its RTU commanders on how well their students were prepared for combat—in fact, there was little feedback from the combat units to the RTUs. Instead, the Air Force rated them on the number of accidents and on whether they graduated the proper number of students on time. It is no wonder that air combat training was toned down and that pilots were often sent off to combat poorly trained (but always on time, of course).

As a result of the increasing demand to replace pilots completing their combat tours, by the beginning of 1967, 200 pilots each month were entering tactical fighter training. While the numbers had increased, the quality had decreased; it was noted that "the decreasing qualifications had reached an alarming point" and "they [the new RTU students] were having a difficult time completing the transition [take off and landing] phase of training." Despite this, the Air Force further lowered the qualifications for tactical fighter training,[35] and "mass production [took] precedence over training to expertness."[36]

The results of these shortcomings quickly became clear: The Air Force's kill ratio dropped from 3:1 in favor of the Air Force from April 1965 to June 1967 to .85:1 in favor of the North Vietnamese during June 1967 to March 1968, as shown in the table on page 166.

It should be noted that just after the June 1967 time period shown in the table, the North Vietnamese Air Force dramatically changed its tactics. The combination of better North Vietnamese tactics and less experienced U.S. Air Force pilots certainly had a synergistic effect on the kill ratio.

Background (percentage)	4/65–6/67	6/67–3/68
Tactical Air Command	64.5%	29.5%
Pilot training candidates	12.5	21.1
Other commands	24	49.4
MiG kill ratio	**3:1**	**0.85:1**

A Road Not Taken

There was, of course, an alternative to the one-year tour policy: Rotate entire squadrons in and out of the war zone. While this would have resulted in some of the squadrons taking a larger share of the load—similar to the situation that developed in the Navy—it almost certainly would have been much more combat effective. It is possible to see how such a system would have worked by looking at the results early in the war, or later, during Linebacker, when entire units were sent temporarily to Southeast Asia. The Linebacker temporary-duty squadrons were very similar to those that had begun the war and were very well regarded by the permanent crews. One MiG killer commented, "We found there was much more talent in the [temporary-duty] squadrons that came to Udorn as a unit . . . than there was in the permanent squadrons because of [the annual] rotation [of aircrews]."[37] The temporary-duty squadrons provided a glimpse of what might have been had the Air Force chosen to rotate entire squadrons in and out of the theater.

Rotating whole squadrons also would have eased the training burden in the combat wings, which had to devote significant resources to bring the constant influx of new aircrews up to combat standard. By the nature of the rotations, the wings had at any given time a number of aircrews who simply were not qualified for the most difficult missions. Had the Air Force rotated entire squadrons, they would have been prepared for their combat tours and would have brought only crews that were combat ready, thereby almost eliminating the need for training in the combat theater.

U.S. Air Force F-4 Back Seaters

The Air Force created a problem with its F-4 aircrews by putting a fully qualified pilot right out of undergraduate pilot training in the back of its F-4s. The idea was that the GIB would learn the F-4 systems and then move to the front seat.[38] But this approach caused a series of difficulties. First, there was no chance to develop a solid long-term program to train GIBs in F-4 systems operation or in working as a team with the front seater, because all the back seat pilots wanted was to upgrade as quickly as possible to the front seat, where they could actually fly rather than simply use the radar. Second, for obvious reasons it was normal in combat squadrons to pair strong GIBs with weak front seaters, but the combination often was tense on both sides. Weak front seaters, often high-ranking officers who had never flown a fighter before, had a tendency to make mistakes in the heat of combat; out of self-preservation, strong GIBs (always lieutenants) were quick to recognize such mistakes and tell the front seaters, sometimes none too gently. Consequently, in the life-and-death situations of combat, confrontations between the two were not uncommon, and as more and more front seaters arrived in combat with little or no fighter background, the problems increased. An additional difficulty was that many experienced fighter pilots flying the F-4 often were not fond of the GIBs. Most of these experienced pilots had flown their entire careers in single-seat fighters where they had developed their own habits—and could make their own mistakes—without any outside interference.[39] Some found having another person in the aircraft very irritating and made no attempt to use the GIB properly; there were many anecdotes of front seaters telling the GIBs not to do anything, including talk, during the entire flight.

The fact that the Air Force had a shortage of pilots made its decision to place two of them in the F-4 especially puzzling. While the Air Force had a shortage of pilots, it had a surplus of navigators, so the practical solution would have been to put navigators in the back seat. Unlike the Air Force, the Navy used navigators—RIOs—in the back seat of the F-4s, and they were a highly trained, respected, and important part of the Navy F-4 force. Both the combat units in Southeast Asia and Air Force Headquarters had asked for a change in policy in order to put navigators in the F-4 back seat,[40] but despite this, the stateside Tactical Air Command (TAC)—who made the final decision—kept pilots in the back seat of F-4s until after Rolling Thunder.

Once TAC adopted the Navy policy and put navigators in the back of the F-4, they became much more productive members of their F-4 crews. Renamed Weapons Systems Operators (WSOs, or "Whizzos"), the back seaters now could focus on learning the F-4s' weapons systems and not on what the pilot in the front seat was doing. The WSOs were quickly accepted and were generally considered better trained and more proficient that the pilot back seaters.[41]

U.S. Navy Problems

Compared to the Navy, the Air Force's personnel problems were small. During Rolling Thunder Navy aircrews on a cruise to Vietnam spent most of their time on Yankee Station and usually flew sixty or seventy missions over North Vietnam each cruise. Since a tour of duty on a carrier involved several cruises, many Navy fighter pilots flew well over 100 missions over North Vietnam—the number that sent an Air Force pilot home for the duration of the war—and still could expect to be sent back again. The situation became so serious that in 1967 the Navy developed a policy that aircrews could have only two combat cruises in fourteen months. This alleviated the situation somewhat, but it still meant that every fourteen months, a Navy pilot could fly about 120 missions over North Vietnam, then do the same thing fourteen months later, while his Air Force counterpart was home for good after 100 missions over North Vietnam.[42]

Also, unlike the Air Force, the Navy could not easily take pilots flying multi-engine aircraft and turn them into fighter or attack pilots. Under the Navy training system, pilots were selected early in the pilot training program for either fighter-type aircraft or non-fighter aircraft. This "two-track" system involved training the two types of Navy pilot entirely differently, making it very difficult to convert a Navy large-aircraft pilot into a fighter pilot, although it was tried, with mixed results.[43]

Not only was it difficult to train Navy large-aircraft pilots to become fighter pilots, but unlike the Air Force the Navy had a structural limit on how bad their new pilot training graduates could be. No matter how many pilots the Navy needed, every pilot—even the large-aircraft pilots—had to be good enough consistently to land on a carrier deck, generally acknowledged as the most difficult task in flying; unlike the Air Force, which could subjectively lower its standards to graduate more pilots, the Navy bar was, in a very real sense, fixed. No matter how badly they needed more fighter pilots, they still had to be good enough to land on a carrier. Finally, because of the extra training required to land on a carrier, it took the Navy about six months longer to train a carrier pilot than the Air Force needed to train a pilot, making the Navy training system slower to respond to the need for replacements.

The result was that the same cadre of Navy pilots flew the missions over North Vietnam—and took the losses. The combination of extensive combat losses with little prospect of relief—and the increasing unpopularity of the Vietnam War in the United States—caused morale problems with Navy aircrews.

U.S. Fighter Tactics

Navy Tactics

The Navy and the Air Force had very different philosophies of air-to-air combat, and their fighters used very different air-to-air formations and tactics during the Vietnam War. The basic Navy fighting unit was two aircraft, called a section, that flew line abreast separated by the distance of a turn radius (generally 6,000–9,000 feet), so that one could turn and instantly be in a position to protect the other. This formation was called "loose deuce"; it was easy to fly, the space between the aircraft allowed the formation to operate at full power, and the relatively long distance between the aircraft gave each crew plenty of chances to look for enemy fighters. The idea was for one fighter to engage the enemy—the "engaged" fighter—while the non-engaged, or "free," fighter stayed close enough to see the engagement, but not so close that he could not look for other enemy aircraft without worrying about the other aircraft in his section. The free fighter also was able to move into the engagement and take a shot if the opportunity arose. The idea was to have both fighters able to engage and make kills while covering each other at the same time. By 1965 the two-ship loose deuce formation was the standard fighter formation for most air forces in the world, including the Israeli Air Force and German Air Force.

Air Force Tactics

The Air Force used a different formation, one from World War II and the Korean War called "fluid four," with the four-aircraft flight as its basic unit. The flight was split into two elements: One element was composed of the flight lead as number 1, with number 2 as his wingman; the second element involved the number 3 aircraft as the element lead, with number 4 as his wingman. In a dogfight the two elements would (in theory) function very much like the two fighters in the Navy loose deuce, with the difference in the function of the two wingmen, numbers 2 and 4. These two flew in a close formation called fighting wing, 1,500 to 2,000 feet behind and offset about 45 degrees from the leaders.[44] In theory, the wingmen's roles were to provide protection for their element leaders, who were designated as the attackers. In reality, the wingman was so close to the leader that he had to spend most of his time keeping in formation, giving him little time to look at the overall battle, but the formation had been acceptable before the Vietnam War because aircraft then were not as maneuverable and because gun-equipped fighters needed to get closer to fire and thus had to fly in front of the wingman to get to the leader.

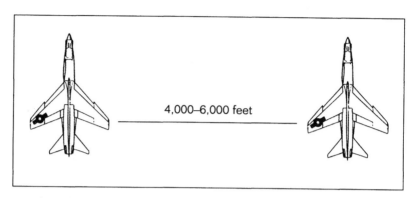

4,000–6,000 feet

Note how the wide split between two U.S. Navy fighters let one quickly turn to help the other if attacked. Loose deuce normally was flown with a "vertical split"; that is, with one aircraft higher than the other.

In Vietnam the situation changed. Missiles meant a fighter could both attack the enemy and be fired upon from long range, and it could close (or be closed on) very quickly, thus increasing the area for which the wingman was responsible. Additionally, the performance of modern fighters, especially the F-4, presented the wingman with many new problems. The F-4's maneuverability in three dimensions was so high and the wingman's position was so close to his hard-maneuvering leader, he was preoccupied with avoiding a collision; he could not look behind the flight to see if they were being attacked, nor could he look around for opportunities to attack a vulnerable enemy. Also, the wingman—less experienced and usually less skilled than the flight and element leads— was trying to fly a position that required a great deal of flying skill, especially in the F-4, with its adverse yaw problems. This led to a problem for the fluid four flight leader: He could not use full power because if he did, he would lose the wingman, who was trying to follow him, so the entire flight had to maneuver at less than full capability against an enemy who was at maximum performance.[45]

Fluid four flights usually had a "single shooter" policy; the leader of the flight usually designated himself as the only "shooter" and used the other three aircraft to protect him while he went after the MiGs. (If there were enough targets, number 3 would be allowed to attack.)[46] When the fluid four leader pursued a MiG the flight tended to spread out into a chain and made the other members of the flight very vulnerable.[47] The wingman was behind the element leader—which meant the leader could not protect him—and a sudden, unanticipated move, the norm in a dog-

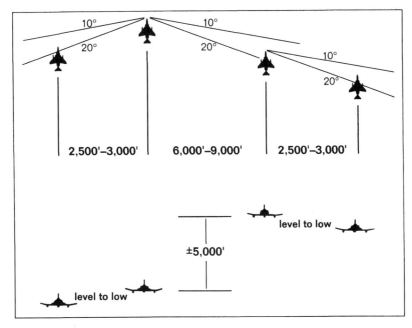

Air Force F-4s in "Fluid Four" Formation. In fluid four the wingmen were on the outside of the formation, where they could not be helped by the other members of the flight. The number 4 position—the F-4 to the far right side of the formation— suffered significantly higher losses during the war because he was not only out- side but behind the rest of the flight, with little hope of assistance if attacked.

fight, could throw the less experienced wingman completely out of posi- tion and leave him alone and open to attack. Most Air Force losses were suffered by the number 3 and number 4 positions in fluid four.[48]

As might be expected, with fluid four formation and the flight leads as the single shooters, in the course of the air war over North Vietnam the Air Force flight leaders shot down most of the MiGs. Since fluid four gave the flight leader a great deal of freedom because he knew he was always protected and could ignore his wingmen while pursuing the MiGs, it was not unpopular with flight leaders, but the formation was much less pop- ular with the other members of the flight.

In addition to giving the inexperienced wingmen little protection, the single shooter concept of fluid four also significantly cut down the offensive power of the Air Force F-4 formations; *a four-ship flight of Air Force F-4s under this doctrine used 25 percent of its potential firepower.* In other words, *two* Navy F-4s operating under Navy tactical doctrine had twice as much firepower as *four* Air Force F-4s operating under Air Force tactical doctrine.

The fluid four formation also caused tactical problems. The North Vietnamese began to realize that a single MiG could pull an entire escort flight of four Air Force F-4s away from the strike force, and from late 1967, often one MiG would feint to pull one escort flight away, then another single MiG would pull the other escort flight away; just two MiGs could tie up eight Air Force F-4s, leaving the strikers unprotected.

The Air Force, at least at the operational level, was aware of the problems with fluid four. As discussed earlier, the Feather Duster II program looked at the effects of formation tactics against a MiG-17 type aircraft, and the engagements showed that fluid four was not an effective formation when it was attacked from behind. The 1965 Feather Duster II report said that when a single F-86H attacked a formation of U.S. fighters, "when the defenders maintained element integrity, that is, when the second aircraft flew fighting wing position, the results were about the same as one versus one engagements";[49] in other words, the wingman in the fighting wing position was useless. Feather Duster recommended that "when attack[ed] . . . it was imperative for the wingman to maintain wide spacing"; in other words, "loose deuce." The recommendation was ignored. These problems soon were noted by the aircrews that had to fly fighting wing in real combat. From the first Air Force engagements with North Vietnamese MiGs, complaints were raised about fighting wing; a report on the Air Force's second MiG engagement of the war said, "Wingmen reported difficulty in maintaining fighting [wing] position during maximum performance maneuvers."[50]

A full analysis of the Air Force's reasons for staying with fluid four goes beyond the scope of this book, but many Air Force officers believed then (and still believe today) that the reason was that the other formation available was a *Navy* formation (as the AIM-9D was a *Navy* missile), and no Air Force officer with an interest in his career would dare suggest the Navy knew better than the Air Force. Suffice it to say that TAC and the unit that developed Air Force fighter tactics—the Fighter Weapons School at Nellis Air Force Base, Nevada—fought like tigers to keep fluid four and fighting wing ("welded wing," as its critics called it) as the basic Air Force fighter formation. They were successful throughout the Vietnam War.

North Vietnamese Tactics

In general, the North Vietnamese Air Force followed standard Soviet tactics, which were heavily dependent on GCI. The North Vietnamese MiGs relied on GCI to position them close to the target before the pilot took over the intercept and to provide protection from attack from the rear, but this dependence resulted in a rigidity in their tactics that made it difficult to respond to a changing situation; often when something unexpected happened, the MiG simply aborted the attack and went home. Despite the tactical rigidity, however, there never appeared to be any attempt to relax GCI control. Under Soviet doctrine, fighters never operated beyond GCI control, and no North Vietnamese aircraft was ever seen flying beyond GCI coverage. In fact, no Chinese, Korean, or Far Eastern Soviet aircraft was ever seen flying outside the range of their GCI, even though the MiG's combat radius often exceeded the range of the GCI radar.[51] The idea of operating in an area without GCI coverage seemed anathema to them. To help expand the operating areas of the MiGs, during Rolling Thunder and later the North Vietnamese tried several times to build GCI sites in western and southern North Vietnam.

MiG Formations

North Vietnam's total reliance on GCI resulted in a basic difference in formation philosophy between the Soviet/North Vietnamese and American formations. U.S. formations tended to try to balance offensive and defensive potential, and U.S. fighters flew formations that were more or less line abreast, so each aircraft could look behind the other. The North Vietnamese formations were based on Soviet ones and tended be trail formations, with one MiG behind the other. Interestingly, often the leader of the formation was not in the first aircraft but in the last, so he could direct the others and make attacks after the Americans had moved to counter the first attack. The MiGs' trail formations were much easier to maneuver and attack from, but they had little defensive protection, especially for the last aircraft; however, because the North Vietnamese counted on their GCI to watch their tails, they accepted this disadvantage. When the MiGs got involved in a turning dogfight, unless the trail formation turned into a wheel, it generally was not a useful formation, so the MiGs tended to drop formation support and fight as single aircraft. While MiG-17s could do this fairly easily, MiG-21s usually were outnumbered, creating a very dangerous situation for them, mainly because of their poor rearward visibility.

By February 1967 two basic formations of MiG-17s had been identified, hi-lo pairs and stacked three. In hi-lo pairs the high pair was at an altitude of 5,000 to 6,500 feet, with the second pair a mile behind at an altitude of 1,500 to 3,000 feet. Generally the first pair attacked the U.S.

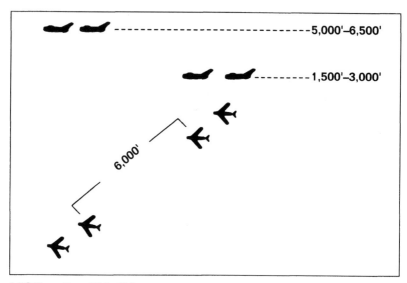

MiG Formation: Hi-Lo Pairs

flight and the second made a follow-up attack after the U.S. aircraft made their defensive move. One of the major advantages of hi-lo pairs was that often the U.S. fighters saw only the first pair and maneuvered against them; the second pair then could get in unobserved.

In stacked three, the lead MiG-17 was at 6,500 to 8,000 feet, with the second MiG one mile behind, flying in echelon about 40 degrees back, at an altitude of about 1,500 to 3,000 feet. The third MiG was about two miles directly behind the lead MiG at an altitude of about 5,000 feet. Generally the first MiG attacked the U.S. formation and the second MiG followed up if the U.S. defender made a descending turn (the normal defensive move). The third MiG would follow up to help either the first or second MiG and, since he could see both, could act as an airborne controller. A variation of this was for all three MiGs to attack different aircraft to force the strikers to drop their ordnance. MiG-17s also flew in wheels, especially when they were waiting to intercept a strike or were heavily engaged by F-4s.

MiG-21s generally flew at much higher altitudes and used slightly different formations with fewer numbers—generally two but never more than four. They flew a variation of hi-lo pairs called hi-lo singles, with single MiG-21s aligned in the same pattern as the pairs of MiG-17s. When

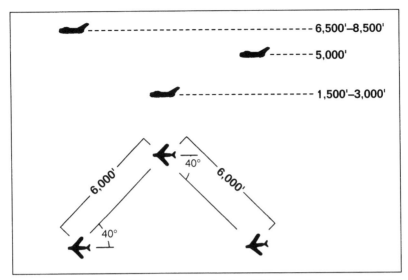

MiG Formation: Stacked Three. Often the leader of this formation was the last air-craft. From the rear position he could direct the attack and follow up with an attack on a vulnerable U.S. aircraft.

the MiG-21s flew in pairs, the wingman also might fly about 6,000 feet behind and 50 degrees to the leader's rear, where the leader could barely see him. Trail formations, especially when attacking, were common. Later in the war, single MiG-21s, with their transponders turned off and with no GCI help, made attacks from behind the strikers. U.S. intelligence speculated that these were North Vietnam's best pilots.[52]

The Most Important Thing

After Rolling Thunder, an important major report, the Weapons System and Evaluation Group's (WSEG) Red Baron I Study, concluded after ana-lyzing the Rolling Thunder engagements that "achieving a position to attack [fire] first was probably the most significant predictor of success in an attack."[53] This conclusion applied to both the Americans and North Vietnamese, but not equally. In engagements where U.S. aircraft destroyed MiGs, 84 percent of the time the fight began from either a posi-tion of U.S. advantage or a neutral position where neither side had the advantage (64 percent U.S. advantage and 20 percent neutral). When a U.S. aircraft was lost, the position was even more important: In 87 per-cent of the losses, the MiG began with an advantage, and in 10 percent

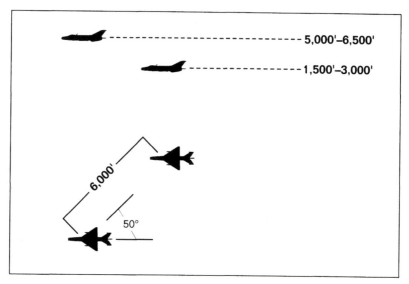

MiG Formation: Hi-Lo Singles

the fight began from a neutral position. (Only one U.S. loss was suffered when the U.S. fighter began with an advantage.)

Surprise most often provided this positional advantage, again on both sides. Forty-four percent of the MiGs that were shot down did not maneuver defensively, indicating that they never saw their attacker, and 58 percent of U.S. aircraft shot down probably were unaware that they were under MiG attack.[54]

In most engagements, the MiGs, with the aid of GCI, knew where the U.S. aircraft were and already had started their attack. The MiG's small size meant that, under normal circumstances, it could close to inside of two miles—Atoll range—behind a U.S. flight undetected, so when a U.S. aircraft saw a MiG-21 behind him, it usually was within a few seconds of firing or already firing. U.S. ground and airborne radar systems, unaided visual search, and existing fighter radar simply lacked the capability to prevent MiGs from making unobserved attacks from behind U.S. aircraft. Adding to the problem was that all of the U.S. fighters had restricted rearward visibility that could be only partially offset by aircraft maneuvering and formations that allowed the members of the flight to look behind each other. After the advent of the pod formations, the problem of seeing a MiG behind the formation increased because pod formations were so tight, they required a great deal of attention to fly; they also left blind spots behind the entire formation, unlike the wider ones flown earlier in the war. One F-105 pilot reflected on the tactical problems of flying a pod formation with MiGs in the area, commenting, "Pod formation is not a good look-out formation in a MiG environment. It's the worst kind of formation you can fly. You have restricted visibility and restricted movement. If you have a MiG shooting at you, it's dangerous to break [make a defensive turn] from a pod formation [because the other aircraft are so close]. It also doesn't lend itself to mutual support."[55]

The WSEG report said that the U.S. crews needed real-time position and direction information on enemy aircraft to reduce the number of undetected attacks from behind, and that *timely position information of the enemy aircraft was identified as the single most important requirement to enable U.S. aircrews to achieve a position to fire first.* If U.S. aircrews had real-time position and direction information on the MiGs, other things being equal, the WSEG believed the MiGs would seldom begin the engagement behind the U.S. aircraft. Since U.S. fighters were very successful in engagements when they detected the MiGs in front of them or to the sides, their kill ratio would have been significantly higher if they could have cut down the MiGs' undetected rear attacks.

Still, while U.S. F-4s and F-8s scored 75 percent of their MiG kills on the first attack, only 27 percent (41 out of 154) of U.S. first attacks resulted in a MiG kill. Most of the U.S. attacks failed because of the low reliability of some U.S. weapons, the limitations of these weapons in a close-in, maneuvering environment, and the tendency for U.S. pilots to fire out of parameters. The WSEG report concluded that any improvement in U.S. weapons or weapon delivery capability would result in an appreciable increase in the number of MiG kills (as the Navy had demonstrated with the AIM-9D).

The conclusion that the MiGs were successful because they could approach undetected was both seductively simple and left unanswered a critical question: If lack of position information was the only cause of the MiGs' successes, *why were the North Vietnamese MiGs more successful after the introduction of QRC-248 (which gave the U.S. aircraft accurate MiG locations) and Rivet Top?* From the middle of 1967, when Rivet Top and the QRC-248 were fully active, U.S. pilots reported that the MiG location information they received was very good, yet losses to MiGs soared.

Accepting that the inability to detect the MiGs was the problem meant it was a one-dimensional, technical one; this relieved the Air Force of having to deal with such troubling questions as why the air-to-air missiles performed so poorly, whether formations and tactics were correct, and if training programs were adequate. If unobserved MiGs were the problem, the Air Force's reasoning went, then the only way the United States could change the situation was to wait years to get a better GCI system, better missiles, better cockpit visibility, and better cockpit layouts. The leadership had done all it could—it simply needed better technology.

Finally, the WSEG report raised a disturbing possibility. When the MiGs approached the U.S. flights unseen, they had a success rate on their first observed firing pass of 13 percent, but according to the analysis, *the frequency of engagements in which the MiGs successfully arrived behind U.S. fighters undetected was **below** the potential achievable for the North Vietnamese GCI against penetrating aircraft dependent on visual detection. If the North Vietnamese were still in the early part of their learning curve, then the relative frequency of unobserved rear quadrant attacks could be expected to increase.* If the North Vietnamese were able to use their GCI more effectively, more North Vietnamese fighters could arrive behind U.S. aircraft before they were detected. In such a case, it was calculated the North Vietnamese would *double* their kills of U.S. aircraft for the same number of North Vietnamese losses.[56] This analysis would prove prophetic.

Part 2

LINEBACKER

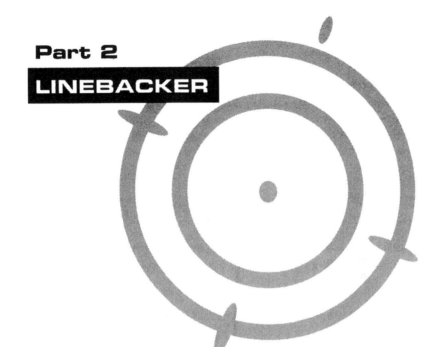

6

Preparing for the Next Round

Air Force and Navy Consider Rolling Thunder

The judgments about air-to-air combat during Rolling Thunder were a Rorschach test for the U.S. Air Force and Navy, and the two services drew almost exactly the opposite conclusions from their battles with the MiGs. The Air Force leadership looked at its losses to MiG-21s attacking virtually unseen from behind and decided that the problem was a technical one, so their solutions were technical; the Navy leadership looked at the results of its F-4 crews against the results of its well-trained F-8 pilots and decided that lack of training was the problem, and set about improving the Navy's air-to-air training program.

The Air Force's technical solutions did address some significant problems. Just after the end of Rolling Thunder the first F-4s with an internal cannon (the M-61 that had been used on the F-105 and in the F-4C and F-4D cannon pods), the F-4Es, arrived in Thailand. The M-61 was tied to an improved radar system that made its gunsight very efficient; overall, it was an excellent system.

The most important F-4 modification was the APX-80, a system similar to the QRC-248 enemy IFF interrogator, which had been so successful on the EC-121s. The new system was added to a few F-4Ds' radar and code named Combat Tree.[1] Tree, as it quickly came to be known, promised to offset the North Vietnamese GCI and finally allow these F-4Ds to tell if a radar target was a MiG so they could use the AIM-7s at long range. It would be a considerable breakthrough for the F-4D crews, but one might ask why it was so long in coming; British Mosquito night fighters in 1945 were using a device called "Perfecto" to interrogate German night fighters' IFF signals.[2]

But the Air Force was considerably less aggressive in trying to solve its missile problems, despite their poor performance in Rolling Thunder. There was no attempt to initiate a broad-based study to examine the causes, only a few disjointed efforts to improve the performance of the specific missiles. Air Force F-4s underwent modifications to their radar

An F-4E. Note the internal 20-mm cannon under the radome. The distinctive "shark's mouth" and the letters "JV" on the tail indicate the aircraft was based at Korat RTAFB. *USAF (courtesy of the National Archives)*

to improve results of firing the AIM-7 in the boresight mode so the mode would give better results,[3] and they tried incremental improvements to its two main air-to-air missiles, replacing the AIM-9B Sidewinder with the AIM-9E and the AIM-7E Sparrow with the improved AIM-7E-2.

The Air Force had high hopes for the AIM-7E-2 "dogfight Sparrow," an AIM-7 modified for use in the short minimum-range and high-G firings required in dogfights. The AIM-7E-2 had two modes, normal and dogfight. Normal provided the same performance as the AIM-7E, but in the dogfight mode the AIM-7E-2 had an electric plug, called a "minimum-range plug," installed in the missile's body. This plug (in theory) gave the AIM-7E-2 a minimum range of 1,500 feet instead of 3,000 feet, better fusing, and better capability against a maneuvering target;[4] virtually all of the AIM-7E-2s carried in combat had the minimum-range plug installed. The dogfight Sparrow was first delivered to the combat theater in August 1968, but when Rolling Thunder ended three months later, the Air Force halted its combat unit deployment. When MiG activity increased in late 1971, Seventh Air Force directed that all air-to-air sorties carry the AIM-7E-2 and deliveries to the theater resumed.

For reasons that remain unclear, the Air Force refused to replace the AIM-9B with the modifications of the Navy's AIM-9D, instead initially opting for the AIM-9E, a "cost-effective" improvement on the AIM-9B and visually almost identical. The "E" incorporated only a few modified components, leaving the AIM-9B's warhead, fuse, and motor untouched.[5] These limited modifications still left the AIM-9E's performance well below the AIM-9D, despite the fact that the AIM-9E was newer by two years.

To further improve its heat-seeking missiles, the Air Force started development of a new AIM-9, the AIM-9J, in November 1968. The AIM-9J was designed to be a "reliable weapon at close range against a maneuvering enemy fighter";[6] it had "cranked" canards and an improved control mechanism, and was expected to have a significantly improved hard turn capability over the AIM-9B/E (but it still kept the old rocket motor, warhead, and fuse). The results of the AIM-9Js' initial test firings against drones were mixed. Twelve of the thirteen test shots—92 percent—were successful, but while the success percentage was good, the average miss distance of 13.5 feet was no better than the earlier AIM-9s. It was clear more testing would be needed before the AIM-9J could be a satisfactory weapon,[7] but following the end of the initial tests in 1969 the test program was stopped and the entire AIM-9J program put on hold, reflecting the low priority the Air Force gave to air-to-air combat.[8] At about the same time, the deployment of the AIM-7E-2 to the combat squadrons in Southeast Asia also was stopped.

While the Air Force made some attempts to improve its missiles, it ignored the far less glamorous area of missile support equipment, despite the fact that it was well known that this equipment was responsible for many of the air-to-air missile failures. One particular area where combat wing commanders had begged for improvement was in missile maintenance. Air-to-air missiles could not be calibrated or checked out on the aircraft; they had to be taken off the aircraft and driven to a special test facility for testing and maintenance. Because this was so time consuming during combat operations and because of the difficulty, periodic maintenance generally was ignored, which clearly contributed to the missile failures. When a wing did make the effort to keep its missiles properly maintained, the missiles had to be carried over rough roads to the maintenance facility on missile transport vehicles that had no shock absorbers. One wing commander wrote, "We cannot now assure careful handling of these costly weapons. Our missiles moved over four miles of poor roads on unsprung trailers whenever they went to calibrations and checkout or storage."[9] The bouncing these delicate weapons received was considered one of the many reasons for the failures.

Training and Tactics

The Air Force essentially ignored the possibility of improving their air combat results by examining their training and tactics. Because of opposition from TAC and the Fighter Weapons School, the idea of looking at new fighter formations was completely out of the question. Additionally, TAC directed that the F-4 RTUs concentrate on training crews to drop bombs, and to reduce the number of air-to-air training sorties—already considered inadequate—from twenty-four to six.[10] The deemphasis of air-to-air combat training was not limited to the RTUs—TAC and the Air Force as a whole cut down on air-to-air training. In fact, one F-4 wing in England did not fly a single air-to-air training mission in over three years![11] A few classes of F-4 crews received advanced training at the Fighter Weapons School every year, but they were trained in both air-to-ground and air-to-air, with the emphasis on air-to-ground. Not only did TAC F-4 pilots do less training in air-to-air combat, but virtually all of their training was against other F-4s—large, smoking, and relatively unmaneuverable. This was hardly good preparation for combat with small, agile MiGs. Handicapped by poor formations, and forbidden to do air-to-air combat training except under the most benign of conditions, the Air Force's operational tactical wings' air-to-air combat skills continued to decline.

An indication of how little emphasis air-to-air combat received can be found in the Fighter Weapons School's official quarterly magazine, the *Fighter Weapons Review*, an unclassified journal featuring articles on various technical-, weapons-, and tactics-oriented subjects. The *Fighter Weapons Review*'s articles emphasize the school's most important current areas of interest, and from 1968 through 1971, out of approximately 112 articles, only seven were on air-to-air combat. One of those seven articles was especially interesting: Written for the Spring 1971 issue by a U.S. Air Force officer, it explained the German Air Force's use of loose deuce—called "double attack"—and pointed out its advantages and disadvantages compared to fluid four. At the end of article the *Fighter Weapons Review*'s editor felt obligated to include a disclaimer stating that the article was not an endorsement of double attack,[12] but apparently this was not enough for the Air Force's leadership. The next two issues included articles giving the party line—that fluid four was the only way for Air Force fighter pilots to fly.[13]

Leadership

It remains difficult to explain why TAC, despite the failures of the last six months of Rolling Thunder, was willing to cut down on air-to-air training, stop the development of improved air-to-air missiles, and not bring in innovative leaders to improve their training programs, since TAC was responsible for "maintain[ing] peak combat efficiency in the tactical missions for fighter, reconnaissance and tactical airlift operations. It [TAC] further trains air and ground crews as required for the overseas commands of the United States Air Forces in Europe and the Pacific Air Forces."[14] Their inaction is especially surprising since the commander of TAC during this period was Gen. William Momyer, the former commander of Seventh Air Force, which had suffered so much at the hands of the MiGs. One might expect that, after watching Air Force losses to MiGs in the later stages of Rolling Thunder, General Momyer would have taken drastic steps when he took over TAC. TAC might have been expected to increase the training levels of air-to-air aircrews going into combat, try to solve the poor performance of the air-to-air missiles, and tell the Fighter Weapons School to reexamine Air Force tactics to offset the new MiG attack patterns. None of these were done, despite the fact that all would not only have been useful in Southeast Asia but also in Europe in the event of a war with the Soviets.

The choice of leaders also reflected TAC's lack of interest in improving its air training. The commander of the 8th TFW was almost universally acknowledged as the best air-to-air leader in Southeast Asia. Under his command, the wing had compiled a remarkable air-to-air record and, more importantly, had consistently come up with new and innovative tactics.[15] Not only was the wing commander an excellent tactician, he was a World War II ace and a four-MiG killer in Vietnam. He was promoted to brigadier general after his tour as the 8th TFW commander, and one might expect that he would have been immediately assigned to TAC to work on improving training and tactics. Not so; he was sent to the U.S. Air Force Academy to supervise the cadets, who were years away from flying combat.

The Navy Reaction

The Navy's reaction to the air-to-air combat results during Rolling Thunder was much more in-depth and far-reaching than the Air Force's. The Navy had introduced some new technology—the AIM-7E-2 dogfight Sparrow was sent to the fleet; an improved F-4, the F-4J, had been deployed in its carriers in the summer of 1968; and the excellent AIM-9D was scheduled to be replaced with an even better heat seeker, the AIM-9G—but the Navy did not believe that these technological improvements would solve their problems in air-to-air combat. The air combat results had sent a clear message: The superbly trained F-8 pilots (using AIM-9s) had thirteen kills in 1967–1968 for no losses versus the poor results of the F-4 crews with the AIM-7. To find a solution, in May 1968 the Navy directed one of its officers, Capt. Frank Ault, to find out why its missiles, especially the AIM-7, had performed so poorly in combat, and to offer suggestions about how to solve the problems of the missiles and other air combat issues.

Ault examined the problem in depth, from the manufacturers, the handling of the missiles en route to the Navy, the handling on the carrier, the maintenance, and the employment by the F-4 crews. He provided an extremely detailed report—the *Ault Report*—that offered a variety of observations and suggestions for improving the missiles. While the analysis of the missiles was meticulous, a small portion of the report attracted much greater attention and had the greatest long-term impact. In this portion, Ault noted that the Navy had lost its air-to-air combat skills and that many of the problems with the AIM-7—and with the Navy's air combat results in general—were simply because Navy F-4 crews especially were poorly trained in air-to-air combat. He recommended that a program be set up to improve their training, pointing out that such a program could be started almost immediately.

This was an idea whose time had come. For many years the Navy had a Fleet Air Gunnery Unit (FAGU) where gunnery skills were taught and practiced, but with the advent of missiles the unit had been abolished. The Navy fighter community believed that ever since the FAGU had been deactivated the Navy's air-to-air combat skills had deteriorated, and the service needed a program—a Navy Fighter Weapons School—to bring these skills back.[16] Navy fighter pilots, led by the F-8 community, had been lobbying for such a program for some time, and several of these "true believers" had been sent to "help" Ault with his report. They freely admitted that they already knew the answer before they began to write the report. The true believers had laid the groundwork well, and the results of Ault's recommendation were almost immediate. A Navy Fighter Weapons School—quickly named Topgun—was approved and set up at the Miramar Naval Air Station in California; unlike the Air Force Fighter Weapons School, Topgun concentrated entirely on air-to-air combat. On March 3, 1969, the first Topgun class arrived, made up of F-4 crews from all over the Navy, and the sole purpose of the course was to teach them how to dogfight in the F-4.

This was not a new idea. Shortly after the beginning of the Vietnam War the Navy recognized that their F-4 crews were not as proficient in air-to-air combat as they should have been, and in early 1966 the chief of naval operations directed a program called Project Plan to review the effectiveness of Navy missiles and air-to-air tactics. Navy Air Development Squadron Four flew Project Plan to determine if "the F-4, notwithstanding the fact that someone forgot to put guns in it, [could] be utilized as an air superiority fighter and how does it compare with other contemporary fighter [aircraft] in this role?"[17]

The tests involved flying Navy F-4Bs against a variety of fighters—Navy F-8s as well as Air Force F-105s and F-104s—to try to develop F-4 tactics. The Project Plan report was not nearly as pessimistic about the F-4's air-to-air capability as the Air Force's Feather Duster. It said that, contrary to what the F-4 pilots might think, the F-4 was the best air-to-air fighter in the world, including the F-8, if the F-4 stayed fast. The Navy emphasized climbing away from the MiGs and then diving on them, called "maneuvering in the vertical." These vertical maneuvers—loops and oblique loops—kept the F-4 in its best performing environment and made it very difficult for any other aircraft to follow it. Project Plan recommended beginning the engagement above Mach 1 and staying low and fast—about 570–600 knots—for best dogfight performance.

Project Plan also emphasized how well the F-4 fit into standard Navy fighter tactics. It found loose deuce especially effective in the F-4 because the back seater could look out the back for attackers while the front seater looked forward at the fight.[18] But despite the Project Plan results, at the time there was no formal mechanism for training the fleet F-4 crews on how to dogfight the Phantom.

Now, with Topgun, the F-4 crews had a place to learn. The Topgun crews did not fight against other F-4s but against other aircraft like the F-8 and A-4; these aircraft simulated the MiGs because they were smaller and more maneuverable than the F-4s, but they lacked the Phantom's power and acceleration. The Topgun crews also flew against Air Force aircraft, usually the delta-wing F-106, which was considered a good MiG-21 simulator. Surprisingly—or perhaps not—the F-106s were not from TAC but from the Air Defense Command, which was responsible for defending the United States against bomber attack.

From the beginning, Topgun emphasized using the AIM-9D rather than the AIM-7. This was a real change in Navy F-4 tactics, but the Ault Report and combat experience showed the AIM-7 simply was not reliable. In addition to learning how to dogfight the F-4, the Topgun instructors (many ex-F-8 pilots) emphasized that the aim of the program was to teach the graduates to train the other crews in their squadrons how to dogfight. The art of debriefing was the heart of air-to-air training; this was where most of the learning took place, and the graduates had to be able to do it accurately and professionally. The student crews were taught how to remember what went on in each engagement and how to debrief it carefully and clearly so that everyone understood what had happened and could learn from it.

The Navy now felt prepared for a new round of air combat anywhere in the world. Project Plan and Topgun had validated the loose deuce tactical formation and brought the Navy's F-4 pilots up to the same skill level as the Rolling Thunder F-8 pilots (although the F-8 pilots would argue that point). Navy F-4 pilots were now trained to eschew the use of the AIM-7 and maneuver for shots with the very reliable AIM-9D and the new AIM-9G. New Navy F-4s also had a new radar, called a pulse doppler radar, with a capability to look down and pick up MiGs at low altitude.

North Vietnamese Improvements

As soon as it became clear that Rolling Thunder was over, the North Vietnamese began to make major improvements in their air defense system. During the ensuing three-and-a-half-year bombing halt the North Vietnamese Air Force steadily increased and improved its MiG force. At the end of Rolling Thunder the North Vietnamese Air Force consisted of approximately 150 MiGs—112 MiG-17s and 38 MiG-21s. By May 1970, the total force had risen to about 265 MiGs—140 MiG-17s, 31 MiG-19s (discussed below), and 94 MiG-21s. Some of the MiG-17s were modified to carry Atoll missiles, and the number of MiG-21s and MiG-19s tripled the modern fighters available to its core of aggressive, confident, combat-skilled pilots.

The high numbers of new MiG-21s were significant, but the MiG-19s were also a major addition. The MiG-19 was a mid-1950s fighter, a contemporary of the American F-100 Super Sabre, but vastly superior in almost every aspect of performance. But while it was the first fighter in Europe capable of level supersonic flight, the MiG-19 was not an instant success. The early versions had severe control and hydraulic problems that caused numerous crashes, and the Soviet Air Force lost confidence in the aircraft. By the time the MiG-19's problems were solved with a later model, the MiG-19S *(Stabilizator)*, the Soviets had become enamored of the Mach 2 MiG-21 and were committed to the more advanced fighter. The MiG-19s mainly were sent to ground attack units or fobbed off on Soviet satellites and allies. Communist China especially built a large number of the improved MiG-19s, first under license and later—after their break with the Soviet Union—on their own.[19]

While lacking the top speed of the MiG-21, the improved MiG-19S turned out to be a fine day fighter. Like the other MiGs it was small, but the MiG-19 was visually distinctive, with very sharply swept wings with a large "fence" on top. Fortunately, the Chinese had supplied MiG-19s to

A post-Vietnam picture of a Chinese-provided Pakistani F-6 (MiG-19S). Note the sharply swept wings with large wing fences and the two heat-seeking missiles outboard of the external fuel tanks. Ironically, these missiles are AIM-9Ps, the export version of the AIM-9J carried by 432nd TRW F-4s during the latter part of Linebacker. Many North Vietnamese MiG-19s carried Atolls on these stations. *Jay Miller*

Pakistan, and U.S. pilots and intelligence officers had the opportunity to fly the aircraft and assess its capabilities.[20] They found the MiG-19's wing loading was slightly higher than the MiG-17 but well below that of the F-4; like the MiG-17, the MiG-19 could easily out-turn the Phantom in a slow- or medium-speed engagement, and it also had maneuvering flaps that, set to 15 degrees, increased its rate of turn below 460 knots. But, unlike the MiG-17, the MiG-19 had excellent acceleration—it could out-accelerate an F-4 out to Mach 1.2—and had a top speed of about 620 knots (Mach 1.6),[21] slower than the MiG-21 and F-4, but still fast enough to make outrunning it difficult. It also had good visibility from the cockpit and a heavy fixed armament of three 30-mm cannon[22] that were notable for their large muzzle flash. Like the MiG-21 and some MiG-17s, the MiG-19 carried two Atoll heat-seeking missiles. U.S. Air Force pilots found the MiG-19 had many shortcomings but overall considered it an excellent fighter.[23] Its major problem was its very short range, and one U.S. pilot who flew it said "in afterburner at low altitude and high speed [the MiG-19 pilot] will be looking for a place to land after about 5 minutes."[24] It was also noted that, unlike other Soviet fighters, the MiG-19 was very difficult to maintain.[25]

The larger number of MiGs required new pilots who were trained by the combat veterans in the weaknesses and strengths of the American air forces and on how to work with their own air defense system. The veteran pilots and GCI controllers, meanwhile, trained hard on their proven tactics and on how to develop new tactics should they have to go back into combat. This North Vietnamese training, coupled with continuing deterioration of the air-to-air training of U.S. Air Force pilots, would greatly improve the relative combat efficiency of the growing MiG force.[26]

The North Vietnamese also continued to expand their radar control network, which the Americans considered the key to their successes during Rolling Thunder. The air defense network was reorganized into five sectors, each with four subsections: air surveillance sites, subcontrol stations, filter centers, and weapons operations centers. The North Vietnamese also increased the total number of radars and built new radar sites in the southern and western parts of North Vietnam, which provided radar coverage deep into Laos and South Vietnam. Also integrated into the system was their extremely effective SIGINT communications intelligence force, which listened in on the American communications and relayed this information to the overall air defense network, apparently without the restrictions that hampered the American SIGINT effort.

Additionally, North Vietnam rehabilitated and expanded its airfields. During Rolling Thunder the North Vietnamese used basically three MiG bases—Kep, Phuc Yen, and Gia Lam. After the end of the bombing, they began to repair the airfields at Vinh and Dong Hoi in the panhandle of North Vietnam and built major new MiG airfields at Doung Suong, Quan Lang, and Yen Bai. These new bases, combined with the new GCI sites, extended the MiGs' potential operating areas to south of the Demilitarized Zone (DMZ) and nearly anywhere in Laos.

In the War Zone

In the combat zone, from November 1968 until mid-1971 the air war was comatose. The American bases in Thailand that had been the backbone of Rolling Thunder now concentrated on interdicting personnel and supplies moving along the road network from North Vietnam through Laos into South Vietnam—a network known as the "Ho Chi Minh Trail"—and supporting U.S. Laotian allies in northern Laos. The Americans considered stopping this flow of supplies vital for a successful end to the war, so day and night U.S. aircraft pounded the trail. The number of Navy carriers off shore also dropped, and their planes bombed either in South Vietnam—where there was virtually no threat—or joined Air Force operations in Laos. For the U.S. aircraft striking the Ho Chi Minh Trail and in northern Laos, compared to the Route Packages, the defenses in Laos were very limited—37-mm and lower AAA without radar control, no SAMs or MiGs—and the American recollection of how to deal with MiGs, SAMs, and high-threat areas gradually faded as the crews rotated annually. Air Force F-4 crews in Thailand realized that their relatively limited air combat skills were disappearing. Paradoxically, the crews of the new F-4Es (which had arrived in Thailand just after Rolling Thunder and were the first F-4s equipped with an internal cannon) said their skills—which they felt were considerable before they arrived in Thailand—"were going steadily downhill" in the combat zone because PACAF prevented them from doing any air combat training after their combat missions. A few months after they arrived F-4E pilots said that they "would be a poor match for MiGs were things to start up again in NVN."[27]

Gradually came the steady drumbeat of withdrawals. In June 1970 the College Eye Task Force left Thailand, and it soon became clear that even the days of the venerable F-105 were numbered. The F-105 production line had closed and losses could not be replaced; its main redeeming characteristic, high speed, was of no use over Laos and South Vietnam, and at that time there were no SAMs in Laos, so the Wild Weasels were not needed. The F-4 carried more bombs, was perceived to be more survivable because of its two engines, and was still in production in improved versions. On November 24, 1969, all remaining F-105s in Southeast Asia (four tactical fighter squadrons) consolidated at Takhli, Thailand, to maximize management efficiency, and less than a year later—in October 1970—F-105 operations in Southeast Asia terminated, with three F-105 squadrons sent to other western Pacific bases or the United States and one squadron disbanded.

There was a brief flurry of activity in early 1970 when, on January 28, a U.S. HH-53 rescue helicopter was waiting in Laos for clearance to go into North Vietnam to attempt a pickup of an F-105 Wild Weasel crew shot down by ground fire. Two MiG-21s, staying at low altitude to avoid U.S. radar detection, ducked in and out of the mountains and pounced on the large, helpless HH-53, shooting it down with Atolls and escaping back across the border to North Vietnam. Three months later, on March 28, a Navy F-4 escorting a reconnaissance flight shot down a MiG-21 with two AIM-9Ds. After that there was very little activity until November 3, 1970, when SAM equipment was photographed in southern North Vietnam in the vicinity of Mu Gia and Ban Karai passes, two of the main centers of activity for the North Vietnamese truck convoys down the Ho Chi Minh Trail. The possibility that the North Vietnamese might be moving

SAMs into Laos quickly brought the F-105s back to Southeast Asia, and in late November the 6010th Tactical Fighter Squadron (TFS), equipped with new F-105Gs, was activated at Korat RTAFB, Thailand.

In 1971, slowly—indeed, almost imperceptibly—the air war began to change. On March 22, an F-4 flying escort for a reconnaissance aircraft was shot down near Dong Hoi, North Vietnam; this was the first U.S. Air Force aircraft lost to a SAM since February 1968. Another loss soon followed on April 26 when an Air Force O-2, a small propeller-driven light plane used to control air strikes, became the first U.S. aircraft lost to a SAM over Laos. By summer of 1971 U.S. intelligence noted that the North Vietnamese were vigorously building up their supplies close to the border with South Vietnam. The U.S. pilots that flew the daily reconnaissance missions saw the supplies piled up in North Vietnam, just inside the border but as untouchable as if they were on the moon, and the pilots were considerably frustrated knowing that these supplies would soon be on their way to South Vietnam.

Gradually the North Vietnamese defenses became aggressive, and more U.S. reconnaissance aircraft flying over North Vietnam were fired on by AAA. Finally the attacks grew so severe that Air Force fighter escorts had no choice but to attack the AAA positions. The first crews that attacked the AAA sites were expecting a negative reaction from Washington; to their surprise their "protective reaction strikes" were greeted not by the critical questions they expected but by, "Attaboy, hit them harder next time" from higher headquarters. A few days later there was another protective reaction strike, with the same reaction. It began to dawn on the pilots that the Nixon administration was not going to nitpick like the Johnson administration had. The U.S. crews, frustrated by flying over the huge buildups of supplies in North Vietnam, needed little encouragement, and soon a protective reaction strike was taking place almost every day.

The North Vietnamese were not long in countering; they gradually began to move their SAMs into Laos and became much more aggressive with the missiles; from October through December 1971 forty-eight SAMs were fired at U.S. aircraft in Laos and southern North Vietnam, as opposed to only two the three months prior. On December 13, 1971, there occurred an event that highlighted poor Air Force training: An F-4 was attacked by SA-2s, and while turning to avoid them, the pilot lost control of his Phantom because of adverse yaw, forcing the crew to bail out. The maneuvers used to avoid SAMs were much the same as those used in a dogfight, and the poor air-to-air training that U.S. crews were receiving began to take its toll.

MiGs were moving, too; by the end of August 1971 the North Vietnamese had moved MiG-21s to the Bai Thuong airfield in southern North Vietnam, and from this point forward MiGs maintained an almost continuous presence south of the 20th parallel. MiG activity from these airfields increased as they began to harass U.S. aircraft conducting attacks on the Ho Chi Minh Trail. Many of the aircraft involved in the interdiction campaign in Laos were "slow movers"—propeller-driven gunships, command and control aircraft, forward air controllers, or helicopters—and B-52s, whose strikes were occasionally very effective and which were much feared by the North Vietnamese. All were very vulnerable to MiG attack.

On October 4, 1971, a MiG from one of the southern airfields attempted to intercept a three-ship formation—called a "cell"—of B-52s on a bombing mission in southern Laos. The MiG closed to within ten miles of the formation before he turned back without firing. In response, on November 8 U.S. fighters struck the Quan Lang airfield in a protective reaction strike. Damage was slight and the North Vietnamese reaction swift. MiGs were sent to southern Laos on November 11, 12, and 13; more seriously, on November 20, a MiG-21 again attacked three B-52s bombing close to the North Vietnam/Laos border. The B-52s were warned of the attack and turned away from the target, but as they did so the MiG attacked from behind. He passed behind the third B-52 and fired his Atolls at the second bomber, but by this time the B-52s were dropping flares to decoy the heat-seeking missiles, and the Atolls missed.[28]

To attack the B-52s, the North Vietnamese GCI watched the bombers while MiG-21s flew at very low altitude—below U.S. radar coverage—until they were in position, and the MiGs climbed to attack; after attacking they dived for low altitude and escaped. The tactics used against the B-52s were not the best for attacking the big bombers, but they ensured that the MiGs would get into position undetected until the last minute and would be very difficult for any fighter escort to counter. This increasing MiG activity forced U.S. planners to provide additional protection for vulnerable missions flown within the threat areas. One form of protection was the activation of air defense alert facilities at Udorn and Da Nang, where air-to-air configured F-4s sat on five-minute alert to protect the missions in Laos.

As an additional counter to the MiG activity, the EC-121s of the College Eye Task Force, which left Thailand in June 1970, were brought back to Korat RTAFB to begin flying missions in an orbit over northern Laos. The College Eye Task Force—now going by the radio call sign Disco—was now flying EC-121Ts, which had replaced the EC-121D in 1971. The EC-121T carried the QRC-248 IFF interrogator and the Rivet Top language stations, called Rivet Gym.[29]

During late November and through December 1971, the MiGs changed the focus of their activities from southern Laos to northern Laos, especially around the Plain de Jars. The Plain de Jars and the surrounding areas were the location of an ongoing "secret" war between Laotian forces, supported by the United States, and the Paphet Lao insurgency group, supported by North Vietnam. Large numbers of U.S. aircraft—both military and from the CIA's air arm, Air America—were active in this area day and night and, as in southern Laos, most were slow movers very vulnerable to MiG attack. The MiGs would sweep down into Laos, often at night, and force the U.S. aircraft in the area to scatter and fall back; then the MiGs would turn back into North Vietnam. Because it was at the closest base to the area, the 432nd Tactical Reconnaissance Wing at Udorn responded to these moves by scrambling its fighters from its alert pad,[30] but the U.S. fighters trying to counter these MiG sweeps found themselves at a severe disadvantage because the MiGs stayed at low altitude. Even with the EC-121s, GCI coverage over northern Laos was very limited at low altitude, while the MiGs had excellent GCI coverage (though their coverage at very low altitude also was limited).

In response to the MiG activity, in early December 1971 the Air Force deployed eight F-4Ds equipped with the APX-80 Combat Tree IFF interrogator to Udorn. The Tree equipment worked as advertised, but despite the vast improvement in detection capability, a Tree return did not automatically give the F-4s freedom to fire at the target. The Tree F-4Ds had strict Rules of Engagement about how close friendly aircraft could be to the MiG before they could fire on the Tree return. If the MiG was coming head on, the friendly aircraft had to be about 15 miles away before the Tree F-4D could fire; if the Tree F-4D was attacking from behind the MiG, it could fire if the friendly aircraft were 5 miles away.[31] Any closer—or if there were any doubt about the range or identity of the target—the Tree F-4D had to identify visually the radar return before firing.[32] In that event, even when the F-4D could not fire early, Tree was still useful because it told the F-4 crew that a MiG was in the area and allowed them to set up their visual identification pass knowing that they were probably attacking a MiG. Tree also vastly cut down on the time and fuel wasted on chasing radar targets that turned out to be friendly, and it allowed the F-4s to locate MiGs on radar without GCI (Red Crown and Disco) help. Since radio communication between the F-4s and the GCI agencies was always problematical, this was another tremendous advantage.

Also in December the MiGs stopped their simple harassment and "got down to business." Beginning on December 18, Air Force F-4s from Udorn and North Vietnamese MiG-21s began seriously to engage, but despite the Tree equipment, these first engagements were a tragic comedy of errors for the F-4s. On that day, Falcon 66, a single F-4D, was covering a helicopter extraction of a CIA combat team in northern Laos when he received a garbled MiG warning. Suddenly there was a large explosion in the back of the F-4; the Phantom went out of control and the crew ejected (it later was determined that he was hit by an Atoll from a MiG-21). Rescue forces headed into the area to pick up the crew, and two more Udorn F-4s, Falcon 74 and Falcon 75, were sent to cover the rescue helicopters. As they began their orbit, Red Crown, the Navy GCI ship, reported MiGs closing on their position. Falcon 74 and Falcon 75 turned toward the MiGs, and the MiGs turned back into North Vietnam with the two F-4s pursuing in full afterburner. The MiGs stayed tantalizingly out of range until the F-4s were low on fuel and had to turn back to Thailand; then several more MiGs began to close from behind. The F-4s turned back to engage, then after a few futile turns again tried to escape. On their way out several SAMs were fired at the flight, and the F-4s became separated as they were forced into a series of fuel-consuming evasive maneuvers. Falcon 74, now critically low on fuel, ran for the border at low altitude to avoid more SAMs; the F-4 just made it to Laos before it ran out of fuel and the crew ejected. Falcon 75 was not so lucky; his last radio call indicated that he had 75 pounds[33] of fuel remaining (a few seconds) and was trying to make it to the coast; the crew was not recovered.

Escalation

In the last three weeks of 1971 the air war increased significantly as ten American aircraft were shot down over North Vietnam and Laos. The North Vietnamese became steadily more aggressive in firing on U.S. reconnaissance aircraft over North Vietnam, and the United States was more aggressive in striking back with protective reaction strikes. The U.S. decided to send a massive, one-time message to the North Vietnamese: Beginning on December 26, after a series of weather delays, it launched Operation Proud Deep Alpha, a five-day, 1,000-sortie bombing attack on supplies and air defenses in southern North Vietnam. Unfortunately, the northeast monsoon was in full swing, and the weather was so bad that most of the strikes had to drop their bombs on instruments. The strikes were not effective; as one official U.S. Air Force history noted, Proud Deep Alpha was "beset with problems and disappointments from initial planning through final execution." The North Vietnamese reacted by expanding and thickening their SA-2 missile network around the DMZ while continuing their massive buildup of supplies on the border of South Vietnam. U.S. intelligence believed the buildup was the prelude to a full-scale invasion.

Despite the occasional protective reaction strikes, the United States generally let the North Vietnamese build up their forces close to South Vietnam from late 1971 through early 1972, much to the distress of U.S. military leaders. What the military did not know was that President Richard Nixon and Secretary of State Henry Kissinger had been conducting a new, secret round of peace talks with Hanoi since late 1971, hoping to end the war before the United States finished its promised withdrawal from South Vietnam. Nixon also was concerned with other foreign policy issues that would have an impact on his Vietnam policy, especially a visit to then-Peking in mid-February 1972 and a planned visit later to Moscow. Thus, despite the North Vietnamese buildup, Nixon and Kissinger took the calculated risk that they would be able to complete the negotiations before the North Vietnamese took military action.

A potential invasion put the United States in a difficult position. Since Nixon's election in 1968, the United States had begun a gradual withdrawal of forces from Vietnam; by the end of 1971, not only had many ground combat troops come out, but the United States had withdrawn more than 400 combat aircraft from Southeast Asia, and there were only two Navy carriers off the Vietnam coast, instead of the four that were there during Rolling Thunder.

Still, as the situation began to deteriorate, the Nixon administration was determined to continue the negotiations but was equally determined not to be seen as backing down militarily. It was politically impossible to send ground troops back, so the United States began reinforcing with more aircraft. The trickle of replacements became a flood: A squadron of Wild Weasels deployed to Korat RTAFB, Thailand; two squadrons of F-4Es deployed to Ubon RTAFB; a squadron of F-4Ds arrived at Udorn; and another squadron of F-4Ds deployed to Da Nang Air Base.

Meanwhile, the MiG-21 flights into Laos continued. In December the MiGs had made twenty-one incursions; in January 1972 the number rose to thirty-three, but despite the Tree equipment no MiGs were shot down as missile problems returned to plague U.S. forces. Late on the afternoon of January 15, Denver, a pair of Tree-equipped F-4Ds, attacked a single MiG-21. Denver 1, using his Tree equipment, was able to locate and lock on to the MiG. The two F-4s fired a total of nine missiles (five AIM-7s and four AIM-4Ds) at the MiG, all well within the missile parameters. All missed (two AIM-4s did not leave the rail), and the MiG escaped. Two days later Phoenix, another pair of Tree F-4Ds, scrambled from Udorn for another early evening intercept of two MiG-21s in Laos. This time the situation was reversed and the MiGs gained the upper hand, but missile malfunctions were not limited to the Americans: All three of the Atolls fired by the MiGs missed.

It was up to the well-trained Navy F-4 pilots to provide the first MiG kills of the new air war. On January 19, Showtime, a flight of two F-4Js, was escorting a reconnaissance flight over North Vietnam when they were fired upon by a number of SAMs. As Showtime 1 maneuvered to escape the missiles at 15,000 feet he saw two MiG-21s passing below him at very low altitude. Showtime 1 dived behind them, but as he prepared to fire the MiGs executed what would become their classic defensive maneuver, with the lead MiG-21 turning into the F-4s while the second continued straight ahead and separated. As the first MiG turned, Showtime 1 realized from his training that he was in the MiG's blind area and that it had not seen him; the North Vietnamese pilot was maneuvering in response to a GCI warning. Showtime 1 stayed in a position where he was out of sight, and soon the MiG rolled out of his turn; Showtime 1 then pulled behind him and fired a single AIM-9 that flew up the MiG's tailpipe and exploded.

The Air Force soon followed with its first kill of 1972. Udorn F-4s were now regularly patrolling over northern Laos, and on February 21 it paid off when Falcon 62 and Falcon 63, two Tree F-4Ds, received vectors in the direction of MiGs coming into Laos. The two F-4s became separated, but Falcon 62 locked on to the radar targets and used his Tree to confirm they were the MiGs, then fired three AIM-7E-2s, the first at 11 miles, the second at eight, and the third at six. The first missile detonated with a small explosion; the second detonated with a similar small explosion, followed by a large secondary explosion that marked the end of the MiG. The F-4s turned to leave, but the engagement was not over. There were two more MiG-21s behind the first one and they chased the F-4s for 30 miles. The North Vietnamese had been expecting an interception by the F-4s and had set a trap; this time it closed empty.[34]

The cat-and-mouse activity between the MiGs and the Tree F-4Ds continued, and on the night of March 1, Falcon 54 and Falcon 55, two Tree-equipped F-4Ds, were flying a night MiGCAP over Laos when they received information of MiG activity. To try to bring the MiGs down, the F-4s made bogus radio calls saying they were short of fuel. The North Vietnamese took the bait, and immediately two MiG-21s turned toward the F-4s. The MiGs closed and the F-4s turned back, dropped low to get under GCI coverage, and after confirming they were MiGs on the Tree, made a head-on pass. Falcon 55 fired three Sparrows; the first two malfunctioned, but the third destroyed the MiG.

While the Air Force was now scoring at night, the Navy continued to dominate the day action. On the afternoon of March 6, a Navy reconnaissance aircraft over North Vietnam was attacked by several MiGs. The F-4 escort engaged, and during the engagement a two-ship section of F-4Bs, Old Nick, was launched from its carrier to help. Under control of Red Crown (at this time the cruiser USS *Chicago*), Old Nick waited south of the fight in the hope of cutting off the MiGs as they returned to their base. After a few minutes Red Crown vectored the F-4s toward a MiG; as the F-4s approached they did not see the MiG, then the Red Crown controller told them to "look low," and Old Nick saw a MiG-17 attacking from below. Old Nick 1 engaged the MiG while Old Nick 2 flew wide support in typical loose deuce formation. Old Nick 1 was unable to get a shot at the hard-turning MiG but forced it down to a very low altitude and very slow airspeed. Old Nick 1 then separated and the MiG turned to follow; Old Nick 2 dropped behind the MiG and destroyed him with a single AIM-9D. As the MiG crashed, Red Crown warned Old Nick they were being attacked by four MiG-21s; now low on fuel, the F-4s separated and outran the MiGs.

The excellent control from Red Crown revealed another aspect of the Navy's emphasis on air-to-air combat: Navy GCI controllers had also had extensive training in controlling fighters in air-to-air combat. It is worth noting that the Red Crown GCI controller this particular day was generally considered the best American GCI controller in the war. He was credited with controlling U.S. fighters—Air Force as well as Navy—to thirteen MiG kills from March through May 1972.[35]

The Blow Falls: The North Vietnamese Invasion

Nixon and Kissinger's gamble—that they could complete peace talks with Hanoi before a North Vietnamese invasion—failed. On March 30, 1972, the North Vietnamese launched a massive, three-pronged attack into South Vietnam, and for the first time the conflict turned into a real conventional war as the North Vietnamese used tanks and regular divisions in the attack. At first the North Vietnamese, with no American ground forces to oppose them, did well. They were able to take advantage of the bad weather at the end of the northeast monsoon: With the weather protecting them from air strikes and encountering poorly trained South Vietnamese Army units, the North Vietnamese Army made good progress.

They also brought a new air defense weapon that was an unpleasant surprise to the American and South Vietnamese air forces: the hand-held SA-7 heat-seeking missile. The SA-7 was an unsophisticated system—the "Saturday night special" of SAMs—but it was very effective against slow-moving aircraft, especially forward air controllers, helicopters, and the propeller-driven South Vietnamese A-1 Skyraiders. In their operational debut, North Vietnamese SA-7s brought down four U.S. aircraft attempting a rescue operation.

Possibly, the North Vietnamese expected a minor, weak U.S. response; if so, they badly miscalculated. Now that the North Vietnamese had made their move and the prospect of successful negotiations had disappeared, Nixon was determined to use air power to its fullest. He assured U.S. air commanders that they would not have to put up with the micromanagement of the bombing campaign they had during the Johnson administration, and he asked for their input as to how to hit at the North Vietnamese. Unfortunately, despite the political decision to strike, most of the U.S. air power was grounded by the bad weather during the first days of the invasion, much to the frustration of the White House. As the North Vietnamese successes mounted, one Nixon administration official decided that "our Air Force consisted of delicate machines only capable of flying in a war in the desert in July" and caustically suggested to the Air Force leadership "that if they could not fly maybe they could taxi north for twenty five miles."[36]

Even more frustrating to Nixon and Kissinger was the mindset of the military. Air Force and Navy commanders were unprepared for the option of a massive use of air power and were somewhat taken aback by Nixon and Kissinger's aggressive stance. Under the Johnson administration, they had been severely criticized when they suggested heavy air strikes into North Vietnam: "Bomb, bomb, bomb, that's all you [the Joint Chiefs of Staff] know," Johnson was said to have commented.[37] Now the Nixon administration expected the military to make the same types of suggestions that had been rejected just a few years before. Initially the process did not go well; Nixon wrote that the "bombing proposals sent to me by the Pentagon could best be described as timid," and Kissinger, after trying to prod the military into action, bemoaned "the frame of mind that had developed among our military leaders during a decade of restraints and three years of withdrawal" and told his advisors that "our [military] commanders have had it drilled into their heads that we want a minimum of activity. . . . They are not aggressive enough."[38]

Eventually the military leaders recovered from their shock and struggled to take advantage of the new situation. A Joint Chiefs of Staff message to the field commanders stated, "According to high level thinking in Washington, we have entered into an entirely new situation . . . in Vietnam. . . . [We] must bring as much air and naval force to bear as possible in order to give the enemy a severe jolt. . . . We have received increased authorities and must make full use of them at every opportunity."[39] The commander of U.S. Forces in the Pacific sent along an additional letter to the commanders saying, "The Chairman [of the Joint Chiefs of Staff] has made it abundantly clear that the constraints which have severely limited our initiative in the recent past are now alleviated. We have been given a fresh opportunity to demonstrate . . . our capability."[40] Clearly, the new bombing operation—called Freedom Train—was going to be different from Rolling Thunder.

On April 5 the Navy and Air Force launched Operation Freedom Train by attacking targets they could find south of 20°N, the weather broke, and the North Vietnamese supply lines were at last visible to U.S. air power. U.S. fighter pilots who had rarely seen an enemy vehicle in the open on the Ho Chi Minh Trail suddenly found large convoys of trucks on the open road in daylight. It was a fighter pilot's dream and they took advantage of it, hitting hard at the convoys while pounding the SAMs and other air defenses that were protecting them. At the same time, the United States deployed even more new forces to the combat area to take advantage of the sudden plethora of targets. Between April 1 and May 13, almost 200 additional tactical aircraft deployed to Southeast Asia, and additional B-52s were sent to Guam and Thailand. By the end of May the United States had over 375 F-4s and 210 B-52s in the theater.

The Battle Begins

To show that this air war would be different, on April 9 B-52s made their farthest strike into North Vietnam, hitting the Vinh petroleum storage area and railroad yards in the central panhandle. While the strike may have "sent a message" to the North Vietnamese, from the U.S. point of view this strike was not satisfactory. Rather than bombing with the B-52s' internal systems, the strike was controlled by Combat Skyspot, a ground-directed instrument bombing system. To everyone's chagrin, the damage was very limited, and post-strike reconnaissance showed that the bombing was "grossly inaccurate."[41] The implications of the B-52s' poor bombing were significant and disturbing: B-52s could carry up to 108 500-pound and 750-pound bombs, and an inaccurate B-52 drop could kill large numbers of civilians—the last thing the United States could stand in such a controversial war. The U.S. headquarters put strict limitations

on future B-52 targets to prevent civilian casualties until "SAC can determine the cause of the . . . [poor performance of the] B-52 system."[42] On
April 12, B-52s hit another target in the center of the North Vietnamese
panhandle, the Bai Thuong airfield. This time they used their own bombing systems, and the bombing was very accurate. Apparently this relieved
the U.S. headquarters' anxiety about the B-52s' accuracy, and more B-52
missions were scheduled, though the planners' awareness of the consequences of a gross error with up to 108 bombs never went away.

The air war escalated further early on the morning of April 16 with the
first B-52 strikes in Route Package VI. The B-52s were preceded by fifteen
Navy A-6s that struck the SAM sites in the Haiphong area. In a change in
tactics that would become the norm for the rest of 1972, twenty F-4s
dropped chaff bombs to form a chaff corridor to protect the B-52s from
SAMs, then, with heavy MiGCAP and Iron Hand support, seventeen B-52s
from U-Tapao, Thailand, struck the major fuel and oil storage area around
the port city of Haiphong.

These were not the end of the day's strikes; two more waves of U.S.
aircraft, one Air Force and one Navy, hit the Hanoi area. The first wave,
which hit five hours after the B-52 strike, was made up of Air Force fighters from Thai air bases hitting the Hanoi petroleum storage area, and
MiGs came up to meet the first strike in force.

The air-to-air missions were flown by the 432nd TRW F-4Ds with Tree;
one of the flights, Basco, was waiting to escort a strike flight, but when it
failed to appear, Basco moved to their secondary mission of MiGCAP. As
they began to orbit, Basco 1 picked up a Tree contact at 20 miles, and the
F-4s turned to engage. At 11 miles the F-4s jettisoned their wing fuel
tanks and soon saw two silver MiG-21s pass overhead. The F-4s climbed
to intercept, but in the turn Basco 3 saw a camouflaged MiG-21 that had
been trailing the first two MiGs at low level beginning an attack on Basco
1 and Basco 2. The F-4s split, with Basco 1 and Basco 2 taking the first
pair of MiGs and Basco 3 and Basco 4 taking the single MiG-21 trailer.
Basco 1 pursued a hard-maneuvering MiG and fired three AIM-7s. The
first Sparrow guided and knocked a piece off the right side of the MiG;
the second failed to guide, but the third hit dead center and destroyed the
MiG.

Meanwhile, Basco 3 and Basco 4 went into the clouds in a game of
hide-and-seek with the third MiG-21. After losing sight of the MiG briefly,
Basco 3 picked him up visually about a mile in front and slightly to the
right—in perfect position for a Sidewinder shot. Basco 3 fired his first
AIM-9; nothing happened. He then rechecked his switches and fired his
next three AIM-9s, but still nothing happened. With the MiG still in front

of them, Basco 3, suspecting an aircraft weapons system malfunction, told Basco 4 to take the MiG. Basco 4 moved into position to attack, but was not carrying AIM-9s and had to rely on his AIM-7s. He closed but could not get a radar lock on the MiG; rather than pass up the opportunity, he fired all four of his AIM-7s ballistically, hoping for a lucky hit. As the MiG dodged frantically all the missiles missed, but his evasive action slowed him down to the point where the F-4s were easily able to stay behind him. With Basco 4 out of missiles (both were F-4Ds without an internal cannon), Basco 3 moved back behind the MiG and got radar lock on for what he believed would be a futile attempt to fire his AIM-7s. To his surprise, the first missile guided perfectly and blew the MiG's right wing off, and the pilot ejected.

Shortly after Basco's two kills, Papa 3 and Papa 4, two Tree F-4Ds, were launched from ground alert at Udorn to a MiGCAP orbit in northern Laos. The F-4s were vectored toward a flight of MiGs, and at 19 miles Papa 4 got a radar contact on the MiGs and was cleared to fire his Sparrows in a head-on pass, but when he tried to fire, all three of his AIM-7s malfunctioned. A flight of two MiG-21s passed overhead and the F-4s turned to engage. Papa 3 fired three Sparrows; the second AIM-7 hit and blew one of the MiGs' tail section off.

Their first missions to Route Package VI in over four years had been an exciting one for U.S. aircrews. While SAM reaction had been heavy—more than 250 were launched—only two U.S. aircraft were lost. The results were excellent—the B-52 strikes and the follow-up attacks that day destroyed about half the known POL storage in the area, and the Air Force had three MiG kills for no losses.

There was a down side, however. Despite the success, it was apparent that the Air Force missile problems that had existed during Rolling Thunder had not been solved. Fifteen AIM-7s had been fired under ideal conditions, but only three hit. Additionally, all four of the AIM-9s had failed. And there was another down side that did not become obvious until the end of the year: the perception that B-52s could operate easily over the most heavily defended areas of North Vietnam at night. One high-ranking general said, "The important lesson we learned [during this first strike in Route Package VI] was that night B-52 strikes were completely feasible even in the most heavily defended region of Haiphong and Hanoi. Also we learned that the support package that we provided, plus the internal ECM capability of the B-52 was perfectly adequate and effective."[43] This belief would come back to haunt the Air Force at the end of the year.

Smart Bombs

One of the most profound changes in the new air was the use of "smart bombs," or precision guided munitions (PGMs), that were accurate down to a few feet. The first of the new smart bombs to be employed in Southeast Asia was the AGM-62 Walleye, developed at the China Lake Naval Ordnance Test Center in California. The Walleye was an electro-optically [television] guided bomb (EOGB) and appeared to have the potential to be an excellent weapon. It was "launch and leave"—that is, once it was dropped, the aircraft no longer had to guide it and could turn away from the defenses—and it had a range of almost eight miles.

The Walleye was first used by the Navy and underwent Air Force combat evaluation in 1967 on the F-4s of the 8th TFW at Ubon under the code name Combat Eagle. The Air Force crews found that the Walleye had some important shortcomings in combat. The television camera that located the target was capable only of locking on to a point where there was a very sharp dark/light contrast, so the Walleye required a target with a very high contrast aiming point. Because of the weather over North Vietnam and the nature of the targets, few of the targets had such contrast at the Walleye's maximum range. To get the contrast needed, the launch aircraft had to get in very close to the target, which made it dangerous to employ, and if the target was low-contrast or camouflaged, there was a still a good chance the Walleye would not see it even if it was close.

A much more useful system was the first of the laser-guided bomb (LGB) systems, called Pave Way I, which arrived at the 8th TFW for combat tests in mid-1968. The LGB was guided by reflected laser light that was beamed from an F-4 to the target; the light beam hit the target and reflected off, and the reflected light created a cone-shaped "basket" of reflected laser energy in the sky. The striking aircraft simply dropped the bomb into the basket, and the seeker and guidance systems in the modified nose section of the bomb homed on the designated laser light spot. The LGB itself consisted of "off-the-shelf" items that were mated to make the weapon. Guidance was provided by a small laser seeker head connected to large guidance and control fins from the AGM-45 Shrike anti-radiation missile. These were attached to the nose of a normal "iron" bomb—usually a Mark 84 2,000-pound general-purpose bomb. The Mark 84 did not penetrate as well as the Walleye, but it had approximately double the explosive warhead weight (946 pounds), and in medium soil it could blast out a crater over 40 feet wide and 13 feet deep. Occasionally the Air Force used a 3,000-pound Mark 118, known as "Fat Albert,"

A 2,000-pound Mark 84 laser-guided bomb mounted on an F-4. The laser-guidance kit consisting of the seeker head and large guidance fins is bolted on the front of the bomb. Note the extra-large fixed fins on the rear of the bomb. *USAF (courtesy of the National Archives)*

with a laser kit. Fat Albert was thin cased and did not penetrate well and had some other tactical limitations,[44] but it made an even more impressive hole.

The second part of the Pave Way I system, the laser designator, was mounted on a gyro-stabilized mount in the back seat of an F-4 and manually operated by the GIB. In operation, the designator aircraft circled the target at fairly low altitude—about 6,000 feet—and the GIB used the laser designator, known as the Zot,[45] to "designate" the target.

There were many advantages to the Pave Way I system. It was spectacularly accurate; in combat tests, over 50 percent of the bombs scored a direct hit—zero error—on the target, and the average circular error for all bombs was eight feet.[46] Almost as important, the bomb could be dropped from high altitude, out of the reach of most of the AAA, and it was very easy for the bomb-dropping aircraft to use—the basket of reflected energy was very large, and virtually any pilot could put a bomb in it. Combat tests showed the Pave Way I system was also extremely reliable and far superior to the Walleye; it was more accurate, far less expensive, and simpler. It did not have the standoff range (under perfect conditions) of the Walleye, but unlike the Walleye, the LGB could be used at night.

The Pave Way I system was not perfect, however. The designator air-craft could not designate for himself, so he did not carry LGBs, cutting down on the number of bombs a flight could carry. Because the laser seeker head had to "see" the reflected laser energy meant that smoke, dust, and haze degraded its effectiveness. Additionally, using the Zot required considerable skill and knowledge by the F-4's GIB, and it required good crew coordination to achieve such pinpoint accuracy. A far more serious potential problem was that, to use the Zot, the designator aircraft was required to fly precision circles around the target while the rest of the F-4s dropped their LGBs. During the bombing runs, the designator aircraft was in a level turn close to the target, and therefore very vulnerable to AAA and SAMs. It would not take the proverbial rocket scientist to figure out that the F-4 orbiting the target had something to do with the accuracy of the bombs, so the defenses were expected to concentrate on it.[47]

By the time Pave Way I finished its combat evaluation in August 1968, the bombing halt restricted U.S. aircraft to targets south of 19°N, and the end of Rolling Thunder a few months later limited its use to targets in Laos and South Vietnam. Still, this was a very useful period because it gave the 8th TFW a chance to train crews, to learn the LGB's and the des-ignator's idiosyncrasies, and to develop tactics. Favorite targets of the LGBs from 1968 until 1972 were small 23- and 37-mm anti-aircraft gun positions in Laos. Striking these targets had dual benefits—it reduced the threat to aircraft attacking the Ho Chi Minh Trail, and it gave the 8th TFW crews experience operating in areas where there was a real threat, so the tactics they developed were useful when the time came to carry the LGBs to North Vietnam.

The Pave Way I systems worked nicely with the new influx of naviga-tors to the back seat of the F-4s. The F-4s' systems were continually becoming more complex and required professionals to operate them. While some of the back seat pilots had done an excellent job, many had not, and the improvement in overall efficiency of the F-4 in multiple roles increased significantly with their replacement by navigators.

The laser designator underwent several changes to make it more tac-tically useful, the most effective being a designator called Pave Knife. Pave Knife consisted of a laser designator in a large pod on one of the external stations on the F-4. It was no more accurate than the Zot of Pave Way I, but the laser designator was gimbal mounted so that this aircraft could maneuver and still keep the laser beam on the target; not only did it allow the designator aircraft to maneuver to avoid defenses, but the pod had enough movement that it could guide LGBs from the designa-tor aircraft.

An F-4 with a Pave Knife pod mounted on the (pilot's) left inboard station and two LGBs on the right inboard and left outboard stations. The limited number of Pave Knife pods was a constant concern during Linebacker. *USAF (courtesy of the National Archives)*

Now Pave Knife designator aircraft could dive on the target and simultaneously illuminate a target for his bomb and the rest of the flight; after he dropped his bomb he went into a turn, but the Pave Knife pod stayed locked on to the target and the rest of the flight timed their roll-ins so that all could drop their LGBs while the leader was still designating the target in his turn. Pave Knife was considered the only designator suitable for consistent use in the high-threat areas, but there were only a few of the complex and expensive pods and delivery was slow; at the beginning of April 1972 only seven Pave Knife pods had been sent to the 8th TFW.[48]

The Air Force did have another guided weapon, a new-model EOGB that operated very much like the Walleye, although externally it looked quite different. This EOGB, however, had the same problem as the Walleye—it required a high-contrast target and was extremely weather sensitive.

From the beginning of the 1972 strikes into North Vietnam, the LGBs were the most important U.S. weapon in the campaign. In addition to the ability to destroy targets in a single strike, they made a whole new set of targets available. During Rolling Thunder many of the restrictions on bombing certain targets were because they were small and in populated areas, and there was great fear of civilian casualties. The LGBs completely changed the U.S. approach to bombing this type of target and led to the change of the Rules of Engagement; the LGBs proved to be so accurate, soon LGB strikes were permitted against targets that were surrounded by heavily populated areas.

Mission Specialization

The new bombing campaign highlighted to the F-4 wings in Thailand the need to specialize in a particular mission. In January 1972, the influx of new weapons and equipment such as the Walleye, the Pave systems, and Combat Tree forced Seventh Air Force to acknowledge *de jure* what had already taken place *de facto,* that each of the wings in Thailand had a specialty. The 8th TFW at Ubon, which had been associated with the Walleye and LGB programs from the beginning, was given the primary strike role; the 432nd TRW at Udorn—the closest wing to Laos and now equipped with the Tree F-4Ds—was given the primary mission of air-to-air. The 388th TFW at Korat, with its F-105Gs and EB-66s, was given the anti-SAM role.[49]

Air strikes into Route Package VI continued sporadically, and the "bomb line"—the northernmost limit of regular U.S. bombing—continued to move north, so by the end of April 1972, it was at 20°25'N. The MiGs continued to respond, and on April 27 the MiGs showed that even the Navy's extensive training program did not work all the time. Late that afternoon Red Crown vectored Norfolk, a pair of Navy F-4Bs on MiGCAP, toward a MiG. The F-4s did not have sight of the MiG as Red Crown called "merged plots," meaning that the F-4s and the MiG were very close, then Red Crown told them to turn. Instead of following tactical doctrine and separating away, the F-4s followed the controller's instructions and turned to look for the MiG. The F-4s' turn apparently placed them directly in front of the MiG; Norfolk 2 was immediately hit by an Atoll and crashed.

The Navy F-4s' revenge was not long in coming. Early on the afternoon of May 6, the Navy launched an Alpha strike against the Bai Thuong airfield in the central panhandle of North Vietnam. (This strike was based on information gathered the night before and demonstrated how much the Rules of Engagement had changed from Rolling Thunder. Striking a North Vietnamese airfield during Rolling Thunder would have required the express permission of the president, or at least the secretary of defense; during Freedom Train an airfield in the approved area for strikes was simply another target.)

As the attack began the strikers were engaged by a large number of MiGs. Old Nick, a flight of two F-4Bs escorting the strike, rushed to help three A-6s being pursued by a MiG-17. Two of the A-6s broke off, but the MiG continued to pursue the single A-6, firing, but well out of range. Old Nick 1 dropped behind one of these MiGs at very low altitude but held off firing a missile for fear that it might guide on the A-6. Unknown to the F-4, the A-6 knew the F-4 was behind the MiG and was planning to break away when the F-4 fired his missile. As Old Nick 1 reached minimum range for his AIM-9, he took a chance and fired; the A-6 saw the missile come off and broke as the missile guided up the MiG's tailpipe and exploded. Later that day, at dusk, Linfield, two F-4Js, escorted another Alpha strike on the same airfield. As the strikers hit, Red Crown vectored Linfield to attack a flight of MiGs coming down from Phuc Yen. As the F-4s closed on the radar contacts, they saw four MiG-21s in a box formation slightly below them. The MiG-21s' poor forward visibility betrayed them again; they apparently did not see the F-4s, who turned behind them and began to close on the trailing pair. At one mile the MiGs became aware of the F-4s and turned into them, but Linfield 2 fired an AIM-9 that guided perfectly and knocked off part of one MiG's wing and tail section. As the MiG went down out of control, Linfield 2 attacked the second MiG and fired two more Sidewinders, but both missiles failed to guide. As Linfield 2 fired his last AIM-9, Linfield 1 also pulled behind the MiG and fired a Sidewinder; Linfield 2's missile damaged the MiG, and seconds later Linfield 1's missile finished the job. The other two MiGs now turned back to the fight, but Red Crown sent in two more F-4s; the MiGs saw the new F-4s, broke off the fight, and fled.

On May 8 Galore, an Air Force flight of four F-4s with Tree, was MiGCAP for a strike in the Hanoi area. The F-4s had just set up their orbit when they visually picked up four MiG-19s in two pairs directly ahead. The F-4s attacked and closed quickly, two F-4s on each pair of MiGs; at a range of 3,000 feet Galore 3 fired a single AIM-7 without a lock on at one MiG, and the MiG pilot, apparently trying to avoid the missile, went out of control and bailed out. As he passed the other MiG-19 head on, the F-4 got a demonstration of the MiG's turning ability: By the time he went by, the MiG was behind him and opening fire from about 4,000 feet, but the F-4s were gradually able to accelerate away. Galore 1 fired an AIM-7 at the other pair of MiGs but missed, and as the MiGs began to out-turn them, the F-4s also disengaged.

A few minutes later Oyster, another Tree MiGCAP, was entering the area when they were called by Red Crown and vectored to the east to engage another group of MiGs. The F-4s got a Tree contact and closed on four MiG-21s. Oyster 1 turned on the trailing MiG—who probably never saw him—and ripple-fired two AIM-7s from a range of about 4,500 feet. The first missile hit the MiG in the right wing; the second hit the MiG in the center of the fuselage as the second MiG broke away and escaped. Oyster 3 and Oyster 4 engaged the second pair of MiGs, which had turned down and away. Oyster 3 was behind the third MiG, and since he had his AIM-4Ds selected and cooled, he fired the two he was carrying. As he expected, "they didn't go anywhere near the MiG," but he "wasn't too concerned because . . . I still had two AIM-7s left." The F-4s were able easily to stay behind the MiG, and Oyster 3 fired his two AIM-7s; both missed. Now he was about 700 feet behind the MiG, out of missiles and without a gun; he stayed close behind the MiG for "about two minutes" trying to think of what to do (being trained in fluid four, it never occurred to him to allow his wingman—who had a full load of ordnance—to fire), until the MiG finally dived away. By now the fourth MiG was working behind the F-4s, so the Phantoms, now low on fuel, disengaged.

Since most of the Freedom Train air strikes had been well south of Route Package V and VI and at the outer limits of the effective range of the North Vietnamese MiG/GCI combination, the most effective North Vietnamese defense system was the SA-2, which shot down nine of the seventeen aircraft lost in Freedom Train (MiGs shot down only one). The North Vietnamese had improved their SAM tactics since Rolling Thunder, when Air Force ECM pods had rendered them relatively ineffective for the last year and a half of the campaign. The North Vietnamese SAM crews were using techniques that considerably reduced the time the Fan Song radar (which triggered American RHAW warning systems) stayed on the air and now used an optical guidance for the SA-2, which also cut down dramatically on the amount of electronic signals needed to guide the missile. To counter the "special pods" that jammed the SA-2 missile guidance systems in late 1967 and throughout 1968, the North Vietnamese had new transponders in the missiles that were resistant to the jamming.

The North Vietnamese also introduced new SAM firing tactics. The most effective was firing three missiles, the first high, the second low, and the third in the middle. This tactic took advantage of the first move of the U.S. SAM countermeasures maneuver, which consisted of diving the aircraft—"taking it down"—and then pulling up sharply to make the missile miss. By firing the second missile low and a few seconds later, the second missile would close on the U.S. fighter as it dived; then, when the fighter pulled up, he flew into the third missile. Additionally, when jamming or chaff blanked out their guidance systems, the North Vietnamese would "barrage fire" SAMs, hoping for a lucky hit and trying to make U.S. aircraft drop their ordnance and break.

7

The Fiercest Battles

BY MAY, the massive air strikes had stopped the main thrust of the North Vietnamese assault, and now the Americans turned their attention to destroying the supply chain. The North Vietnamese had large armies in the field that were in constant combat, and these forces had to be supported with a steady stream of supplies. Cutting this massive supply flow was expected to be much easier than before the invasion, when North Vietnamese forces simply refused to fight if supplies were low.

On May 9, 1972, the Nixon administration made its next move as the president decided to move the air campaign back into Route Package VI to seal off North Vietnam from China and destroy the supplies already there. This escalation of the air war was first called Rolling Thunder Alpha,[1] but it was quickly renamed Operation Linebacker (later called Linebacker I), allegedly because of the president's fondness for football. It soon became clear that Linebacker was going to be different from Rolling Thunder, and even Freedom Train. The first mission of Linebacker, called Pocket Money, was the dropping of delayed-action mines in Haiphong harbor and all of the other smaller harbors in North Vietnam; three days later they were activated, and the harbors were effectively closed for the duration of the war. Few events were as symbolic in showing the difference between Linebacker and Rolling Thunder, when the Joint Chiefs of Staff had asked for permission to mine the port of Haiphong and other ports on the North Vietnamese coast from the beginning of the war and the Johnson administration had denied it. Now, expectations were high that Linebacker operations would seriously cut the flow of supplies into North Vietnam.

Linebacker was in many practical ways unrestrained, especially when compared to Rolling Thunder. In general, Nixon allowed the military to make all the decisions on targets once the general guidelines and Rules of Engagement were established. There was no policy of "gradual escalation" in Linebacker; most of the major targets in Vietnam were quickly put on the target list, and once on the list there was no time limit; the target could be struck when tactically feasible. The commanders were given tactical latitude about how and when to strike targets on the list and were allowed to choose the weapons the wings thought were appropriate.[2] The expanded target list not only allowed a more tactically flexible bombing strategy, but also ensured that, when the weather over a target was bad, there was a list of lucrative alternate targets that could be struck. All this made Linebacker strikes much more effective—with many fewer casualties—than Rolling Thunder strikes.

In concept, the overall aim of Linebacker was the same as Rolling Thunder—interdiction of the North Vietnamese supply lines—but in execution it was very different. Linebacker's standing operations order was to disrupt transportation from the DMZ to the Chinese buffer zone (30 nautical miles wide to 106°E longitude, then 25 miles from the 106° line to the Gulf of Tonkin) but, unlike Rolling Thunder, all of the North Vietnamese air defenses—SAM sites, most airfields, GCI radars—were included in the targeting plan.

To keep the pressure on, one Air Force Linebacker strike was planned to the Hanoi area every day and flown if the weather permitted. The original list of Linebacker targets was intended to isolate Hanoi and Haiphong by neutralizing their defenses, destroying the rail and road links to the north and south, and then destroying all war material in storage or in transit.[3] Still, not all of the restraints were removed. Fixed transportation targets (bridges, railyards, etc.) within ten nautical miles of Hanoi and Haiphong and the Chinese buffer zone needed Joint Chiefs of Staff approval, and the secretary of defense had to approve B-52 strikes above Route Package I. Linebacker bombing strikes were also instructed to avoid prisoner of war camps, churches/shrines, hospitals, and third-country shipping, and to minimize civilian casualties. There were also occasional short-term restrictions. From May 21 through June 5, Hanoi was not bombed to avoid casualties during Nixon's visit to Moscow,[4] and the Haiphong area was off limits from May 25–30 for the same reason. Following the president's return, strikes resumed.

But even with the restraints, Linebacker felt very different to the combat aircrews. Approval for new targets was quickly granted, and as the operation continued, many of the Rules of Engagement were gradually or temporarily relaxed;[5] in August and September, for example, there were twice the number of sorties into the upper route packages as there were from May to July.[6] The military was quite pleased with the rules for Linebacker; the Seventh Air Force commander summed up their feelings when he said, "We were not constrained. In some of the sensitive areas, for example, I was allowed the take out all power [major electric power plants] in a very short time, with the exception of one power plant and that was the thermal power plant for Hanoi itself."[7]

Linebacker: The First Day

On the morning of May 10, the Air Force launched its first strike of Linebacker against the Paul Doumer bridge in Hanoi and the Yen Vien railroad yard. Oyster was the first Combat Tree MiGCAP in the area and was patrolling at low altitude when they picked up MiG activity on their Tree equipment. The F-4s turned toward the MiGs and set up a head-on pass, knowing that since they were the only U.S. fighters in the area they could fire their AIM-7s head on without visually identifying the MiGs. Oyster's radars showed there were four MiGs, and the F-4s locked on and closed; the F-4s were below the MiGs and seemingly undetected, in what looked like a perfect attack setup. Once in range Oyster 1 fired his first Sparrow; it went about 1,000 feet in front of the F-4 and detonated prematurely, so Oyster fired a second AIM-7 at what he could now identify as four MiG-21s. The missile guided well and hit the second MiG in the flight. Oyster 2 fired two AIM-7s at almost the same time at the third MiG and also scored a hit. As the missiles hit, the first MiG flashed by and Oyster 1 turned to pursue him; meanwhile Oyster 3 and Oyster 4 attacked the fourth MiG. As the MiG started a right turn Oyster 3 fired two AIM-7s; the first went under the MiG without detonating, but the second hit the MiG amidships. At this point, all was going well for Oyster flight; three MiGs were fireballs and Oyster 1 was behind the last MiG, maneuvering for the kill.

Oyster 1 was flying an F-4D without a cannon and found himself too close to the MiG to fire a missile. As he maneuvered to drop back far enough behind the MiG to fire, suddenly four MiG-19s appeared behind the F-4 (they apparently had been trailing the MiG-21s at low altitude). The MiGs flew poorly; they overshot Oyster 1 and were slightly in front of and close off the left wing—in easy sight had the crew looked in that direction—but despite warning calls from Oyster 2 neither Oyster 1's pilot nor the WSO (who was temporarily distracted) saw the MiGs, and Oyster 1 continued his attack. The MiG-19s pulled back behind the F-4 and slid in close; as Oyster 1 fired and missed with an AIM-7 at the MiG in front of him, the MiG-19s opened fire with their 30-mm cannon. Oyster 2 saw the long flames from the MiG-19s' guns and again warned, "Hey lead, break right, break right, they're firing." It was too late; the MiGs hammered the F-4 with their heavy cannon and it went into a flat spin. The back seater asked the front seater to bail out but he demurred and said he would stay with the burning aircraft.[8] The back seater ejected and, after several weeks on the ground, was eventually picked up. The front seater was killed in the crash.

A few minutes later Cleveland, four F-4s escorting an LGB flight, was attacked by a MiG-19, and was introduced to the maneuverability of the new fighter. The four F-4s saw the MiG crossing behind them perpendicular to their flight path at very high speed and Cleveland 1 said to himself, "There is no way he can make that turn. . . . I just knew he couldn't make the turn, but he cranked in the bank, pulled it around, made a square corner and stopped" very close behind Cleveland 4. The MiG began to fire, hit Cleveland 4 in the wing, and the F-4 went down in flames. Cleveland 1 pursued the MiG, who apparently lost sight of the F-4. He pulled behind the MiG at low altitude and began to fire missiles, first an AIM-9 that went ballistic and then two AIM-7s. The first AIM-7 exploded off the MiG's wing, forcing the startled North Vietnamese pilot to jerk back on the stick and snap his aircraft out of control into a spin. Cleveland 1 pulled off and "was going to watch him and see him hit the ground, just for the satisfaction of saying I got him. A kill is a kill." Just as the MiG was about to hit the ground, "he [the MiG-19 pilot] recovered the damn thing right in the weeds. When he came out of the spin he was in a stall, just staggering along pretty close to the ground . . . still headed home."[9] Overall that day the Air Force shot down three MiGs for two losses, both to MiG-19s.

That same afternoon, after the Air Force strike, the Navy struck in the Haiphong area with Alpha strikes, and a large number of MiGs attacked the strike force. The Navy was waiting for the MiGs and had two surprises: the Topgun-trained F-4 crews and a tactic that it had used successfully in the last engagements of 1968—communications jamming. Navy jammers, operating from close off shore, jammed the North Vietnamese communications, leaving the MiGs to fend for themselves, without GCI to warn them that the F-4s were attacking.[10] Both tactics showed their effects; the well-trained Navy F-4 crews had a field day against the MiGs.

In the morning Silver Kite, two F-4Js on Target CAP (TarCAP) sighted two MiG-21s taking off and shot one down. During the afternoon strikes the MiGs were up in force, and as the battle began, the Navy specialists began jamming the MiGs' communications with their GCI. Despite their loss of communications, the MiGs stayed to fight; it was a mistake. An F-4J on Iron Hand escort destroyed one MiG-17, and a few minutes later two F-4Bs on MiGCAP engaged and destroyed another MiG-17.[11] At almost the same time another F-4 MiGCAP, Showtime, attacked a MiG-17 who was chasing an A-7. More MiG-17s poured in and a large dogfight erupted; in the melee, Showtime 106 destroyed two MiG-17s. The MiGs kept coming. Another Showtime flight on a flak suppression mission on the Haiphong rail yards had just dropped their bombs when two MiG-17s attacked them from behind. Showtime 100 forced the first MiG to over-shoot and fired an AIM-9 as the MiG flew in front of him, blowing it up. As the second MiG closed from the rear, Showtime 100 accelerated away to "drag" the MiG in front of his wingman. Unfortunately, his wingman had his hands full with two more MiGs that had attacked him, so Show-time 100 outran the MiG and rejoined with his wingman, and the two F-4s turned back to the battle.

As they returned to the target area, the F-4s saw a low-altitude wheel of eight MiG-17s with three F-4s in the middle. Showtime 100 saw that one of the F-4s had three MiGs behind and dived in to help; as he did, he saw several MiG-21s in the area and was attacked from behind by two MiG-19s. Showtime 100 stayed fast—550 knots—to keep the MiGs from closing and continued toward the F-4 that was under attack. At first Showtime 100 was unable to fire because he was afraid his missile would home on the F-4 instead of the MiG, but after several radio calls the F-4 broke away and Showtime 100 fired his missile. It hit the MiG and the pilot ejected. As the missile hit, several MiG-21s began to attack Show-time 100; severely outnumbered and with no F-4s in sight, Showtime 100 broke off the engagement at high speed and headed for the coast.

On the way, Showtime 100 saw a single MiG-17 and turned for a head-on pass; as he passed, the F-4 went into a climb to turn back after the MiG, but to his surprise, the MiG began to climb with him. Showtime 100 thought this would be an easy kill if he just out-climbed the MiG and then dropped behind him, but before he could out-zoom the MiG, it pulled behind him and opened fire, forcing the F-4 to dive away. The F-4 and the MiG-17 went through several more vertical maneuvers; Show-time 100 took a chance in one of the zooms and slowed down rapidly; the MiG flew in front of him, and Showtime 100's Sidewinder ended the fight. This was Showtime 100's fifth kill, and made the crew the first American aces of the Vietnam War.

Showtime 100 then turned and joined with another F-4 in the area and departed; on the way out they passed very close behind several more MiGs, but low and fuel and without a gun for a quick kill, the F-4s had to continue out. At the coast Showtime 100 was hit by a SAM that knocked out his hydraulics, but he was able to get off shore and eject. The crew was picked up by a helicopter.

The Navy plan had worked to perfection; supported by the jamming of the North Vietnamese GCI, the well-trained Navy pilots shot down eight

MiGs without losing an aircraft. In the melee, several F-4s were very close to MiGs and reported they would have had several more easy kills if they had had a cannon. Most of the kills were in dogfights with the supposedly more agile MiG-17s, and all of the kills had come with AIM-9s; it was a stunning success for the Navy's post-Rolling Thunder training program.

At the end of the first day of Linebacker, six U.S. aircraft had been lost, two to MiGs. U.S. fighters had shot down eleven MiGs for their biggest day of the war, but the day had not been a good one for the Air Force. Despite their Tree equipment, they shot down only three MiGs for the loss of two F-4s. The loss of Oyster 1 had been especially disturbing; he had been the wing weapons officer at Udorn and was generally acknowledged as the "guru" of the 432nd tactics and the most knowledgeable pilot in the wing about the Combat Tree system. He had scored his third kill just before he was shot down, and he appeared to have been well on his way to being the first Air Force ace. After the back seater was picked up and explained how the front seater had deliberately ridden the aircraft down rather than take a chance on being captured and interrogated by the North Vietnamese, no one was surprised—"He was that kind of a guy" was the common opinion.

The next day, May 11, the MiGs were active again, and the North Vietnamese tried new tactics. Tuna, a flight of four Iron Hand F-105Gs, was inbound into the target area when they were fired on by a barrage of unguided SAMs; distracted, the F-105s failed to see two MiG-21s attacking from below, and one of the MiGs shot down Tuna 4 with an Atoll. A few minutes later, a MiGCAP flight, Gopher 1 and Gopher 2, pursed an aircraft they could not identify. Gopher 1 closed to make an ID pass from the rear; as he approached he saw the target was a MiG-21, so he broke away and cleared Gopher 2 to fire an AIM-7. Seconds after Gopher 2 fired, he saw a missile hit Gopher 1 in the rear and down the F-4. This distracted Gopher 2's attention, and he did not see the result of his missile. During post-mission debriefings the possibility was raised that Gopher 1 had been hit by the other F-4's malfunctioning AIM-7. (It was not until over two years later that the event was successfully reconstructed. Gopher 1 had been hit by an Atoll from a trailing MiG-21, unseen by either of the F-4s, and Gopher 2's AIM-7 had hit the lead MiG—probably a decoy—and destroyed him.)

The following day the F-4s continued to have missile problems but still scored. Harlow, a four-ship F-4D MiGCAP, was flying near Yen Bai airfield when they saw four MiG-19s taking off. Harlow 1 attacked the leader and fired four AIM-7s, but all missed. Harlow 2 attacked the other three and fired three AIM-7s at the fourth MiG; the last AIM-7 hit and the MiG crashed. There was no more MiG activity until May 18, when the

Air Force struck a large POL storage area just northeast of Hanoi; using LGBs, the strike flights destroyed more that 5.5 million gallons of fuel. The MiGs were active that day; two flights of F-4Ds on MiGCAP intercepted two MiG-21s and probably damaged one. Fifteen minutes later, four F-4s were engaging a MiG-21 when, in an attack reminiscent of May 10, they were attacked by two MiG-19s, who shot down number 4.

Meanwhile, the Navy's F-4s continued to set a fast pace. That afternoon a section of two Navy F-4Bs, Rock River, was on MiGCAP for an Alpha strike over North Vietnam when it received a call from Red Crown that there were MiGs airborne over Kep airfield. As the F-4s turned toward the airfield, they saw two silver MiG-19s in front of them, in trail at low altitude. Rock River 1 began an attack knowing the MiGs had been using decoys to set up trailing MiGs for attacks, and Rock River 2 went high to cover and look for these trailers.

As Rock River 1 began his attack the MiGs saw him, jettisoned their external tanks, and began to turn into the F-4. The agile MiGs soon began to out-turn Rock River 1, so Rock River 2 moved in to help and fired an AIM-9; the MiGs split up, one turning to defeat the missile and one heading off in the other direction. Each of the F-4s now was in a turning engagement with a MiG-19, and the MiGs were working toward an advantage when, inexplicably (perhaps they lost sight of one of the F-4s),[12] both MiGs rolled out and one flew in front of Rock River 1. As the F-4 began his attack, the second MiG-19 pulled behind him but in front of Rock River 2. Rock River 2 fired an AIM-9D; the missile detonated about five feet behind the MiG, and pieces began to come off. As Rock River 2 passed, the MiG pitched straight up with more pieces coming off, and the pilot ejected. Rock River 1 continued after the first MiG and shot him down with an AIM-9.

Unfortunately for the Air Force, on May 20 another aspect of their poor training program reappeared. An F-4D MiGCAP was attacked by two MiG-21s; in a hard break to avoid the MiGs, one of the F-4s—untouched by MiG fire—went out of control because of adverse yaw and crashed. On May 23 MiGs were again very active and challenged both Air Force and Navy strikes. Balter, an Air Force flight of four F-4Es, was assigned as a chaff flight escort, then was supposed to convert to MiGCAP when the chaff flight completed its mission. After completing its escort role uneventfully, Balter was enroute to a MiGCAP orbit when the F-4s passed a few miles north of Kep airfield and saw several MiG-17s, -19s, and -21s in the traffic pattern. Balter 1 turned to attack two of the MiG-19s but overshot his original pass and repositioned for a Sparrow shot. Dropping low so his radar and missile had a "look up" angle to avoid ground clutter problems, Balter 1 fired two AIM-7s; the first hit and destroyed the MiG. Balter 1 then turned back and found that the MiG-19s had set up a wagon wheel; he made several passes on the wheel without results. As Balter 1 pressed the wheel, Balter 2 saw two MiG-21s attacking and turned to engage. He pulled his F-4 behind one of the MiGs and opened fire with his cannon; the MiG slowly came apart, rolled over to the left, and hit the ground.

The Navy scored well that same afternoon. Rock River, a section of two F-4Bs on MiGCAP for an Alpha strike on Haiphong, received vectors for MiGs over Kep and turned toward the airfield. As they approached at 3,000 feet, the F-4s passed head on with two MiG-19s; they turned to engage, then found themselves surrounded by MiG-17s. The MiGs had been flying in the trail of the MiG-19s, hoping to "sandwich" the F-4s, but they had been too close. The two F-4s were now in a low-altitude engagement with the two MiG-19s and about four MiG-17s. After several turns with the MiGs and after firing two AIM-9s, which the MiGs outmaneuvered, Rock River 1 found a MiG-17 close behind him, firing. The F-4 pulled into the MiG to try to make the MiG overshoot, but this simply allowed the very maneuverable MiG-17 to get in very close. As he closed, Navy training took over. Rock River 1 realized the MiG was pulling so much lead to fire his cannon that the pilot was in a position where he could not see Rock River 1 over his nose; he was simply expecting the F-4 to continue his turn. Rock River 1 abruptly stopped his turn; the MiG continued on and flew in front of the F-4, who fired a Sidewinder that blew off the MiG's tail.

Meanwhile, Rock River 2 had another MiG-17 behind him, so Rock River 1 called for him to accelerate away and fly toward him to "drag" the MiG in front of him. As Rock River 2 accelerated away with the MiG behind him, Rock River 1 pulled behind the North Vietnamese and fired his last missile, not expecting a good result because the missile had not worked in the pre-takeoff ground checks. To his surprise the missile guided perfectly and hit the MiG; the MiG pilot ejected, and the F-4s departed the area.

Air Force Linebacker Missions

Concept

Air Force Linebacker missions depended on the LGB; the LGBs and their designator aircraft changed the relative value structure of aircraft in the strike force. Relatively few LGB-carrying aircraft could destroy any target in North Vietnam, but the small number of Pave Knife pods and LGB-carrying aircraft meant that the relative value of each was vastly increased. In a thirty-six ship Rolling Thunder strike each aircraft had equal value—

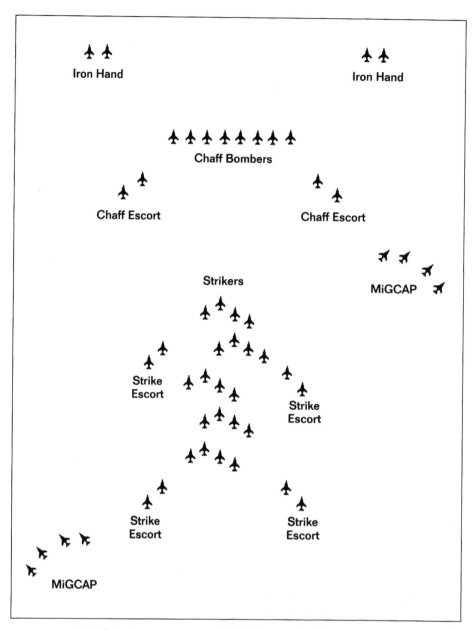

Typical Air Force Linebacker Strike. Note the chaff formation leading the strike and the much larger number of support aircraft as compared to a Rolling Thunder strike.

the loss of two, for example, had little impact. An LGB strike, however, usually consisted of only eight to twelve aircraft, so the loss of two strikers represented a much greater percentage of loss for the strike force. More importantly, only one aircraft in each flight carried the Pave Knife laser designator that was absolutely critical for the success of the mission. At the beginning of Freedom Train, there were only about seven Pave Knife pods, and two of those proved difficult to maintain, so the practical number of pods was five.

The Air Force decided to protect the limited number of Pave Knife guidance pods at all costs, but they realized that the combined threat of North Vietnamese MiGs and SAMs meant that the ECM pod formation flown in Rolling Thunder could not provide the protection the Pave Knife pod-carrying aircraft required. This forced a tactical decision that would influence Air Force operations over North Vietnam for the rest of the war: The Air Force decided that rather than the Rolling Thunder pod formation, the major protection for the Pave Knife strike force would be a relatively high-altitude chaff corridor laid down by F-4s flying in front of LGB-carrying strikers. This chaff corridor meant a significant increase in the size and complexity of the support package compared to Rolling Thunder strikes, and Linebacker missions into the high threat Hanoi/Haiphong area had a large number of support aircraft for relatively few strikers. A Rolling Thunder visual strike mission penetrating North Vietnam might have had twenty-four strike aircraft with eight Wild Weasels and eight MiGCAP escorts flying with them, or a support-to-strike ratio of two support aircraft for each three strike aircraft. On the other hand, a typical Linebacker mission into Route Package VI might have twelve smart bomb strikers and forty-eight support aircraft flying with them, or a support-to-strike ratio of 4 to 1; often it was much higher. The larger number of aircraft also meant a larger number of tankers and increased coordination, since it was necessary for each part of the force to drop off the tankers and go into North Vietnam at the proper time. Overall, the requirement for the very large support forces essentially limited the Air Force to one strike a day during much of Linebacker.[13]

First Flights In

On a normal Linebacker mission, the first Air Force flight that took off was assigned to perform weather reconnaissance of the target. Because of the large force and the sensitivity of the guided bombs to weather, these "weather recce" aircraft had to report the refueling area and target weather twice, once four and a half hours before and once two and a half hours before the target time. At first the weather reconnaissance missions were flown by two F-4s, but in June 1972 an RF-4 joined the flight because the F-4's radio was so poor; the RF-4 carried a long-range, high frequency (HF) radio to call the weather back to each wing's ground command post to pass to the strike forces, who were refueling.[14] In addition to the weather reconnaissance aircraft, before the strike force entered North Vietnam, two flights of Air Force F-4s were set up as a Barrier CAP—BarCAP—between North Vietnam and the tanker forces. (Experience showed that this eight-ship BarCAP took a great deal of Air Force F-4 resources and was rarely needed, and in July land-based Marine F-4s began to provide these CAPs over Laos while Navy F-4s provided them over the Gulf of Tonkin for eastern entries.)[15]

MiGCAP

Air Force MiGCAP tactics had undergone tremendous change since Rolling Thunder. The Air Force had always known that the most effective way to stop MiGs from attacking the strike flight was to intercept them with MiGCAP flights before they could start their attacks, but for most of Rolling Thunder the escort F-4s had to stay close to—or in formation with—the strike flights. This allowed them to share the ECM coverage from the rest of the strike flight's pods, but the main reason was that the North Vietnamese GCI kept the MiGs away from separate MiGCAP flights. When the QRC-248–equipped EC-121s arrived, they tried to guide F-4s to MiGs based on the MiGs' IFF returns, but once the F-4s broke off after QRC-248 contacts, they left the strike force unprotected. The Air Force quickly learned that, because the F-4 radar could not detect the MiGs at low altitude and because the MiGs were too small to see visually, they had little chance of finding them. The result was that the F-4s moved back and stayed close to the strikers, but this allowed the MiG-21s to set up their attack and build up such a speed advantage that it was very difficult for the F-4s to counter the attack or catch the MiGs after they struck.

With Combat Tree this situation changed. Tree F-4s could see and identify the MiGs on their own radar even at low altitude; now flights of F-4s with Tree could be sent on MiGCAP into North Vietnam, arriving before the strikers and setting up patrols between the MiG airfields and the target to cover the strike and chaff flights as they entered North Vietnam. With the help of the QRC-248s' information, Rivet Gym intercepts, and their Tree equipment—supplemented when possible by excellent Navy GCI from Red Crown—these MiGCAPs planned to aggressively hunt down the MiGs before they got to the strikers or chaffers. To pick up any MiGs that leaked through the MiGCAP, a traditional close escort of air-to-air armed F-4s was attached to the strike and chaff missions.

A MiGCAP flight ideally contained two Tree F-4Ds in the number 1 and number 3 positions and two cannon-armed F-4Es as number 2 and number 4; unless absolutely unavoidable, there was always one Tree aircraft in the flight. Analysis showed that MiGs were most likely to attack the first third of the strike package (which included the chaff bombers), so to counter this the MiGCAPs were "front loaded" so that the largest number of MiGCAPs arrived on station just prior to the chaffers. Early in Linebacker the MiG-21s approached at high altitude, so through June the MiGCAPs patrolled between 15,000 and 20,000 feet to try to counter these MiGs.

The first MiGCAP into the area, known as the "ingress cap," was the most popular with the F-4 crews because of the high level of MiG activity and because there were no U.S. aircraft in the area, making it easy to meet the requirements for using AIM-7s head on without having to visually identify the target as a MiG. Ideally the MiGCAP would have liked to be in place fifteen minutes prior to the force, but fuel considerations prevented this, and normally the MiGCAP was in place five to ten minutes before their arrival. To be ready to engage at any time the MiGCAPs had to fly at high speed—between 450 and 500 knots, depending on their altitude—and this high speed burned fuel quickly. Fuel was always a serious problem for the MiGCAP, and the MiGCAP flights shuttled in to try to have fully fueled F-4s available, but the large numbers of flights to be protected on a normal Linebacker mission meant fuel was always a critical issue for the MiGCAPs.[16] Some MiGCAP aircraft were lost when they ran out of fuel during or after engagements.

The MiGCAPs flew a variation of a fluid four formation called "tactical patrol," which was basically a line abreast formation with a few changes to allow the formation to be turned quickly; in certain situations the MiGCAPs also used a weave between the two elements that allowed them constantly to look behind the other pair. Tactical patrol offered little help to the vulnerable wingmen, who were still trapped in "fighting wing," while the "one shooter" philosophy was stronger than ever. The policy was described by a flight leader and MiG killer as follows: "The leader is the primary and generally the *only* shooter. Number three is the alternate shooter when cleared by the leader."[17]

With their early arrival times, separate orbit points, and distinctive formations, the MiGCAPs were easy to identify on North Vietnamese radar, giving the North Vietnamese a choice of engaging them or trying to avoid them and attacking the strike flights or the chaffers. As a rule the MiGs did not deliberately engage the MiGCAPs except when they had an advantage or were trying to set a trap. But the MiGs' advantage with their GCI was somewhat offset by the new U.S. systems; by using the Tree and

GCI from Red Crown and Disco, the MiGCAP forces often were able to locate the MiGs early. They were by far the most likely flights to engage; and when they *did* engage MiGs, they usually were in a good or at least neutral position.[18]

Chaff

Once the weather was confirmed as good and the ingress MiGCAPs were inbound to their CAP points, the chaff aircraft moved in to lay a chaff corridor. Since they arrived over the target ten to twenty-five minutes before strike flight, they also served as the final target weather reconnaissance and could divert the strikers if the weather was bad.

The use of chaff corridors was the most significant tactical change instituted by the Air Force for its 1972 bombing campaign. Chaff, in conjunction with ECM, degraded the Fansong radar performance, affected the fusing of SA-2 missiles, and blocked the fire control and AAA radars. Aircraft flying in the chaff corridor were almost untouchable by SAMs and radar-guided AAA, and a Seventh Air Force general said after the campaign that chaff was "essential for survival of the strike force in an SA-2 and radar-directed AAA environment." He pointed out that of seven losses to SAMs during Linebacker, "only one may have occurred in a chaff corridor."[19]

In the beginning of the campaign chaff corridors were laid by from eight to as many as twenty F-4 "chaff bombers" using Mk-129 chaff bombs. Each F-4 carried nine chaff bombs and dropped one bomb every twenty seconds. The chaff corridor laid by these bombs was five to six miles wide and about 32 miles long, and began and ended at the edge of the SAM threat. At first the chaff flights laid their corridor in a formation of eight aircraft line abreast, but as the North Vietnamese adjusted, the chaffers developed more and more sophisticated tactics to confuse the defenses and make their very predictable operation less predictable.

The chaff from the bombs took about ten minutes to fully deploy and form a corridor, and after about twenty-five minutes it dissipated and became so thin it was useless, so the strike flights had a fifteen-minute "window" to hit the target.[20] Varying the time on target within the fifteen-minute window made the strike somewhat less predictable, but as the delay moved toward twenty-five minutes, it left the Iron Hand and MiGCAP flights (who had to support both the chaffers and the strike mission) so low on fuel that they could not attack SAM sites or MiGs. Generally it was determined that fully fueled support flights were worth more than the small amount of deception in a few minutes' delay, and normally the strikers arrived about fifteen minutes after the laying of the chaff corridors.[21]

Tactically, there was a high price to pay for laying a chaff corridor. It was an arrow pointing to the target and gave the North Vietnamese at least ten minutes to organize their defenses. When the chaff bombers began to drop their chaff they became highly visible and easy to track on the North Vietnamese radar, making the chaff flights vulnerable to SAMs, even though they carried ECM pods. The chaff flights were also an easy target for MiGs because, to lay the corridor, the F-4s had to fly straight and level at a set altitude, a relatively slow airspeed, and in a straight line.[22] Additionally, the spacing in normal fluid four formation was so wide that the resulting chaff corridor was not dense enough to hide the strike force, forcing the chaffers to fly a tighter formation that cut down on their ability to look behind each other for MiGs. Because the chaff flights were so vulnerable they required a full support package, including Iron Hand, MiGCAP, and four to eight F-4s as close escorts.

At first aircraft from both the 432nd TRW at Udorn and the 8th TFW at Ubon flew the chaff mission, but for efficiency all of the chaff activities were moved to the 8th TFW,[23] where they could more closely coordinate with the Pave Knife strike flights they were supporting. U.S.-based squadrons that were temporarily assigned to the 8th TFW, the 334th and 335th TFS from Seymour-Johnson AFB in North Carolina,[24] flew most of the chaff missions, which many considered the most consistently dangerous missions during Linebacker.

Close Escorts

The F-4s of the close escort flights flew behind the strikers or chaffers to try to protect them against MiGs that leaked through the MiGCAPs. The close escort flights were very vulnerable, tied to F-4s that could not fly at high speed—either the chaffers or the heavily loaded strike flights—so the escorts had to fly slowly, often weaving to stay in position. This weave had the advantage of letting the escorts constantly look behind the flight to look out for MiGs. However, the weaving pattern had a disadvantage in that it made it easy for both the North Vietnamese GCI and the MiGs see where the close escorts were in the force.[25]

For close escort for the chaffers and the strikers, initially four F-4s were assigned to each flight, flying an "outrigger" formation with a pair positioned on the flanks about two and a half miles back. While it was a good formation for escorting the rather tight strike formations, the outrigger formation presented a problem for the chaff escorts—to cover the wide-spaced chaff flight they had to split into two pairs of two, and Air Force pilots had not been trained to fight in a two-ship formation.[26] This caused many problems throughout Linebacker, and a postwar report noted that "lack of . . . knowledge [of how to fight as a two-ship formation] seriously limited mutual support, visual lookout capability, and offensive potential."[27]

Once the MiGs penetrated the MiGCAP, they had a relatively easy time. The larger numbers of F-4s that made up the strike or chaff flights were easy to find, closely bunched together at medium altitude, and leaving a huge smoke trail. The MiGs essentially had their choice of targets; to make their own escape easier they usually attacked the rearmost flights or the flights on the flanks.

When the MiGs were sighted, the escorts would warn their charges and turn to engage, often firing a missile (usually unguided) at the MiG to try to distract him and make him break off his attack.[28] The AIM-7, with its large smoke trail, was particularly useful for this. At first the escorts had to stay with the forces they were guarding and could not aggressively pursue MiGs. Only when the MiGs committed could they counter, and realistically they had little chance to engage a MiG who came ripping through their formation from behind at high speed and then dived away, accelerating as he went.

Because they were behind the valuable strike and chaff flights, the escorts took the brunt of the MiG attacks and felt—probably correctly[29]—that their mission was to soak up Atolls meant for the more valuable chaffers and strikers. Of the eighteen F-4s lost to MiGs in air-to-air combat in Linebacker I, nine—half—were flying as either chaff or strike escorts.[30] In one sense the escorts of the strike flights were slightly better off than the chaff escorts, because the strike flights had more flexibility in their choice of formations and altitudes,[31] but the strike escorts had a problem the chaffers did not have—they had to wait for the strikers to drop and then escort them out. LGBs especially took a long time to drop, so the strike escorts were in a difficult position; at first they orbited near the target, but this made them easy targets, so soon they moved away and set up a Bar-CAP between the target and the nearest MiG threat.

Once the strike flights had hit their targets and were leaving the area, another group of MiGCAP F-4s, called the "egress CAP," dropped off the tankers and passed through the exiting F-4s looking for MiGs that might be trailing them.

SAM Countermeasures

ECM pods, the mainstay of Rolling Thunder, were still carried by U.S. fighters and continued to be effective in the proper formations, and flights outside of the chaff corridor—especially MiGCAP flights and the chaffers themselves—depended on ECM pods and maneuvering[32] almost exclusively to defeat the SAMs. Despite their age, U.S. crews still felt the pods were effective.[33]

In addition to the chaff corridor and the MiGCAP, the strike force had much the same support as a Rolling Thunder strike with both standoff jamming from EB-66s and SAM suppression from Wild Weasels. EB-66s provided the same valuable standoff jamming as in Rolling Thunder, but the very high level of MiG activity was a major concern for the EB-66s, which were the only Air Force jamming aircraft in Southeast Asia. Their vulnerability to MiGs and the large number of escorts required to protect them meant either cutting into the strike force protection or increasing the overall size of the MiGCAP. Neither of these were possible, so beginning on May 17, 1972, the EB-66s were withdrawn from many missions, and only chaff support and pod formations were provided. From that day forward the EB-66s were used only to support deep penetration strikes into SAM areas.[34]

One mission that had changed relatively little since Rolling Thunder was the Wild Weasels' SAM suppression. As part of the specialization of the wings, the SAM suppression mission was taken on by the 388th TFW at Korat flying the F-105G, an improved F-105F. The F-105G had more sophisticated equipment to detect SAM sites and better self-protection systems, and it now carried two types of anti-radiation missiles to attack the sites once they had been detected. The newest missile—and the missile of choice—was the Standard ARM, a large missile based on a Navy system with a heavy warhead, long range—longer than the SA-2—and a memory device that allowed it to home on a radar site even if the radar shut down. It was a great improvement over the venerable Shrike, which had been in use for most of Rolling Thunder and was still carried. The Shrike had been improved but still had many tactical shortcomings—short range and a very small warhead—and was still easily countered by shutting off the SAM radar.[35]

While none of these defensive measures alone gave complete protection, together they sharply limited the SAMs' effectiveness, but SAMs nevertheless remained an important part of the North Vietnamese defense system. SAMs were deployed as a barrier around Hanoi, in a blocking line in the Red River delta, or as a point of defense around a particularly lucrative target. During Linebacker the North Vietnamese had about nine SAM regiments, each with about four battalions. Each battalion was composed of six launchers, twelve missiles, and the associated radars and transporters, and generally a single battalion manned a site, so there were usually over thirty manned SAM sites in North Vietnam. While shooting down relatively few aircraft in the Hanoi area, the SA-2s continued to dictate the American tactics—such as the use of chaff corridors and the large support force requirements—that gave the MiGs more targets.[36] In May and June SAMs shot down about fourteen U.S. aircraft, but during that period the heaviest areas of SAM suppression activity were in the Hanoi area,[37] and almost all of the SAM kills were in areas where the suppression activities were much less.

GCI Support

The two U.S. GCI agencies used during Linebacker were much the same as they had been during Rolling Thunder—Air Force EC-121s and Navy radar ships. Seven EC-121s (generally called Disco) were based at Korat RTAFB. (These were EC-121Ts equipped with the Rivet Top equipment, including the QRC-248 and Rivet Gym equipment, used to listen in on radio conversations between MiGs and their controllers.) Disco still had the disadvantages of limited radio range, and because of the characteristics of the airborne system—the need to turn in orbit and the slow movement of the radar antenna—it still had only a limited ability to control U.S. fighters. Because of the large number of flights in the air during a Linebacker mission, it was difficult for the EC-121s—with only five radios, eight frequencies, and two controllers—to keep track of everything that was taking place, but the EC-121 crews found that the more combat missions they flew the more proficient they became.

The Navy's ship-based GCI, usually called Red Crown, was on a Navy cruiser or destroyer stationed off North Vietnam in the Gulf of Tonkin. These ships had the advantage of having their radar relatively stationary and had much the same capabilities as the EC-121s, but more of it. Red Crown had four control consoles, one non–air control console, and five controllers dedicated to Linebacker mission support, as well as the QRC-248 and access to Vietnamese linguists listening to the MiG radio calls. But Red Crown's greatest asset was its staff of exceptionally good GCI controllers. The Red Crown controllers were another byproduct of the Navy's air-to-air combat training program; they had been working with the Topgun-trained Navy pilots for years and knew what information to give the fighter pilots and when to give it to them. Because of these assets, Red Crown was the controller of choice for the Navy F-4s and was also the choice of the Air Force crews, one of whom commented after the war, "Red Crown has a GCI that is so far superior to our Rube Goldberg agencies that it is absolutely no contest. If we had two or three Red Crowns we would have doubled our MiG kills."[38]

For most of Linebacker, with the new equipment, U.S. controllers could now determine the MiG types and gave each type a different color code—Red Bandits were MiG-17s, White Bandits were MiG-19s, and Blue Bandits were MiG-21s. Additionally, the controller gave the F-4s other vital information, with color codes used for this information as well—a Black Bandit was a MiG that was returning to base low on fuel, and the call "heads up red" meant the best North Vietnamese pilots were up. (This was later changed to "heads up green" to avoid confusion with the MiG-17's code name.)[39]

But though the new equipment gave the U.S. forces many advantages, the old problem of radio communications between the GCI agencies and the strike forces over the Hanoi area continued. Communications between GCI and the Air Force strikes were usually poor; there were radio relay aircraft to pass messages from GCI to the strikes, but these were notoriously unreliable and by their nature imposed a delay on the information. One U.S. MiG killer commented, "On a number of occasions we were unable to engage and MiGs were able either to shoot us [the MiGCAP] down or shoot down friendly airplanes because we just did not get the information. Many times the information was there but there were radio relay problems, and just plain old radio problems."[40]

Despite its limitations, U.S. GCI served a vital function for Air Force strikes, giving warnings and other MiG information that was otherwise unavailable to U.S. crews. Defensively, it alerted Air Force strikes that MiGs were in the area and that they should be prepared to take action; offensively, as one of the leading Air Force MiG killers said, "It [GCI] was the primary reason we were able to engage MiGs and effect kills."[41]

The MiGs Change Tactics

The chaff corridors appeared to have completely disrupted the SAM defenses, and it was left to the MiGs to try to break up the chaff formations so the SAMs could have some influence on the air battle. On May 26, an Air Force strike of sixteen LGB-carrying F-4s was scheduled to attack the Son Tay storage area. The force was preceded to the target by three chaff flights and their escort, and for the first time MiGs attacked the chaffers. The chaffers were flying at high altitude—28,000 feet— because of the fusing of the chaff bombs, and as the force turned over the border to begin their long, straight run in to the target they were attacked by three MiG-21s. The MiGs overshot their first attack but forced one flight of chaffers to jettison the chaff bombs, then three more MiG-19s and another MiG-21 attacked from below, and three more chaffers jettisoned their bombs. Chaos reigned; one of the chaffers fired an AIM-7 that missed the MiG and clipped the wing tip of another F-4, and the MiGs fired at least seven Atolls while the F-4s fired four AIM-9s and six AIM-7s and made several cannon attacks. There were no hits by either side, but after the MiGs' attacks only five of the twelve chaffers completed their mission. A postwar report said, "Coordination and discipline between the F-4s broke down completely."[42]

This was the first time the MiGs had attacked the chaff flights, and it would put additional pressure on the escort and MiGCAPs. The chaff flights began to experiment with different formations both to make a better corridor and for protection against MiGs. Initially they flew eight aircraft line abreast, but this formation was hard to maneuver and therefore very vulnerable to MiGs; it later was switched to one flight of four leading and one flight trailing by three miles and offset to the side, so the entire force was more maneuverable and the trailing flight could fire at MiGs that attacked the first flight.[43]

Initial Missile Results

The 432nd TRW had noted missile problems from December 1971, when it began to engage MiGs over Laos, and the wing made a serious effort to try to solve the problems, concentrating first on the Tree aircraft, which carried the bulk of the air-to-air missions. In May 1972, despite the number of MiG kills and the favorable kill ratio, the Air Force F-4s were still having major problems with the missiles, and the failure to improve Air Force missiles after Rolling Thunder was now revealing itself in combat results.[44] The missile problems were especially unfortunate because they often offset the advantage of the Tree equipment, which allowed F-4s to enter the dogfights knowing where the MiGs were and to fire AIM-7s at long range.

An Air Force message sent on May 24 said, "The low reliability of our AIM missiles during combat since 1 January 1972 had promoted much concern at all command levels. The number of missile firings vs. the number of aircraft kills is indeed discouraging."[45] The heat-seeking AIM-9E, which had replaced the AIM-9B, was especially disappointing. From January to June 1972, Air Force F-4 crews fired twenty-five AIM-9Es and achieved worse results than they had during Rolling Thunder, scoring only three kills (12 percent)[46] compared to 15 percent for the AIM-9B in Rolling Thunder (and that figure had been considered inadequate). Seventh Air Force noted that while the Air Force's AIM-9E was performing worse than the AIM-9B, the Navy had gone from strength to strength and was even more successful with their replacement for the AIM-9D, the AIM-9G. The AIM-9G was so clearly superior to the AIM-9E that Seventh Air Force swallowed its service pride and requested that AIM-9Gs be made available to the Air Force "at the earliest possible date."[47] Unfortunately, the AIM-9G, like the AIM-9D, was an exclusively Navy missile, incompatible with Air Force launchers and electronics. Since the AIM-9G could not be used on Air Force aircraft without major modifications, Seventh Air Force dropped the request.

While acknowledged as unreliable, the AIM-7E-2 "dogfight Sparrow" was now the weapon of choice of Air Force F-4 crews. The Tree equipment now gave more opportunities to fire the AIM-7E-2 head on, which was its most effective mode. The dogfight Sparrow also had a longer range and larger envelope than the AIM-9E, and it could be fired when the F-4 was in a high-G turn, unlike the AIM-9E's two-G limit.[48] This large firing envelope was especially attractive since the poorly trained Air Force aircrews felt they did not have to maneuver as skillfully to use the dogfight Sparrow as they did to use the AIM-9.

Unfortunately, the improvements of the AIM-7E-2 did not include solving the reliability problems. From January to June, the AIM-7E-2's kill rate was less than 13 percent, despite being fired under perfect conditions much of the time, and the missile suffered major failures over 70 percent of the time.[49] The most disconcerting failure of the dogfight Sparrow was its tendency to detonate prematurely about 1,000 feet in front of the F-4, but it also displayed many other anomalies: Frequently the rocket motor did not fire and the missiles simply dropped like a bomb; when the motor *did* fire, often the flight path was erratic and/or the missile fused early, late, or not at all. These were problems that had plagued the AIM-7E-2 since it was first brought into service, and they simply had not been solved. An official U.S. Air Force history said, "These . . . missile problems resulted in a relatively unsuccessful employment of the AIM-7E-2 in combat."[50]

Some help for Air Force F-4 crews did appear to be on the horizon, however. As hostilities increased, in January 1972 the Air Force had restarted the AIM-9J program,[51] and in April the test program began again. AIM-9Js were fired at drone targets to try to improve the missile's earlier performance. Unfortunately, the Air Force had not changed its procedures for testing missiles, meaning the AIM-9J tests were carried out in a highly controlled environment. The drones flew at high altitudes and made no hard maneuvers—the exact opposite of the conditions that could be expected over North Vietnam. In this controlled environment, the Air Force concluded that, when compared to the AIM-9E, the AIM-9J had improved maneuverability, a wider launch envelope, a much shorter minimum range (1,000 feet instead of 3,000), greater maximum range, and the capability to be fired while the launch aircraft was in a seven-G turn.

But despite the touted improvements, even in the ideal test conditions the AIM-9J had some problems, including a warhead/fuse combination that was ineffective when the missile detonated more than 16 feet from the target. These deficiencies should have required further testing, but because of the poor combat performance of the AIM-9E, the Air Force decided to send the AIM-9J missile into combat as soon as possible, and in early June the decision was made to send them to the 432nd TRW at Udorn.

It was a month before the first missiles arrived at Udorn and training began, and on July 31 the 432nd received permission to carry the AIM-9Js into combat. During August no AIM-9Js were fired (one missile was launched unintentionally), but missiles had some problems simply being carried on the aircraft in combat conditions; four returned from missions with their seeker heads damaged from maneuvering.[52]

Weather

Weather had a huge impact on Linebacker operations, since the LGBs and EOGBs required good weather to drop. Because of the small number of Pave Knife pods and the large support forces required, it was possible to fly only one Linebacker mission a day, making Seventh Air Force very reluctant to cancel the mission for bad weather. To give the best chance of getting the missions off, the strikes were scheduled to hit the targets early in the morning; if the weather was bad, rather than cancel, the entire strike force would be put on weather hold for periods as long as eight hours. Despite the delays, weather caused about one-third of Linebacker mission to be canceled or recalled. The large number of aircraft involved in the daily Linebacker strike meant that during bad weather a large percentage of Air Force fighters in Thailand were sitting on the ground rather than striking targets in areas where the weather was good— a huge waste of resources. Some of the blame had to go to the mission planners, who for much of Linebacker paid little attention to the weather forecast—targets were selected on the basis of priority, not the target weather. Finally, by mid-July, the next day's forecast began to be considered in the selection of targets.[53]

The weather problems and the concomitant low number of sorties flown made the Joint Chiefs of Staff uncomfortable and led to proposals to try to expand the number of Linebacker missions from one a day to two a day by reconfiguring and streamlining the support packages. Scheduling two strikes a day would allow Seventh Air Force to put less of a premium on flying the first mission and it could be canceled sooner, allow-

The seeker head of an AIM-9J shows the distinctive front fins. Apart from these fins, the missile was externally similar to the other AIM-9s. *USAF (courtesy of the National Archives)*

ing the forces to be used on other missions. There were several suggestions on how to reduce the size of the support force. One way was to allow area targets—ones that did not require PGMs—to be scheduled for strikes by aircraft carrying "dumb" bombs, thus having two types of strike forces. Another proposal was to try to reduce the number of chaff aircraft by experimenting with different size corridors, trying for the maximum result with the minimum of chaffers.[54] However, because Seventh Air Force still believed that reducing the support force size would put the Pave Knife aircraft at excessive risk, through July just one Linebacker mission per day was scheduled.

There was one major benefit for the 432nd TRW F-4 MiGCAPs when a mission was canceled due to bad weather. After the mission was scrubbed, the flights scheduled for the day's MiGCAPs took off and flew training missions over Thailand, often at low level, to work on fundamental formation procedures such as proper positioning in turns and radio calls. This training proved very helpful, especially when the MiGCAPs changed from medium altitude to low altitude in July.[55]

The MiGCAPs needed all the extra training they could get; despite the limited time that their fuel permitted them to stay in their CAP orbits,

MiGCAPs were involved in more than half of the Air Force engagements in Linebacker I (forty-three out of eighty-two), and they scored the vast majority of Air Force MiG kills. They also suffered: Out of the eighteen F-4s lost to MiGs during Linebacker I, six were from MiGCAP flights. But MiGs were not the only threat; operating in small flights at medium altitude outside of the chaff corridor, the MiGCAPs suffered losses to SAMs and AAA.

May 31, 1972, was a very active MiG day as the North Vietnamese launched thirty-two MiG sorties. Icebag, an F-4 Tree MiGCAP flight, took advantage of the North Vietnamese radio monitoring and the MiGs' attacks on the chaff flights by simulating a chaff mission using chaffer call signs and radio calls. The ruse worked; when the chaff radio calls were made, two MiG-21s were scrambled from Gia Lam to intercept the "chaffers." With Red Crown watching the MiGs carefully, the F-4s waited until the MiGs had committed to their attack and then turned toward them. The lead MiG broke away as Icebag 1 fired four AIM-7s at the trailer (by now the air-to-air missiles were acknowledged to be so unreliable that tactical doctrine in the 432nd TRW was for the F-4 to fire all the selected missiles when a MiG was attacked).[56] The first Sparrow corkscrewed away from the MiG and headed for parts unknown and the second and third detonated prematurely. The fourth missile began by turning well in front of the MiG, and it appeared it would miss too, but it made a last-second correction and hit the MiG in the cockpit, completely destroying the front part of the North Vietnamese fighter.

June 1972: The MiGs Dominate

In early June the air-to-air war was slow, with only a few inconclusive engagements. The action picked up on June 11 when two Navy F-4Bs on MiGCAP intercepted four MiG-17s and destroyed two. On June 13 the Air Force suffered another loss in a well-coordinated attack. Sparks, a MiGCAP flight, was being vectored toward MiG-19s at medium altitude when they missed a radio warning call as two MiG-21s attacked from below. Sparks 4 was downed; as the MiGs tried to escape, one of the other F-4s fired four AIM-7s at a MiG but missed a kill because of poor coordination between the front seater and the WSO.

After this flight the criticism of the Air Force fluid four formation was vehement. The flight leader (who later went on to be a multiple MiG killer) said after this loss: "We brought the wingmen in to 1,000 feet [from about 2,500 feet, standard for fluid four], almost a welded wingmen, to keep them from getting shot down. . . . A wingman never did me any good in Linebacker. I always worked with the number 3 man. The wing-man was always just another airplane in the air. I would have preferred to have gone into Route Package 6, under the conditions we were operat-ing, with two highly qualified crews [flying Navy loose deuce] rather than four. . . . I had to spend 90 percent of my time keeping somebody in the flight from getting shot down [and] could not go about the business of MiGCAP."[57]

On June 21 the MiGs continued to press the chaffers. On the afternoon mission Iceman, a flight of four F-4Es, was escorting a chaff flight when three MiG-21s crossed in front of them starting an attack on the chaff bombers. Two off the MiGs saw Iceman 1 and Iceman 2 so they broke off their attack on the chaffers and switched to the escorts while the lead MiG-21 pressed his attack and fired at the chaff flight, who had missed the radio call to break. The MiG's Atoll hit the number 3 chaffer and it "went straight up his tailpipe and just blew it apart. The tail came off and was floating down [and] there was chaff all over hell."[58]

As the F-4 went down, the other MiGs continued attacking and fired two more Atolls that exploded behind Iceman 1 and Iceman 2 but caused no damage. Now the situation changed; the MiGs apparently failed to see Iceman 3 and Iceman 4, who were high and off to the left. Iceman 3 turned behind the MiGs, got a radar lock on to one of them, and began to fire missiles. First he fired two Sparrows, but neither left the aircraft; he then switched to the AIM-9 and ripple-fired three Sidewinders at the MiG, who was in a gentle left turn, apparently unaware he was being attacked. The first AIM-9 detonated prematurely, but the second guided up the MiG's tailpipe, and the MiG exploded into flames from the canopy back.

Iceman 3 then turned his attention to the MiG that had fired on Ice-man 1 and Iceman 2. He pounced on the MiG, who began a violent series of evasive maneuvers while diving for the ground. As Iceman 3 closed on the MiG, he began to fire short bursts from his cannon, but missed. As he closed, it appeared that the sight was malfunctioning so he pulled more lead and emptied the F-4's cannon at the MiG, scoring hits on the wing as the cannon ran out of ammunition; then he departed the area with Iceman 4. Iceman 4 had been sitting with a full load of missiles in perfect position to attack the MiG after Iceman 3 missed his cannon attack, but because of the "welded wingman" concept, Iceman 3 never thought of allowing him to shoot the MiG down. Iceman 4 later commented in a masterpiece of understatement: "It was kind of frustrating to sit there with a full system lock-on and a full load of missiles" and not be allowed to fire.[59]

Improving MiG Tactics

The Air Force's Tree equipment clearly had thrown the MiGs and their controllers off a bit during their night encounters over Laos and during their day engagements in April and May, and the Navy's newfound dog-fighting skills had been another nasty surprise.

During Freedom Train and the first part of Linebacker, the MiGs appeared to be experimenting with tactics. At first the MiGs engaged in large numbers, apparently believing that their new pilots and aircraft would bring more kills, but after their heavy losses in May, the MiGs gave up that tactic. To counter their losses to the Navy the MiGs simply began to avoid Navy strikes and concentrated on Air Force strikes. Not only were the Navy F-4 pilots shooting down the MiGs, but Navy strikes were not using LGBs, were striking fewer targets in the Hanoi area, and did not use chaff corridors, so they seemed to be better targets for the SA-2s.

As Linebacker continued and the North Vietnamese began to sense the rhythm of the American operations, the effectiveness of the MiG force dramatically increased. U.S. combat reports indicated that the North Vietnamese had MiG-19s and MiG-21s that were faster and more maneuverable than U.S. intelligence had expected. Late in May and early in June MiG-17s and MiG-19s appeared to be firing Atolls for the first time; during Rolling Thunder such capabilities had been postulated but not seen. Additionally, a MiG-21 appeared to fire four Atolls in downing an F-4 in mid-June; up until that time U.S. intelligence believed that North Vietnamese MiGs could carry only two Atolls. This new capability was consistent with the later-model MiG-21J, which had not been expected in the North Vietnamese inventory.[60]

The North Vietnamese were operating their steadily improving GCI from three control centers at Bac Mai, Phuc Yen, and Kep. The centers had increased in sophistication since Rolling Thunder and were now capable of controlling SAMs, MiGs, and AAA in the same area, and the new Air Force tactics gave them an additional advantage. Now, in addition to the massing of support forces to warn them that an Air Force raid was coming, a chaff corridor pointed like an arrow to the target area and gave them up to twenty-five minutes to prepare and mass their defenses.

The North Vietnamese also monitored U.S. radio calls and integrated this information with their radar picture, especially listening for calls that might indicate a flight was unusually vulnerable, such as having a damaged flight member or being low on fuel. A postwar Air Force report commented, "It was quite obvious that the [North Vietnamese] monitored and reacted to U.S. low-fuel or 'bingo'[61] calls. MiGs attempted on several occasions to engage U.S. aircraft after 'bingo' fuel calls were made."[62]

The MiGs generally operated out of only four airfields—Phuc Yen, Kep, Gia Lam, and Yen Bai—with three alternate/emergency airfields at Kien An, Duong Soung, and Hoa Loc.[63] The MiGs were very well dispersed from the runways, and could be parked as far as several miles away. Often MiGs were moved from their far dispersal or maintenance areas by one of four Mi-6 "Hook" helicopters based at Gia Lam, where they could not be attacked. The MiG-21 force—the force primarily responsible for air defense—operated for most of the war from Phuc Yen, but later moved to Gia Lam when Phuc Yen began to be bombed.[64]

There were four to six MiGs on alert at each base, and the total number of MiGs that engaged the strike force rarely exceeded the number on alert. When the U.S. forces were committed and the control center decided to attack, the MiG pilots (staying in bunkers close to their aircraft) were told to go to "Condition One," where they were sitting in their aircraft ready to take off. It took about five minutes to launch the first alert aircraft, and as soon as they took off another set took their place; the second set could be launched in two to three minutes. Occasionally North Vietnamese GCI would launch a separate flight sitting in Condition One to attack a U.S. formation that appeared particularly vulnerable, rather than use MiGs already airborne.[65] If a flight was launched "cold," before being brought to Condition One, it usually took seven to eight minutes from the scramble order to take off. Normally the North Vietnamese did not take off if U.S. aircraft were over the field. In principle, the North Vietnamese did not keep their pilots in Condition One for long; they either launched or went back to their bunkers.[66]

Once airborne the MiG pilots were given initial heading and altitude information, then turned over to their GCI controller. The MiGs would launch up to forty-five minutes prior to the first time on target and continued to launch until about forty-five minutes after the strike. It took about fifteen minutes from detecting the forces over Laos until the first MiGs were in a position to intercept the strike. By launching early, the MiGs were able to intercept the U.S. strike forces as they entered North Vietnam very heavy, loaded with bombs and with their external tanks full of fuel; the second preferred time for attacks was when the strikes were egressing, when the U.S. aircraft were low on fuel. MiG-21s were allowed to roam over North Vietnam following GCI instructions to intercept U.S. aircraft, but the slower and lower flying MiG-17s and MiG-19s invariably stayed within 30 miles of their bases. Generally the MiGs did not fly over Hanoi and appeared to avoid the immediate Hanoi area, leaving the defenses to SAMs and AAA.[67]

To attack the Air Force flights, the MiGs returned to using a few skilled pilots under good GCI control, the tactics that had been so successful for them from September 1967 until the end of Rolling Thunder. MiG-17s—and later MiG-19s—were seen in their classic wheel formations at low altitude while the MiG-21s would go to orbit points and wait to be sent to attack using the "one pass, haul ass" tactics. These tactics were initially successful, but the Tree MiGCAPs were now able to locate the MiGs in orbit and try to hunt them down, so the North Vietnamese stopped orbiting and began to launch a pair of MiGs who would fly at full speed directly to the U.S. flights, make a quick attack, then return to base, often low on fuel. As the first pair of MiGs recovered, a second pair would launch.[68]

Once the U.S. strike was in the SAM area, the North Vietnamese tried to integrate their SAM and MiG attacks, apparently hoping that one would distract the U.S. aircrews and make them vulnerable to attack from the other. This degree of coordination appeared to be within the North Vietnamese capabilities, but while it was successful occasionally, it proved to be very difficult in Route Packages VIA and VIB, because of the large number of aircraft and the U.S. ECM and chaff jamming that saturated the radars. Still, the effort to integrate the systems appeared to give the North Vietnamese an overall improvement in their air defenses, and from time to time there appeared to be cases of successful coordinated MiG/SAM attacks against U.S. forces.

Despite their successes, however, the North Vietnamese continued to operate relatively few MiG-21s, and there was much discussion on the U.S. side as to why they did not use more. Some thought it was because of the limits of their GCI system; others thought it was because of a lack of skilled pilots.[69] While the MiGs often changed tactics and improved their efficiency, the MiG pilots generally displayed the same shortcomings as they had in Rolling Thunder. If the MiGs' GCI setup was good and they were in a good position to attack, they did well; but while the MiG pilots were aggressive offensively, when their few stereotyped maneuvers failed, they had difficulties and usually resorted to a hard turn to defeat a missile and a dive to leave the area quickly. When they stayed they often were shot down.[70]

There had been few modifications in MiG formations since Rolling Thunder. In addition to the formations described earlier, MiG-17s and -19s were seen in a formation known as "sharp bearing," where the wingman was almost behind the leader and 650 to 2,000 feet out (this formation was not used by MiG-21s because of their limited rearward visibility). The MiGs, especially the MiG-21s, continued to fly in closer formation or in their preferred trail formations of two or three, and it was noted that the flight leader—the best MiG pilot—often was in the last air-

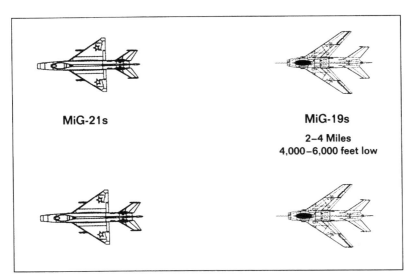

MiG-21s   MiG-19s

2–4 Miles
4,000–6,000 feet low

MiG Formation: Kuban Tactics. This was a very popular North Vietnamese attack formation during Linebacker and caused heavy U.S. losses to the trailing pair of MiGs.

craft, so he had a chance to attack after the American fighters were distracted by the first MiG in the formation. A modification of the hi-lo pairs/hi-lo singles was observed, called "Kuban tactics," where the trailing flight was not flying off of the lead flight but was controlled by GCI to a position to attack any American aircraft that attacked the first flights. Kuban tactics often were used at lower altitudes with MiG-21s in the lead and MiG-19s/17s as the trailers. The MiG-21s would carry out a hit-and-run attack and the trailers would engage the scattering forces.[71]

The Battles Continue

In mid-June 1972 the weather over North Vietnam changed, and normally there was a mid-level (10,000 feet) cloud deck over much of Route Package VI. The MiGs began to fly under this deck, where they could not be seen, then on a call from GCI they would climb up through the cloud deck to surprise the Air Force strikes. At first the MiGCAP F-4s continued to patrol at their usual altitude above the deck, but the new MiG tactics soon began to cause losses. On June 23 Barstow, an F-4 MiGCAP flight with Tree, was intercepted by MiG-21s in a coordinated pincer attack. Two MiG-21s came in below the cloud deck and popped up through the clouds to attack; one attacked from the left of the formation

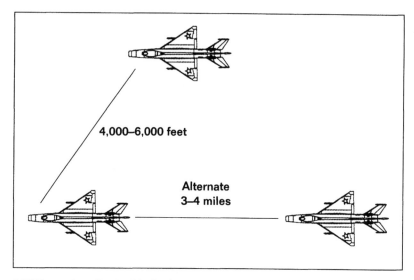

MiG Formations. During Linebacker, MiG-21s operating in pairs usually used one of these two formations. When one was three to four miles behind, he was usually the leader and directed the attack.

and one from the right, and the F-4s were caught in between. The F-4s saw both the MiGs, and one pair of F-4s turned into one MiG and the other pair into the second MiG. The fourth F-4 was lagging, and one of the MiG-21s fired an Atoll at him; it missed, but as the F-4 broke to avoid the missile, he went out of control because of adverse yaw. The F-4 crashed and the crew had to bail out about 30 miles west of Hanoi. That afternoon, in a rescue that was described as "miraculous," the front seater was picked up, but the WSO was captured.

The next day, in very bad weather, the MiGs were successful again. The chaff force dropped its chaff and was leaving the target area as the LGB flight was inbound, and as the strike force turned left around a large thunderstorm they met the exiting chaff force head on. As the two American forces dodged each other the MiGs struck, and one of the escort F-4s exploded as an Atoll hit. The strike force continued in and hit the target, but on the way out two of the strike F-4s, Brass 3 and Brass 4, were departing the area under the overcast when a pair of MiG-21s dropped down out of the clouds. The first MiG turned Brass 4 into a fireball, and as Brass 3 turned after the first MiG, the second MiG attacked him from behind, but the Atoll missed and Brass 3 escaped.

But the worst was yet to come. On June 27, an F-4 chaffer was shot down by an SA-2 in the target area, and as the force was departing, four F-4s on MiGCAP received indications of a SAM launch and maneuvered to avoid the missile; no missiles were fired, but in a "perfect example of a coordinated SAM/MiG attack," while the F-4s were looking for the SA-2, they were attacked by a single MiG-21, and a Phantom went down. Both of the F-4 crew bailed out, and since the crew was outside the Hanoi defensive area, the decision was made to attempt a rescue.

Unfortunately, the North Vietnamese were apparently listening to the radio calls starting the rescue attempt and made a full-scale attempt to stop it, turning the rescue into a disaster. A little over three hours after the second F-4 was downed Memphis, a flight of F-4Es, was covering the downed crew when it was attacked by two MiG-21s; Memphis 4 was damaged. Twenty minutes later, Tampa, another flight of F-4Es, was diverted to join in the rescue. Tampa orbited, covering the search and rescue, then called they were low on fuel and began to exit the area. As they left, they were told two MiGs were in front of them. The F-4s turned toward the MiGs and prepared to engage as the MiGs closed to ten miles. Suddenly Tampa 3 exploded, followed by Tampa 4; two more MiG-21s had slipped in behind the distracted F-4s, fired their Atolls almost simultaneously, and downed the two Phantoms.[72] It was the worst air-to-air day for the Americans in the Vietnam War; MiG-21s shot down three F-4s and damaged one for no MiG losses.

By June 1972 the Air Force had lost a total of thirteen aircraft in air-to-air combat while shooting down seventeen, but that month seven Air Force aircraft were lost to MiGs for only three kills, and during the last week of the month the Air Force lost five F-4s to MiGs without a kill in return. The trend was going the wrong way, and the losses to MiGs forced the Air Force to further increase the size of the support package by increasing the number of escorts, making the ratio of strike escorts to strikers 1:1.[73] The commander of Seventh Air Force noted that the growing MiG aggressiveness, combined with their superb GCI and tactics, had brought the situation back to where it was at the end of Rolling Thunder.[74]

But despite the talk of GCI, U.S. pilots knew what the cause of most of their losses were—they had simply not trained against small aircraft that could turn well and were hard to see, and they were having a very difficult time simply seeing a MiG-21. One postwar guide for new F-4 pilots stated bluntly: "If you know a MiG-21 is in your area or you lose sight of one and want to find it again: ROLL OUT WINGS LEVEL [for] 15 SECONDS THEN LOOK IN YOUR SIX O'CLOCK [directly behind] ABOUT 1.5 [miles]. IT WILL BE THERE. PROBABLY YOU'LL SEE MACH 2

ATOLL SMOKE TRAIL FIRST BEFORE YOU SEE THE MiG, BUT REMEMBER THAT'S WHERE THE -21 IS! JUST ASK ONE OF THE 20 AIRCREWS SHOT DOWN DURING LINEBACKER THAT NEVER KNEW THEY WERE UNDER ATTACK."[75]

Meanwhile, the Navy had scored twenty kills for one loss,[76] but the North Vietnamese were no fools, and for the Navy this high kill ratio was about to change. The North Vietnamese no longer engaged Navy F-4s unless they had an advantage, and from June 14 until the end of Linebacker the Navy shot down only two MiGs, while MiGs shot down two Navy F-4s and a third F-4 ran out of fuel after a dogfight.

A Threat to the LGB Force

While the summer MiG losses were serious, it was the attrition of the Pave Knife pods that was causing the most concern to the Air Force. The Pave Knife/LGB combination had exceeded all expectations, and combat experience was showing that an average of two LGBs were required to destroy or damage any intended target. The entire Air Force interdiction effort in Route Packages V and VI was built around the capabilities of the Pave Knife pods, but there had been no replacements since Linebacker began. When one of the Pave Knife F-4s was shot down by a SAM in late June the commander of Seventh Air Force wrote with concern: "We have built our entire strike program around a few Pave Knife pods. . . . We have carefully tailored the force to provide maximum protection for the strike aircraft. This has meant extensive use of chaff dispensing aircraft and heavy MiGCAP protection. . . . Until yesterday, we have been extremely successful in avoiding losses to SAMs. This has been due to our strike jamming POD discipline and, of course, the use of chaff to protect the strike aircraft in the target area. Of the six [Pave Knife] pods available to us, two are considered substandard because of parts shortages, and four are maintained at acceptable standards with maximum [maintenance] effort." On July 5 another Pave Knife pod was lost on takeoff when the F-4 crashed, reducing the total number of Pave Knife pods to five (only three of which were reliable), and the situation began to look critical.[77]

There were still twelve Pave Way I (Zot)-equipped F-4s available, but Pave Way I—with its requirement for the designating aircraft to circle around the target—was not considered safe to use regularly in the high-threat areas around Hanoi and Haiphong. Early in Linebacker the 8th TFW did develop tactics to use Pave Way I in high threat areas,[78] and it was used effectively against targets in the less heavily defended areas of the northern Route Packages such as the northeast and northwest rail lines. However, as the interdiction program continued, the enemy extended its SAM defenses northward along the rail lines, particularly the northeast one, and the threat increased to a level that provoked Seventh Air Force generally to prohibit Pave Way I deliveries. At least, that was the headquarters point of view. A very sore point with the 8th TFW was that Seventh Air Force Headquarters—who had little expertise with LGB systems—told them which Pave system to use on a given target, instead of letting the 8th TFW Tactics Shop decide. After much discussion, eventually it was left up to the wing to decide which system to use.[79]

With the shortage of Pave Knife pods, 8th TFW tried to use the EOGB against targets in the Hanoi area. Although the employment of EOGBs in the low-threat areas of southern North Vietnam showed some success, results of strikes in the high-threat areas around Hanoi generally were not satisfactory, and by the end of July, only nine sorties had dropped EOGBs in the high-threat areas. The Seventh Air Force commander clearly preferred the LGB over the EOGB and summed up the situation in a July 24 message: "The 8th TAC Fighter Wing has used the EOGBs with some success in Route Pack 1 . . . where they are able to get down to the proper delivery altitudes. They have been releasing at about 6,000 feet [above the ground] . . . with aircraft recovery at 4,500 feet. This is much too low for operations in Route Packages 5 and 6. . . . We will continue to work with this weapons system to get the most out of it, but the very strong feeling in the wing is that it is not a suitable weapon for the high-risk areas." He said in a later message: "We will continue to make every effort to optimize the use of the EOGB. Nonetheless, it is apparent that in the current state of the art, the LGB is a far superior weapons system and the one we must rely upon to assure best possible accuracy and highest probabilities of destruction."[80] Fortunately, no more Pave Knife pods were lost in July and the immediate concerns eased.

Overall, guided bombs allowed U.S. forces to maintain crucial interdictions in the northeast and northwest rail lines, and at this point it was estimated they had cut off practically 100 percent of the sea- and rail-borne supplies to North Vietnam. North Vietnam's supplies were reduced by an estimated 80 percent; the major portion of the remaining 20 percent had been pre-positioned before the bombing, and North Vietnamese forces fighting in South Vietnam were short of many critical items such as POL, ammunition, and food. The accuracy of the guided bombs also permitted strikes against strategic targets with far less danger to noncombatants, and targets such as the rail sidings and rail yards, which often were located in populated areas and which had been off limits in Rolling

Thunder, were now fair game for LGBs, as were other high-value targets such as the power plants, industrial targets, and repair facilities clustered in the heavily populated Red River basin area. The LGBs also allowed Air Force aircraft to bomb the Haiphong port facilities without endangering neutral shipping in the harbor.

New Chaff Tactics

The chaff bombs dropped by the F-4 formations provided good protection for the strikers, but the chaff bombing F-4s carried only nine chaff bombs each, so the chaff corridor from the bombs extended only for a relatively short distance over the heavily defended target areas. To counter the small area of chaff coverage, the North Vietnamese began to expand their defenses by occupying previously empty SAM sites outside the Hanoi/Haiphong area so that the SA-2s would be able to fire on the strike aircraft before they got into the chaff corridor.[81] To protect the strike force, beginning in mid-June the chaffers' changed equipment, and the F-4s began using the ALE-38 chaff dispenser instead of the chaff bombs.[82] The chaff dispensers distributed chaff in a stream rather than all at once, like a bomb; using the dispensers, the chaffers could sow a chaff corridor 5 miles wide and 105 miles long—long enough to reach from the Laos/North Vietnamese border to any target in North Vietnam. Later the chaff flights began to carry five chaff bombs to supplement the chaff from the dispenser; the chaff from the bombs gave separate false returns over the target to help the bombers in the dive-bombing attacks,[83] further adding to the defenses' problems.

Because of their vulnerability, the chaff flights continued to develop a variety of tactics to protect themselves against increasing MiG attacks while they were setting up to lay the corridor.[84] One of the most common techniques was to use MiGCAP call signs and pretend to be MiGCAP flights on their way to their CAP points, expecting the North Vietnamese GCI to keep the MiGs away from them. At other times, since the chaff corridor could be laid either inbound to or outbound from the target, the chaffers would fly with the MiGCAPs to the target area, then turn outbound and lay the corridor from the target out to the strike force entry point.[85]

July 1972

Despite losses and problems with the North Vietnamese defenses, the blockade of the harbors and bombing had brought the North Vietnamese invasion of South Vietnam to a halt, and it was clear they could not achieve a military victory as long as U.S. air power was available. Politically, the North Vietnamese were getting almost no help from China or Russia; neutralized by Kissinger's diplomacy, there were no indications that either of the two were willing to pressure the United States to stop the bombing. The North Vietnamese position was looking more and more tenuous, and toward late June Hanoi called all its negotiators home from Paris for a strategy session; progress in the peace talks seemed possible.

Meanwhile, bad weather was causing more and more delays in the daily Linebacker missions. In early July, under heavy pressure from Washington to keep the campaign going, the Air Force decided to try bringing its daily Linebacker strike in from the east, over the Gulf of Tonkin, hoping for better weather to complete the strike.[86] The eastern Gulf of Tonkin or "feet wet" entry and exit were not popular with the crews. The Chinese buffer zone and the heavily defended Haiphong area forced the strikes to enter North Vietnam in a very narrow area where it was easy for the North Vietnamese to concentrate their defenses. Additionally, fuel was more of a problem (entering from the Gulf of Tonkin increased the number of tankers required by 30 percent), and there was less chance of a rescue for a crew on the flat areas of coastal North Vietnam than in the mountains of the west.[87] Still, the eastern "feet wet" route had some initial success and appeared to offer the hope of ending some of the long weather delays that were handicapping the Linebacker strikes.

Meanwhile, the MiG successes had forced the Air Force to increase its MiGCAP and escort forces again, and in July the support-to-strike ratio increased to 5.2 support aircraft for each strike aircraft.[88] The MiGs also forced the Air Force to devote more resources to escort and MiGCAP in the target area, and so in July Marine Corps F-4s took up responsibility for protecting the tankers and search and rescue forces on the border between Laos and North Vietnam to free up Air Force F-4s. Over North Vietnam there continued to be a cloud deck at about 10,000 feet, and after the successful MiG pop-up attacks Air Force F-4 MiGCAPs changed tactics and began to patrol below the cloud deck at between 3,000 and 8,000 feet, hoping to catch the MiGs before they began their attack. The low altitude meant the F-4s used more gas, were more exposed to AAA, and often lost radio contact with the GCI agencies, but the MiGCAP crews considered it worth it.[89]

In another attempt to slow down the MiG successes, on July 4 the Air Force daily strike attacked the Air Defense Command and Control Center at Hanoi's Bac Mai airfield, and an LGB with a long delay fuse for maximum penetration scored a direct hit on the center. Seventh Air Force believed that the control center was severely damaged, but if the damage bothered the North Vietnamese they did not show it, and the next day was another bad one for the Air Force. MiGs took advantage of the strike escorts' dilemma—what to do during the relatively long period it took for the LGB flights to drop their bombs. As Kingman, a strike escort flight, made an easy turn over the cloud-covered target area, a MiG-21 popped up from the low cloud deck and fired two Atolls at Kingman 2, trying to fly "fighting wing"; the F-4 exploded, the right wing came off, and the crew ejected. The F-4s maneuvered to cover the downed crew, and as Kingman 4 maneuvered in fighting wing, he was hit by an Atoll from a MiG-21 that had been in a classic trail formation; both crew members bailed out. After the mission, it was learned that a Disco EC-121 had kept an Iron Hand flight informed of the MiGs' progress and knew the MiGs were attacking, but the information was never passed to Kingman; review of the tapes showed that both Kingman 2 and Kingman 4 had been told to "break," but the calls had been drowned out by other radio transmissions on Guard frequency.

These kills brought Air Force losses to MiGs to seven F-4s in less than two weeks, without a MiG kill in return. After the July 5 losses, the Air Force set up another Disco orbit off the coast of North Vietnam, in much the same location as the EC-121 Alpha orbit flown during Rolling Thunder, to try to get better low-altitude coverage of the Hanoi area.

On July 8, the string of F-4 losses was finally broken. Brenda, a flight of four F-4s, was departing after their chaff escort mission when Red Crown warned them that MiGs were attacking. Two MiG-21s swept in from behind, damaging Brenda 1 so badly that the crew had to bail out, but one of the MiGs overshot and would up in front of Brenda 3. He fired an AIM-9 that failed to guide, then fired three more Sidewinders, but none of the AIM-9s even came off the rail. With the MiG still in front of him, he fired two AIM-7s; the first hit the MiG in mid-fuselage and the second guided on the wreckage.

Ten minutes later two MiG-21s began to approach the strike force when the North Vietnamese GCI controller had a problem and told the two MiGs to break off the engagement and return to base, but the MiG leader told the GCI controller he had F-4s in sight, so the controller gave the pair permission to attack.[90] The F-4s were Paula flight, four F-4Es on MiGCAP covering the exiting strike; unknown to the MiGs, Paula had received a call from an EC-121 that they were under attack by the MiG-21s two miles off to their left. The F-4s turned into the MiGs and saw one passing overhead, but rather than turn and attack the F-4s continued straight ahead. Paula 1 had been part of Oyster flight on May 10, when Oyster 1 had been caught and shot down by trailing MiG-19s as he attacked a flight of MiG-21s; Paula 1 realized if he turned to attack the first MiG he might be turning the flight in front of a trailing MiG. He made the right decision; a few seconds later the F-4s saw a second MiG-21 about two miles behind the first, and as this MiG passed they turned to attack. Paula 1 attacked the second MiG from below, got a radar lock on, and set up to fire an AIM-7. The MiG-21 did not see the F-4s at first, but in the five seconds the F-4 required to lock on and fire the Sparrow, he saw the American fighters and made a hard turn into them. Paula 1 fired two AIM-7s from the very edge of the envelope; the first missile guided and hit amidships, blowing the MiG in half, and the second went through the fireball.

Meanwhile, the first MiG-21 had turned back and now was attacking Paula 4, who in the best fluid four tradition was guarding the rear of the flight but was unprotected himself. Paula 1 saw the second MiG approaching and cut across the turn toward the North Vietnamese; as he approached in a five-G turn he fired a Sparrow from 3,000 feet, on the edge of the missile's maneuvering capability and inside the missile's minimum range. Paula 1 expected the missile to miss, and as he fumbled to select the cannon for a follow-up attack (the cannon switch position was in an awkward spot) he saw to his surprise that the missile made a sharp right turn and guided perfectly; the MiG disintegrated after the AIM-7 hit.

Despite the MiG successes, the U.S. anti-MiG forces were very successful in their main mission (preventing strike force losses), and only one strike aircraft was shot down by MiGs between April and June (and only three strike aircraft were lost to MiGs during all of Linebacker I). Several factors combined for the low losses to MiGs in the strike forces. The ability of the Tree MiGCAPs to intercept many MiGs well away from the strike force, coupled with more effective command and control (especially from Red Crown), proved very effective and cut off many MiG attacks. Additionally, once they penetrated the MiGCAP it was very difficult for the MiGs—especially the MiG-21s with their poor forward visibility—to sort out the different groups of F-4s. Unlike Rolling Thunder, when the majority of strikes were flown by F-105s and the MiGCAPs were F-4s, in Linebacker virtually all the aircraft—MiGCAP, chaff bombers, strikers, and escort—were F-4s; despite the different patterns each flew, in the press of battle it appeared difficult for the MiGs to tell who was a bomb carrier, who was a chaffer, and who was an escort. Also, unlike Rolling Thunder, when the strike and MiGCAP often were in the same formation, now the strike aircraft were in the center of a large group of support forces, with almost all F-4s carrying some air-to-air missiles. If the MiGs had consistently tried to penetrate all the way to the middle of the force—where the Pave Knife aircraft were—they would have been under attack from the moment they penetrated the outer ring of U.S. forces. Under these circumstances MiG losses surely would have risen, perhaps even skyrocketed. The large number of support forces gave the MiGs plenty of targets, so the North Vietnamese generally attacked the most vulnerable flights—the strike or chaff escorts on the flanks or single MiGCAP flights—rather than risk trying to fight their way through to the strike flights.

Causes of the MiG Successes

The commander of Seventh Air Force, like other Air Force general officers, still believed that the main reason for the MiG successes was the North Vietnamese GCI and insisted that if the loss rate was to be reversed, the North Vietnamese GCI would have to be countered by improved American warning systems. In fact the answer was much more complex, and a PACAF Headquarters report during this period concluded that the high Air Force losses were a combination of factors: enemy tactics, enemy GCI capabilities, friendly tactics, friendly warning and GCI capabilities, air-to-air missile capabilities, *but especially the lack of F-4 air-to-air crew training.*[91] The report said, "New F-4 Replacement Training Unit (RTU) graduates arriving in SEA [Southeast Asia] were not fully qualified in the air-to-air role."[92] The commander of the 432nd TRW, tasked with flying the MiGCAP missions in Linebacker, added: "The single most deficient area of aircrew preparation for SEA operations has been that of aerial combat training."[93] The combat wings were paying a heavy price for TAC's decision to neglect air-to-air training.

There were other problems, too. Because of the length of the war and the Air Force policy of prohibiting nonvoluntary second tours, most of the experienced pilots in the Air Force—and virtually all of the fighter pilots[94]—had already flown a combat tour. Now a larger percentage of the new F-4 pilots were recent graduates of undergraduate pilot training who had been sent directly to the F-4 RTU, where they were given rudimentary fighter skills and then sent off to combat. When these new pilots arrived in Southeast Asia, they were taken from a strictly supervised student environment where "flying safety was paramount to completion of the mission" to a very difficult combat situation where they were expected to fly in bad weather, dodge SAMs, and fight MiGs. They simply were not prepared for this; one post-Linebacker report said, "Lack of experience among aircrews newly assigned to SEA, together with inadequate air-to-air training, manifested itself in lack of aggressiveness, excessive radio/intercom chatter, erroneous maneuvers when attacked, failure to act on timely information when provided, and break-down of flight/formation integrity."[95] The low caliber of many of the new pilots forced the combat F-4 wings to increase their training for new crews after they arrived. This put a huge additional burden on the wings; it took a new crew an estimated three to six months in theater to reach a stage where they were ready for the air-to-air environment over North Vietnam. The wing weapons officer in the 432nd commented, "Many ACs [aircraft commanders] . . . [and] men in the back simply were not qualified. It certainly was not their fault. . . . [T]he combination of unqualified, inexperienced AC[s] and unqualified, inexperienced WSO[s] was a serious problem."[96] A joint service report on Linebacker missions said, "The RTU graduates arriving in-country without operational experience are at an even greater disadvantage. The initial high loss rate of [Air Force] F-4s to MiGs is an indication of this deficiency."[97] The incoming crews agreed; in postwar interviews most said they arrived in the combat theater unprepared because of a lack of realistic training at their previous bases. They attributed this to an "overconcern with safety" that led commanders to remove or water down the realistic aspects of air-to-air training.[98]

At the same time the inexperienced RTU graduates were flooding the combat wings, two other events helped soften the blow. The Air Force had almost run out of fighter pilots that had not flown a combat tour, so it began pressing experienced fighter pilots to return for a second tour; many did, and they were arriving in the wings just in time for Linebacker. Even more helpful were the large numbers of F-4 squadrons that came to Thailand on temporary duty (known as TDY) to augment the permanent squadrons. The TDY squadrons were made up almost entirely of experienced combat veterans (not all of whom were happy to be back) who did yeoman service throughout Linebacker.

However, even these squadrons were not prepared by TAC for air-to-air combat. A postwar critique of the most common problems with Linebacker missions said, "The validity of sending aircrews into a high threat environment with only standard [Tactical Air Command training] requirements is highly questionable. [Air-to-air combat] training was deficient because of the requirement to complete [TAC required] training events. . . . [V]ery little opportunity was provided for training in the single most demanding phase of flying [air-to air-combat]. . . . By contrast, the Navy crews were prepared for the [air-to-air combat] role."[99]

The 432nd TRW realized that the complex environment over North Vietnam and the maintenance problems of keeping more than a few F-4Ds with Tree "peaked" for air-to-air combat dictated that only a small number of crews be designated for MiGCAP. For this reason, MiGCAP crews were a carefully selected group, and the flight leaders—the "shooters"—tended to be pilots on their second combat tour, and were often graduates of the Fighter Weapons School.

While it was possible to send the best crews out for MiGCAP, this arrangement did not solve the basic problem of the poorly trained crews arriving from the RTUs. Because of the wildly varying skill levels, all of the wings tried to fly missions to Route Package VI with their best and most experienced crews, but despite their best efforts, the sheer numbers of aircraft required for a Linebacker mission meant that often less-qualified crews were sent on many missions.

The Attacks Continue

Combat Tree continued to be a major part of MiGCAP operations. The Tree was so good that often the F-4Ds could see the MiG's transponder at very long range—50 to 60 miles—while a MiG-21 under normal circumstances could be seen only on radar inside of about 20 miles. From time to time Tree F-4 crews called out over the radio that they were locking on to MiGs at very long ranges; the North Vietnamese certainly monitored the MiGCAP's radio calls and must have been able to tell the Udorn F-4Ds had some way of detecting the MiGs at very long range. As a result, their MiGs began to cut down on the use of their IFF equipment except at critical moments, thus limiting the usefulness of Tree.

Like the Pave Knife pods, Tree had a numbers problem. By July 1972 the eight Tree-equipped F-4Ds had been reduced to three because of combat attrition, and since they were in daily combat the possibility of more losses was always present. There was a push to get more Tree-equipped F-4s into the theater, and during July twenty more arrived, ending the crisis.[100]

As the MiG successes mounted, attacking the MiG bases was considered to reduce the MiG threat, but this was considered even less profitable during Linebacker than it was during Rolling Thunder. Now the North Vietnamese had a greater number of MiG-capable bases, most of them in the Hanoi area, where they were well defended, and for the United States to keep them closed would have required a major, continuing effort with possibly severe losses. The United States simply did not have the resources to do that and at the same time pursue the main aims of Linebacker. Still, from time to time large strikes hit the airfields to force the North Vietnamese to keep their defenses up. These attacks occasion-

ally destroyed MiGs on the ground and often cratered the runways, closing the fields for short periods. It was possible to attack the southern
bases, which were less well defended, and for most of Linebacker the
U.S. air strikes kept these bases closed. Another possible target was the
command and control network, but the dispersed, redundant system was
a difficult target. When the Bac Mai Command and Control Center was
wiped out by an LGB on July 4 it should have had an effect on the air
defenses, but the next day MiGs were up shooting down F-4s, controlled
by the two other centers at Phuc Yen and Kep.

By mid-July the MiGs introduced new tactics; they returned to high-
altitude (30,000 feet) attacks[101] from orbit points while continuing to
launch alert flights to quickly attack U.S. flights that were having problems. On July 29 two MiG-21s took off from Gia Lam and less than four
minutes later attacked a chaff-escort flight; the lead MiG shot down number 4 with an Atoll, but one of the escorts shot the second MiG down
with an AIM-7, and a MiGCAP F-4 shot down another MiG-21.

8

Stalemate

August Changes

THE JOINT CHIEFS OF STAFF were continuing to press for more bombs on North Vietnamese targets and less support flights, and beginning in August 1972 Seventh Air Force changed the number of mass Linebacker missions from one to two a day and committed to having at least forty-eight bombers on these missions. Since the size of the LGB force could not be increased because of the shortage of Pave Knife pods, the second mission of the day would be a "dumb bomb" strike, with a much smaller support:strike ratio.

The two missions gave the planners much move flexibility to work around bad weather and increase pressure on the North Vietnamese defenses. Now missions could involve

—guided or unguided bombs
—east or west entry
—chaff or no chaff, depending on the defenses
—target times very close or separated

Bad weather and other factors initially limited the dual day missions, and only twice in August were two missions flown on the same day. These were so successful this became the Air Force norm for the rest of Linebacker I. To add to the Air Force's flexibility, it began using a new all-weather bombing system, LORAN, for bad weather strikes. Postwar reports indicate that LORAN was ineffective, but it was widely used during Linebacker and allowed the Air Force to bomb North Vietnam almost every day no matter what the weather.

Teaball

The GCI agencies of Disco and Red Crown were effective at guiding U.S. fighters when the MiGs or their transponders could be seen on radar with the QRC-248, but when the MiGs were at low altitudes west of Hanoi—

where they intercepted most of the Air Force strikes—Disco and Red Crown were less useful. There was considerable SIGINT and other information about the MiGs available from a variety of sources, but this information was jealously guarded by the American agencies that collected it; just because American aircrews were being shot down for lack of this information they saw no reason to release it. Part of the problem was that this information was so secret only a few people knew it existed, but those who did pressed hard to find some way to use it. Finally, the heavy air-to-air losses in June and July led to the establishment of a facility that would combine all of this information. This long-range, integrated "all source" control center, named Teaball, was established at Nakhon Phanom RTAFB, very close to the border between Thailand and Laos in late July 1972.[1]

Teaball was an attempt to establish a single location where information from all of the U.S. early warning and MiG activity sources would be taken in, collated, and passed on to advise all the forces over North Vietnam of MiG activity. One of the key sources of information to Teaball that had not been available before was a variety of "very sensitive" sources, among them Vietnamese-speaking U.S. personnel who listened to North Vietnamese radio transmissions. Teaball's intelligence information came from many sources. The problem, however, was a recurring one from Rolling Thunder—the information was so highly classified by the U.S. government that the pilots who were under attack could not be told the MiGs were there because it was a security violation. Many Air Force generals either knew this information existed or knew who had access to it, and some (but not all) pressed hard to have it given immediately to the aircrews where it could do some good. (One later commented, "No one in the intelligence community could ever explain to me why we were gathering this information when we couldn't—actually wouldn't— pass it on to the crews being attacked.") These generals' efforts finally resulted in the expanded intelligence sources being incorporated, to a limited degree, into Teaball, where they made a significant contribution.[2]

One of the main sources was the Seventh Air Force "Green Room," which had a special secure radio net directly to Teaball; this information was passed from Teaball through Luzon, a KC-135 radio relay aircraft, out to the Navy Red Crown ship via another special secure radio net, the Air Force Green Net. Other sources were RC-135s known as Combat Apple and Burning Pipe and the Navy's Big Look EC-121s and Sea Wing A-3s,[3] as well as the Disco EC-121s and many more sources. All of these support agencies were supposed to provide Teaball with a position of both U.S. forces and MiGs every minute. Teaball processed the data,

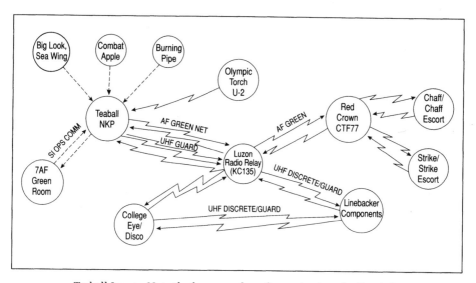

Teaball Inputs. Note the large number of organizations feeding information into Teaball. Note also how all Teaball communications had to go through the unreliable Luzon radio relay aircraft. Luzon's unreliability was one of several reasons the U.S. Air Force crews had a low opinion of Teaball.

then relayed the information through a radio relay aircraft, Luzon, to the Linebacker flights over North Vietnam.

Unfortunately, as part of the arrangement to supply information to Teaball, the American intelligence community insisted that the crews not be told of the sources of the information. The result was that many, if not most, of the crews thought that Teaball was just another warning from the agencies with no special credibility, so they did not pay particular attention to the warnings.[4] Gradually, however, the aircrews figured it out; one said, "Some of the controlling agencies were definitely monitoring [North Vietnamese] radio frequencies because you could hear them call, 'They [MiGs] have jettisoned their fuel tanks and are engaging.' So someone was monitoring these radio frequencies and providing us, although somewhat delayed, some information on what the enemy was doing at the time."[5]

The first operational use of Teaball was in late July when it was given permission to pass all-source information to Disco, who could then pass it on to the MiGCAP aircraft, but this procedure was very time consuming, and the information invariably reached the MiGCAP too late.[6] To shorten the time, Seventh Air Force then decided that Teaball would be the central piece in the overall control and warning system, and beginning

August 22 several procedural changes were implemented to ensure that Teaball would be the main source of MiG information.[7]

The changes were confusing, however. Seventh Air Force first made Disco responsible for controlling the three MiGCAP missions—ingress MiGCAP, mission MiGCAP, and egress MiGCAP—when there were no MiGs airborne, but when MiGs were airborne, Teaball took over, controlling the MiGCAP with Disco as back up. (Disco and Red Crown were designated as back up control centers when Teaball communications failed.) Red Crown controlled all the strike, chaff, and escort forces, and Teaball could warn these forces on Guard it they were being attacked. Red Crown could also give warnings to the MiGCAP forces (who were not on their radio frequency) on Guard if they were being attacked.

While Teaball controlled the MiGCAP, Disco could, with a consistent QRC-248 IFF radar contact on a MiG, take over control if Teaball chose to pass it. Additionally, if Teaball went down, Disco would take over; if both were down, then Red Crown would take over.[8] While this was confusing enough, these instructions were combined with almost daily minor procedural changes, often increasing Air Force crew confusion about the critical matter of who was to warn them about MiGs.[9]

Linebacker Conferences

After the first few months of Linebacker I, it was clear the problems of coordinating a single air strike involving aircraft from four (or more) bases was much more difficult than previously anticipated. On July 10–11, the U.S. military held a conference in Saigon to try to solve some of the many problems with the Linebacker missions. The problems discussed ranged from the large ones—how all the MiG position information input could be combined into a single source that could give the Linebacker crews better MiG warning—to smaller ones, such as how to keep Air Force strike flights entering North Vietnam over the Gulf of Tonkin from mixing with Navy flights carrying out their missions in the same area. (It was agreed that the Air Force flights would stay at 16,000 feet and above and the Navy flights at 14,000 feet and below, and that the strikes would be separated by one hour.)[10] Even with its broad scope and limited results, the July conference bore the seeds of major improvements in Linebacker operations. The response to the conference was so enthusiastic that the Air Force began to explore the possibility of more such conferences, including daily meetings to discuss the previous day's Linebacker missions.

Beginning in August Seventh Air Force decided to hold daily postmission debriefings and critiques of the Linebacker missions, called Linebacker Conferences, to try to quickly solve problems as soon as they arose.[11] At first the conferences involved only the tactical wings, but they quickly expanded, with representatives from the support agencies—GCI, planners, and tankers[12]—meeting at Udorn and discussing what went wrong (and right) and looking at ways to solve the problems. The initial Linebacker Conferences were chaired by a general officer—the commander of Seventh/Thirteenth Air Force, a hybrid organization based at Udorn;[13] Seventh Air Force in Saigon also sent representatives.

At first, the idea of a mass debriefing in front of the Seventh Air Force staff and a general officer was not at all popular with the combat wings and the aircrews.[14] The crews knew there were problems with the operation, but they also understood the "fog of war" and that mistakes were part of any combat operation. Based on bitter past experience, the crews were afraid that discussing mistakes made on missions in front of noncombat flying staff—who would report these mistakes to higher headquarters—would be another way for the leadership to try to heap blame on the combat aircrews.

Fortunately, the crews' fears were unjustified. Seventh Air Force leadership was much more interested in "getting the job done" than in hanging people, and the mass debriefings were used as a tool for improving operations and passing on suggestions for improving tactics and procedures. The crews quickly appreciated the value of the conferences, and it quickly became clear that, until the implementation of the Linebacker Conferences, most crews had not known what the other flying and support organizations were really doing or what their problems were. While the crews in each wing had all the expertise on how to improve the missions in their particular areas, the press of the daily operations had prevented them from passing it on. Briefings for Linebacker missions often took place at 5:30 A.M., and with regular weather delays, the missions often were not over until late in the afternoon. After a mission came the debriefing, preparation for the next morning's mission, and then finally bed; the days often were fifteen hours long. With such a schedule, the experienced crews who flew the high-threat missions every day simply did not have the time or energy to relay suggestions for improvement to headquarters.[15]

This all changed with the Linebacker Conferences. Once started, the face-to-face interchange and the debriefings proved extraordinarily valuable; each mission was reviewed in detail—a normal Linebacker Conference debriefing took about six hours—and while they were "lemon squeezes," they were also very professionally done. The strike forces now were able to get instant feedback and make changes quickly, and coordination began to improve dramatically (if sporadically).

Preparing for the conferences was serious business. Each tactical unit documented all the problems its crews had during the mission, then a wing representative who had flown the mission took the problems to the conference to discuss with other unit representatives. The benefits were many: Each unit could learn the others' problems, workable solutions could be achieved quickly, and the solutions could be implemented immediately when the representatives returned to their bases. Problems that could not be solved immediately or that required higher-level help were relayed by the Seventh Air Force representative to headquarters.

One of the main uses of the Linebacker Conferences was finding solutions to the many problems U.S. forces encountered because of poor radio communications and poor coordination. While some of these problems seemed trivial, the synergistic effects of all of the problems had a very serious, negative impact on operations. As an example of how common such problems were, in the ninety-seven Linebacker missions flown from August to December 1972, MiGCAP aircraft reported thirty-seven problems with communications and sixteen with coordination; the strike forces reported seventeen with communications and twenty-seven with coordination, and the support forces twenty-seven with communication and fifty-one with coordination. It should be noted that these problems covered only the period from August to December, after the Linebacker Conferences started. The problems had been much worse from May through July, the first three months of Linebacker.

Probably the worst problem area of Linebacker operations—and the most intractable—was poor radio communication. Crowded communications had been a problem for Air Force strikes during Rolling Thunder, but (as might be expected) nothing had been done to improve them. Since a normal Air Force Linebacker mission had almost twice the number of tactical aircraft flying into Hanoi as a Rolling Thunder mission, the communications problem grew exponentially. During Linebacker the Air Force strikes over North Vietnam were on several different frequencies, each force—chaff, strike, escort, and MiGCAP—talking to a different agency and none talking to each other. The only way to talk to the entire force was on Guard channel, but Guard channel was used by many other organizations—with very powerful radios—to broadcast their messages. Most of these messages on Guard had nothing to do with the Linebacker strikes (one of the most common was warnings of B-52 Arc Light strikes in extreme southern North Vietnam) and further clogged the radio channels, and often on Linebacker missions U.S. forces managed to completely jam their own communications.

The structural problems were combined with the extremely poor-quality radios of the F-4. This was another area that the Air Force and the builder of the F-4, McDonnell, had not tried to correct; amazingly, even after several years of war McDonnell claimed to be unaware of the problem.[16] The F-4 radios were bitterly criticized in postwar analyses; one report said, "Effective modern fighter operations are heavily dependent upon clear, reliable radio communications. The radios now installed in the F-4 do not meet these criteria." Another analysis said, "A solution must be found to the radio problem if the F-4 is to compete effectively in the modern warfare arena."[17] One report noted the confusion caused by the poor U.S. radios and the large numbers of aircraft on a single frequency and commented, "The combined effect of these factors may well explain the apparent [North Vietnamese] lack of interest in . . . [radio] jamming."[18]

Teaball took over in August 1972 as the agency primarily responsible for MiG warnings, but it quickly became clear to the crews that it had been brought on line too quickly. While Teaball had very sophisticated intelligence-gathering arrangements, it had very poor radios and in general could not communicate directly with the strikes; instead, Teaball was entirely dependent on the radio relay aircraft, Luzon, to pass information to the flights over North Vietnam. Unfortunately, Luzon proved to be extremely unreliable in general, and specifically their radios regularly failed. Even when the system was working, having to use a radio relay meant that any warnings received were sixty seconds old by the time the flight got them. Another continuing problem was interference on the frequency used by the relay aircraft; some thought it was jamming by EB-66s, but this was never confirmed.

Because of the radio relay aircraft and other technical problems, Teaball regularly failed, and when this happened, the MiG warnings to the Linebacker flights suffered because it took time for Teaball to pass the responsibility to Disco and/or Red Crown. August 26 was a classic example of where Teaball's failure cost the American forces dearly. MiGs were continuing to launch early to try to intercept U.S. forces as they entered North Vietnam, so the first F-4 flights of each mission were sent as BAR-CAP to protect the tankers as they refueled the strike force. On this day two Marine F-4Js, Motion Alpha, were BARCAP for the daily Linebacker mission when Red Crown warned them of MiGs in the area. Instead of leaving the mission to Red Crown, Teaball took over control of the F-4s (who did not have radar contact with the MiGs) and turned the Phantoms to make a head-on pass on the North Vietnamese. As the F-4s closed on the MiGs, Teaball had a systems failure and went off the air without passing control to Disco or Red Crown, and the F-4s went into the engagement without the MiGs in sight or on radar. Red Crown came up just as the

MiGs and F-4s passed, but it was too late; the small MiGs had already seen the large, smoking F-4s. Motion Alpha 1 saw Motion Alpha 2 explode; a camouflaged MiG-21 flashed over the fireball, dived into the cloud deck, and escaped. It was later learned that, in addition to Teaball, the radio relay aircraft had failed.

Because of Teaball failures, MiG-21s were regularly able to elude the MiGCAP and get to the strike/chaff flights, and this put pressure on the close escort flight either to go after the MiGs as soon as they were warned of their presence—leaving the chaff/strike force unprotected— or wait until the MiGs hit and hope for the best. To counter these MiG attacks, at the Linebacker Conference on August 20 the wings agreed to change the MiGCAP and escort tactics. MiGCAP flights would fly immediately in front of the chaff and strike forces instead of patrolling near the MiG airfields, so they could be diverted quickly to engage MiGs approaching the chaff/strike flights; this would allow the escort force to remain as a back up if the MiGCAP's engagement proved unsuccessful. The conference participants also agreed to allow some of the close escort flights to use some variations in tactics, even allowing them to operate as two-ship flights and vectoring one pair in a spoiling attack against MiGs when they were about 20 miles away, as long as they were under radar control by Red Crown or Disco. Experience had shown that, if the MiGs perceived that they were being threatened before they started their final attack, there was an excellent chance they would break off, but once they began their attack run they were very aggressive and almost impossible to divert.[19] While this proved fairly effective (even though it smelled of the Navy's two-ship formations), the Air Force pilots were not trained to engage with only two F-4s and could not take advantage of this new flexibility.[20]

By August SAMs were becoming more effective, and the Linebacker Conferences began to reflect this as the wing representatives pressed for destruction of certain specific SAM sites. This led the 366th TFW at Korat to develop SAM "hunter-killer" teams of F-105Gs and F-4Es armed with cluster bombs.[21] The hunter-killer idea had been under discussion for some time, and within a week the Iron Hand flights were flying these missions. In practice, a pair of F-105Gs flew ahead to locate the SAM sites with their sensors and then fired their anti-radiation missiles to take out the radar or force it to shut down; the F-4Es followed up with CBU-52s, a new, very effective type of cluster bomb. The CBUs made it possible for the hunter-killer teams to wipe out a site—the radar vans, missiles, and other equipment—whereas in the past all the ARMs could do was knock out the radar antenna. The F-4Es also played a useful role in protecting the F-105Gs from MiG attack.

The hunter-killer teams were usually directed to support the chaff or the strike forces and for the first part of the mission focused on keeping the SAM radars off the air by firing ARMs. The Weasels aggressively orbited the SAM sites trying to draw the North Vietnamese into an attack; the North Vietnamese tried to avoid engaging the Weasels while waiting for the strike force. After the force left the area, if there had been no SAM activity the F-4Es accompanying the Weasels would attack known SA-2 sites or other targets—including airfields—with their CBUs. From the beginning, the hunter-killer missions worked well and proved extremely effective, forcing the North Vietnamese to move their missiles more often, pay more attention to camouflaging the SAM sites, and be very careful in turning on their radar.

An early Linebacker Conference noted that the MiGs had returned to orbiting at high altitude—about 30,000 feet—before descending for their attacks, and this information quickly proved useful.[22] A few days later, on August 28, Teaball had communications problems again and Disco stepped into the gap. As Buick, a Combat Tree MiGCAP, was leaving the area, Disco turned them toward two MiG-21s. Two other F-4 MiGCAP flights converged on the two MiGs, but Buick got there first. Buick 1 remembered from the Linebacker Conference to look for the MiGs at a high altitude, and as the flights passed he saw the MiGs above him at about 28,000 feet and made a climbing turn behind them. Buick 1 fired two AIM-7s from maximum range—a little over four miles—and missed, then closed and fired two more Sparrows, still at long range. The first missed off one of the MiGs' left wing, but the startled MiG made a sharp turn that reduced the range the second missile had to travel; the missile hit and destroyed the MiG, making the F-4 front seater the first Air Force ace.

At the end of August, the Linebacker Conferences and many of the changes the Air Force made in July seemed to be working. The MiG kill ratio had improved significantly, and though only a few had been flown, the two daily strike missions had brought the support:strike ratio down to 3.65 support aircraft for each strike aircraft.

Navy F-8/Udorn Tactics Exchange

In August and September a group of F-8 pilots from carrier USS *Hancock* spent several weeks at the 432nd TRW at Udorn to fly air-to-air training missions with the F-4 crews there. Udorn was responsible for most of the Air Force MiGCAP missions and was the Air Force's premier MiG-killing wing; they had a good deal of pride in their accomplishments, and it was hoped that both sides might learn something.

It did not work out that way. The well-trained F-8 pilots, using their loose deuce tactics, embarrassed the 432nd TRW F-4 crews flying fluid four. The F-8s were consistently able to surprise the F-4 formations, herd them around the sky, and generally dominate the engagements. The F-8 pilots, used to dueling with the Navy's Topgun F-4 crews, were appalled by the Air Force tactics and formations and by the crews' lack of skill in air combat maneuvering—especially considering this was the base responsible for air-to-air missions. One of the F-8 pilots said, "The contest between the F-4s and our F-8s was so uneven at first we [the F-8 pilots] were almost ashamed of the disparity. . . . The sight that remains in my mind from this is a chilling one, for any number of MiG pilots must have identical views; the pitiful spectacle of four super aircraft [the Air Force F-4s] in front of you, all tucked in close finger four, pulling a level turn. An Atoll fired anywhere in parameters would find itself in the position of the proverbial mosquito in the nudist colony. It would hardly know where to begin."[23]

It was a tense situation. The F-8 pilots felt the Air Force crews needed basic instruction, not just training missions. Air Force tactics were predictable and standardized, their formations were wrong, and they did not use the F-4s' primary advantages in a dogfight by keeping the fight fast and using vertical maneuvers. They found the Air Force crews were "Sparrow-tuned" (like Navy F-4 crews before Topgun) and did not try to maneuver to use the much more reliable AIM-9. To add to the problems, the F-8 pilots were used to rough-and-tumble air combat debriefings and were willing to call a mistake a mistake, which did not always sit well with the Air Force crews, who were not used to losing, much less having their mistakes aired in the debriefings. Further, many of the Air Force pilots were graduates or even instructors of the Air Force Fighter Weapons School, which had developed and preached fluid four for years and violently resisted any attempts to change.

After the exchange, the Navy sent a report to PACAF Headquarters, where they toned down the F-8 pilots' comments considerably but said that there appeared to be some deficiencies in Air Force tactics and training. But rather than examine the training deficiencies the report pointed out, PACAF said the report was an example of interservice bias and disregarded it.[24] On the other hand, the Udorn crews found the exchange helpful, and one Air Force pilot later commented that this training helped him shoot down two MiGs.[25] In the long term it would be even more helpful because it confirmed what most Air Force F-4 crews already knew—that they had a long way to go in air combat training. But they also knew that somebody—albeit in a different uniform—knew the way.

September 1972

In September the Air Force was regularly scheduling two strike sorties a day, one with LGBs and a heavy escort (about 3:1 support to strike ratio) and one "dumb bomb" strike with about a 1.5:1 support to strike ratio; overall the support:strike ratio was down to about 2.25 support aircraft for every striker, the best of the campaign. The strikes also added tactical flexibility—they could be executed sequentially or close to the same time and from different directions to put additional pressure on the North Vietnamese defenses.

Two daily missions had a side benefit that was somewhat unexpected—the percentage of missions attacked by MiGs dropped significantly. The North Vietnamese continued to fly the same number of MiG missions but appeared unable to increase them to keep pace with more U.S. strikes; U.S. intelligence speculated it was because of a limited number of pilots (possibly caused by attrition), interdiction of the airfields, damage to the GCI,[26] or a combination of the three.

While the percentage of U.S. strikes attacked by MiGs declined, the MiGs continued to be very aggressive. On September 2 Eagle, a hunter-killer flight of two F-105Gs (1 and 2) and two F-4Es (3 and 4) was flying a SAM suppression mission near Phuc Yen airfield when they heard a radio warning—"White bandits [MiG-19s] attacking Phuc Yen"—and the second F-105 saw an Atoll heading for Eagle 1. The F-105s made a hard turn and the missile missed, but the MiG continued on and made a cannon attack on the lead F-105, missing again. The MiG-19 set up to attack again when the two F-4Es closed on the battle. The F-4s could not see the small MiG and simply headed for the F-105s; as they got closer, they finally saw the MiG still focused on the F-105s. The F-4s pulled behind him and Eagle 3 fired an AIM-7, but shortly after he fired he had to break to avoid a SAM. When he turned back the MiG was gone, but his wingman and one of the F-105 crews saw the missile hit the MiG and the pilot eject.

On September 9, eight MiGs (six MiG-21s and two MiG-19s) from Phuc Yen and Gia Lam attempted to intercept an Air Force strike on bridges close to the Chinese border. Olds, a Tree MiGCAP flight carrying the new AIM-9Js, was vectored toward a "black bandit" (a MiG that was almost out of gas) that was trying to land at the Phuc Yen airfield. As the F-4s approached, they saw a silver MiG-21, an easy target flying slowly with its landing gear and flaps down, preparing to land. Olds 1 pulled in behind the MiG and fired two AIM-7s; both missed (the radar was not locked on), and the gunless F-4D found himself inside minimum range for his other missiles. The MiG was now aware of his danger and pulled up his gear and flaps and began to maneuver against the F-4D; this was not a good situation for the gunless F-4, in a slow speed fight with a MiG-21. The Olds 1 wingman commented later, "I can recall . . . thinking this was not the best thing. It was a little uncomfortable with the MiG back there at 8 o'clock; there was some doubt in my mind who was going to win. I didn't like the airspeed. It all worked out in the end because 03 was in the right position."[27] Olds 3—an F-4E with internal cannon—was now in position and was cleared by Olds 1 to attack. As Olds 3 closed rapidly on the MiG, Olds 1 dropped out of minimum range and tried to have Olds 3 break off the attack on the slow-flying MiG so he could get the kill, but Olds 3 was in perfect position and (not surprisingly) did not hear the call to let Olds 1 have the kill. Olds 3 closed and fired two AIM-9Es that failed to guide, then opened fired with his 20-mm cannon, scoring hits all over the MiG, which crashed close to the airfield.

Olds flight then turned back toward its CAP point when they were told by Teaball that they had MiGs behind them. The F-4s turned back at low altitude and Olds 1 got a Tree contact on the MiGs at 15 miles. Two MiG-19s and the F-4s passed head on, and the F-4s began their attack, apparently unseen. As the F-4s pulled behind, one of the MiGs saw them and dived away; Olds 1 fired two AIM-9Js at the turning MiG, but before he saw the results he turned after the second MiG-19. The second MiG was in a hard turn as Olds 1 closed and fired another AIM-9J from a high angle off—about 50 degrees—and with both aircraft in a five-G turn. This was well out of the envelope of the earlier AIM-9s, but the new missile worked perfectly and hit the MiG in the tail; the North Vietnamese rolled over and crashed. As the flight left the area, Olds 4 was hit by anti-aircraft fire and began to lose fuel rapidly; the F-4 made it to Laos, where the crew ejected and were later rescued. When the flight landed, two of the other F-4s reported that Olds 1's first missile detonated about 20 to 25 feet behind the first MiG. Intelligence later reported that the MiG had caught fire and crashed on landing, so Olds 1 received credit for his second MiG. The AIM-9J's debut had been impressive—it had scored two kills for two launches, and more importantly, the missile had been fired at the very edge of the envelope, where it might have been expected to perform poorly. The double kill also made Olds 1's back seater the second Air Force ace.[28]

While the air battles raged, intelligence reports were beginning to show that, despite the massive effort and the new guided bombs, the bombing campaign was not meeting its aims. An analysis of Linebacker strikes from August 22 to September 26 showed that only 25 percent of North Vietnam's oil storage capacity had been destroyed, and electric power plant and transformer attacks had few long-lasting results. The analysis also showed that the North Vietnamese were able to keep the major highways open. Based on this, there was a shift in Linebacker targeting emphasis in late September and October to focus on targets in Route Packages V and VI that supported resupply from the Chinese border and to try to isolate the triangle of Hanoi, Haiphong, and Ninh Binh by concentrating on fewer targets with greater force and consistency. Additionally, the wing commanders were given maximum flexibility to strike when weather was good.

To the MiGCAP crews, it was becoming clear that the North Vietnamese realized the United States was reading their IFF, and in August the 432nd TRW reported, "We are certain that [the North Vietnamese are] aware or our ability [to read their IFF]. . . . This has been reflected in a change in their tactics from constantly squawking . . . to use of their IFF only during critical phases of the GCI intercept and recovery." Still, the MiGs had to use their IFF at times and the Tree still helped. To try to counter the non-IFF MiGs, the MiGCAP flights would from time to time make a radio call that their Tree had failed and then operate in a passive mode to entice the MiGs within range for an attack.

With the bad weather, the North Vietnamese moved back to more high-altitude attacks and the MiGCAPs moved back up above the overcast to their medium-altitude CAP altitudes. September 11 was a bad day for both the Air Force and the Navy. On the morning strike the first MiGCAP flight into the area, Chevy, got Tree contacts on MiG-21s, but the MiGs turned off their IFF and Chevy lost contact. As Chevy looked for the MiGs the force timing broke down and the chaff flight entered North Vietnam early, allowing the MiGs to set up an attack before the MiGCAP could find them again. Finch, the chaff escort, saw MiG-21s pass through their formation attacking the chaff flights. The escorting F-4s told the chaffers to break, but the chaffers turned the wrong way and exposed their tails to the MiG-21s; one of the chaffers was shot down. Later that day two Navy F-4s on MiGCAP intercepted two MiG-21s over Phuc Yen; the F-4s destroyed one and damaged the other, but while departing the area one of the F-4s was shot down by an SA-2 and the other ran out of fuel and crashed.

On the morning of September 12 equipment problems again plagued Teaball and its radio relay aircraft, but Air Force escort flights—who usually took a back seat to the MiG-killing MiGCAPs—nevertheless shot down two MiGs on the morning mission. The battles began when Red Crown began to call MiGs approaching the chaffers from the north, but the radio calls were not clear. Finch, the chaff escort flight, elected to stay with the chaffers rather then turn after the MiGs. Finch saw the MiGs behind them and turned into them, but the MiGs ignored the escort and pressed their attack on the chaffers and began to fire Atolls. One missile hit a chaffer; on fire, the F-4 tried to make it to the coast, but the crew had to bail out before they reached the water.

Finch now intervened; as a MiG-21 dived away, Finch 1 fired two AIM-7s that missed, followed by two AIM-9s. The second AIM-9 hit the MiG's left wing, and Finch 1 followed up with a cannon attack for the kill. At the same time, Finch 3 attacked a second MiG-21. He had similar missile problems: He fired his two AIM-7s but they failed to guide, then followed up with three AIM-9s, which passed close to the MiG but did not detonate. Finch 3 continued to close and fired 400 rounds of 20-mm, scoring hits all over the MiG. The MiG pulled into a steep climb, slowing rapidly. As Finch 3 passed he saw the pilot slumped forward in the cockpit, and the MiG rolled off and crashed in a large fireball.

By mid-September it was clear that the GCI control of Air Force strikes had to be revised and the best agency allowed to control the forces. Seventh Air Force still insisted that Teaball be the primary control agency despite its unreliability, but now the Navy's Red Crown was moved to second position. The new arrangements were still confusing, but at least the very effective Red Crown had more responsibility. Now it had control of all MiGCAP flights until the MiGs were airborne, then Teaball took over. However, if Red Crown had a good radar picture and IFF contact with both the MiGs and the U.S. aircraft, it would remain the primary controller. Red Crown was also to take over when Teaball went down. Disco took the strike, chaff, and escort flights and the MiGCAP if both Teaball and Red Crown went down.[29]

On September 16 Teaball was down again when the radio relay aircraft malfunctioned, but Red Crown and Disco were able to take over. Chevy, an F-4 MiGCAP armed with the new AIM-9Js, was vectored by Red Crown to attack a single low-flying MiG-21. In the low-level chase Chevy 1 fired four AIM-9Js; two hit the ground and two missed. Chevy 1 then tried to fire his AIM-7s; two fired but failed to guide, and two failed to launch. Chevy 3 then took over and fired four more AIM-9Js; the first two failed to guide, the third guided but failed to detonate, but the fourth hit the MiG in the tail. The MiG started to turn, then abruptly pitched down, and the pilot ejected just before the MiG hit the ground.

Chevy had fired seven AIM-9Js before the eighth hit, and seven misses in a nonmaneuvering environment was discouraging, even though they had been fired from as low as 50 feet during the chase. The recent misses put AIM-9J's performance back with the rest of the Air Force missiles, and an investigation revealed that the AIM-9J's maximum range at low altitude was much less than had been thought. This had not been caught in the AIM-9J precombat test program because it did not include low-altitude test launches, thus effectively ignoring the large number of combat MiG engagements at low altitude.[30]

On September 30 MiGs were up in strength and both the Americans and the North Vietnamese suffered from missile problems. Olds, a MiGCAP flight, engaged a MiG-21 almost head on and Olds 1 fired three AIM-7s; all missed, and Olds turned behind the MiG and fired four AIM-9Js, which also missed. Olds 1 then fired his last AIM-7; after he watched it hit the ground, he turned the attack over to Olds 2, a cannon-armed F-4E. Olds 2 closed on the MiG, firing his cannon, but he missed as the MiG dived into the clouds. Meanwhile, Olds 3 had engaged a second MiG; he fired an AIM-7 that did not launch, then two AIM-9Js that also missed. Another MiGCAP flight fired three more AIM-7s at another MiG, but all missed. The MiGs had no better luck with their missiles, firing at least five Atolls at strike flights and escorts but scoring no hits.

October 1972

To try to counter the MiG attacks, on October 1 the United States made some of its heaviest attacks on the North Vietnamese airfields during all of Linebacker, destroying five MiGs on the ground and damaging nine more. But despite Teaball, the airfield attacks, and the new GCI arrangements, for most of the rest of October the MiGs were up in force and able to get through unobserved again and again to attack the Air Force missions. On the afternoon of October 1 Chevy, a MiGCAP flight, was attacked from behind by two MiG-21s; an Atoll hit Chevy 2 but did not explode, and the F-4s recovered safely. One of the F-4 strike escort flights was attacked by two MiG-21s, but the F-4s were able outmaneuver the MiGs and two were able to fire missiles, but all missed. One AIM-7 headed for an F-4, but the shooting F-4 broke lock and the missile went ballistic. Other MiGs shot down an F-4 that apparently missed a break call and attacked several other strike flights, firing Atolls from well within the envelope but having one missile after another miss.

On October 2 MiGs got through again. On the morning LGB mission Buick, one of the MiGCAP flights, was being vectored toward six MiGs (four MiG-21s and two MiG-19s) when the MiGCAP F-4s had to maneuver to avoid SAMs. While they were maneuvering, the MiGs slipped past and closed in on the strike flights, with Buick pursuing in full afterburner. The MiGs harried the strike flights, scoring no kills but putting so much pressure on the bombers that only one of the six flights dropped accurately on their target. Before Buick could catch the MiGs to engage, they had to break off because of low fuel; as they tried to reach a tanker, a series of errors resulted in Buick 3 running out of fuel and ejecting. A few minutes later Eagle, an F-105G/F-4E hunter-killer team, was warned by Red Crown that MiGs were attacking. The two F-105s turned to leave the area while the two F-4s began to move to cut off the MiGs. Suddenly two MiGs, a MiG-21 and MiG-19, appeared behind the F-4s and began an attack. The MiG-19 pressed Eagle 4 and opened fire, and the F-4 rolled into a vertical dive with the MiG in hot pursuit; Eagle 3 rolled in behind the MiG, followed by the MiG-21. The fight was now a vertically diving daisy chain: Eagle 4, the MiG-19, Eagle 3, and the MiG-21. Eagle 3, Eagle 4, and the MiG-21 pulled out of their dive about 300 feet above the ground; the MiG-19 could not make the pullout and hit the ground at full speed, still firing at the F-4. An American general read an account of the battle and scribbled, "Guts!" on the side of the report.[31]

On the afternoon of October 8, a single MiG-21 penetrated to the strike flights; he unsuccessfully attacked the bombers but forced several of them to jettison their ordnance. Lark, the strike escort, then attacked the MiG. Lark 1 fired two Sidewinders that did not come off the rail, then closed and shot the MiG down with his cannon. On October 12, a MiGCAP flight, Vega, was leading the strike force into the target when it was vectored toward two MiG-21s. Vega began to pursue; as the F-4s closed on one MiG it turned into them, rolled inverted, and plunged vertically for a cloud deck at 8,000 feet, pulling all four F-4s with him. Later, intelligence reported that the MiG had crashed and Vega 1 was credited with the kill, but while Vega was involved with that MiG the other MiG-21 had gotten to the strike force. The strike escort flight, Sparrow, tried to escape, but the MiG hit Sparrow 3 with an Atoll and the F-4 exploded. The rest of his flight did not see the missile hit; the explosion was seen by Vega flight as they pulled off their chase.

While the American and North Vietnamese air forces were locked in their daily struggle, the peace talks in Paris to halt the war moved on. Suddenly, on October 8, the chief North Vietnamese negotiator, Le Duc Tho, announced the North Vietnamese acceptance of practically all the U.S. proposals. It was a stunning development; as Kissinger was to write later, "Peace came in the guise of the droning voice of an elderly revolutionary. . . . It was less dramatic than we ever imagined."

The announcement had little effect on the air war, however. American aircrews got up in the morning, read the headlines about a breakthrough in the peace talks in the *Stars and Stripes,* the Armed Forces newspaper, then climbed into their aircraft for another trip to Hanoi. On the afternoon of October 15 there was a large series of dogfights, and MiGs again forced U.S. strikers to jettison their ordnance, but the F-4s made them pay. Chevy, a Tree MiGCAP flight, was vectored by Red Crown toward

MiGs that had taken off from Phuc Yen. The F-4s turned toward the MiGs but were unable to get a radar contact when suddenly they saw contrails slightly to their right and passed a MiG-21 in a right descending turn. Chevy 1 turned behind him, firing and missing with three AIM-7s (fired without a radar lock on). The MiG continued his downward spiral and Chevy 1 fired three AIM-9Es; the first two missed but the third hit the MiG in the tail, turning it into a fireball from the wing back as the pilot ejected. A few minutes later, several MiGs ripped through the strike flight, missing with their Atolls but forcing two flights to jettison their ordnance. After the attacks Buick, another Tree F-4 MiGCAP, engaged several MiGs. Buick 1 attacked a MiG-21, but his radar malfunctioned so he cleared Buick 3 to attack. Buick 3 fired an AIM-7 that detonated prematurely immediately in front of his aircraft, fired another AIM-7 that failed to guide, then followed up with a cannon attack; two bursts hit the MiG, and the pilot ejected. In the chase, Buick passed through Parrot flight, an orbiting strike escort flight waiting for the strike force to egress. A few minutes later Parrot saw a chute floating down. Unsure if the chute were American (it was actually the pilot of the MiG Buick shot down), the F-4s turned toward it and, as they approached, found a silver MiG-21 lazily orbiting the same chute. Parrot 1 slid behind the MiG and fired a single AIM-9E that hit the MiG in the tail, blowing off the right elevator. On fire, the MiG snap rolled to the right and dived into the ground.

On October 23 the results of the Paris peace talks finally took effect, and strikes north of the 20° line terminated. Linebacker I was over, but the war was not. The peace agreement was supposed to be signed by October 31, but the secret negotiations were so secret that the South Vietnamese did not know the specifics of the agreement. When they learned the details of the deal Kissinger had made they balked, and Kissinger and Le Duc Tho were forced back to the negotiating table in November for a new round of talks.

Going for Broke: Linebacker II

While it was continuing bombing operations, the United States was also continuing its withdrawal from South Vietnam, and after the bombing halt, the U.S. withdrawal from South Vietnam was hurried on by the very real possibility of a peace settlement; in November 1972, the last Air Force installations in South Vietnam were transferred to the Vietnamese Air Force. The constant high tempo of operations over North Vietnam had put severe pressure on the Navy's carrier force, which was showing the strain of keeping four carriers on Yankee Station; with the end of

Linebacker I, the Navy requested permission to drop to three carriers. Initially this request was denied because of the need for Navy aircraft to continue to support interdiction operations below 20°N and the counteroffensive in South Vietnam, but by the end of November permission was given to reduce the carrier force off Vietnam.

New Air Force F-4s

The final improvement to the Air Force's counter-MiG forces came in late 1972 with the introduction of new F-4Es with leading edge slats on the wings, a program called Rivet Haste. The leading edge slats gave the new F-4s dramatically better maneuverability and handling; not only could the slatted F-4 out-turn the "hard wing" version, but its low speed handling was vastly improved, and more important, the slats virtually eliminated its adverse yaw problems. One official U.S. Air Force publication aimed at F-4 crews said, "This new F-4 will warm the cockles of your heart. . . . [A]dverse yaw is significantly reduced . . . and the ailerons . . . can be used in most all flight conditions."[32] The down side of the slats was minimal; landing was slightly more difficult (the early F-4s, designed for carrier landings, were notoriously forgiving), and the increased drag from the slats decreased the acceleration and forced the new F-4s to slow down faster in a turn, but overall the slats were a major improvement.

The Rivet Haste F-4 improvements did not stop with the slats. All the new F-4s were equipped with the Tree enemy IFF interrogator and also with what was essentially a long-range telescope in the left wing, called a TISEO (Target Identification System, Electro-optical). The TISEO could look the same direction the radar did, and was supposed to give the F-4E capability to visually identify a radar target at long range in time to shoot him with an AIM-7 (in fact, on one occasion TISEO prevented a Rivet Haste F-4 from shooting down another F-4).[33] Finally, the slatted F-4E's cockpit armament switches were vastly improved. As discussed earlier, the arrangement of the armament switches in the cockpits of American fighters had been terrible. While the F-4 was not as bad as the F-105, an official U.S. Air Force magazine devoted to tactical aviation commented in 1972, "A common bond between the oldest 'old head' and the youngest, newest F-4 aircraft commander has been the long time frustration over the front cockpit [switches] . . . undoubtedly laid out by a left-handed, cross eyed pigmy engineer with a demented sense of humor. Not laughing, however, were the many pilots . . . who have lived with the inadequacies far too long."[34]

The new cockpit layout carried most of the air-to-air armament switches on the left throttle and all of the other armament switches and

This superior photograph of a Rivet Haste F-4E shows the leading edge slats on the outboard wing section, the rails for the inboard slats under the inner wing, and the TISEO projecting from the leading edge of the wing directly under the back seater. The white area behind the back seater's head is a hood used for instrument training. *Author's collection*

lights on the upper left-hand side of the instrument panel, where they were easy to see. Now the pilot could select any of the F-4 air-to-air weapons—the gun, the heat-seeking missile, and the AIM-7—by moving a switch on his throttle (where his hand was all the time). No longer did the pilot have to look inside the cockpit and reach for a rotary switch between his legs to select the cannon or feel for a small switch low on the instrument panel to switch from the Sparrow to the Sidewinder. The new cockpit layout—called the 556 Mod (modification)—was a real breakthrough, and the best part was that it was not limited to the new Phantoms, but could be quickly retrofitted to the older F-4Es. By the fall of 1972 older F-4Es in Southeast Asia were being modified, to the delight of the crews.

The Rivet Haste crews were specially trained in air-to-air combat, including missions against the Have Drill MiG-17 and the Have Donut MiG-21, and logically they were sent to the MiGCAP specialists at the 432nd TRW at Udorn. However, rather than follow past procedures of sending new aircraft to a selected squadron or two and letting the combat crews take them over, Air Force leadership decided to form a new squadron stateside, including crews, and send them *en masse* to Udorn.

This idea delayed the deployment of the Rivet Haste F-4s and kept them from being used during Linebacker I, but otherwise the idea of introducing a new aircraft with fully qualified crews appeared sound; unfortunately, the implementation was extraordinarily clumsy. Instead of making the Rivet Haste crews and aircraft a new squadron, as had been done in the past[35] the Air Force decided that they would take over the name and building of the 555th TFS, known as the "Triple Nickel," the leading and most famous MiG-killing squadron in Southeast Asia.[36] The "Nickel" had been in the air-to-air business the entire war; it had begun at Ubon during Rolling Thunder and coincidentally moved to Udorn in 1970, where it continued its MiG-killing ways when Udorn took over the air-to-air role in Linebacker. By the end of Linebacker I the 555th TFS had shot down more MiGs than any other squadron (and most wings) in Southeast Asia, had two (of the three) Air Force aces, and like the other squadrons at Udorn, was manned by the most experienced Air Force air-to-air pilots in Southeast Asia.

It came as a considerable to shock to the 555th TFS aircrews when they were told in the fall of 1972 that many of them were being transferred to other squadrons to make room for the Rivet Haste crews, who would take over much of the Nickel and its illustrious history lock, stock, and barrel. There was considerable grumbling; no one could understand why the new organization simply didn't take a new name rather than usurp the 555th's. When the Rivet Haste aircraft and crews arrived on November 20, 1972, the situation did not improve. The pilots of the "new Nickel," as it quickly became known, expected to be sent immediately on the most lucrative MiGCAP missions, despite the fact that few had recent combat experience. This increased the resentment of the "old Nickel" combat veterans and the rest of the F-4 squadrons at Udorn. But timing made the debate moot; Linebacker I was over, and the Rivet Haste F-4Es went, with the rest of the Air Force fighters in Thailand, to bombing attacks in Laos and against North Vietnamese forces still in South Vietnam.[37]

Increasing the Pressure

Despite the halt to the bombing in extreme North Vietnam, to increase the pressure on the North Vietnamese in October and November B-52s began to move regularly into the southern part of North Vietnam to bomb North Vietnamese supply depots. The B-52s limited their strikes to areas where there were no SAMs and were under orders to break off the mission if they so much as saw a single SAM (much to the amusement and derision of the tactical crews who fought through the SAM defenses around Hanoi every day). The North Vietnamese soon realized this and moved SAMs into the area; as the B-52s approached, the SAM site's radar would come up briefly—long enough to be detected on the B-52's electronics but not long enough to be located—and a missile would be fired, often unguided. As soon as the B-52s saw the SAM radar on their electronic gear and the missile fired, they would divert to a safer target. Soon so many of the B-52 missions were being aborted that the B-52 crews were told to go on in spite of the threat from MiGs and SAMs (still very low in the areas where the B-52s flew).

The North Vietnamese were learning, too. They realized now that the feints on the B-52 strikes were not working, and after watching the B-52s and charting their electronic emissions patterns, on November 5 they struck. Despite the heavy support packages, chaff corridors, and the B-52 jamming, a SAM that was fired using new guidance techniques hit a B-52, causing extensive damage, but the big bomber was able to land safely. On November 22 a B-52 on a mission in the central panhandle of North Vietnam was hit by a SAM and badly damaged; the B-52 was able to drag itself into Thailand, where the crew successfully ejected before it crashed. This was the first B-52 lost in seven years of combat.

Analysis determined that the SAM operators had guided the SAM on the B-52's jamming patterns rather than on the aircraft itself. It was also discovered that the chaff corridor had been blown off by high winds and that the B-52 was out of the corridor, highlighting the vulnerability of a B-52—even with its ECM systems—outside a chaff corridor.[38]

The Peace Talks Collapse

The final peace arrangements were not going well. After the South Vietnamese had objected to parts of the peace plan, the peace talks resumed in Paris on November 20 in an effort to try to iron out the differences. Suddenly, on December 4, the North Vietnamese returned to their old position and became intransigent. Meetings took place on December 6, 7, 11, and 13, but there was no movement, and for practical purposes it appeared the North Vietnamese had broken off the peace talks. The reasons the North Vietnamese took this action remain speculative, but they were certainly aware that Congress had cut off funds for the war and that the days of U.S. military action in Vietnam were numbered. It is possible they were emboldened by the bad weather that marked the onset of the northeast monsoon, which historically had meant a pause in the serious bombing of North Vietnam. The North Vietnamese still did not understand the military mindset of the Nixon administration, despite the mining of Haiphong and other, more aggressive activities, and made a serious mistake in timing—they chose to be intransigent at a time when Congress was out of Washington on Christmas recess. On December 14 Kissinger and Nixon began discussing their alternatives, and Nixon sent Hanoi an ultimatum—serious negotiations would have to resume in seventy-two hours or the bombing would resume. The North Vietnamese did not respond.

The Die Is Cast

Now Nixon decided to execute a massive, maximum-effort bombing campaign, Linebacker II, starting almost immediately. Linebacker II was completely different from the interdiction policy of Rolling Thunder and Linebacker I; Linebacker II would be a sustained maximum effort to destroy all major target complexes in the Hanoi and Haiphong areas. This could not be done by Phantoms, even with LGBs; it required a massive application of force, which could only be exerted by B-52 strikes. Linebacker II also involved the removal of many of the restrictions surrounding the previous operations over North Vietnam, except an attempt to "minimize the danger to civilian population to the extent feasible without compromising effectiveness" and to "avoid known POW compounds, hospitals, and religious structures." In essence, Linebacker II finally gave advocates of air power the opportunity to see if massive concentrated bombing could yield the promised results.

The planning for the operations had begun as early as August 1972,[39] and on the afternoon of December 15 the tactical wings were notified of the coming campaign.[40] Under the guise of a massive strike into southern North Vietnam preparations began,[41] and on December 18 the attacks themselves began, described in the mission execution message as a "three day maximum effort, repeat, maximum effort, of B-52/TACAIR [tactical aircraft] strikes in the Hanoi/Haiphong area. . . . Object is maximum destruction of selected military targets in the vicinity of Hanoi/Haiphong. Be prepared to extend operations past three days, if directed." The bombing was originally authorized against thirty-eight targets in six areas: the Hanoi target complex (thirteen targets), the Haiphong target complex (eight targets), three electric power facilities, three radio communications facilities, four air defense targets, and a transshipment point. Additionally, strikes were authorized against all air defense targets.

B-52 Operations

The B-52s were the key to Linebacker II. By all accounts they were the weapon the North Vietnamese most feared, and the shock effect of B-52s bombing the North Vietnamese cities was expected to be profound. Additionally, the B-52 bombing systems were virtually immune to weather—they bombed by radar, so day, night, or bad weather made no difference. The northeast monsoon would not protect North Vietnam. Still, the decision to send them was not an easy one. All U.S. B-52s had a nuclear commitment, and the production lines had long since closed, so any B-52 losses would diminish America's strategic nuclear force and could not be replaced. And there would be losses—the North Vietnamese were expected to use everything in their defensive arsenal to stop the big bombers.

To support the B-52 strikes into Route Package VI the fighter wings in Thailand made a maximum effort to provide chaffers, SAM suppression aircraft, and MiGCAP, dividing the support about equally between anti-SAM activity and MiGCAP/escort flights. North Vietnamese MiGs were expected to be the biggest danger to the B-52s. They had come very close to shooting a B-52 down before, and since the MiG-21 was designed specifically to intercept the B-52 it was probable they would be the main weapon. The most likely tactic, at least initially, was expected to be the one tried over Laos, where the MiGs stayed low below U.S. radar coverage and then, in full afterburner, executed a steep climb to behind the B-52 formation. To counter the MiGs the Air Force would use its standard tactics, with Tree MiGCAP flights patrolling between the MiG bases and the bomber stream supported by a close escort force. Since the B-52s were to fly at very high altitude—35,000 to 40,000 feet—the close escort F-4s would fly alongside the bomber stream at an altitude of about 25,000 feet and about five miles behind the last aircraft in each B-52 cell. This was far enough behind the B-52s that the F-4s could fire their AIM-7s and be sure the Sparrows would not home on the B-52s' jamming (the AIM-7 had a "home on jamming" feature where the missile guided on a jamming source). If the MiGs tried to pop up from a low position to get behind the B-52s, they would have to fly through and in front of the trailing escort F-4s. As an added advantage for the F-4s, the MiG-21s would have to use their afterburner to get to the B-52s' altitude, and the single flame from a MiG-21 afterburner—clearly different from the two flames from the F-4—would make the North Vietnamese fighters easy to identify at night. The United States had another advantage because the Rivet Haste F-4s had almost doubled the number of Tree F-4s, and it was expected that a MiG-21 with Atolls would be no match for a Tree-equipped F-4 with AIM-7s. The F-4 close escorts planned to escort one B-52 cell, then after the B-52s dropped their bombs, the F-4s would turn back and pick up another B-52 cell, flying an elongated racetrack pattern; the F-4s planned to use their radar to locate the B-52 cells they were to escort and also to keep the proper spacing.

The F-4 crews had escorted B-52s at night early in 1972 and had had problems with using two-ship formations. They had found it very difficult to fly maneuvering formation at night, and when the wingman was thrown out of position, it was impossible for him to get back; after the first severe maneuver the formation would became two single aircraft trying to find each other. Two-ship formations also vastly increased the chances of midair collision. Based on this experience, the F-4 wings asked Seventh Air Force for permission to fly the MiGCAP and escort missions with single F-4s, the classic night fighter technique for as long as night fighters had been flying. The logic of the combat F-4 crews was lost on higher headquarters, however,[42] who decreed that the escort should be flown by two-ship F-4 formations, with the wingman flying—of course—fighting wing. The lead F-4 would be a Tree aircraft and the second would provide additional ECM pod support, as well as backup weapons and radar should the radar on the first F-4 go down. Also, it was felt that the second aircraft would "protect" the Tree aircraft.[43] While this assignment for the wingman sounded impressive, it was impossible to perform. It was, for example, unclear how at night the wingman could see MiGs approaching from behind. The crews believed that the main mission of number 2—who would be behind the Tree-equipped number 1— was, as usual, to simply absorb the Atoll.

The insistence on two-ship formations had a real cost. It doubled the number of F-4s required for B-52 escort duty—F-4s that could have been used to escort day operations. In the event, because of the requirement for two-ship flights at night, the strain of flying night escort missions limited the number of F-4 escorts available for day missions, and from time to time day MiGCAP and escort missions had to be canceled to support the higher-priority night MiGCAPs.[44]

The B-52 Night Missions

The story of the eleven nights of B-52 raids—Linebacker II—over North Vietnam is too long and complex to be told here. At first the B-52s used tactics dictated by Strategic Air Command Headquarters in Omaha, Nebraska. The tactics were not discussed with the fighter crews who went to the Hanoi area every day, but were developed by SAC planners halfway around the world who had no experience in a heavy SAM and MiG environment. The tactics the B-52s used the first three nights over the Hanoi area were exactly the same ones they had used for years over North Vietnam and Laos, down to the same formations, altitudes, and airspeeds—tactics that the North Vietnamese were very familiar with. Additionally, SAC Headquarters sent the B-52s into the target in a string, all flying about the same heading and the same altitude; then, after the B-52s dropped their bombs, they performed a maneuver—the "post target turn"—that blocked their ECM equipment and left them vulnerable to SA-2 attack.

The North Vietnamese took advantage of the U.S. tactical mistakes and during the first three nights shot down so many B-52s that SAC was forced to stop going into the Hanoi area and chose less well defended areas while they developed new tactics. SAC Headquarters began to listen to the B-52 aircrews and finally agreed to let the combat B-52 organizations develop their own plan and tactics. As might be expected, the combat wings developed an excellent plan that gradually overwhelmed the North Vietnamese defenses with relatively few losses.

Defensively, the MiG-21s were expected to be a—if not the—major threat to the B-52s, but they were used relatively little, and their main mission appeared to be to pass information to the SA-2 sites. There were few engagements between F-4s and MiGs, and most were inconclusive and marked by U.S. missile failures.

Linebacker II Day Missions

While the most important part of Linebacker II was the night B-52 strikes, the Air Force and the Navy launched daily tactical strikes against various targets in Route Package VI to keep the pressure on the North Vietnamese defenses. Unfortunately, generally the weather was bad and the flights were forced to drop using their all-weather systems.

The first few days the weather was bad, and U.S. aircrews bombed using these systems; the North Vietnamese provided only a modest defensive reaction, and no MiGs came up. Finally, on December 21, the weather cleared and Air Force and Navy fighter bombers were able to strike visually. The Hanoi power plant, which had long been off limits, was struck by LGBs, which knocked out the power plant and disrupted electrical power to the entire city; this strike was another message to the North Vietnamese that this time the U.S. was serious.

The weather was good again on December 27 and Air Force and Navy aircraft struck targets all over the Hanoi and Haiphong area, using both conventional bombs and LGBs to destroy several important radio sites used for command and control of the North Vietnamese defenses. The hunter-killer teams also used the clear weather to attack the SAM sites that had been most effective against the B-52s. For the first time in Linebacker II day operations MiGs were active and, unfortunately, very effective. On the afternoon mission Vega, a MiGCAP flight entering on an ingress CAP ahead of the strike, was vectored by Red Crown on a MiG-21; as the F-4s approached the MiG Vega 1 fired two Sparrows, but one misfired and the other exploded inside the MiG's turn. The MiG dived for the clouds; Vega 1 and Vega 2 followed while Vega 3 and Vega 4 lost sight of the battle in the clouds and left the area. Vega 1 continued to pursue the MiG through clouds, but after he fired and missed with a Sidewinder the F-4 developed flight control and electrical problems and lost an engine. Meanwhile, Vega 2 lost sight of his leader and, flying alone in the clouds, was attacked and shot down by a prowling MiG-21. Vega 1, after a harrowing low-speed exit from North Vietnam and a botched emergency tanker rendezvous, was able to recover safely.

The force that Vega was to cover struck the target and was departing when two of the escorts, Desoto 3 and Desoto 4, saw a MiG-21 and, in the best fluid four discipline, asked Desoto 1 for permission to attack. In the best single-shooter tradition, Desoto 1 refused permission for his wingman to attack and the two F-4s lost sight of the MiG. As they were leaving the area Desoto 4 saw Desoto 3's centerline tank come off, fire break out in the F-4's belly, and the crew eject. The MiG they had pursued earlier had returned and not missed his opportunity. This was the last significant day engagement of the war, and it ended like the first daylight engagement in April 1965, with two Air Force aircraft down and no MiG losses.

The next day the weather was again good enough for visual strikes and LGBs dropped on the Hanoi highway/railroad bridge. At the same time, hunter-killer teams attacked and destroyed several SAM sites, including one that had been responsible for shooting down or damaging five B-52s. Defensive reaction was minimal, and despite their success the day before, no MiGs were airborne. The once-feared North Vietnamese SAM defenses had become essentially impotent: The chaff corridor—once a *sine qua non* for attacks over Hanoi—was blown away by unusual and unpredicted high winds, making the LGB strike flights vulnerable to attack by SAMs, but the B-52 attacks had reduced the North Vietnamese defenses so much that they were unable to take advantage of the opportunity, and the strike flight returned with no losses.

The End

Now North Vietnam lay prostrate before the B-52s, and the North Vietnamese leadership realized their options were almost gone. Their Soviet and Chinese allies had issued *pro forma* denunciations of the bombings but took no substantive actions, and Kissinger noted that even the North Vietnamese protests were "surprisingly mild"; North Vietnamese negotiators quickly indicated they were willing to return to the peace talks and be more flexible. In recognition of this, the United States stopped the bombing on December 29.[45] This time the North Vietnamese stayed at the peace talks and there was no breakdown; after considerable technical haggling a peace agreement was signed on January 23, 1973. Lyndon Johnson had died the day before.

MiG Activity

The low level of MiG activity was one of the major surprises of Linebacker II. MiG-21s were expected to be the main threat to the B-52s, and the commander of Seventh Air Force commented, "There was a great deal of concern on the part of SAC that the MiGs would get to them, and many of the SAC people felt that the MiG would be a greater threat than the SAMs. This did not turn out to be the case."[46] Post–Linebacker II analysis indicated that the early strikes against airfields and intensive jamming appeared to be the major contributors to the low level of MiG activity; there were only twenty-six MiG reactions to Linebacker II operations, all by MiG-21s.

In retrospect there were a number of possible reasons for the limited MiG reaction to the B-52s. At night, the North Vietnamese GCI was completely dependent on the MiGs' transponders for control; if the MiGs did not use their transponders they could not be guided to the B-52s and might be fired on by their own SAMs. At the same time, using the transponder made the MiGs vulnerable to the large number of Tree-equipped F-4 escorts. The MiG-21s with their primitive radar and short-range, stern-only Atolls were no match for the powerful radar and all-aspect missile of the F-4s.

It should be noted here that the MiGs were not particularly active during the daylight missions. The North Vietnamese GCI network had to work all night against the B-52s, and the GCI controllers—and certainly the best were on at night—might simply have been exhausted.

As a final footnote, when Linebacker II began on December 18, the Air Force was determined to show that the Rivet Haste program was a success, and the new Nickel crews were given the best MiGCAPs in an effort to get them a MiG kill. Despite these efforts, the North Vietnamese did not cooperate. Only four MiGs were shot down by the Air Force during Linebacker II, all by the 432nd TRW and three by the 555th TFS—but to most of the wing's intense satisfaction, all were shot down by old Nickel pilots flying F-4Ds. The Rivet Haste F-4s and their crews came up empty.

9

Looking Back, Looking Ahead

Assessing Linebacker

THE SINGLE MOST significant statistic that came out of Linebacker I and II was a stark, simple one: The Air Force shot down about forty-eight MiGs and lost twenty-four aircraft to MiGs, for a kill ratio of about 2:1. The Navy lost four aircraft to MiGs and shot down twenty-four,[1] for a kill ratio of 6:1.[2] Not only was the Navy's kill ratio much better, but in Linebacker, as in Rolling Thunder, Navy fighters had a much higher rate of kill per engagement than Air Force fighters. In twenty-six Linebacker engagements, the Navy F-4s scored twenty-four kills, or .92 kills per engagement, with four losses, or .15 per engagement. The Air Force F-4s had eighty-two engagements and scored forty-eight kills, or .58 kills per engagement, and lost twenty-four aircraft, or .29 aircraft per engagement. To put it another way, *the North Vietnamese scored a kill about every three times they engaged the Air Force, and about one kill every six and a half times they faced the Navy;*[3] *the North Vietnamese lost a MiG about every two engagements with the Air Force but lost a MiG almost every time they faced the Navy.* Looking at the cold numbers, it is little wonder that from early in Linebacker the MiGs concentrated almost exclusively on Air Force sorties.

The differences between the Air Force and Navy kill ratios were well known even during Linebacker, and after the operations were over the Air Force was forced to address the serious questions about why the Navy had a vastly superior exchange ratio with the North Vietnamese MiGs.[4] The numbers were especially interesting since the Air Force F-4s appeared to have significant advantages over the Navy F-4s in air-to-air combat. Most of the Air Force MiGCAP F-4s carried Combat Tree equipment that allowed them to identify the MiGs at long range, and the Air Force had a number of cannon-armed F-4Es (which scored seven kills with their cannon).

Postwar interviews with Air Force F-4 crews showed that they thought *the first and most important reason for the Navy's higher kill ratio was its*

aggressive training program (Topgun) initiated in 1968. Other causes the
crews listed were as follows:

—The Navy engaged MiGs in a relatively confined area near the coast
while Air Force missions were vulnerable to surprise attacks for a
much longer period of time as they flew over North Vietnam in and out
of Laos (though these same conditions existed in Rolling Thunder
when the Air Force and Navy kill ratios were about the same).

—The Air Force flew mainly against the MiG-21 and MiG-19 while the
Navy flew mostly against the older MiG-17 (68 percent of Air Force
engagements were against the MiG-21s versus 42 percent of the Navy's;
the Navy flew 48 percent of its engagements against the MiG-17,
whereas the Air Force rarely encountered it).

—The Air Force flew most of its missions at relatively high altitude
because of the chaff corridors. While this reduced the danger from
ground defenses, it gave the North Vietnamese a great deal of warning
about the strike and put the MiG-21 in its best environment. (On the
plus side, the AIM-7 Sparrow—the Air Force's weapon of choice—was
much more effective at higher altitude.)

—The Navy usually flew near the coast where it had excellent GCI support from Red Crown; while the Air Force utilized Red Crown whenever
possible, many of its flights were out of Red Crown's range, forcing the
Air Force to rely on Disco and Teaball.[5]

Equipment Performance

Overall Air Force missile performance continued to be poor during Linebacker, even worse than during Rolling Thunder. After a good start the
AIM-9J's performance in combat was unimpressive. Thirty-one were
fired; four hit, four failed to launch, and twenty-three missed the target
(at least four because of crew error), for a hit rate of about 13 percent. The
Air Force fired sixty-four AIM-9Es and scored five kills for 8 percent, and
overall the Air Force fired ninety-five AIM-9s and scored nine kills for a
success rate of 11.5 percent. The Air Force took pains to point out that
the AIM-9J's hit ratio was better than that of the AIM-9E, but this certainly was damning by faint praise. The comparison was also deceptive
because the AIM-9Js were usually carried by the best air-to-air crews, who
should have been more successful no matter which missile they used. In
fact, combat and later tests on the AIM-9J showed that it offered only a
small improvement over the AIM-9E, and in some areas it was actually
not as good as the earlier Sidewinder. Many of the AIM-9J's problems

were later overcome, and if the Air Force had not stopped testing the AIM-9J between Rolling Thunder and Linebacker Air Force F-4 crews might have had a reliable heat-seeking missile for Linebacker. The Navy's AIM-9G still proved much superior to the Air Force's AIM-9E and AIM-9J; it had fired fifty AIM-9Gs for twenty-three kills (46 percent).[6]

About 281 AIM-7E-2 dogfight Sparrows had been fired and had scored about 34 kills, for about 12 percent; the percentage of hits was about the same for both services. As Topgun had forecast, the AIM-7 reliability was terrible—about 66 percent of the AIM-7s fired by both services malfunctioned.[7] Because of its considerable reliability problems Air Force crews' opinions of the dogfight Sparrow varied greatly, probably because different wings put a different level of effort into maintaining the missile. Not surprisingly, the 432nd TRW at Udorn, with its MiGCAP mission and Tree aircraft, put considerable effort into keeping its crews trained on the AIM-7E-2 and its Sparrows "peaked," and the results showed it. The Air Force's first ace—an Udorn pilot—got all of his kills with the AIM-7E-2 (five kills in thirteen firings), often scoring hits on the very edge of the missile's envelope, and proclaimed himself "very pleased with the [F-4's] weapons system . . . particularly the performance of the AIM-7E-2 dogfight missile."[8]

Air Force general officers shrugged off the missile problems with an "I don't want to talk about it" attitude. One high-ranking general with a fighter background who had been at Seventh Air Force for part of Linebacker—an officer who should have been very familiar with the various missiles—showed impressive ignorance when he said, "The AIM-9E was disappointing and I really don't know why. The Navy Sidewinder [AIM-9D/G], *which is really not too much different than the missile we had,* performed better. I think one of the reasons was that our [Air Force] crews felt that the AIM-7 was just a better missile" (emphasis added).[9]

The differences in the Air Force and Navy air-to-air training programs and weapons employment philosophy were clearly shown in their weapons results. The Air Force used the AIM-7 for thirty of its forty-eight kills while the Navy scored twenty-three of its twenty-four kills with the AIM-9. The Air Force scored nine kills with the AIM-9E/J and seven with the F-4E internal cannon, and two were "maneuvering" kills, where the MiG hit the ground trying to avoid an attack.

There was a very interesting difference in the tactical missile firing philosophy of the two services that reflected both the difference in training and the reliability of their missiles. In at least one wing, the 432nd (which scored thirty-three of the Air Force's forty-eight kills), when an F-4 was in firing position on a MiG with one type of missile selected, *the general policy was to fire all of this type of missile at this single MiG.*[10]

This meant that Air Force crews practically had only two firing passes—one where they fired all of their AIM-7s and one where they fired all of their AIM-9s—and consequently Air Force crews scored relatively few multiple kills with missiles. The well-trained Navy crews, on the other hand, usually fired one AIM-9 at a time; with four AIM-9s a Navy F-4 had four firing passes, and the Navy had a significant number of multiple missile kills on a single mission.

Combining the Air Force Linebacker missile firing philosophy and the Air Force tactical formation philosophy produced an interesting result that also helps explain the difference in kill ratios. An Air Force fluid four formation consisted of four F-4s carrying a total of thirty-two missiles (sixteen AIM-9s and sixteen AIM-7s). If this tactical unit used standard Air Force engagement techniques—single shooter and firing all missiles of a type in one pass—*the four F-4s had two firing passes against MiGs.*

On the other hand, the Navy's tactical unit, loose deuce, carried sixteen missiles (eight AIM-9s and eight AIM-7s), but using a single AIM-9 for each pass and having each F-4 free to attack, the two Navy F-4s had *eight firing passes against MiGs.* In other words, *two Navy F-4s had four times the firepower of four Air Force F-4s.*

Finally, another equipment problem that had not been resolved between Rolling Thunder and Linebacker was the F-4's 600-gallon centerline tank. The F-4 manual said the centerline could be jettisoned up to 425 knots, but one F-4 pilot commented, "Experience at our base indicated that, regardless of how we jettisoned the centerline tank, one out of six was going to hit the aircraft. We finally settled on [jettisoning them at] 300 knots straight and level. . . . They still continued to hit the aircraft, but they did less damage at 300 knots than at 425 knots."[11] Even worse, during Linebacker the nose cone of the centerline tank sometimes broke off; when this happened, the F-4 pitched up violently and went out of control.[12] The Air Force lost one of its multiple MiG killers when, doing mild maneuvers while returning home after a mission, the centerline tank's nose cone tore off and the F-4 snapped up, went out of control, and crashed, with no survivors.

Significant Engagement Factors

The Air Force looked carefully at Linebacker and Rolling Thunder engagements to see if they could identify the significant factors that influenced the outcomes. According to the postwar U.S. Air Force studies, *the most important element in the loss of both U.S. aircraft and MiGs remained the element of surprise;* almost 60 percent of the aircraft lost in combat were unaware of the attack, and another 21 percent were aware of the attack only when it was too late to initiate successful maneuvers. A logical outcome of this was that positional advantage was the second most significant factor in the outcome of an engagement. Most—about 75 percent—of the attacks were initiated when the attacker was behind the defender and when the defender was in a 60-degree cone off the attacker's nose. This led the Air Force to the same conclusion that had been reached at the end of Rolling Thunder: Many of these aircraft could have successfully defended themselves if they had had adequate, real-time warning of MiGs behind them.

For general officers explaining the Air Force's lack of success, lack of warning came to mean lack of GCI; in fact, as in Rolling Thunder, the explanation for the high Air Force loss rate was more complex than just lack of radar warning. Many times the Air Force F-4s knew that there were MiGs in the area; they simply did not see them until the MiGs began their attack. While the MiGs were small and hard to see, poor training,[13] poor formation lookout, and poor cockpit visibility were at least as responsible as poor GCI for the Air Force's inability to locate the MiGs visually.

In addition to surprise and position, speed and altitude were also significant factors in the engagements. In about 75 percent of the losses on both sides the victor had a speed advantage over his victim. During Linebacker the chaff corridors made high-altitude engagements a common occurrence and at high altitudes the MiG-21 had a significant performance advantage over the F-4. U.S. weapons systems, especially airborne radar and the AIM-7 missile, were much more effective at high altitude than low, but notwithstanding this, the MiGs were more effective in engagements above 15,000 feet and F-4s more so below 7,000 feet; over 60 percent of MiG losses happened below 7,000 feet.

The Air Force also looked to other factors that influenced the outcome of engagements. Offensively, the most important factors—by far—in getting kills over North Vietnam were (1) flying MiGCAP (as opposed to escort) missions and (2) flying as the leader of a MiGCAP flight. MiGCAP flight leaders usually flew F-4Ds equipped with Tree and often arrived in North Vietnam early so they could fire AIM-7s without having visually to identify the target, and also were free to pursue the MiGs aggressively. Additionally, in fluid four the MiGCAP leader was the only one who was automatically free to fire, with three F-4s whose sole role was to support and protect him, so it was not surprising the MiGCAP flight leaders got the most kills.

There was also a strong correlation between previous air-to-air combat training and air-to air success, and the study (conducted by the Fighter Weapons School) noted that the Fighter Weapons School graduates had most of the kills during Linebacker. In fact, there was a correlation, but it was not clear that the cause of their success was the skills learned in the Fighter Weapons Schools. Graduates generally had more F-4 and fighter experience than the other pilots in the squadron, and flight leaders were invariably chosen on the basis of experience. Since a disproportionate number of flight leaders were Fighter Weapons School graduates, they had a disproportionate share of the kills, but there is no evidence that Fighter Weapons School flight leaders scored a higher percentage of kills than non-Fighter Weapons School flight leaders.

Yet another factor that was highly correlated to kills was total missions and the number of missions over North Vietnam; however, since pilots with the most missions over North Vietnam were usually chosen to be flight leads, once again the main causative factor in scoring MiG kills seemed to be flight position, no matter what criteria were used to be chosen for that position. (Interestingly, because of the loose deuce formation, the Navy found flight position seemed to be unimportant in scoring kills.)

Defensively, formation position was also very important—number 3 and number 4 in the fluid four formation, especially number 4, suffered disproportionately. The amount of fighter time and total flying time were also important (probably because both generally dictated the pilot's flight position) while other types of flying time and pilot age were not. The causation between flight position and loss rates was clear, and the report recommended that the Air Force "review doctrine for tactics and formations and reduce the vulnerability of the second element . . . if the decision is made to retain four ship flights."[14]

In escaping from a MiG attack combat experience appeared to be the most important factor; the more combat experience a pilot had, the better his chances of survival when he was attacked. The study did not examine why, but it is probable that an experienced pilot was more likely to be on the lookout for MiGs, was probably better at seeing a MiG or an Atoll, and was more likely to quickly jettison his bombs and maneuver immediately when he was attacked.

Teaball

Losses to MiGs fell substantially after mid-August 1972, and this success against the MiGs was initially credited to Teaball. U.S. Air Force histories point out that from the time Teaball was activated until the end of Linebacker I the Air Force kill ratio went from less than one MiG shot down for each Air Force fighter lost to almost four MiGs for each Air Force loss.[15] The "godfather" of Teaball and commander of Seventh Air

Force, General J. W. Vogt, was effusive in his praise, saying, "With the advent of Teaball we dramatically reversed this [loss-to-victory ratio], and in August, September, and October . . . during Linebacker I, we were shooting down the enemy at the rate of four to one. Same airplane, same environment, same tactics; largely [the] difference [was] Teaball. It was one of the most impressive developments we've had out here."[16]

The change in kill ratio made Teaball seem successful, but in fact, the number of MiGs shot down continued at about the same rate after Teaball came on the air; it was because Air Force losses began to sharply decrease beginning in August that the F-4:MiG exchange ratio changed. Teaball supporters were quick to give it the credit, but in fact Teaball was mainly responsible for controlling the MiGCAP forces; if there was an indicator of success, it should have been in more MiG kills, not less losses. In fact, the percentage of kills by the MiGCAP dropped significantly after Teaball took over control.[17]

Despite General Vogt's enthusiasm for his brainchild, objective postwar reports about Teaball were not flattering. The most in-depth U.S. Air Force assessment of Linebacker operations, Red Baron III, said:

> Although it [Teaball] had the potential capability to provide timely information to Linebacker forces, several serious deficiencies affected Teaball's ability to perform its mission and made questionable its effectiveness in supporting offensive air-to-air operations. These deficiencies included the following:
>
> a. A shortage of personnel with the necessary training, experience, and security clearances limited its ability to support Linebacker day missions and made it nearly impossible to support missions at night.
> b. [Teaball] was totally dependent on the radio relay aircraft for direct communications with the Linebacker forces.
> c. Lack of automated equipment for handling and displaying certain types of information [prevented it from having] real-time capability.
> d. Vulnerability to UHF jamming.
> e. Lack of redundancy in equipment.
> f. Dependence on outside agencies for sources of information.
> g. Frequent changes in procedures created confusion in the minds of the aircrews.
> h. Security requirements [that] prevented the aircrews from fully appreciating the significance of Teaball's information.[18]

This last item was a particular problem with Teaball. As late as the October 1, 1972, Linebacker Conference—after Teaball had been in service for almost two months—the Teaball representative had to plead with the aircrews to make some sort of a defensive move when Teaball told a flight that MiGs were attacking; the crews simply did not attach much credibility to Teaball's information.

The F-4 crews that used Teaball in combat gave final proof that it was much less useful than its advocates claimed. A typical comment was, "Disco and Teaball tried . . . [but] for some reason they were always behind as far as sending information to aircrews. By the time we learned of MiGs from Disco or Teaball one of our compadres was already in flames or in a break turn."[19] Red Baron III concluded, "Red Crown was the major source of warnings during the Linebacker period. It generated the same number of warnings when Teaball was in operation as it had before. It appears Teaball did not make a very big contribution compared to Disco and Red Crown."[20] Finally, in a postwar survey of the relative effectiveness of control agencies, Air Force F-4 combat crews rated Red Crown the best control agency, Disco second, and Teaball last.[21]

There are several possible reasons—not including Teaball—the Air Force F-4:MiG kill exchange ratio changed beginning in August. First, the relatively small number of engagements do not make this drop statistically significant, and a careful look at the descriptions of individual engagements from the time Teaball was activated shows that, despite Teaball, the North Vietnamese MiGs were still getting into position to make kills. The MiGs were not scoring kills simply because of missile malfunctions, pilot ineptitude, or just plain bad luck. There were several periods like this in Rolling Thunder and Linebacker, and it affected both sides. What Teaball was supposed to stop, or at least reduce, was unobserved MiG attacks (it had no control over whether the MiG pilots scored), and the evidence suggests it was not successful in doing this.

Another explanation was suggested in Red Baron III, which said Teaball could take some credit for reduced losses, but that "two other factors, however, undoubtedly affected U.S. losses: (1) USAF aircrew experience was increasing as the war progressed, and (2) the bombing campaign may have affected the NVNAF's capability to generate and control sorties. Any conclusion regarding Teaball's effectiveness must be viewed in light of these factors."[22]

Finally, it should be noted that the losses began to drop after the Linebacker Conferences began. Using the criteria of Teaball's alleged success—that losses dropped in August after Teaball came on line—it is equally easy to say the losses dropped in August after the Linebacker Conferences began and coordination improved.

One thing is clear: Giving Teaball so much responsibility so early was a mistake. Teaball was put on line before its communications were reliable, and several U.S. aircraft were shot down after it came into service, when it had radio problems and there was confusion about who was in charge of the warnings.

Another thing is clear: There was considerable pressure at the time to make Teaball look responsible for the improvement in the kill ratio. The explanation appears to be because General Vogt strongly supported it and because Teaball's success would validate the Air Force leadership's view that the Air Force's poor F-4:MiG exchange ratio was entirely due to lack of GCI. But despite the official praise for Teaball, the combat crews knew the real reasons the MiGs were successful. One experienced fighter pilot said of the losses to MiGs: "In almost every loss, there was a mistake made and sometimes very bad mistakes. A lot of this had to do with air crews that, frankly, were not prepared for the mission in Route Pack 6, and a lot of it was training and experience. . . . [T]here were many other associated problems. But in almost every loss we had in Route Package 6, there was a mistake that cost the loss."[23]

Looking Ahead

After the end of the war, both the Air Force and the Navy had to look ahead and see what changes needed to be made to prepare for future air-to-air combat. The changes covered two basic areas: new technologies required for air-to-air combat and improved tactics and training. Of the two, the technology issue was by far the easier. There was general agreement between the Air Force and the Navy about what was needed, and the new technologies were nonthreatening to the leadership—no generals or admirals objected to getting new weapons systems. Many of the technical changes were based on what had happened in Rolling Thunder and were already well along. The technologies also brought other changes; for example, the missile test programs were quietly changed to provide more realistic target maneuvers and tests at low altitude.

New Technologies

Virtually every report written on the technological improvements needed by U.S. aircrews identified three areas: improved detection and identification of enemy aircraft, improved weapons, and better man-machine interface.[24]

Improved Target Discrimination against the Ground Return and
Improved Location and Detection Information
Probably the most critical problem for U.S. aircraft over North Vietnam was detecting and identifying a low-flying enemy before he had a chance

to move into a firing position. U.S. analysis showed that the Vietnam-era "visual search patterns, airborne radars, and MiG warning techniques were inadequate" and that "if a MiG was visually detected behind a U.S. aircraft he was able to fire first 95 percent of the time."[25] The F-4 radar was considered "inadequate against the low-flying targets which . . . characterized many of the air battles in SEA," and the North Vietnamese MiGs and GCI exploited the radar's shortcomings; additionally, once an F-4 had located and locked on to a MiG, if the MiG dived, the ground clutter often made it impossible for the F-4 to keep a radar lock on, and losing radar contact allowed the small MiG to escape from an engagement. EC-121 radar suffered the same problems. The report also pointed out that, if there was a requirement to identify aircraft as hostile before they could be fired on, the U.S. fighters had to be able to identify the targets as friendly or hostile at the same range they could pick them up on radar.

One of the most difficult technological problems was how to locate low-flying aircraft on radar when they were in the "ground return"—in other words, how to develop a radar with a real "look down" capability. The technological solution was to develop a radar, known as a doppler radar, that operated on movement; that is, it would filter out stationary objects (such as the ground) and see only those with relative movement. A low-flying aircraft that was moving toward a doppler radar would show up even if it was very low because the radar detected its movement; the stationary ground, on the other hand, was filtered out. By 1968 new Navy F-4Js were carrying early versions of such a radar, and by the time Linebacker began very sophisticated pulse doppler radars were undergoing tests.

In addition to the radar problems, the poor visibility from the cockpit, especially to the rear, of all of the U.S. fighters was considered a major factor in the MiGs' successes. This helped the MiGs when they attacked from behind, and contributed to the American crew losing sight of the MiGs in an engagement and either being attacked again or allowing the MiG to escape.

Limited solutions to the identification problem were in place during Rolling Thunder when the QRC-248 was mounted on all Air Force EC-121s and Navy GCI ships. Before Linebacker, the Combat Tree enemy IFF interrogator had been developed and mounted on selected F-4Ds, and in Rolling Thunder and Linebacker the ability to interrogate the MiGs' IFF proved very effective, even if the North Vietnamese were able to counter them to some extent by using their IFF sparingly.

Improved Weapons Reliability and Increased Weapons Versatility
For the entire war, the missile figures were unimpressive. About 612 AIM-7s had been fired for about 56 kills, a success rate of less than 10

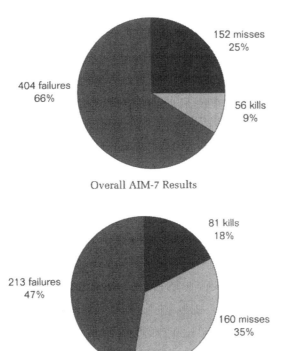

152 misses
25%

404 failures
66%

56 kills
9%

Overall AIM-7 Results

81 kills
18%

213 failures
47%

160 misses
35%

Overall AIM-9 Results

percent. Even worse, 66 percent of the AIM-7s did not function properly. The AIM-9s were better—about 454 were launched for 81 kills, or a success rate of 18 percent, but if the AIM-9Gs used in Linebacker are removed from the statistics, the success rate drops to 14 percent. The AIM-9 was more reliable than the AIM-7; still, 47 percent of the AIM-9s did not function properly.[26] The requirements for new missiles were predictable—larger firing envelopes, including shorter minimum range and higher G capability, greater reliability, and shorter time from lock on to firing. The Navy had solved the missile reliability problems with the AIM-9D and the later AIM-9G, and by making the tactical decision not to use the AIM-7. The missile problems were essentially ignored by the Air Force in the period between Rolling Thunder and Linebacker, but this was a political decision; the technology for a reliable heat seeker was available.

It was not until some time after the war that the Air Force and Navy found real solutions for their missile problems. The two services jointly participated in developing a new AIM-9, the AIM-9L, which finally fulfilled the heat seeker's promise. The AIM-9L would prove extremely reliable with an excellent fusing system and warhead; as a bonus, it had a very real all-aspect capability (it could be fired from in front as well as from behind). Both services also cooperated on an improved AIM-7, the AIM-7F, which finally added reliability to a long-range, all-aspect missile.

Rolling Thunder and Linebacker also settled the argument for the foreseeable future about whether or not fighters should have a cannon. For the entire war 40 of the Air Force's 135 kills—29 percent—were scored by cannon, despite poor gunsights on many fighters and emphasis on using missiles.

Increased Man-Machine Compatibility

The WSEG report found that poor man-machine compatibility—mainly awkward switch positions, weapons, and complicated steps to change from one system to another—caused many problems. First, it often forced the pilot to choose between looking inside the cockpit to change switches or looking outside to try to keep track of a maneuvering MiG. Second, it increased the possibility of a pilot making a mistake and arming, firing, or jettisoning the wrong weapon. Third, it required a great deal of training to get to even minimum efficiency with the switches. The report pointed out that these man-machine compatibility problems were accentuated by the character of the war, which was a visual environment with close-in maneuvering that required the pilots to keep their head out of the cockpit as much as possible.[27] It was clear that future fighter cockpits would have to allow the pilot to change weapons switches without putting his head inside the cockpit. The "556 Mod" on Air Force F-4Es, which concentrated all the weapons switches on the throttle or high on the instrument panel where they were easily seen, was a major step toward a "user friendly" cockpit.

Truly user friendly cockpits and greater cockpit visibility, of course, required an entirely new aircraft, and the first prototypes of new fighter aircraft, based on the lessons of Rolling Thunder, were actually off the drawing boards and in the air before Linebacker was over.

Training and Tactics

After reviewing the air-to-air results of Linebacker, the Navy was understandably satisfied with its training and tactics. The Topgun-trained aviators had done extremely well; the tactic of using AIM-9s instead of AIM-7s had been validated; loose deuce had proven itself the best tactical formation for modern air-to-air combat; and, most importantly, with Topgun the Navy had a structure to develop future tactics and train its fighter pilots.

The Air Force was in a much different position. Many of the generals who were responsible for training and tactics were still in the Air Force at a very high level, so the postwar criticisms of training and formations had to walk a fine line—they had to be accurate enough to be useful, yet could not seem overly critical, not only of TAC but also of the powerful Air Force Fighter Weapons School. While Fighter Weapons School graduates had done relatively well in air-to-air combat (though nowhere near as well as the Navy), the school had failed to develop training plans for the rest of the Air Force. Additionally, it had failed to develop modern formations, adequate night escort tactics, and most importantly, had not developed counters to the MiG-21s' attacks after Rolling Thunder.

As the combat veterans came back to the peacetime Air Force, they began to bring profound changes to the training programs. The feelings of the combat veterans were summed up by one wing commander who said, "There is no substitute for realistic counterair training. Frequent [air-to-air training missions] against dissimilar aircraft is absolutely essential for those specializing in the counterair role. [F-4 vs. F-4] engagements are of dubious value once the crew has progressed beyond the [basic] phase."[28]

Still, this new generation of Air Force leaders was relatively low ranking, and they had to try to bring changes to the Air Force fighter force without implying that the programs and decisions that now-senior generals and the Fighter Weapons School had made were wrong. It was a tough tightrope to walk, and trying to give the Air Force a realistic air combat training program after the war would cost many dedicated officers their careers. It was not until the late 1970s, when Vietnam-era fighter pilots were relatively high-ranking officers, that the corporate Air Force began to feel free to really criticize Air Force training during the war.

From November 26 through December 2, 1972, TAC hosted a Tactical Fighter Symposium where combat veterans had the opportunity to discuss the problems from Linebacker I with TAC general officers and commanders of the tactical air forces. The keynote speaker of the symposium (from which the commander of TAC, General Momyer, was noticeably absent) admitted, "Things have changed a lot and we [TAC] have not kept pace." One official TAC journal noted the symposium focused on the idea that "we [the Tactical Air Command] may have concentrated too extensively on improving the machine and have not spent enough effort on the man who must fly it or on the training which he must have to make that machine an exploitable advantage."[29] At the conference, the combat aircrews had a forum where they could criticize TAC's poor training programs; gradually the problems began to come out in the open.

To continue the momentum, after the end of Linebacker the Air Force conducted a survey among its F-4 pilots who had participated in air combat engagements from 1971 to 1973, asking what they felt were the most important aspects of air combat. The four questions were as follows:

1. What factors contributed most to the ability to *achieve* an offensive posture in an air-to-air encounter?
2. What factors contributed most to the ability to *maintain* an offensive posture in an air-to-air encounter?
3. What concepts should the USAF stress in preparation for future air-to-air conflicts?
4. What factors contributed most to an enemy pilot's effectiveness in an air-to-air encounter?[30]

In response to the first three questions, the Air Force pilots asked for improvements in areas where the Navy had a considerable advantage over the Air Force—more and better training (provided at Topgun), better warning and detection capabilities (Red Crown), better tactical formations (loose deuce), and better missiles (the AIM-9D/G); the pilots also asked for "better aircraft performance."

New Training
To provide better training, the Air Force formed an "Aggressor squadron"—one that specialized in flying Soviet tactics to give air-to-air training throughout the Air Force. The Aggressors took the Soviet tactics and small smokeless fighters on the road to fly against regular F-4 squadrons to work on air-to-air combat, and they were soon described as "the greatest boon to air combat training since the beginning of air warfare."[31] At first the Aggressors embarrassed the F-4s, but soon new tactics and training took hold and the engagements became much more even. At the same time, visionary Air Force officers developed a program called Red Flag, an exercise in the Nevada desert that allowed Air Force units to come from all over the world to fly in Linebacker-type missions against the Aggressors and mock missile defenses. Red Flag was soon expanded to include Navy and allied aircraft as well.

Air Force Formations
It was clear to most veterans of Linebacker that the four-ship fluid four formation was inadequate for modern air combat and that the Navy's two-ship loose deuce was much more effective; in their classified reports and in private forums many Air Force fighter pilots were highly critical of

fluid four.[32] Gradually TAC and the Fighter Weapons School began to realize their mistakes, and in the fall 1975 issue of *Fighter Weapons Review* the lead article, "F-4 Air-to-Air Training," discussed the shortcomings of fluid four and recommended a two-ship formation called "Fluid Two," which was "very similar to USN Loose Deuce." The article went on to describe how the Fighter Weapons School instructors trained against the Navy's Topgun instructors and had been constantly outflown "for two reasons, lack of proficiency and outmoded tactics."

The article further described the well-known faults of fluid four. "Fighting wing is not easier to fly" than the new formation, it pointed out, and the idea that "the fighting wingman provides visual lookout [is] Horsefeathers! . . . The average F-4 wingman is required to devote almost 100% attention just to flying formation. When does he check six [look behind the flight]? He doesn't." The close formation of fighting wing also led to "large overlapping zones of vulnerability which neither [the leader or the wingman] could clear."[33]

The publication of the article marked the last stage in the evolution of the Air Force's air-to-air training program. By 1975, air-to-air training was at the top of the TAC training agenda.

The New Technologies

The F-14

To replace the F-4, the Navy merged its ill-fated F-111B (the interceptor version of the F-111 produced for the Navy) and the requirement for a fleet interceptor into the Grumman F-14 Tomcat. The F-14 was a very large, variable geometry ("swing-wing") two-seat fighter, with a very long range missile system, the Phoenix, and its associated pulse-doppler radar system, the AN/AWG-9. In addition to the long-range Phoenix, the F-14 solved many of the close-in dogfighting shortcomings of the F-4—it had a large, bubble canopy that gave the crew excellent visibility; a "user friendly" cockpit with a "heads-up" display (HUD) of airspeed, heading, and other information on the gunsight and all of the weapons control systems on the throttles; and an internal Vulcan M-61 20-mm cannon. The variable geometry wings made it an excellent turning aircraft at slow speeds, and the pulse doppler radar allowed it to see targets at low altitude. Except for its large size, the F-14 seemed to solve the complaints about the F-4; now the Navy had a fighter with an internal gun, good cockpit visibility, and the ability to fight at high and low speeds. The Navy also decided to stay with the two-seat fighter; they felt the RIO had proved his worth over North Vietnam.

The engine that had been planned for the F-111B, the Pratt and Whitney TF-30, was used for the F-14, but unfortunately the engine was not up to the rest of the design. From its first flight in October 1972, the Tomcat was plagued with difficulties—the prototype crashed on its first flight, and a total of three of the first ten prototypes were lost to various causes— but it went into service in 1973 and went on its first carrier cruise in 1974, ironically covering the evacuation of U.S. personnel and others from Saigon in 1975.

Despite its general success, problems with the F-14's TF-30 engine continued; it was hard to maintain and did not produce enough power, and it was clear that for the F-14 to reach its full potential it would need a better engine. Unfortunately, the new engine would not come for almost two decades, but even with the TF-30 the performance of the F-14 was excellent, and it was able to dominate the F-4 and any of the 1970s and mid-'80s MiGs. The Tomcat's performance, combined with the superb Topgun training of its crews, made it an excellent fighter in any situation, and the long-range Phoenix missiles gave it an added dimension for fleet defense.

A Grumman F-14 "Tomcat" prepares to launch from the aircraft carrier USS *Forrestal. USNI Photographic Collection*

The F-15

At about the same time the Navy was developing the F-14, the Air Force was also looking for its F-4 replacement, initially called the "F-X." The shortcomings of the F-4 in air-to-air combat during Rolling Thunder had a tremendous impact on the selection of the type of aircraft, and in 1968 the Air Force gave the new aircraft a numerical designation—the F-15— and the highest priority for development funds; it also decided that, while the F-15 would carry AIM-7-type missiles, its main mission would be to engage in close-in air-to-air combat. The Air Force's F-15 design request asked for a fighter with low wing loading and buffet-free turning capability at .9 Mach (for maneuvering dogfights), a high thrust-to-weight ratio, a look-down shoot-down pulse doppler radar, long range, good cockpit visibility, and—somewhat surprisingly—a single seat. It also asked for—and in the end never got—a top speed of Mach 2.5. The Air Force was determined that the F-15 would never be a multirole fighter; the informal slogan of the F-15 program became "not a pound for air-to-ground."[34] After evaluating many proposals, on December 23, 1969, McDonnell-Douglas, the builder of the F-4, was selected to build the F-15.

The F-15 was in many ways similar to the F-14. It was big, with a huge, high wing with an area of more than 600 feet, twin vertical tails, and underslung engines. The pilot sat high in a bubble canopy with excellent visibility in all directions—"like sitting on the end of a pencil," one pilot commented. The engines were also a major breakthrough—two Pratt and Whitney F-100 turbofans with 25,000 pounds of thrust. The turbofan design gave the F-15—dubbed the Eagle when it was first rolled out—great range as well as acceleration. The F-15's armament was the same as the F-4E—four AIM-7s, four AIM-9s, and an internal M-61 Vulcan cannon—but it was much more efficient because the F-15 had a large HUD and all of its armament controls on the throttle, similar to but more advanced than the F-4E with the 556 Mod. Additionally, for its new AIM-7Fs, the F-15 had an APG-63 pulse doppler radar with look-down, shoot-down capability, and the ability to find targets at low level. The pulse doppler radar and HUD proved to be an extremely efficient combination.

The F-15's performance was incredible, and it was able to dominate all existing fighters, but like the F-14 it had its share of teething problems. While the performance of the F-100 engine was excellent, it was very difficult to maintain, and this, combined with a shortage of spare parts, handicapped the F-15 for some time after its service introduction in 1976. It was not until 1980 that the F-15 really became a reliable weapons system.

A USAF F-15 Eagle flies over the Atlantic with the TAC's 1st Tactical Fighter Wing. *USNI Photographic Collection*

Finally, as the F-15 came into the inventory, it was possible to change formations. The F-15s moved to a variation of loose deuce as their standard tactical formation, and this change gradually worked its way through the rest of the Air Force; by 1980, fluid four was a distant (and unpleasant) memory. By the early 1980s, the Air Force's air-to-air training program was virtually unrecognizable from the program that had existed in the early 1970s. Air-to-air training was given top priority in the fighter force, and to the surprise of many, Air Force training accidents actually dropped as the pilots became better and better trained in handling aircraft in high performance maneuvers and as they became able to recognize dangerous situations before they occurred.

AWACS

While the F-14 and the F-15 were the glamour aircraft of the post-Vietnam era, possibly the most useful new system was the E-3A Airborne Warning and Control System, universally known as "AWACS." The AWACS was a C-135 with a huge saucer-shaped radome on top, carrying a huge antenna for a pulse doppler radar with an advertised range in excess of 200 miles. The pulse doppler radar gave it a look-down capa-

One of the Air Force's E-3As. *USNI Photographic Collection*

bility, and low-flying targets that had previously been safe from radar detection were visible, and the AWACS carried powerful and sophisticated new radios. The AWACS replaced the College Eye EC-121s and gave the Air Force an accurate, long-range flying GCI site. No longer would ground radar stations be required—American fighters could take their GCI with them.

This was the one system that everyone agreed the U.S. military needed, a real flying GCI station that had a long-range, look-down capability. On a chauvinistic note, many Air Force officers felt one of the main benefits of the AWACS was that the Air Force was no longer forced to rely on GCI from Navy ships, something that had considerably bothered many of the Air Force commanders in Vietnam.[35]

Epilogue

But the ultimate test was still combat. In the 1980s, in two engagements over the Gulf of Sidra, Navy F-14s shot down Libyan MiGs in engagements that lasted a matter of seconds. Then, in 1993, the United States went to war in the Persian Gulf. While the Navy F-14s were limited in their activities, Air Force F-15s, controlled by AWACS aircraft, shot down thirty-two Iraqi fighters in air-to-air combat with no losses.

Appendix 1

Notes on the MiG Pilots

In the Korean War it was well known (and later confirmed) that Russian pilots flew MiGs against U.S. aircraft in combat. From available information, this was not the case in Vietnam. When asked in a classified report, "Did you ever have any indication there were other than North Vietnamese [pilots]?" one of the leading Air Force aces said, "No. We have every indication they're [the pilots] . . . North Vietnamese."[1] In answer to another question he said, "We do think the Russians were flying training missions, test missions, and instructing on the ground, but we do not have any knowledge they were flying combat missions. . . . From everything we know, there were nothing but North Vietnamese flying combat."[2] Another pilot said in answer to the same general question, "I was told specifically that our monitoring of their radios, and the information we had gathered from the North Vietnamese, was that they would not even let their [North Korean, Chinese, and Soviet] advisers fly when we had a strike mission going on."[3]

In a further note, several Air Force pilots spoke about the best North Vietnamese pilots. In response to a question about intelligence reports on a specific North Vietnamese pilot, one U.S. pilot said, "[One] was supposedly head of their [unit] . . . comparable to our Fighter Weapons School. . . . [Colonel or General Nguyen] lived right outside of Hanoi. . . . I've been told he possibly had 18 kills."[4] Another U.S. pilot said, "It is my understanding that he has been shot down . . . a couple or three times and has several F-4s to his credit. I've seen him a couple of times. Of course, I didn't find [that] out until after the action. The guy can really turn the airplane—really maneuver the airplane."[5]

Appendix 2

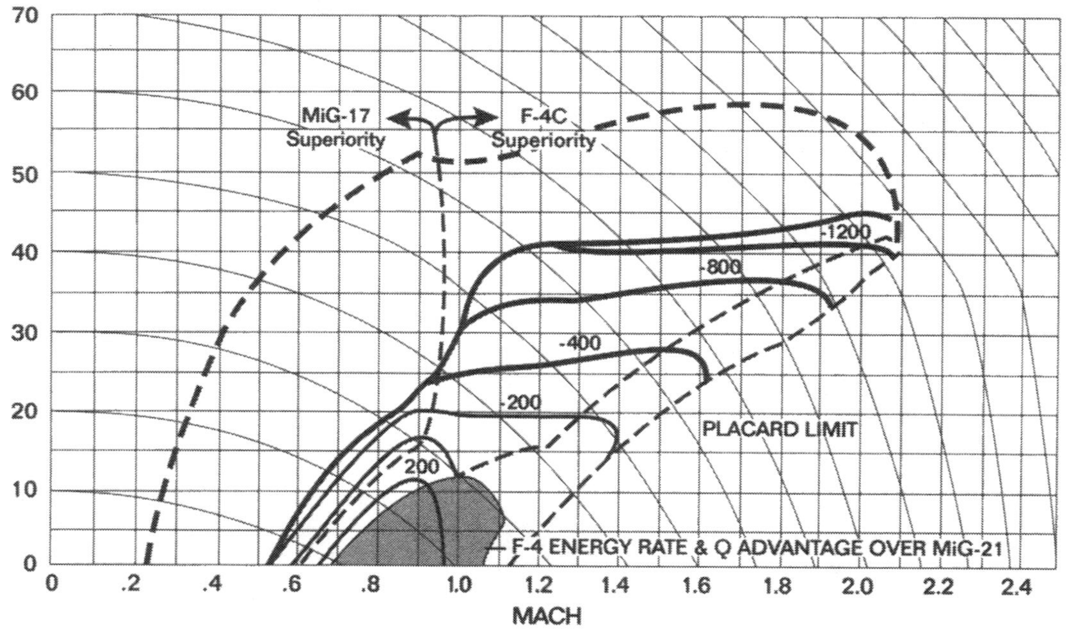

A basic energy maneuverability chart comparing the F-4 to the MiG-17 and the MiG-21. The chart shows the F-4 has an advantage over the MiG-17 at speeds from .6 Mach to .95 Mach, depending on altitude, and an advantage over the MiG-21 below about 12,000 feet at speeds from .7 Mach to Mach 1.05 (the cross-hatched area).

Appendix 3

ROLLING THUNDER F-4 PHANTOM CONFIGURATIONS

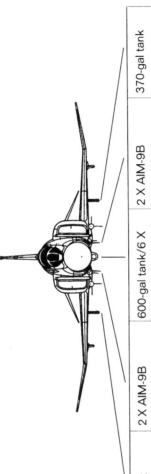

Early (pre-pod)	370-gal tank	2 X AIM-9B	600-gal tank/6 X 500-lb bombs or 5 X 750-lb bombs	2 X AIM-9B	370-gal tank
Early 8th TFW pod	QRC-160 ECM pod	2 X AIM-9B	600-gal tank	2 X AIM-9B	370-gal tank
366th TFW air-to-air May 1967	370-gal tank	2 X AIM-9B QRC-160 ECM pod	SUU-16 cannon pod	2 X AIM-9B	370-gal tank
8th TFW "slow CAP" late 1967	370-gal tank	1 or 2 X AIM-4D QRC-160 ECM pod	SUU-16 cannon pod	1 or 2 X AIM-4D QRC-160 ECM pod	370-gal tank
8th TFW "fast CAP" later 1967	370-gal tank	2 X AIM-9B QRC-160 ECM pod	600-gal tank	2 X AIM-9B	370-gal tank
U.S. Navy (all)		2 X AIM-9B/D	600-gal tank	2 X AIM-9B/D	

Appendix 4

ROLLING THUNDER F-105 CONFIGURATIONS

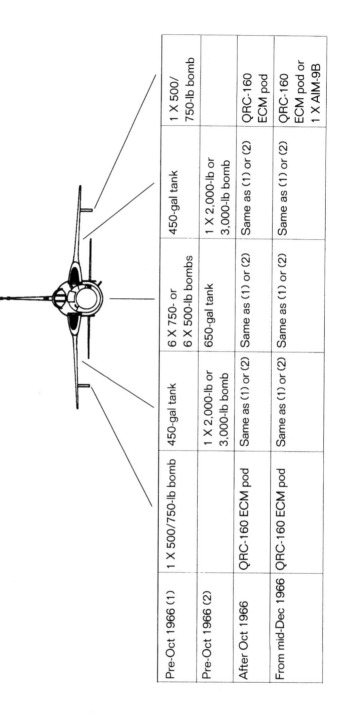

Pre-Oct 1966 (1)	1 X 500/750-lb bomb	450-gal tank	6 X 750- or 6 X 500-lb bombs	450-gal tank	1 X 500/750-lb bomb
Pre-Oct 1966 (2)		1 X 2,000-lb or 3,000-lb bomb	650-gal tank	1 X 2,000-lb or 3,000-lb bomb	
After Oct 1966	QRC-160 ECM pod	Same as (1) or (2)	Same as (1) or (2)	Same as (1) or (2)	QRC-160 ECM pod
From mid-Dec 1966	QRC-160 ECM pod	Same as (1) or (2)	Same as (1) or (2)	Same as (1) or (2)	QRC-160 ECM pod or 1 X AIM-9B

Notes

1. Opening Fire

1. The AIM-9 followed a zigzag pattern to its target, so it was named the Sidewinder.
2. This trait of F-8 pilots is well documented. See, for example, Cdr. J. B. Nichols and B. Tillman, *On Yankee Station: The Naval Air War over Vietnam* (Annapolis, Maryland: Naval Institute Press, 1988), 71–72.
3. For example, the commander of the first Navy F-4 training unit was quoted as saying, "The 'Gun Club Crowd' was pushing for a gun [in the F-4]. I didn't want a gun because I didn't want a gun going off right under the radar while you were trying to use the scope." J. Lake (ed.), *McDonnell F-4 Phantom: Spirit in the Skies* (London: Aerospace Publishing, 1992), 75.
4. 44th TFS, "Defensive Tactics for Air-to-Air Guided Missiles." Japan: Itsinch AB, November 10, 1958, 1–4. Quoted in Maj. J. E. Witt, USAF, "F-4 Employment of Air-to-Air Missiles in Southeast Asia," Project Corona Harvest Report (February 1970).
5. The AIM-7 warhead was a "continuous-rod" warhead, an improvement of the high-explosive warhead of the AIM-9. When the warhead exploded, it threw out a large number of thin rods, which added to the destruction.
6. Robert S. McNamara, Secretary of Defense, June 4, 1964. Quoted in *USAF Fighter Weapons Review* (Fall 1989): 43.
7. H. Nordeen, *Air Warfare in the Missile Age* (Washington, D.C.: Smithsonian Institution, 1981), Appendix 1, 224.
8. *USAF Fighter Weapons Newsletter* 1 (March 1966): 21–26.
9. *PACAF Tactics and Techniques Bulletin 45 (Summary of Feather Duster I and II)* (July 26, 1966): 1.
10. *USAF Fighter Weapons Newsletter* 1 (March 1966): 25.
11. Alfred Price, *The Last Year of the Luftwaffe, May 1944–May 1945* (London: Arms and Armour, 1991), 50.
12. Alfred Price, *World War II Fighter Conflict* (London: MacDonald and Co., 1975), 114–15 and 127.
13. Mach is the speed of sound and is a common measure for jet fighter speed. The speed varies directly with temperature—the lower the temperature, the slower the speed of sound—and therefore inversely with altitude, because high altitude is colder than low altitude. As a rule of thumb, the speed of sound—Mach 1—is about 600 knots at sea level.

14. Those whose eyes do not glaze over at this point should see Robert Shaw, *Fighter Combat* (Annapolis, Maryland: Naval Institute Press, 1985) for a far more in-depth discussion of these factors.

15. "Project Feather Duster (TAC Test 1965–1966)," IIF-4.

16. SEACAAL Study, H-5.

17. The Chinese claimed the F-4B was hit by an American missile. Red Baron I, Weapons System and Evaluation Group, vol. I, Event I-3.

18. Ubon's F-4s also flew a large number of night ground attack missions.

19. See, for example, K. Bell, *100 Missions North: A Fighter Pilot's Story of the Vietnam War* (Washington, D.C.: Brassey's, 1993), 131 and 172; and Col. Scott G. Smith, Commander, 432nd TRW, Udorn RTAFB, April 1972–March 18, 1973, End of Tour (EOT) Report, May 31, 1973, 32.

20. The jettison limits on the F-4 centerline were straight and level flight, 1G, 175–425 knots, a speed one wing commander said was "totally unacceptable in a high threat environment." Smith EOT Report, 32.

21. Carriers that supported the war in South Vietnam were stationed off the coast of South Vietnam and were based in an area known, logically enough, as "Dixie Station."

22. Remarks by Adm. James Holloway, "Command and Control of Air Operations in the Vietnam War," Colloquium on Contemporary History, Naval Historical Center, January 23, 1991, 8.

23. Ibid., 9; see also R. Francillon, *Tonkin Bay Yacht Club: U.S. Carrier Operations off Vietnam* (Annapolis, Maryland: Naval Institute Press, 1988), 43–45.

24. For example, napalm and the CBU-2 cluster bombs. Red Baron II, USAF Fighter Weapons Center, vol. I, III-2–3.

25. Ibid., III-4–5.

26. Bernard C. Nalty, "Tactics and Techniques of Electronic Warfare: Electronic Countermeasures in the Air War against North Vietnam, 1965–1973," Office of Air Force History, August 16, 1977, 3–4.

27. The B-66 had been originally developed from a Navy jet bomber, the A-3, which was designed as a carrier-based nuclear-capable jet bomber.

28. "PACAF Rolling Thunder Operations Handbook," March 1968, 29.

29. "Tactics of Electronic Warfare," Project CHECO Report, July 1974, 19.

30. Three EB-66Cs were shot down by SAMs during Rolling Thunder.

31. E. H. Tilford, *Setup: What the Air Force Did in Vietnam and Why* (Maxwell AFB, Alabama: Air University Press, 1991), 124.

32. Ibid., 54.

33. "Tactics and Techniques of Electronic Warfare," 31–32.

34. Red Baron II, vol. I, II-7.

35. Ibid.

36. Gen. William W. Momyer, *Airpower in Three Wars (WWII, Korea, and Vietnam)* (Washington, D.C.: Government Printing Office, 1978), 135.

37. Red Baron II, vol. I, III-7.

38. *PACAF Tactics and Techniques Bulletin* 50 (October 26, 1966).

39. Red Baron II, vol. I, III-7, 24.
40. 388th TFW commander, August 1966. Quoted in "Air Superiority Tactics over North Vietnam, 1964–1972" Air Command and Staff Study (n.d., probably 1975), 31.
41. "Rolling Thunder Operations Handbook," 29.
42. "Tactics and Techniques of Electronic Warfare," 22.
43. Ibid., 51–54.
44. Ibid., 40.
45. "Air Superiority Tactics over North Vietnam," 63.
46. "Air-to-Air Encounters over North Vietnam, 1 July 1967–31 Dec 1968," Project Corona Harvest Report 1970, 6.
47. "Tactics and Techniques of Electronic Warfare," 65–66.
48. "Tactical Electronic Warfare Operations in SEA, 1962–1968" (n.d.), 18.
49. "Tactics and Techniques of Electronic Warfare," 53–54.
50. H. Kissinger, *White House Years* (Toronto: Little, Brown and Co., 1979), 1112.

2. The Battles Begin

1. This was the U.S. designation. The Soviet designation was MiG-21F-13.
2. Red Baron I, vol. IV, I-63. The Atoll was thought to be a direct copy of an AIM-9B; legend has it that in 1958 a Chinese Communist MiG-17 had been hit in the tail by a Nationalist Chinese AIM-9B that did not explode. The MiG-17 carried the AIM-9B back to its base, where it was copied by the Soviets.
3. Red Baron I, vol. IV, I-34.
4. Ibid., Event I-28.
5. Ibid., Event I-24.
6. Red Baron II, vol. I, D-5–6.
7. May 13, 1995, interview with Don Mace, former maintenance officer (1967), College Eye Task Force.
8. College Eye Special Report, Project CHECO, November 1, 1968, 37.
9. "Mark X IFF Problem" TF-77 proposal to ComSeventh Fleet, March 1966.
10. Ibid.
11. "Tactics and Techniques of Electronic Warfare," 127.
12. Ibid., 127–28.
13. Ibid., 155.
14. College Eye Special Report, Project CHECO, 46.
15. Ibid., 129.
16. Ibid., 3.
17. "Tactics and Techniques of Electronic Warfare," 146–56.
18. Red Baron I, vols. I-III, passim.
19. Ibid., vol. I, I-38.
20. Ibid., vol. IV, 71.
21. R. Tillman, *MiG Master: The Story of the F-8 Crusader,* 2d ed. (Annapolis, Maryland: Naval Institute Press, 1990), 76.

22. Red Baron II, vol. I, VI-5.

23. Ibid., VI-8.

24. *Setup*, 118.

25. Ibid., 120.

26. "Air-to-Air Encounters over North Vietnam," 2.

27. *100 Missions North*, 135.

28. Ibid., 107–109; review of Red Baron I engagements from October–December 1966.

29. Red Baron I, vol. III, F-105 events of December 1966.

30. "388th (F-105) TFW 1968 Tactics Manual" (1 February 1967): 7.

31. It should be noted that this was based on the judgments of the pilots. The F-105 gun camera film of engagements was so poor it was impossible to judge why most cannon attacks missed the target.

32. D. Anerton, *The F-105 Thunderchief* (London: Osprey Publishing Ltd., Osprey Air Combat, 1983), 74.

33. "Rolling Thunder Operations Handbook," 13.

34. "Tactical Electronic Warfare Operations in SEA," 44.

35. The QRC-160 was later designated the ALQ-71. For purposes of clarity, it will be referred to as the QRC-160 for the entire book.

36. "Tactics of Electronic Warfare," 135.

37. "Tactics of Electronic Warfare," 132.

38. "Rolling Thunder Operations Handbook," 72.

39. "Air-to-Air Encounters over North Vietnam," 29.

40. These figures are approximate, since it was difficult to tell how many SAMs were actually fired.

41. Red Baron I, vol. I, Event I-52.

42. Ibid., Event I-53.

43. Ibid., Event I-57.

44. Ibid. See F-4 aircrew debriefs after May 1966.

45. The two-seat F-105F had virtually no rearward visibility for the back seat electronic warfare officer and was, in this sense, a single seater.

46. Red Baron I, vol. IV, 35.

47. See, for example, *Tactical Analysis Bulletin* (TAB) 74(1) (March 30, 1974): 22.

48. "Tactics and Techniques of Electronic Warfare," 145.

49. Ibid., 143.

50. *Air Superiority Tactics over North Vietnam*, 56.

51. Ibid., 57.

52. "SEACAAL Briefing for USAF Headquarters," February 10, 1967, 6.

53. Project CHECO SEA Report (March–June 1965): 53.

54. Because of a wiring anomaly, the F-4s initially had to carry the QRC-160 pod on the outboard wing pylon where they normally carried a wing tank, meaning they carried two external fuel tanks (a centerline and a wing tank) instead of the normal three.

55. Maj. Gordon Y. W. Ow, *Operational Analysis of Mission Bolo*, working paper 67/3, PACAF Tactical Air Analysis Center, February 13, 1967.

3. The American Victory

1. Red Baron III, USAF Fighter Weapons Center, vol. I, June 1974, A-2.
2. Red Baron II, vol. I, A-2–3.
3. End of tour interview with Col. Robin Olds, 8th TFW commander, July 12, 1967, Corona Harvest, 23.
4. Interview with Maj. Frederick G. Tolman, wing weapons officer, 355th TFW, July 15, 1967.
5. Olds, quoted in M. D. Scutts, *Wolfpack* (Osceola, Wisconsin: Motorbooks International, 1988), 82.
6. R. Cunningham with J. Ethell, *Fox Two* (Mesa, Arizona: Chaplin Fighter Museum, 1984), 77.
7. "Air-to-Air Encounters over North Vietnam," 17.
8. Ibid., 11.
9. The first MiG-21s had two 30-mm cannon, but one had been removed to provide room for the Atoll's electronics.
10. Red Baron III, vol. I, 16.
11. "8th TFW (F-4) Tactics Manual" (1968): 13.
12. Ibid. Quoted in "Air-to-Air Encounters over North Vietnam."
13. Red Baron III, vol. IV, 128.
14. There are several different types of turns in a dogfight, and they are subject to a variety of complex variables. For a more in-depth explanation, see *Fighter Combat,* 17–19, passim.
15. Red Baron I, vol. IV, 110–12.
16. Ibid., 111.
17. See, for example, Olds EOT interview, 2–4, 20.
18. End of tour interview with Capt. Richard S. ("Steve") Ritchie, Air Force Oral History Interview #K239.0512-630, October 11 and 30, 1972, 3.
19. "F-4 RTU Flight Manual," 31st TFW, Homestead AFB, Florida (1972), 31–32. See also comments by Captain Ritchie, ibid., 4–5.
20. See, for example, *Fox Two,* 110.
21. J. Broughton, *Thud Ridge* (New York: Bantam Books, 1969), 37.
22. "8th TFW History" (January–March 1968): 57; Ritchie EOT interview, 2.
23. Ritchie EOT interview, 41.
24. This problem was widely noted; see, for example, Red Baron III, vol. I, 9.
25. Ibid., 43–44.
26. Ibid., 41.
27. Ibid., 27.
28. For example, U.S. Air Force and Navy Forward Air Controllers (FACs) had several radios so they could also talk to ground troops. Also, one of the first modifications the Israeli Air Force made to U.S. fighters when they were delivered was the addition of another radio.
29. Red Baron I, vol. IV, 42–43.
30. Red Baron II, vol. I, III-49–50.
31. Olds EOT interview, 6.

32. Red Baron II, vol. I, III-50.
33. Olds EOT interview, Special Notes.
34. This was first noted in Red Baron I, vol. III, Event III-102.
35. Now at least two F-105s in each flight carried an AIM-9B.
36. Olds EOT interview, cited in "Air-to-Air Encounters over North Vietnam," 48.
37. Red Baron III, vol. I, III-20.
38. Ibid., 31. This was the first time an entire strike was abandoned for a search and rescue. It is an interesting commentary on the force commander's authority over the priorities of the aircrews bombing North Vietnam.
39. Red Baron I, vol. IV, 27.
40. "388th TFW Tactics Manual," 40.
41. Red Baron II, vol. I, III-20.
42. Red Baron I, vol. III, Event III-191.
43. "Tactics and Techniques of Electronic Warfare," 129–30.
44. College Eye Special Report, Project CHECO, 18.
45. "Tactics and Techniques of Electronic Warfare," 129–30.
46. Interview with Lt. Col. George Anderson, Vice Commander/DCO of the College Eye Task Force, July 11, 1969.
47. College Eye Special Report, Project CHECO, 20.
48. *USAF Fighter Weapons Newsletter* 4 (December 1965): 4.
49. Red Baron II, vol. I, IV-6.
50. College Eye Special Report, Project CHECO, 19.
51. History of the 366th TFW, 1 April 1967–30 September 1967, vol. I: Narrative and Docs, 1.
52. Maj. Gen. Frederick C. Bleese, *Check Six: A Fighter Pilot Looks Back* (New York: Ballantine Books, 1992), 148–53.
53. Ibid., 149.
54. "History of the 366th," 2.
55. "Air-to-Air Encounters over North Vietnam," special notes from the 366th TFW (no page nos.).
56. Ibid.
57. SEACAAL Briefing, H-14.
58. Red Baron I, vol. IV, Appendix D, 191–200.
59. Because it was very difficult to load F-4 wing tanks while on a carrier, Navy F-4s generally carried only centerline tanks. Carrying a centerline cannon would have eliminated all Navy F-4s' external fuel and would have left them very little fuel for combat, a situation exacerbated by the carriers' limited air refueling capability. There was also a perception that the cannon jammed often (not borne out by Air Force experience), that it could not be sighted accurately on the ship, and that it would have required a manufacturer's technical representative on the carrier. (Chief of Naval Operations Public Affairs News Desk response to a query, facsimile received May 26, 1995.)
60. "Combat Snap: AIM-9J Southeast Asia Introduction" (circa 1974), 3.
61. Red Baron I, vol. IV, 72.

62. *Spirit in the Skies,* 36.
63. *Wolfpack,* 44–45.
64. Red Baron III, vol. I, IV-9–10.
65. Olds EOT interview, 10.
66. Ibid., 3.
67. "Combat Snap," 3.
68. *USAF Fighter Weapons Review* (Winter 1974): 30.
69. "Combat Snap," 7.
70. EOT interview with Maj. William Kirk, 8th TFW, 7–8.
71. "History of the 366th," 3.
72. "Air-to-Air Encounters over North Vietnam," 48.
73. "Rolling Thunder Operations Handbook," 29.
74. College Eye Special Report, Project CHECO, 26.
75. "Tactics and Techniques of Electronic Warfare," 124.
76. Red Baron II, vol. I, D-4.
77. Ibid., 146.
78. Ibid.
79. College Eye Special Report, Project CHECO, 27.
80. This problem remains; a U.S. F-16 was shot down over Bosnia in early June 1995, reportedly because he was not given available intelligence information on SA-6 SAMs in the area. See the Washington *Post,* November 15, 1995, A20.
81. "Rolling Thunder Operations Handbook," 13.
82. "Air-to-Air Encounters over North Vietnam," 4, and figure 2.
83. "Rolling Thunder, June 1967–Oct. 1968," Project CHECO Report (n.d.), 5.

4. The MiGs Strike Back

1. Statements made August 12, 1967.
2. Red Baron I, vol. IV, 55.
3. Lt. Col. J. T. Miller, USAF, "Analysis of Aircrew Personnel Flying Out of Country Interdiction Missions," AWC Report #3651, April 1968, 49.
4. Ibid., 55.
5. Lt. Col. Howard F. Hendricks, USAF, "Air Force Liaison Officer Report, September–October 1966," 2.
6. For a more detailed description of these problems, see P. B. Mersky and N. Pulman, *The Naval Air War in Vietnam* (Baltimore, Maryland: Naval and Aviation Publishing Company of America, 1990), 62–63; and *On Yankee Station,* 34–47.
7. "Air Force Liaison Officer Report," 3.
8. ECM pods continued to arrive; there were 100 by January, 107 in February, 170 in March, and 205 in April. "Air Tactics against NVN Air Ground Defenses, December 1966–November 1, 1968," Project CHECO Southeast Asia Report, 4.
9. "Rolling Thunder Operations Handbook," 25.

10. Olds EOT interview, 1–2.
11. *Naval Air War in Vietnam,* 103.
12. Most of the support aircraft supported both strikes, and some supported all four.
13. *Airpower in Three Wars,* 223.
14. This CIA/military-operated, very secret navigation station, located deep in Laos close to North Vietnam, was extremely useful during Rolling Thunder; it was finally overrun by the North Vietnamese.
15. "Rolling Thunder Operations Handbook," 55.
16. Red Baron II, vol. I, III-55.
17. "8th TFW History," 57.
18. The radar site was overrun in early March 1968, ending the Commando Club operations.
19. "Tactical Electronic Warfare Operations in SEA," 29.
20. "Air Tactics against NVN Air Ground Defenses," 22–23.
21. "Rolling Thunder Operations PACAF Briefing," November 1967, 3.
22. "Rolling Thunder Operations PACAF Briefing," August 28–September 17, 1967, 2.
23. "Squadron History," 497th TFS, 8th TFW, January–March 1968, 4.
24. "Air-to-Air Encounters over North Vietnam," 61–62.
25. "Tactics and Techniques of Electronic Warfare," 130.
26. Ibid., 131.
27. College Eye Special Report, Project CHECO, 41–42.
28. Red Baron II, vol. I, D-3.
29. Ibid., vol. IV, 47.
30. Ibid., 52.
31. "Air-to-Air Encounters over North Vietnam," 62.
32. "Air Tactics against NVN Air Ground Defenses," 25.
33. "Air-to-Air Encounters over North Vietnam," 63.
34. Red Baron II, vol. IV, 59.
35. "Tactics and Techniques of Electronic Warfare," 59–60.
36. Ibid., 64.
37. "Air Tactics against NVN Air Ground Defenses," 20–21.
38. "North Vietnamese Fighter Patterns," PACAF Briefing, January 1968, 5.
39. Red Baron II, vol. I, III-62.
40. Ibid., III-59–60.
41. Ibid, III-61.
42. Ibid., vol. IV, 73.
43. Ibid., 79.
44. Albert H. Dell, "Navy, Marine Corps, and Air Force Fixed Wing In-Flight Combat Losses to MiG Aircraft in Southeast Asia from 1965 through 1972," report for the Center for Naval Analyses, March 28, 1978.
45. Ibid., 123.
46. "Air-to-Air Encounters over North Vietnam," 123.
47. "NVNAF Fighter Patterns," DCS/Intel PACAF Briefing, 1968, 2–10.

48. Olds EOT interview, 17.
49. "Tactics and Techniques of Electronic Warfare," 138–39.
50. "North Vietnamese Fighter Patterns," 4.
51. Ibid., 5.
52. Red Baron II, vol. I, III-62.
53. Ibid., III-65.
54. Ibid., III-65–66.
55. Ibid., III-66.
56. Ibid., vol. IV, I-37.
57. Ibid., I-38.

5. The End of the Beginning

1. Red Baron II, vol. I, III-71.
2. The actual number of missiles fired and kills achieved varies from report to report, though usually by a small amount, depending on when the report was written. Intelligence and combat analyses were constantly adjusting the actual numbers.
3. Red Baron I, vol. IV, 72–73.
4. Ibid., 71.
5. Ibid., 10.
6. Ibid., 72–74.
7. Ibid., 115.
8. Ibid., 11.
9. See Red Baron I, vols. I and III, passim.
10. Red Baron II, vol. VI, VI-11.
11. "Employment of Missiles and Guided Weapons in Southeast Asia," briefing by General Eggers, Deputy Director for Operations (Strategic and General Operations), J-3, n.d. (probably late 1972), viewgraph number 8.
12. "Analysis of Aircrew Personnel," 59–60.
13. Red Baron I, vol. IV, 57.
14. Red Baron I, vol. IV, 98.
15. "F-4 Employment of Air-to-Air Missiles in Southeast Asia," 22–24.
16. It is worth noting that the U.S. Navy's 1970 Ault Report, which was given credit for initiating the famous Navy Topgun program, was mainly devoted to the care and maintenance of the AIM-7 missile.
17. *Spirit in the Skies,* 76, passim.
18. *USAF Fighter Weapons Review* (Fall 1973): 2.
19. Red Baron I, vol. IV, 57.
20. This large increase happened with the gunsight in the secondary air-to-air mode. The primary air-to-air mode of the F-105 gunsight required a radar lock on, but in the approximately 140 F-105 gun attacks not a single F-105 obtained a radar lock on because the system was not capable of being used in a fast-moving engagement.

21. "Air Tactics against NVN Air Ground Defenses," 31–32.

22. Quotes from Brig. Gen. Robin Olds, then commander of the 8th TFW, cited in *Fighter Combat,* 69. It should be noted this is the chapter on "Basic Fighter Maneuvers," not the more complex ones.

23. *Air Superiority Tactics,* 32.

24. This is well documented. See, for example, "U.S. Navy Air Development Squadron Four, Project Plan" and "Challenge over North Vietnam: Carrier Aviators Battle with the NVAF MiG," *The Hook* (Winter 1983): 25–28.

25. Red Baron II, vol. I, II-16.

26. Interview with Sasha Prokorov, former Soviet Air Force officer, St. Petersburg, Russia, July 1995. His comments are based on "Vietnam Lessons Learned" briefings he received while in the Soviet Armed Forces Staff College in 1987.

27. In the Navy's case, fighter/attack pilots. For brevity, the term "fighter pilot" is used; when it refers to Navy pilots, it should be read as "fighter/attack pilots."

28. "Analysis of Aircrew Personnel," 56.

29. Red Baron III, vol. I, 27.

30. "Analysis of Aircrew Personnel," 54.

31. The length of time for the RTU was driven partially by personnel policies. Any course longer than six months required that the students have a "permanent change of station" (PCS) move. This was much more expensive and disruptive to the personnel system than a move of less than six months, which was classified as temporary duty (TDY). The Air Force opted not to make an exception for RTUs to allow better combat training.

32. "31st TFW RTU F-4 Training Syllabus," 1972.

33. Ibid., 91.

34. "Analysis of Aircrew Personnel," 76.

35. Ibid., 42.

36. Ibid., 46.

37. Ritchie EOT interview, 102; see also end of tour interview with Maj. Upton D. Officer, July 11–13, 1973, Maxwell AFB, Alabama, USAF Oral History Program, 233.

38. "Analysis of Aircrew Personnel," 62.

39. See, for example, J. Broughton, *Going Downtown: The Air War against Hanoi and Washington* (New York: Pocket Books, 1988), 163.

40. "Analysis of Aircrew Personnel," 61–62.

41. Ritchie EOT interview, 30–31.

42. *Naval Air War in Vietnam,* 63.

43. *Alpha Strike Vietnam,* 201–3.

44. Major G. I. Clouser, "A Critical Analysis of USAF Combat Tactics," Air Command and Staff College Research Study, May 1974, 7.

45. Ibid., 61–62.

46. See, for example, Smith EOT Report, 31; and Ritchie EOT interview, 14.

47. Officer EOT interview, 99–100.
48. Red Baron III, vol. I, 10.
49. "Project Feather Duster" (TAC Test 1965–1966), IIF-4.
50. *PACAF Tactics and Techniques Bulletin* 25 (September 27, 1965): 1.
51. "North Vietnamese Fighter Patterns," 3.
52. *Defense Analysis Bulletin 30* (February 1968), cited in Red Baron II, vol. I, B-3.
53. Red Baron I, vol. IV, 97.
54. Red Baron II, vol. I, II-16.
55. Ibid., vol. IV, Part I, 76.
56. Red Baron I, vol. IV, 55.

6. Preparing for the Next Round

1. Ritchie EOT interview, 84.
2. *Last Year of the Luftwaffe,* 94.
3. Combat experience showed it was very desirable in a maneuvering engagement to be able to go from a boresight lock on to a full-system lock on so that the AIM-7 could be used effectively; a switch could be activated by the F-4 back seater to go from the boresight to a full-system situation, but frequently during this operation the radar broke lock. Now a modification automatically sent the radar from a boresight lock on to a full-system lock on.
4. Red Baron III, vol. III, section II, 3.
5. Robert K. Wilcox, "State of the Art," *USAF Fighter Weapons Review* (Winter 1974): 30–31.
6. "Combat Snap," 16.
7. Ibid.
8. Ibid., 16–17.
9. Smith EOT Report, 2.
10. July 7, 1968, interview with three pilots (Maj. Perry Smith, Capt. J. Alley, Capt. R. B. Battista [MiG killer on his previous tour]) of the 555th TFS, Udorn RTAFB, Doc. no. 0283988, Maxwell AFB Air Historical Center.
11. Maj. Donald Gish, "F-4 Air-to-Air Training," *USAF Fighter Weapons Review* (Fall 1975): 2.
12. Maj. Vincent P. Roy, "Double Attack Revisited," *USAF Fighter Weapons Review* (Spring 1971): 27–32. Editor's disclaimer, 32.
13. *USAF Fighter Weapons Review* (Summer 1971): 14–16, 33; (Fall 1971): 32.
14. Description of the responsibilities of TAC taken from the beginning of the biography of Gen. William M. Momyer, produced by the Secretary of the Air Force Office of Information, current as of May 1, 1971.
15. Except, as mentioned earlier, its initial reluctance to use the pod-mounted cannon.
16. Robert K. Wilcox, *Scream of Eagles: The Creation of Top Gun and the U.S. Air Victory in Vietnam* (New York: John Wiley and Sons, 1990), 102–3.

17. "Project Plan Report," PACAF Special TAB, September 1966.

18. Ibid., 7–8.

19. The Chinese MiG-19s, many of which were supplied to the North Vietnamese, were designated the F-6. It was essentially the same aircraft and will be referred to as the MiG-19 in the text.

20. Red Baron III, vol. III, 17.

21. Some F-6s were modified to fly up to 675 knots, but it was described as "a pretty hairy ride." Red Baron III, vol. III, 17.

22. A two-second burst fired 90 rounds weighing 81 pounds. Each gun carried 90 rounds of ammunition, giving the MiG-19 a firing time of about six seconds.

23. Ritchie EOT interview, 3.

24. Red Baron III, vol. III, 17.

25. Ibid., 18–19.

26. Red Baron I, vol. I, Appendix A, 1–2.

27. July 7, 1968, interview with Smith, Alley, and Battista. These are the comments of Major Smith.

28. "USAF Operations against North Vietnam, 1 July 1971–30 June 1972," Project Corona Harvest Report, April 1972–18 March 1973, PACAF Headquarters in cooperation with Strategic Air Command, dated 31 May 1973, 12–13.

29. "Tactics and Techniques of Electronic Warfare," 141.

30. The wing originated as the reconnaissance wing in Thailand. It accumulated more and more fighter squadrons and by the time of Linebacker was the home of four F-4 squadrons and only one reconnaissance squadron. Eventually—long after the war—the name was changed to the 432nd Fighter Wing.

31. Ritchie EOT interview, 84.

32. This was because the radar beam was so wide it might have two aircraft in it—the MiG giving a Combat Tree return and a U.S. aircraft—and the AIM-7 might go after the U.S. aircraft.

33. U.S. fighters measured their fuel in pounds, not gallons.

34. Red Baron III, vol. II, 37.

35. This radar controller was later awarded the Distinguished Service Medal for his accomplishments as a controller; he became only the second Navy enlisted man in history to receive this medal.

36. White House Years, 1098.

37. Setup, 47.

38. White House Years, 1111.

39. "USAF Operations against North Vietnam," 57.

40. Ibid., 58.

41. Ibid., 69.

42. Ibid., 70.

43. Gen. Alton Slay, Director of Operations, PACAF, End of Tour Report, April 1972, 58.

44. Ibid., 79. The extra drag from the appropriately named Fat Albert's large diameter meant the F-4 used too much fuel to carry it deep into North Vietnam, and it was less accurate because it was too heavy to maneuver well.
45. From the comic strip "B.C." by Hart.
46. "Linebacker Operations September–December 1972," Project CHECO Southeast Asia Report, 31 December 1978, 38–40. The LGB was essentially an "all or nothing" weapon. If it guided, it scored a direct hit; if it did not guide, it missed by several thousand feet.
47. Interestingly, it seems that the North Vietnamese never really accepted the fact that the orbiting F-4 was guiding the bombs to the target.
48. "USAF Operations against North Vietnam," 159.
49. "Linebacker Operations, September–December 1972," 29.

7. The Fiercest Battles

1. "Linebacker Operations, September–December 1972," 8.
2. "Linebacker: Overview of the First 120 Days," Project CHECO Southeast Asia Report, September 27, 1973, 14.
3. Ibid., 11–12.
4. "Linebacker Operations, September–December 1972," 3–4.
5. Ibid., 7.
6. Ibid., 8.
7. "Linebacker: Overview of the First 120 Days," 43.
8. April 14, 1995, interview with Gen. (then Col.) Charles A. Gabriel, Commander, 432nd TRW, October 1971–June 1972.
9. Red Baron III, vol. IV, part I, 117–18.
10. "Tactics and Techniques of Electronic Warfare," 65.
11. The F-4 pilot on this mission had been a project pilot for Have Drill and was very familiar with the MiG-17's maneuverability. Red Baron III, vol. IV, 128.
12. It appeared that the MiGs were trying the Navy's "drag" technique, where one F-4 would lead a MiG pursuing him in front of another F-4 so the second could get a kill. This technique, needless to say, required skill and excellent timing.
13. "USAF Operations against North Vietnam," 120.
14. Ibid., 29.
15. Ibid., 45.
16. "Linebacker Operations, September–December 1972," 45.
17. Ritchie EOT interview, 14. Emphasis added.
18. "Linebacker Operations, September–December 1972," 45.
19. "Linebacker Study" (draft), Military Assistance Command, Vietnam (MACV), January 20, 1973, VI-3.
20. The most common chaff was quite heavy because it had rope mixed in. The United States did have an ultra-lightweight chaff that stayed in the air longer,

but it was in short supply and saved for support of B-52 operations. Eventually the light and heavy chaff were combined for the tactical missions. Slay EOT Report, 65.

21. "Linebacker Study," 8.
22. "Linebacker: Overview of the First 120 Days," 44.
23. "Linebacker Study," 3.
24. Officer EOT interview, 133–34.
25. "Linebacker: Overview of the First 120 Days," 44.
26. Ibid. (includes diagrams).
27. Red Baron III, vol. III, section I, 46.
28. "Linebacker Study," VI-8.
29. The commander of Seventh Air Force said, "We have tailored our force to provide maximum protection for the strike aircraft. These tactics have allowed us to avoid the loss of strike aircraft and take our lumps in the escort categories." "Air Force Operations over North Vietnam," Project Corona Harvest Report, PACAF, n.d. (approximately September 1972), 169.
30. "Linebacker Operations, September–December 1972," Appendix 3. The actual breakdown was six on strike escort and three on chaff escort.
31. "Linebacker Study," VI-7.
32. Because of the nature of their mission, MiGCAP flights did not carry heavy ordnance—such as bombs—and so were generally able to outmaneuver the SAMs if they were fired.
33. Ritchie EOT interview, 15.
34. "USAF Operations against North Vietnam," 128.
35. "Linebacker Operations, September–December 1972," 23, 65.
36. Red Baron III, vol. I, 9.
37. "USAF Operations against North Vietnam," 122.
38. Red Baron III, vol. III, section I, 92.
39. Officer EOT interview, 157–59.
40. Ritchie EOT interview, 8.
41. Ibid., 13.
42. Red Baron III, vol. VI, 40 and 41.
43. "Linebacker Operations, September–December 1972," 48–49.
44. All from "Combat Snap."
45. Ibid., 13.
46. Ibid., 12.
47. "USAF Operations against North Vietnam," 146.
48. "Combat Snap," 11.
49. Ibid., 8.
50. Ibid., 9.
51. Ibid., 17.
52. Ibid., 22.
53. Red Baron III, vol. III, section I, 114.
54. Ibid., 156.

55. Smith EOT Report, 33.
56. Ibid., 34. This increased the chance that at least one missile would work, but it also meant that if one missile was fired out of the envelope, so were the rest of them.
57. Red Baron III, vol. IV, 252.
58. Ibid., vol. IV, section I, 262.
59. Ibid., 263.
60. "Air Force Operations over North Vietnam," 135–36.
61. The term "bingo" was used by U.S. pilots to indicate that they had just enough fuel to leave the area safely.
62. Red Baron III, vol. III, section I, 30.
63. Ibid., vol. I, 13.
64. Ibid., 28.
65. Ritchie EOT interview, 19.
66. Red Baron III, vol. III, section I, 97.
67. Ibid., 96.
68. Ibid., 17.
69. Ibid., 74.
70. Ibid., 60.
71. Ibid., 26–27.
72. Ibid., Event 58.
73. "Linebacker Study," 3.
74. "Air Force Operations over North Vietnam," 136–37.
75. Red Baron III, vol. I, 23.
76. Ibid., 136.
77. "USAF Air Operations against North Vietnam," 159.
78. Slay EOT Report, 84.
79. Message, Seventh Air Force to PACAF, September 2, 1972, Subject: Linebacker Mission August 27, 1972 (DTG 021135Z).
80. Although a cost analysis was not considered—mission effectiveness was the only criterion by which bombs were measured—it is interesting to note that an EOGB cost approximately $17,000 as compared to about $4,000 for an LGB.
81. "Linebacker Study," 3.
82. "Linebacker Operations, September–December 1972," 48.
83. Officer EOT interview, 134.
84. Karl J. Eschmann, *Linebacker: The Untold Story of the Air Raids over North Vietnam* (New York: Ivy Books [Ballantine], 1989), 38–39.
85. "Linebacker Operations, September–December 1972," 49.
86. Smith EOT Report, 4.
87. Ritchie EOT interview, 68–69.
88. Linebacker Study, 4.
89. Smith EOT Report, 31.
90. This was reported by SIGINT after the engagement. Ritchie EOT interview, 22.

91. "Air Force Operations over North Vietnam," 138.
92. Ibid.
93. Smith EOT Report, 11.
94. But not all. Some Air Force fighter pilots never went to Southeast Asia, even after seven years of war; how they avoided it is unclear.
95. "USAF Operations against North Vietnam," 139.
96. Ritchie EOT interview, 33–34.
97. "Linebacker Study," 5.
98. Red Baron III, vol. III, section I, 39.
99. "Linebacker Study," 5.
100. Smith EOT Report, 4.
101. Ritchie EOT interview, 59.

8. Stalemate

1. Red Baron III, vol. I, 50.
2. Ibid., vol. II, 87.
3. "Linebacker Operations, September–December 1972," 18.
4. Red Baron III, vol. I, 34–35.
5. Officer EOT interview, 156.
6. Red Baron III, vol. III, section I, 89.
7. "Linebacker Operations, September–December 1972," 50–51.
8. Red Baron III, vol. III, section I, 89–90.
9. Ibid., 92.
10. "Linebacker Study," 7.
11. Ibid., 26–30.
12. Red Baron III, vol. III, section I, B-1.
13. "Linebacker Operations, September–December 1972," 26.
14. Ibid, 27.
15. Ritchie EOT interview, 67–68 and 98–99.
16. Ibid., 41–42.
17. Red Baron III, vol. I, 9.
18. Ibid., vol. III, section I, 38.
19. Ibid., 41.
20. Ibid., 46.
21. Message, Seventh Air Force to PACAF, August 23, 1972, Subject: Linebacker Mission August 19, 1972 (DTG 230834Z).
22. Message, Seventh Air Force to PACAF, September 5, 1972, Subject: Linebacker Mission August 26, 1972 (DTG 051232Z).
23. On Yankee Station, 87.
24. "Linebacker Operations, September–December 1972," 28.
25. Ibid.
26. Red Baron III, vol. III, section I, 105.
27. Ibid., vol. II, section II, 122–23.

28. In both Navy and Air Force F-4s, the front seater and the back seater—pilot or navigator—were all given credit for a kill.
29. Red Baron III, vol. III, section I, 91–92.
30. "Combat Snap," 11.
31. Message, Seventh Air Force to PACAF, October 13, 1972, Subject: Linebacker Mission October 6, 1972 (DTG 131333Z).
32. "Super Phantom," *USAF Fighter Weapons Review* (Winter 1972): 18–24.
33. See Red Baron III, Event 124.
34. "The New Phantom Switchology," *USAF Fighter Weapons Review* (Summer 1973): 26–30.
35. For example, when the first F-4E models came to Southeast Asia in 1968 they came as a completely new squadron.
36. Smith EOT Report, 38.
37. "Linebacker Operations, September–December 1972," 55–71.
38. *Linebacker II: A View From the Rock*, USAF Southeast Asia Monograph Series, Monograph 8 (Washington, D.C.: Office of Air History, 1985), 26.
39. Smith EOT Report, 7.
40. Ibid., 8–9.
41. Ibid., 35.
42. Ibid.
43. Ibid., 9.
44. *White House Years*, 1457.
45. "Linebacker Operations, September–December 1972," 65.

9. Looking Back, Looking Ahead

1. Navy pilots on exchange duty with the Air Force shot down two MiGs, but these are counted as Air Force kills.
2. Red Baron III, vol I, part I, Appendix A: Air-to-Air Losses in Southeast Asia, A-2–3. This does not include U.S. "induced losses," where MiGs were credited with causing the indirect loss of a U.S. aircraft. The Air Force suffered seven induced losses and the Navy two; with induced losses the kill ratio was about 1.5:1 for the Air Force and 4:1 for the Navy.
3. Notes from a General Dynamics presentation to the NATO Fighter Symposium, Skydstrup Air Base, Denmark, September 21–October 9, 1987, B-100.
4. Red Baron III, vol. I, 9–10.
5. Ibid., 27–28.
6. Employment of Missiles and Guided Weapons in Southeast Asia, viewgraph numbers 6–13.
7. Ibid.
8. Ritchie EOT interview, 45.
9. Slay EOT Report, 90.
10. Smith EOT Report, 34.
11. Red Baron III, vol. III, section I, 37.

12. Officer EOT interview, 163.
13. The Air Force learned after the war that training significantly enhanced the pilots' ability to see small aircraft at long distances; the Navy had learned this in 1968 at Topgun.
14. Red Baron III, vol. I (Summary), June 1974, 26.
15. "Linebacker Operations, September–December 1972," 52.
16. Ibid., 53–54.
17. Red Baron III, vol. III, section I, 100.
18. Ibid., vol. I, 26.
19. Red Baron III, III-165.
20. Ibid., vol. III, part I, 93.
21. Ibid., vol. I, 9.
22. Ibid.
23. Ritchie EOT interview, 106.
24. See, for example, Red Baron I, vol. IV, 5.
25. Ibid, 6.
26. TAB 74(1) (March 30, 1974), 22.
27. Red Baron I, vol. IV, 4.
28. Smith, EOT, 16.
29. *USAF Fighter Weapons Review* (Winter 1972): 9–10.
30. Red Baron III, vol. I, 2–13.
31. "F-4 Air-to-Air Training," 3.
32. See, for example, Officer EOT interview, 110–12.
33. "F-4 Air-to-Air Training," 5.
34. In the late 1980s, the Air Force finally developed a ground-attack version of the F-15, the F-15E. It—like the fighter version—was tremendously successful.
35. Smith EOT Report, 2.

Appendix 1. Notes on the MiG Pilots

1. Ritchie EOT interview, 21.
2. Ibid., 53.
3. Officer EOT interview, 119.
4. Ibid., 121.
5. Ritchie EOT interview, 23.

Glossary

AAA anti-aircraft artillery

adverse yaw the tendency of an aircraft to yaw away from the applied aileron while at a high angle of attack

AGM air-to-ground missile

AIM air intercept missile

all aspect a term applied to a missile that can be fired from any target angle, including the front, not just from behind. The AIM-7 Sparrow was an all-aspect missile.

angle of attack the angle between the mean chord line of the wing and the relative wind

ARC Light B-52 strike

Atoll the NATO designation for the Soviet K-13 missile, equivalent of the AIM-9B

back seater the occupant of the backseat of a fighter aircraft (see GIB, RIO, WSO)

bandit an enemy aircraft

BarCAP barrier combat air patrol; set up between a strike and the area of the expected threat

bingo a preagreed amount of fuel needed to return to base, alternate airfield, or tanker

black bandit code word for a MiG that is low on fuel and returning to base; a "cripple"

blue bandit code word for a MiG-21

boresight mode a method of firing the AIM-7 quickly where the radar beam was aligned to the roll axis of the F-4

break maximum performance defensive turn

CAP combat air patrol

CBU cluster bomb unit; a bomb carrying a number of smaller bomblets inside for maximum spread over the target

chaff thin, narrow, metallic strips cut to various wavelengths and dropped to create false impressions on radar screens

Channel 97 a TACAN station located in eastern Laos and used extensively in Rolling Thunder before it was captured

Combat Tree the APX-80 carried on some F-4Ds and the Rivet Haste F-4s. It was similar to the QRC-248 in that it was an EIFF (enemy IFF) detector that could read the transponders of the North Vietnamese MiGs.

Disco call sign for EC-121 aircraft that provided MiG warnings and other forms of radar control

dumb bombs unguided bombs

ECM electronic countermeasures

ECM pod a pylon- or fuselage-mounted pod housing multiple transmitters and associated electronic devices to provide self-protection for aircraft penetrating an electronically controlled ground-to-air defense system

EOGB electro-optically guided bomb

Falcon AIM-4D heat-seeking air-to-air missile

Fan Song NATO designation for the guidance radar of the Soviet SA-2 missile

feet wet over water

fighting wing standard U.S. Air Force two-ship tactical formation where the wingman flew close to the leader to provide protection

flak anti-aircraft fire

flight standard U.S. Air Force fighting unit, usually consisting of four aircraft

fluid four standard U.S. Air Force four-ship tactical formation consisting of two pairs of aircraft with the number 2 and number 4 aircraft flying fighting wing

FWS U.S. Air Force Fighter Weapons School

GCI ground-controlled intercept

GIB guy in back; back seater, usually a pilot, in an Air Force F-4

Guard emergency frequency (243.0 MHz UHF) usually monitored by all aircraft and ground stations

IFF identification, friend or foe; an aircraft transponder that gives a unique return on a radar screen

Iron Hand mission to destroy SAMs and radar-guided AAA flown by specially equipped fighter aircraft

Jolly Green Giant call sign for U.S. Air Force search-and-rescue helicopters

knot a speed of one nautical mile per hour

LGB laser-guided bomb

lock on to follow a target automatically by means of a radar beam

Loran a long-range, all-weather navigation/bombing system used by Air Force aircraft during the latter part of the Vietnam War

M-61 six-barreled 20-mm cannon, called the Vulcan

M-129 a bomb designed for the distribution of chaff (and other light materials)

Mark 12 Colt cannon carried on the F-8 Crusader

Mark 82 500-pound low-drag general purpose bomb

Mark 84 2,000-pound low-drag general purpose bomb, often used with a laser seeker head to make an LGB

Mark 117 750-pound low-drag general purpose bomb

Mark 118 3,000-pound low-drag general purpose bomb

MiG Mikoyan/Gurevich series of Soviet fighters

MiGCAP anti-MiG combat air patrol

nm nautical mile

NVN North Vietnam(ese)

Pave Knife laser designator pod mounted on the left inboard pylon of specially modified F-4Ds

PGM precision guided munitions; generic name for the family of laser and electro-optically guided "smart" bombs

pipper a small dot in the center of a gunsight used for aiming

PIRAZ positive identification radar advisory zone; used by the U.S. Navy in the Gulf of Tonkin

P_k probability of kill

pod formation a formation of ECM pod-carrying aircraft to give the best combination of overlapping jamming, tactical maneuverability, and visual lookout

POL petroleum, oil, lubricants

pop up a maneuver where an aircraft comes in very low and fast, then pulls up rapidly

red bandit code name for the MiG-17

Red Crown code name for the U.S. Navy GCI ship located in the Gulf of Tonkin

ResCAP rescue combat air patrol

RHAW gear radar homing and warning equipment that points out the direction of radars and warns of changes in missile launch and guidance status

RIO radar intercept officer; the U.S. Navy term for the back seater in the F-4

Rivet Haste specially modified F-4s with slats, TISEO, Combat Tree, and the 556 modification sent to Udorn RTAFB, Thailand, in late 1972

ROE rules of engagement

Route Package one of the six areas North Vietnam was divided into to allow for better coordination of U.S. Air Force and Navy strikes

RTAFB Royal Thai Air Force Base

RTU (USAF) replacement training unit

SA-2 Soviet-built surface-to-air missile

SAC strategic air command

SAM surface-to-air missile

Shrike name for the AGM-45 anti-radiation missile

Sidewinder name for the AIM-9 series of missiles

SIGINT signal intelligence

six, six o'clock the position directly behind an aircraft

smart bombs guided bombs; see EOGB and LGB

Sparrow name for the AIM-7 series of missiles

TAC tactical air command of the U.S. Air Force

TACAN a navigation system that gives both range and bearing to the station

TarCAP target combat air patrol; a Navy name for CAP missions flown in the vicinity of the target

Teaball code name for the all-source warning agency located at Nakhon Phanom RTAFB; began operations in late July 1972

TFW (Air Force) tactical fighter wing

Thud Ridge American nickname for the Tam Dao mountain range that begins about 20 nautical miles north-northwest of Hanoi and extends about 25 miles farther northwest. Often used for terrain masking from radar by U.S. aircraft.

TISEO target identification system electro-optical; a long-range television-type system mounted in Rivet Haste F-4s

Topgun advanced air-to-air training course for U.S. Navy F-4 crews begun between Rolling Thunder and Linebacker

TRW tactical reconnaissance wing

VID visual identification

white bandit code name for the MiG-19

Wild Weasel code name for specially configured fighters and specially trained crews used to hunt, suppress, and attack SAM sites

WSO weapons system operator; a navigator in the back of U.S. Air Force F-4s

ZOT nickname given to the Pave Way I laser designator mounted in the backseat of some Air Force F-4s

Bibliography

Notes on Sources

There are three principal types of sources used in this book. First, and by far the most important, are a large variety of official military staff studies, analyses, and other official reports on the air war over North Vietnam. Second are a smaller number of unofficial reports, including various types of term papers written by students or staff members at the various service schools, especially the U.S. Air Force's Air Command and Staff College and the Air War College at Maxwell Air Force Base, Montgomery, Alabama. Third are "self-reports"—commercial books, end of tour (EOT) reports written by wing commanders and senior staff officers, interviews, and other personal accounts where actual participants in the air war discuss what happened from their point of view. The author has tried to blend both the relatively objective headquarters perspective and the passion of the perspective of those actually flying the missions. Sorting between them is no easy matter.

To understand why requires a brief explanation of how the military staffing process works. A staff report or analysis is not written in isolation. While one person or office is assigned the task of writing the report, once the report is completed, it is circulated in draft form to most—if not all—of the contributors for accuracy checks and general comments. This process tends to make these reports accurate in terms of numbers and events because they have been verified from several sources, including the originators. Additionally, the contributors can—and often do—comment on the actual findings and conclusions of the report, and many times the report will not go forward until the conclusions and especially recommendations are agreed upon by the contributors. While this leads to the curse of the staffing process—watering down conclusions and recommendations to the lowest common denominator—this has little effect on the researcher, who is more concerned about the facts in the reports.

The second set of sources are a mixed bag. Students tend to write reports in their own areas of expertise and/or experience and have access to a great deal of information (much of it classified). This expertise and information usually makes the papers factually accurate, but often the conclusions, arrived at in isolation and usually from a very narrow viewpoint, are less reliable.

Finally, there are the self-reports. Commercial books often are good but depend largely on their sources for accuracy, and writers without a military flying background are at the mercy of their sources. It is therefore no surprise that most of the best are written, at least partially, by military officers who participated in the campaigns. The danger of these books is that the authors may have their own ax to grind and/or may move outside of their areas of knowledge and expertise in the course of their narrative. As for end of tour reports, interviews, and "there I was" accounts—while large events are composed of individual stories, these sources are much more difficult to judge for accuracy and raise the classic problem of how to evaluate the accuracy of statements given by interested parties. The author has dealt with the problem in two ways. First, the self-reports have generally been used for information that is value-neutral to the source—i.e., altitudes and speeds for MiGCAPs—and for other small bits of technical information that fill in the details of operations. Second, the self-reports are used as quotes or anecdotes to confirm information generally found elsewhere in official sources—the problems with jettisoning centerline fuel tanks, for example—or to make a point that might run counter to a noticeable trend, i.e., the comments of one Air Force ace that he thought the AIM-7 was an excellent missile.

As for the engagements, the author has read all available records carefully and used his personal experience to analyze them. Any mistakes are his alone.

Books

Anerton, D. *The F-105 Thunderchief* (London: Osprey Publishing Ltd., Osprey Air Combat, 1983).

Bell, K. *100 Missions North: A Fighter Pilot's Story of the Vietnam War* (Washington: Brassey's, 1993).

Bleese, Fredrick C., Maj. Gen., USAF (Ret.). *Check Six: A Fighter Pilot Looks Back* (New York: Ballantine Books, 1992).

Broughton, J. *Going Downtown: The Air War against Hanoi and Washington* (New York: Pocket Books, 1988).

———. *Thud Ridge* (New York: Bantam Books, 1969).

Cunningham, R. *Fox Two* (Mesa, Arizona: Chaplin Fighter Museum, 1984).

Eschmann, Karl J. *Linebacker: The Untold Story of the Air Raids over North Vietnam* (New York: Ivy Books [Ballantine], 1989).

R. Francillon. *Tonkin Bay Yacht Club: U.S. Carrier Operations off Vietnam* (Annapolis, Maryland: Naval Institute Press, 1988).

Futrell, et al. *Aces and Aerial Victories: The United States Air Force in Southeast Asia, 1965–1973* (Washington, D.C.: The Albert F. Simpson Historical Research Center, Air University, and the Office of Air Force History, 1976).

Hartsook, E. H. *Air Power Helps Stop the Invasion and End the War 1972* (Montgomery, Alabama: Maxwell AFB, Office of Air Force History, 1978).

Kissinger, H. *White House Years* (Toronto: Little, Brown and Co., 1979).

Lake, J., ed. *McDonnell F-4 Phantom: Spirit in the Skies* (London: Aerospace Publishing, 1992).

Levinson, J. *Alpha Strike Vietnam: The Navy's Air War 1964–1973* (Novato, California: Presidio Press, 1980).

Linebacker II: A View From the Rock, USAF Southeast Asia Monograph Series, Monograph 8 (Washington, D.C.: Office of Air History, 1985).

Mersky, P. B., and N. Pulman. *The Naval Air War in Vietnam* (Annapolis, Maryland: Naval and Aviation Publishing Company of America, 1990).

Momyer, William W., Gen., USAF (Ret.). *Air Power in Three Wars (WWII, Korea, Vietnam)* (Washington, D.C.: U.S. Government Printing Office, 1978).

Nichols, J. B., Cdr., and B. Tillman. *On Yankee Station: The Naval Air War over Vietnam* (Annapolis, Maryland: Naval Institute Press, 1988).

Nordeen, H. *Air Warfare in the Missile Age* (Washington, D.C.: Smithsonian Institution, 1981).

Price, Alfred. *The Last Year of the Luftwaffe, May 1944–May 1945.* Paperback ed. (London: Arms and Armour, 1991)

———. *World War II Fighter Conflict* (London: MacDonald and Co., 1975).

Scutts, M. D. *Wolfpack* (Osceola, Wisconsin: Motorbooks International, 1988).

Shaw, Robert. *Fighter Combat: Tactics and Maneuvering* (Annapolis, Maryland: Naval Institute Press, 1985).

Tilford, E. H. *Setup: What the Air Force Did in Vietnam and Why* (Maxwell AFB, Alabama: Air University Press, 1991).

Tillman, B. *MiG Master: The Story of the F-8 Crusader.* 2d ed. (Annapolis, Maryland: Naval Institute Press, 1990).

Wilcox, Robert K. *Scream of Eagles: The Creation of Top Gun and the U.S. Air Victory in Vietnam* (New York: John Wiley and Sons, 1990).

Magazine Articles

"Challenge over North Vietnam: Carrier Aviators Battle with the NVAF MiG," *The Hook* (Winter 1983): 25–28.

Drenkowski, Dana. "The Tragedy of Operation Linebacker II," *Armed Forces Journal* (July 1977): 24–27.

Gish, D. L., Maj., USAF. "F-4 Air-to-Air Training," *USAF Fighter Weapons Review* (Fall 1975): 2–5.

"The New Phantom Switchology," *USAF Fighter Weapons Review* (Summer 1973): 26–30.

Roy, Vincent P., Maj., USAF. "Double Attack Revisited," *USAF Fighter Weapons Review* (Spring 1971): 27–32.

"State of the Art," *USAF Fighter Weapons Review* (Winter 1974): 28–33.

"Super Phantom," *USAF Fighter Weapons Review* (Winter 1972): 18–24.

USAF Fighter Weapons Newsletter 1 (March 1966).

USAF Fighter Weapons Newsletter 4 (December 1965): 4.

USAF Fighter Weapons Review (Summer 1971): 14–16, 33.

USAF Fighter Weapons Review (Fall 1971): 73.

USAF Fighter Weapons Review (Winter 1972): 9–10.

USAF Fighter Weapons Review (Fall 1989): 43

Contemporary Historical Examination of Current Operations (CHECO) Reports

"Air Tactics against NVN Air Ground Defenses, December 1966–November 1, 1968," Project CHECO Southeast Asia Report (various dates).

"College Eye Special Report," 1 November 1968.

"Combat Snap (AIM-9J Southeast Asia Introduction)," (n.d.—circa 1974).

"Linebacker Operations, September–December 1972," Project CHECO Southeast Asia Report, 31 December 1978, 38–40.

"Linebacker: Overview of the First 120 Days," 27 September 1973.

"Southeast Asia Report, March–June 1965" (n.d.).

"Tactical Electronic Warfare Operations in SEA," 1962–1968 (n.d.).

"Tactics of Electronic Warfare," July 1974.

End of Tour Reports and Interviews

Interview, Lt. Col. George Anderson, Vice Commander/DCO, College Eye Task Force. Dated July 11, 1969.

Interview, Gen. (then Col.) Charles A. Gabriel, Commander, 432nd TRW, October 1971–June 1972. Dated April 14, 1995.

End of Tour Interview, Maj. Upton D. Officer. U.S. Air Force Oral History Program, Maxwell AFB, Alabama. Dated July 11–13, 1973.

End of Tour Debriefing, Col. Robin Olds, 8TFW Commander, July 12, 1967, Corona Harvest.

End of Tour Interview, Capt. Richard S. ("Steve") Ritchie. U.S. Air Force Oral History Interview #K239.0512-630. Dated October 11 and 30, 1972.

End of Tour Report, Gen. Alton Slay, Director of Operations, PACAF. Dated April 1972.

End of Tour Report, Col. Scott G. Smith, Commander, 432nd TRW, Udorn RTAFB, April 1972–18 March 1973. Dated May 31, 1973.

Interview, Maj. Frederick G. Tolman, wing weapons officer, 355th TFW. Dated July 15, 1967.

Corona Harvest

"Air Force Operations over North Vietnam," Project Corona Harvest Report, PACAF. (n.d.—circa September 1972).
"Air-to-Air Encounters over North Vietnam, 1 July 1967–31 Dec 1968," Project Corona Harvest Report 1970.
"USAF Operations against North Vietnam, 1 July 1971–30 June 1972," Project Corona Harvest Report, April 1972–18 March 1973, PACAF Headquarters in cooperation with Strategic Air Command, dated 31 May 1973, 12–13.
Witt, James A., Maj., USAF. "Employment of Air-to-Air Missiles in Southeast Asia." Project Corona Harvest (February 1970).

Messages

Message, Seventh Air Force to PACAF, August 23, 1972. Subject: Linebacker Mission 19 August 1972 (DTG 230834Z).
Message, Seventh Air Force to PACAF, September 2, 1972. Subject: Linebacker Mission 27 August 1972 (DTG 021135Z).
Message Seventh Air Force to PACAF, September 5, 1972. Subject: Linebacker Mission 26 August 1972 (DTG 051232Z).
Message, Seventh Air Force to PACAF, October 12, 1972. Subject: Linebacker Mission 5 October 1972 (DTG 121233Z).
Message, Seventh Air Force to PACAF, October 13, 1972. Subject: Linebacker Mission 6 October 1972 (DTG131333Z).
Message, Seventh Air Force to PACAF, December 28, 1972. Subject: Linebacker Missions 18, 19, and 20 December 1972 (DTG280405Z).
Message, Mark X IFF Problem. Navy proposal forwarded to ComSeventh Fleet, March 1966.

Miscellaneous Works

8th TFW (F-4) Tactics Manual 1968.
31st TFW (Homestead AFB, Florida) RTU F-4 Weapons Employment Manual (1972).
388th (F-105) TFW Tactics Manual (1 February 1967).
497th TFS, 8th TFW, Squadron History (January–March 1968).
Clouser, Gordon I., Maj., USAF. "A Critical Analysis of USAF Air Combat Tactics." Air Command and Staff College Research Study, May 1974.
Command and Control of Air Operations in the Vietnam War. Colloquium on Contemporary History, January 23, 1991, Naval Historical Center. Remarks by Adm. James Holloway, 8.
"Counter Air Tactics" (Summary of Feather Duster I and II). *PACAF Tactics and Techniques Bulletin* 45 (July 26, 1966): 1.
Dell, Albert H. "Navy, Marine Corps, and Air Force Fixed Wing In-Flight Combat Losses to MiG Aircraft in Southeast Asia from 1965 through 1972." Report for Center for Naval Analyses, March 28, 1978.

Dickson, John R., USAF. "Electronic Warfare in North Vienam: Did We Learn Our Lessons?" Air War College Research Report. EB-66C Out of Country Reconnaisance, 1965–1967. (n.d.—probably 1969).

"EC-121D Operations in SEA." *PACAF Tactics and Techniques Bulletin* 35 (February 8, 1966): 388.

"Effectiveness of the QRC-160-1 Pod." HQ PACAF Working Paper no. 31, March 16, 1967.

Hendricks, Howard F., Lt. Col., USAF. Air Force Liaison Officer Report, September–October 1966.

History of the 366th Tactical Fighter Wing, 1 April 1967–30 September 1967.

Linebacker Study (draft). Military Assistance Command, Vietnam (MACV), January 20, 1973.

Miller, J. T., Lt. Col., USAF. Analysis of Aircrew Personnel Flying Out of Country Interdiction Missions. April 1968.

Nalty, Bernard C. "Tactics and Techniques of Electronic Warfare: Electronic Countermeasures in the Air War against North Vietnam, 1965–1973." Office of Air Force History, August 16, 1977.

Notes from a General Dynamics presentation to the NATO Fighter Symposium. Skydstrup Air Base, Denmark, September 21–October 9, 1987.

PACAF Rolling Thunder Operational Handbook (March 1968).

PACAF Tactics and Techniques Bulletin 50 (October 26, 1966).

"Project Plan." Report, U.S. Navy Air Development Squadron Four (1966).

Red Baron I, Weapons System and Evaluation Group. Vol. I October 1967, vol. II April 1968, vol. III September 1968, vol. IV February 1969.

Red Baron II, USAF Fighter Weapons Center. 5 vol. January 1973.

Red Baron III, USAF Fighter Weapons Center. 4 vol. June 1974.

"SEACAAL Study." Briefing presented to HQ USAF February 10, 1967.

"USAF Combat Victories in Southeast Asia." USAF Museum (list of U.S. Air Force victories by aircraft type and tail number).

Briefings

Employment of Missiles and Guided Weapons in Southeast Asia. Briefing by General Eggers, Deputy Director for Operations (Strategic and General Operations), J-3 (n.d.—probably circa late 1972).

NVNAF Fighter Patterns. DCS/Intel PACAF Brief 1968.

Rolling Thunder PACAF Briefing, November 1967.

Index

About the Author

Marshall Michel is a native of New Orleans who attended Georgetown and Harvard Universities. He joined the U.S. Air Force in 1966 and went to flight school at Webb Air Force Base, Texas. In 1970 he was assigned to the 432nd Tactical Reconnaissance Wing, Udorn Royal Thai Air Force Base, Thailand, first flying RF-4Cs and later F-4Es. From 1970 to 1973 he flew 321 combat missions.

Mr. Michel was the assistant air attaché at the American embassy in Tel Aviv from 1977 to 1980, when he returned to the United States to fly F-15s at Langley Air Force Base, Virginia. He later served as the Israel desk officer for the Joint Chiefs of Staff in the Pentagon, as a fellow at the Jaffee Center for Strategic Studies at Tel Aviv University, and on the NATO staff in Brussels, Belgium. He retired as a colonel from the Air Force in 1992.

Mr. Michel is an avid scuba diver who has pursued his hobby all over the world. His identification of the hulk of the MS *Dunraven* was the basis for the BBC television documentary *The Mystery Wreck of the Red Sea*. He currently lives again in both New Orleans and Brussels while he works on a novel about the Russian mafia and the European Commission, set in Brussels, Washington, and Moscow.